Angel Diary

vol.2

Kara · Lee YunHee

ice
Kunion

WORDS FROM THE CREATORS

It's already volume two of <Angel Diary>! We're so glad that our second book is out. When we first started working in Manhwa, we promised ourselves that we'd try to deliver the kind of books people wouldn't regret picking up. We feel we still have a long way to go, but we do try our best with each and every page!

-Kara (Artists)

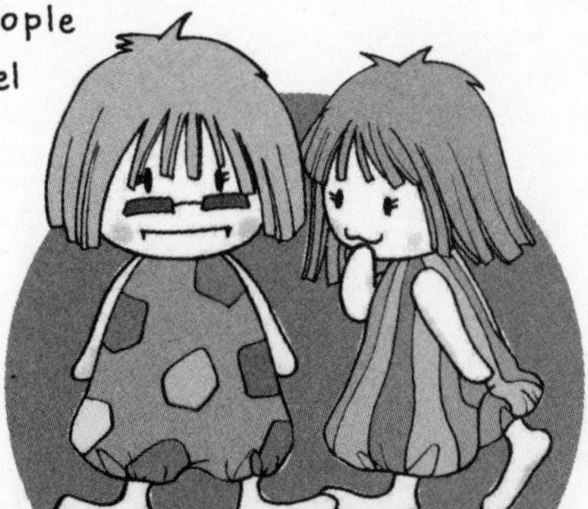

<Angel Diary> has so many lovable characters! I think they're the cutest, too. On the other hand, people often say I have odd taste in comic book characters. So, maybe I don't know what I'm talking about.

-Yun-Hee Lee(Writer)

PROFILE OF THE CHARACTERS

Dong-Young

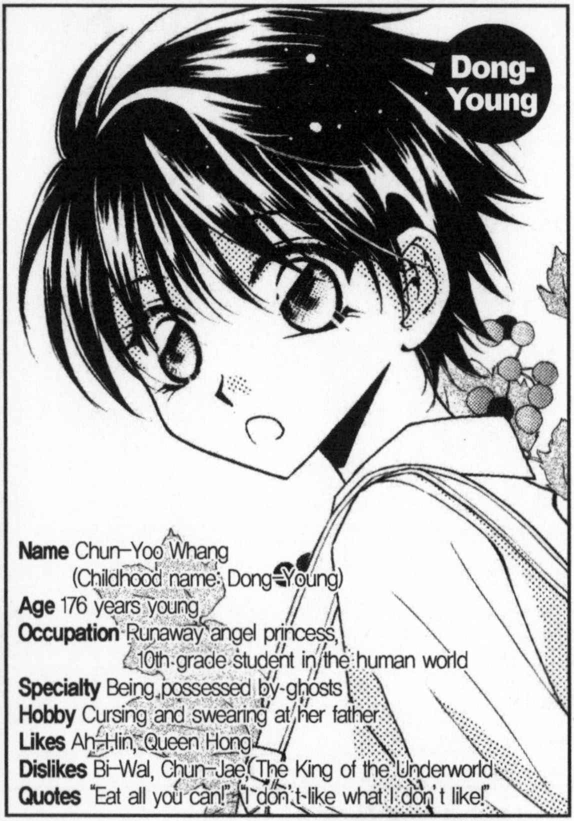

Name Chun-Yoo Whang
(Childhood name: Dong-Young)
Age 176 years young
Occupation Runaway angel princess,
10th grade student in the human world
Specialty Being possessed by ghosts
Hobby Cursing and swearing at her father
Likes Ah-Hin, Queen Hong
Dislikes Bi-Wal, Chun-Jae, The King of the Underworld
Quotes "Eat all you can!" "I don't like what I don't like!"

Bi-Wal Jin

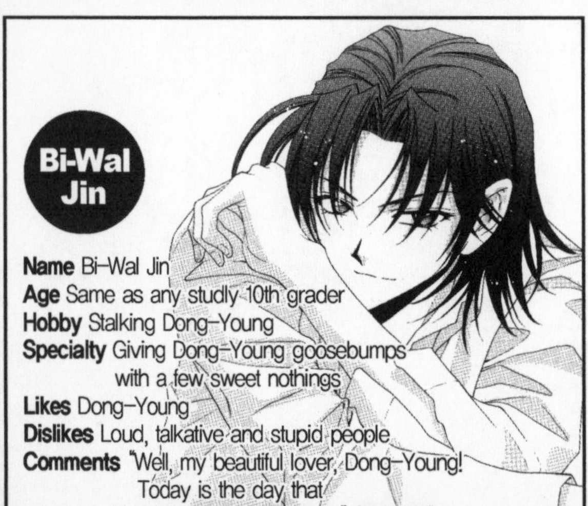

Name Bi-Wal Jin
Age Same as any studly 10th grader
Hobby Stalking Dong-Young
Specialty Giving Dong-Young goosebumps
with a few sweet nothings
Likes Dong-Young
Dislikes Loud, talkative and stupid people
Comments "Well, my beautiful lover, Dong-Young!
Today is the day that
we will prove our love..." (SMACK!)

Mya-Oh

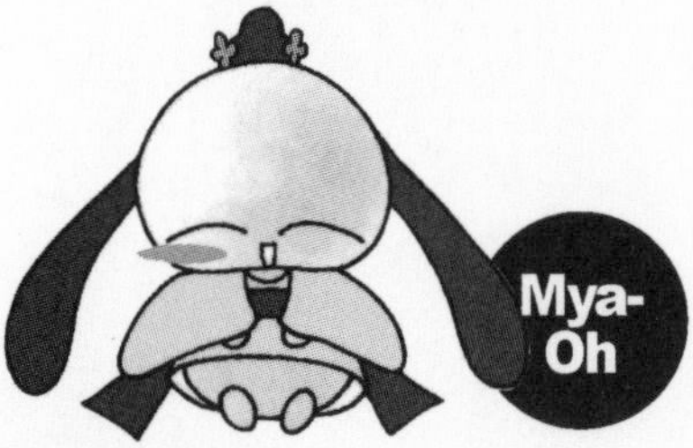

Name Mya-Oh
(but most people don't remember)
Occupation Unlucky servant of
a runaway angel princess (sigh)
Specialty Fleeing from dangerous situations
Likes Queen Hong, Dong-Young-Nim
Dislikes Scary people
Comments "Pray that Dong-Young-Nim
blossoms into a beautiful woman."
(I realize this is as likely as
the stars falling out of the sky)

Queen Hong

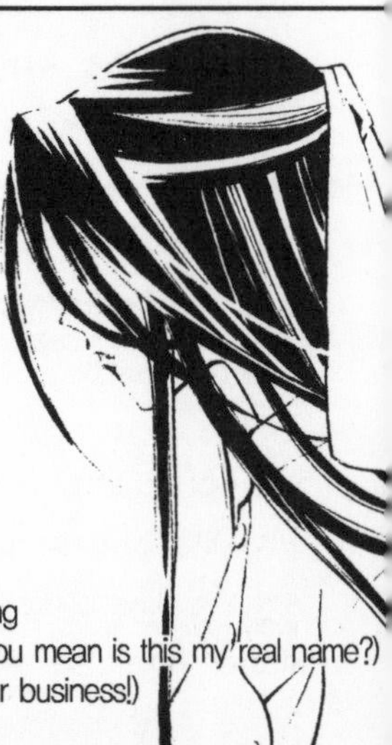

Name Queen Hong
(What do you mean is this my real name?)
Age (None of your business!)
Hobby Well...
Specialty I don't remember...
Likes Hmm... what do I like?
Dislikes Secrets!
Comments "How dare you ask me such
personal questions?
How rude! Enough of this prying!"

THE FOUR GUARDIANS

Name Ah–Hin
Age 176
Occupation White Tiger of the Four Guardians
Description Pretty, kind, and lively (but her friends know better)
Motto "Beautiful people should never have to apologize!"

Name Ee–Jung
Age 175
Job Red Phoenix of the Four Guardians
Hobbies Following his sister everywhere
Description Lazy, a whiner, complains about everything
Note Dependent on sister Ah–Hin who is the center of his universe
Motto "What Ah–Hin says goes!"

Name Woo–Hyun
Age 175
Job Blue Dragon of the Four Guardians
Hobbies Sleeping (anywhere and anytime)
Description Very cute, adorable and fairly independent
Goal To somehow find a girlfriend while in school!

Name Doh–Hyun
Age 178
Job Black Turtle of the Four Guardians
Hobbies Pondering life, the universe, everything
Description Perfect! Handsome, kind and good at school, sports, everything
Note He is worldly wise.
Goal To smooth things (everything) over (somehow).

CONTENTS

II FIELD TRIP

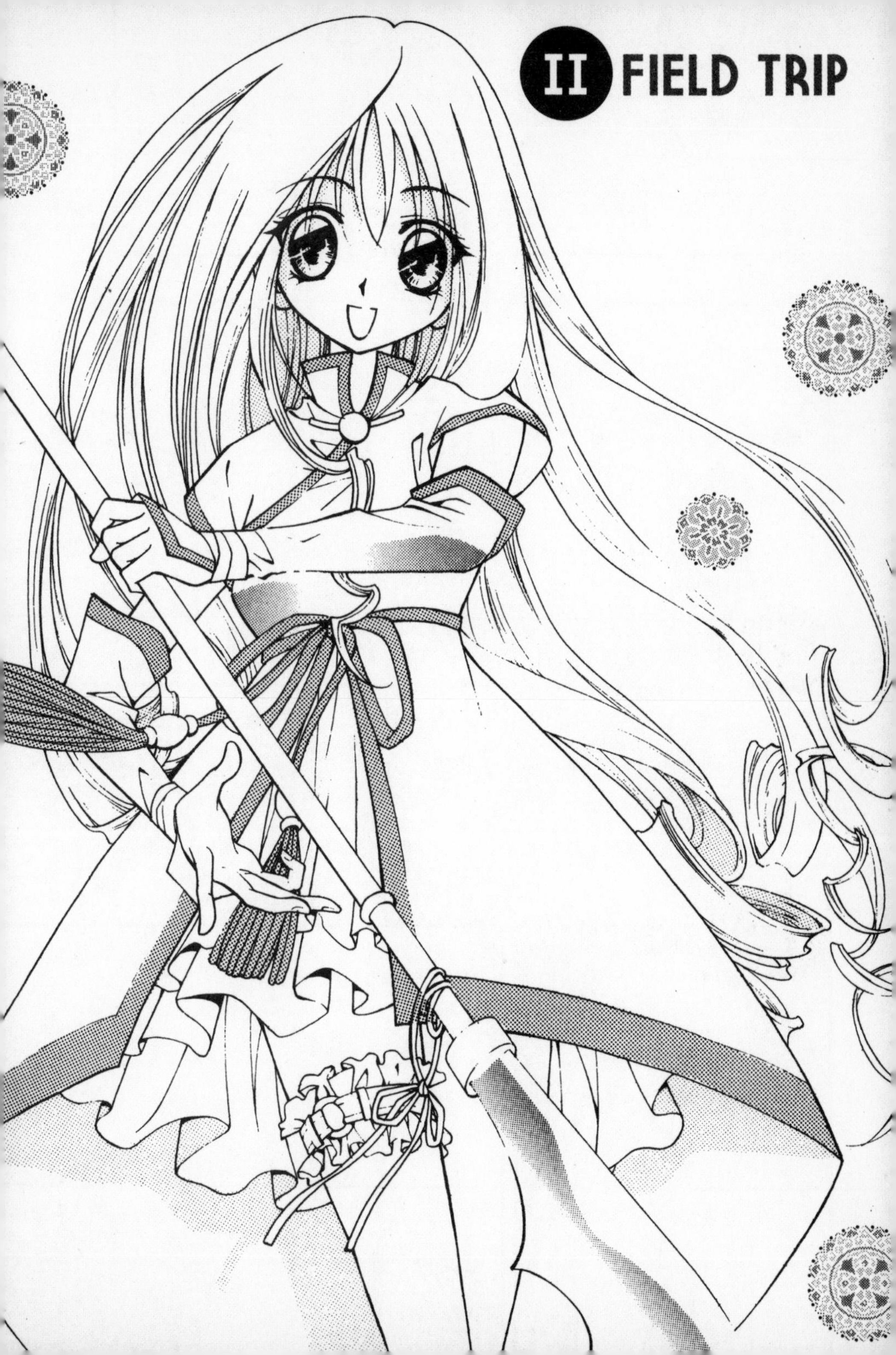

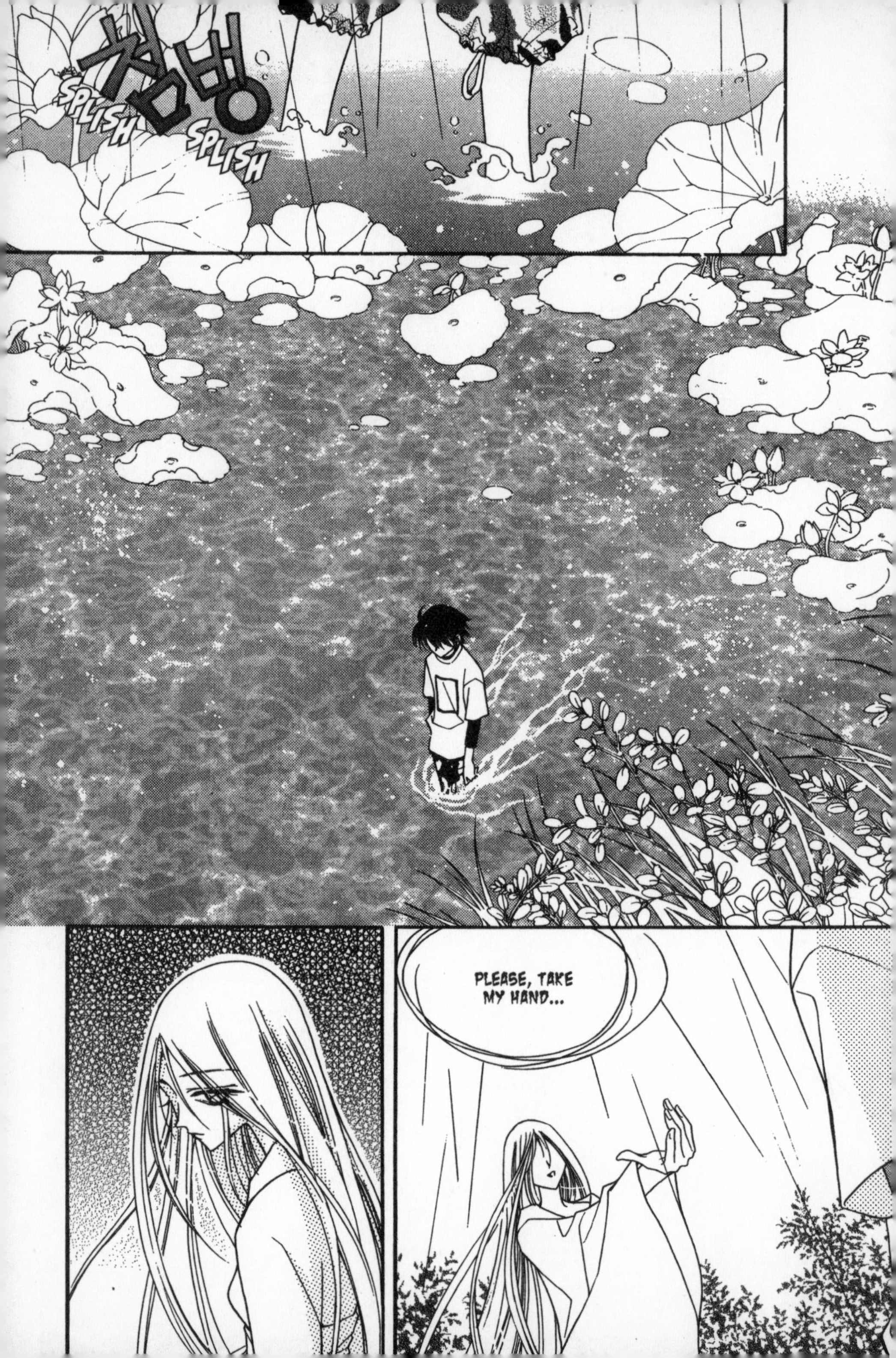
첨벙
SPLISH
SPLISH
PLEASE, TAKE MY HAND...

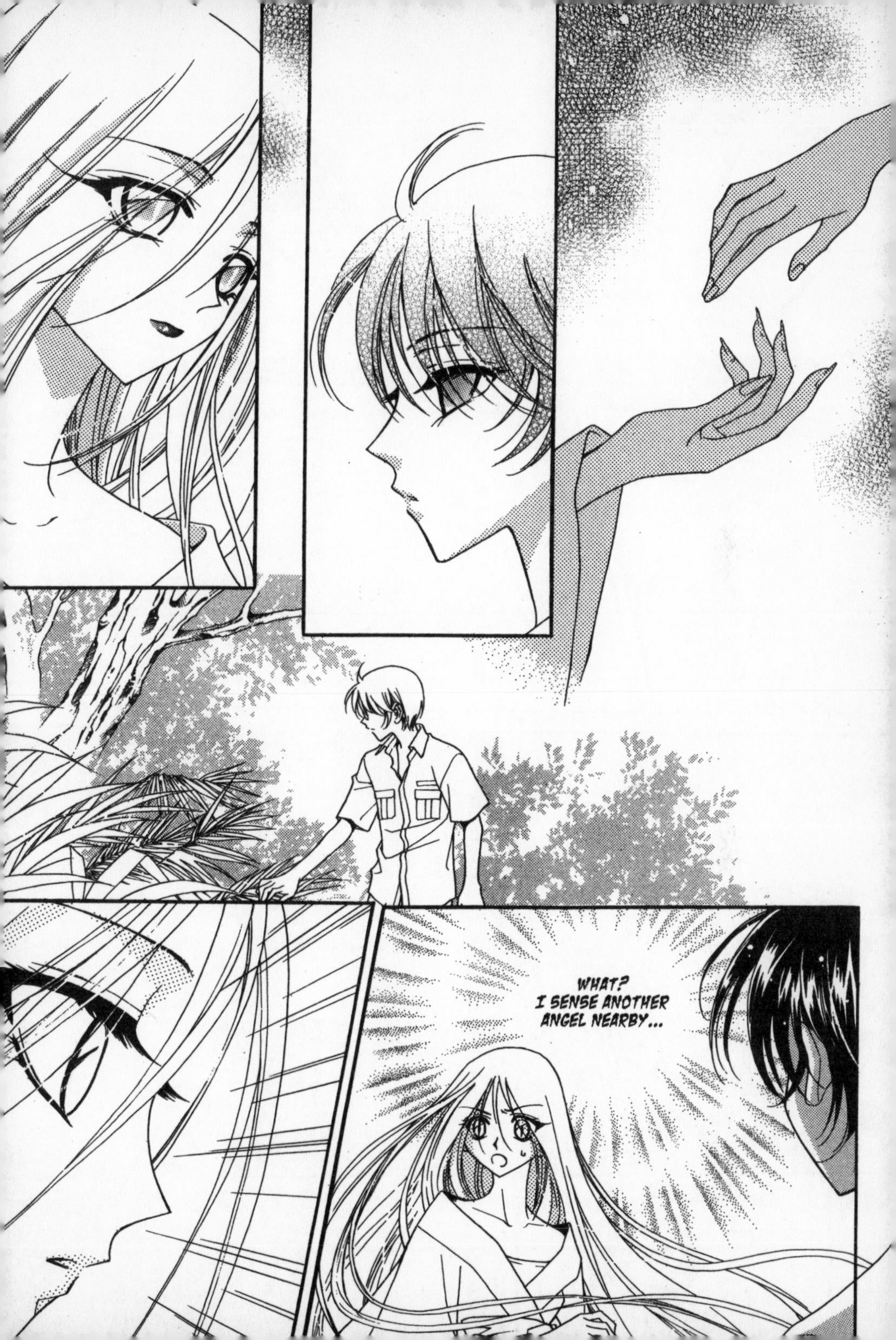
WHAT? I SENSE ANOTHER ANGEL NEARBY...

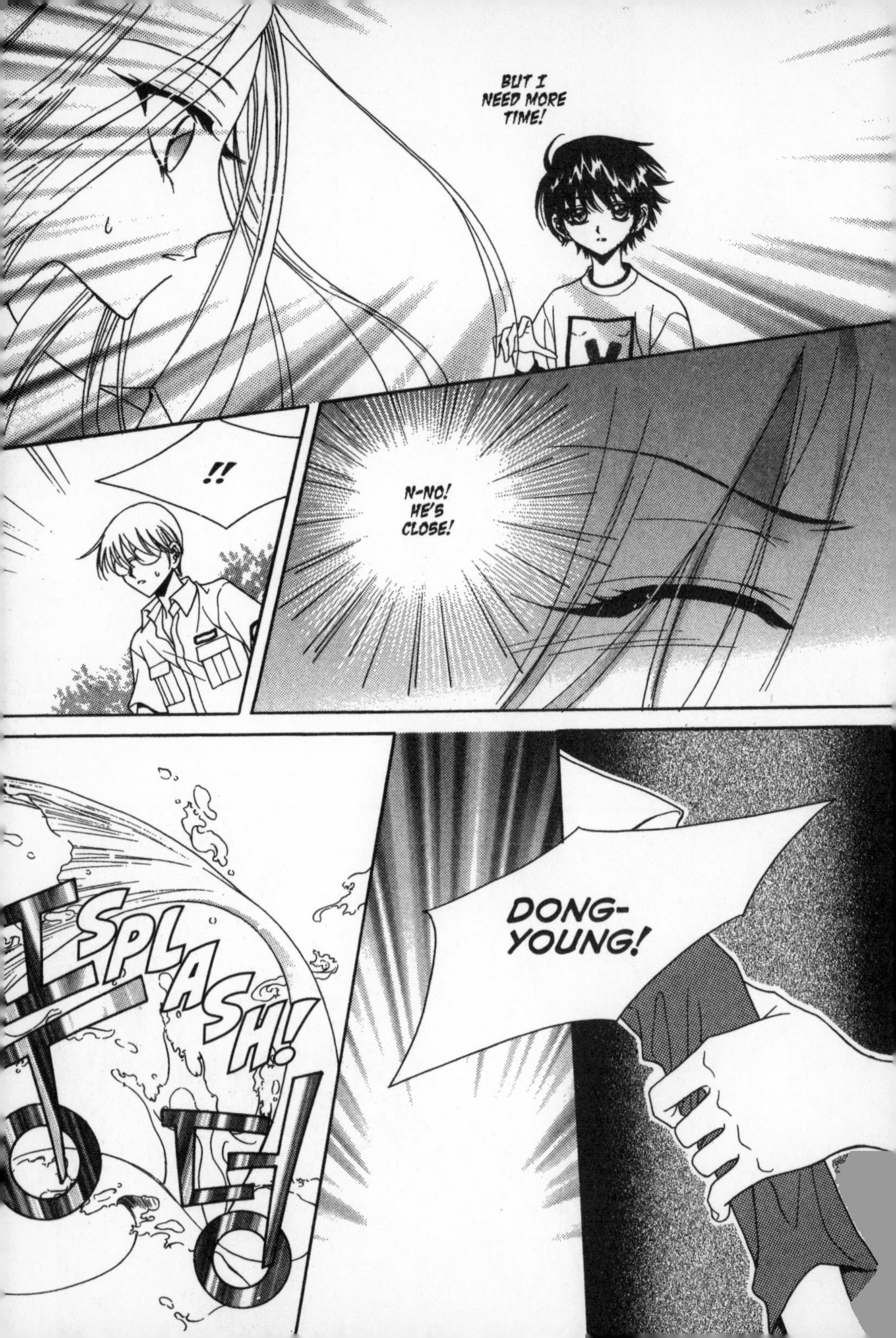
BUT I NEED MORE TIME!
!!
N-NO! HE'S CLOSE!
SPLASH!
DONG-YOUNG!

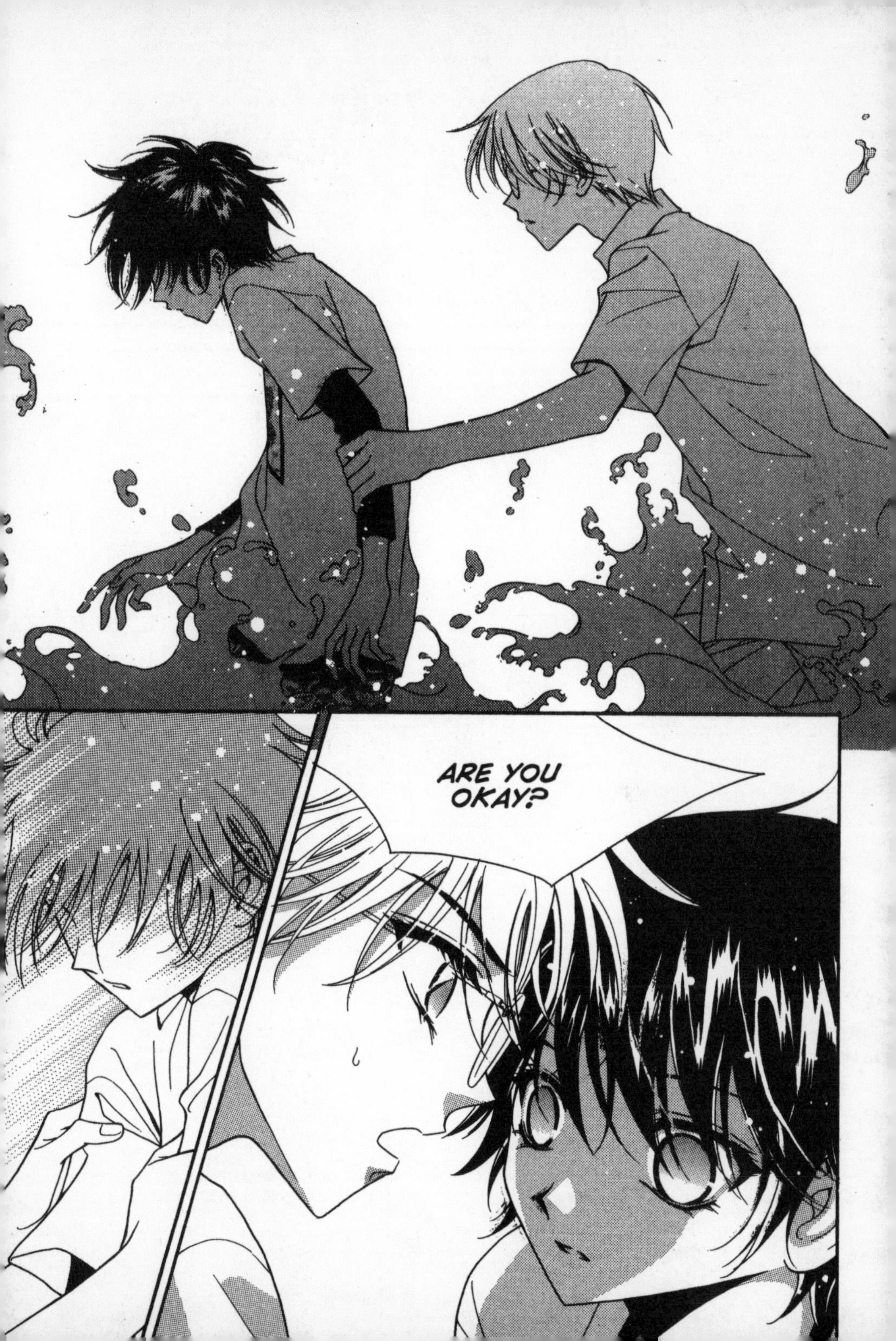
ARE YOU OKAY?

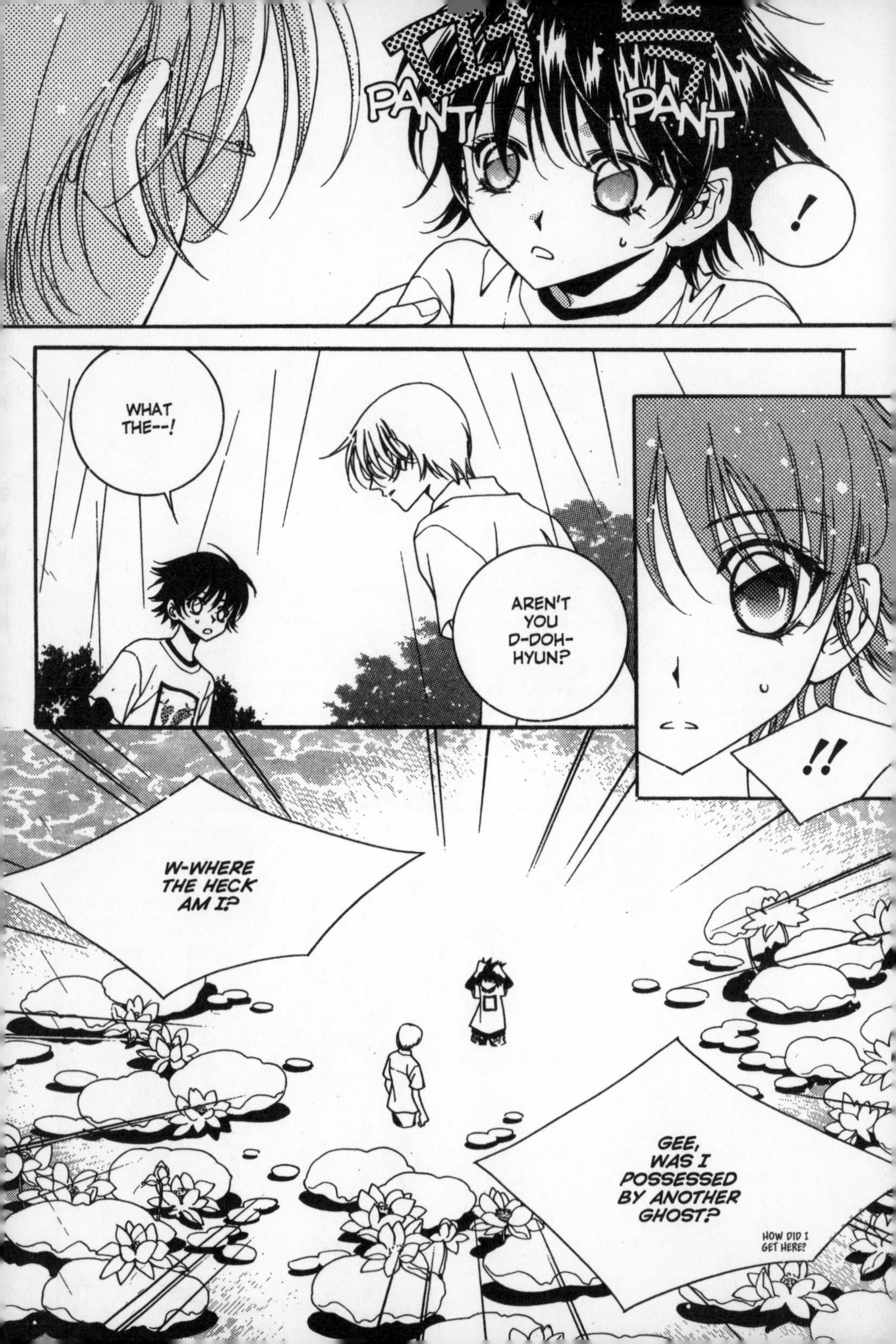
PANT PANT
!
WHAT THE--!
AREN'T YOU D-DOH-HYUN?
!!
W-WHERE THE HECK AM I?
GEE, WAS I POSSESSED BY ANOTHER GHOST?
HOW DID I GET HERE?

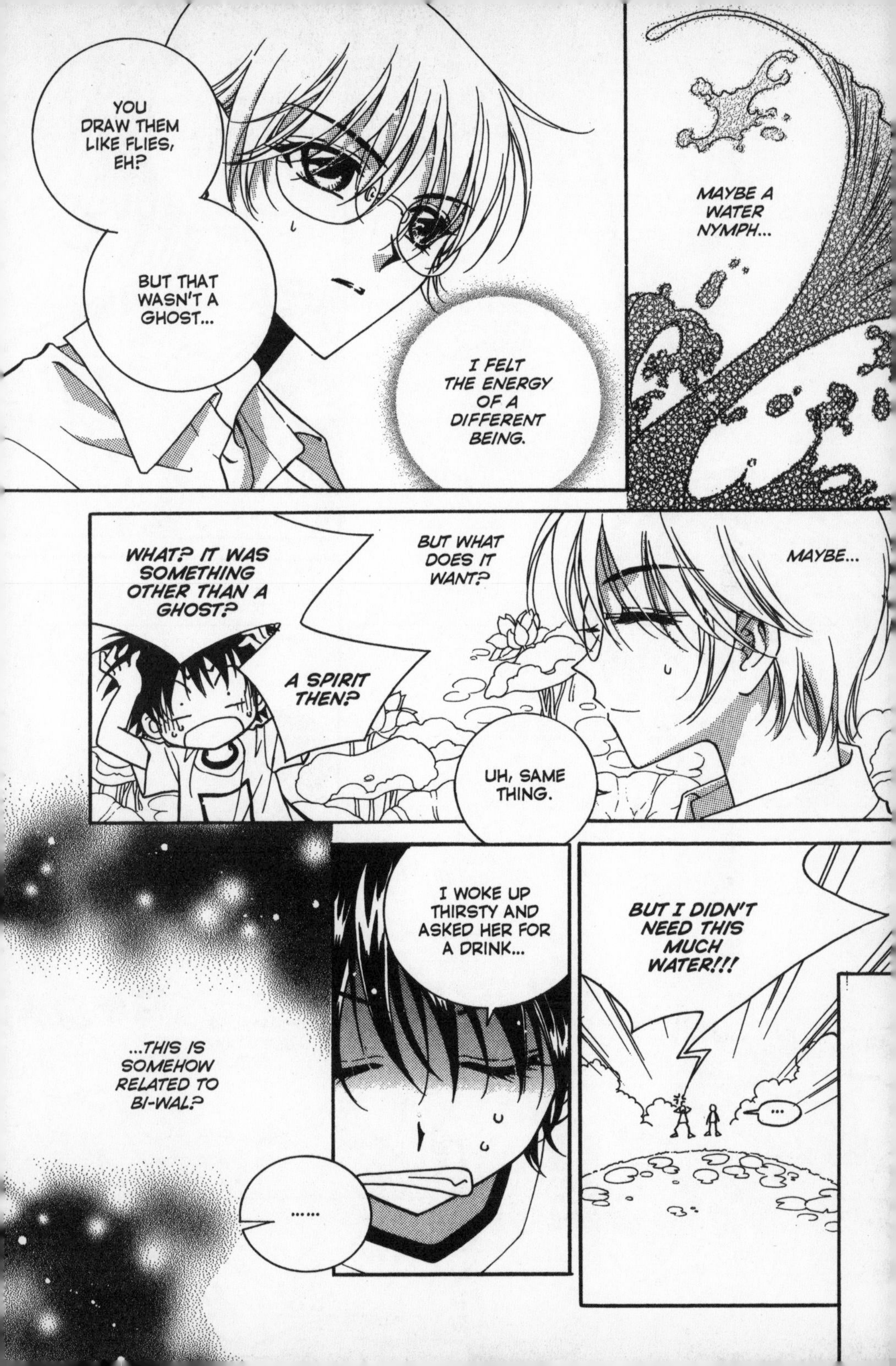
YOU DRAW THEM LIKE FLIES, EH?
BUT THAT WASN'T A GHOST...
I FELT THE ENERGY OF A DIFFERENT BEING.
MAYBE A WATER NYMPH...
WHAT? IT WAS SOMETHING OTHER THAN A GHOST?
A SPIRIT THEN?
BUT WHAT DOES IT WANT?
UH, SAME THING.
MAYBE...
...THIS IS SOMEHOW RELATED TO BI-WAL?
I WOKE UP THIRSTY AND ASKED HER FOR A DRINK...
......
BUT I DIDN'T NEED THIS MUCH WATER!!!
...

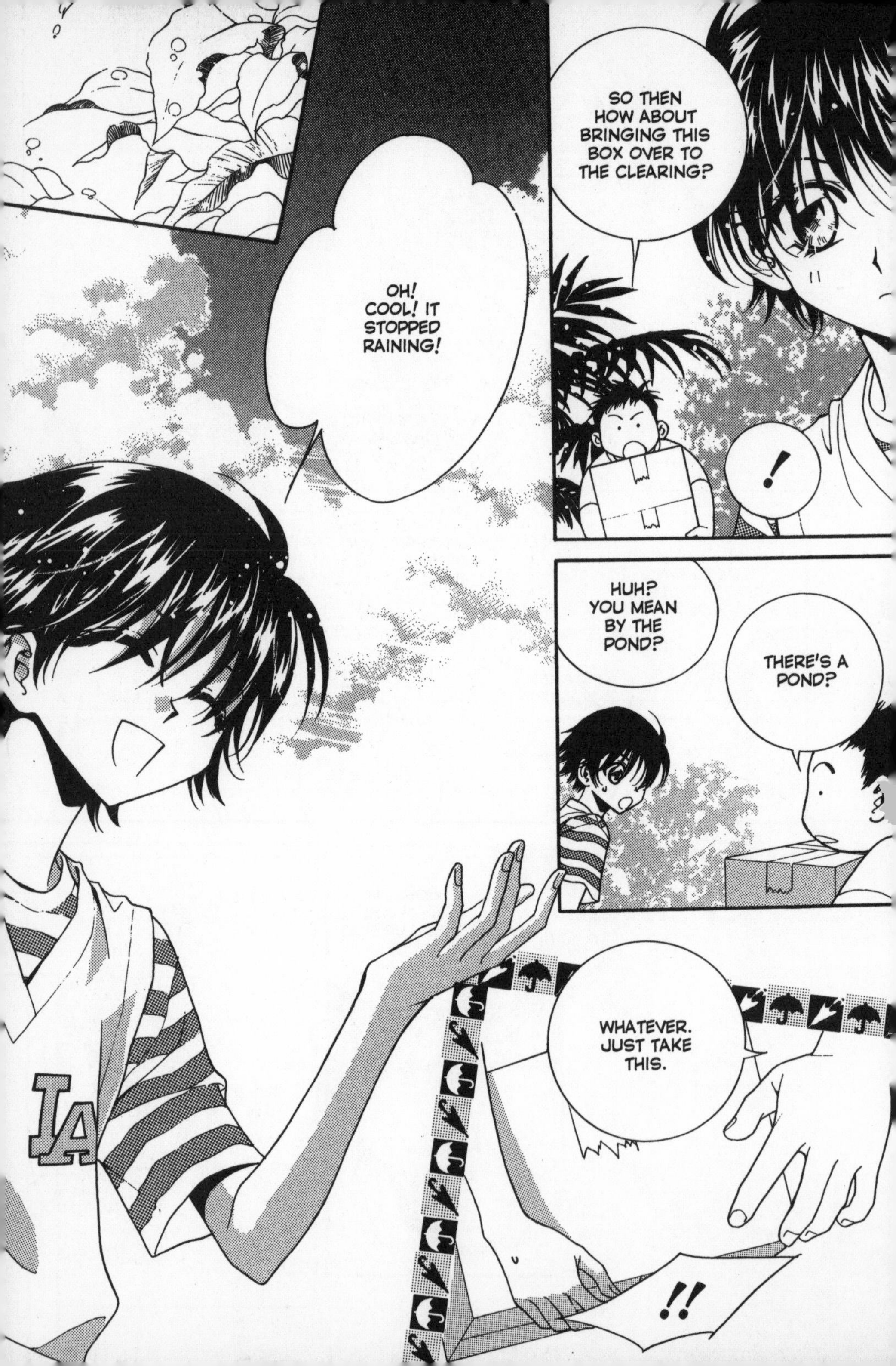
OH! COOL! IT STOPPED RAINING!
SO THEN HOW ABOUT BRINGING THIS BOX OVER TO THE CLEARING?
!
HUH? YOU MEAN BY THE POND?
THERE'S A POND?
WHATEVER. JUST TAKE THIS.
!!

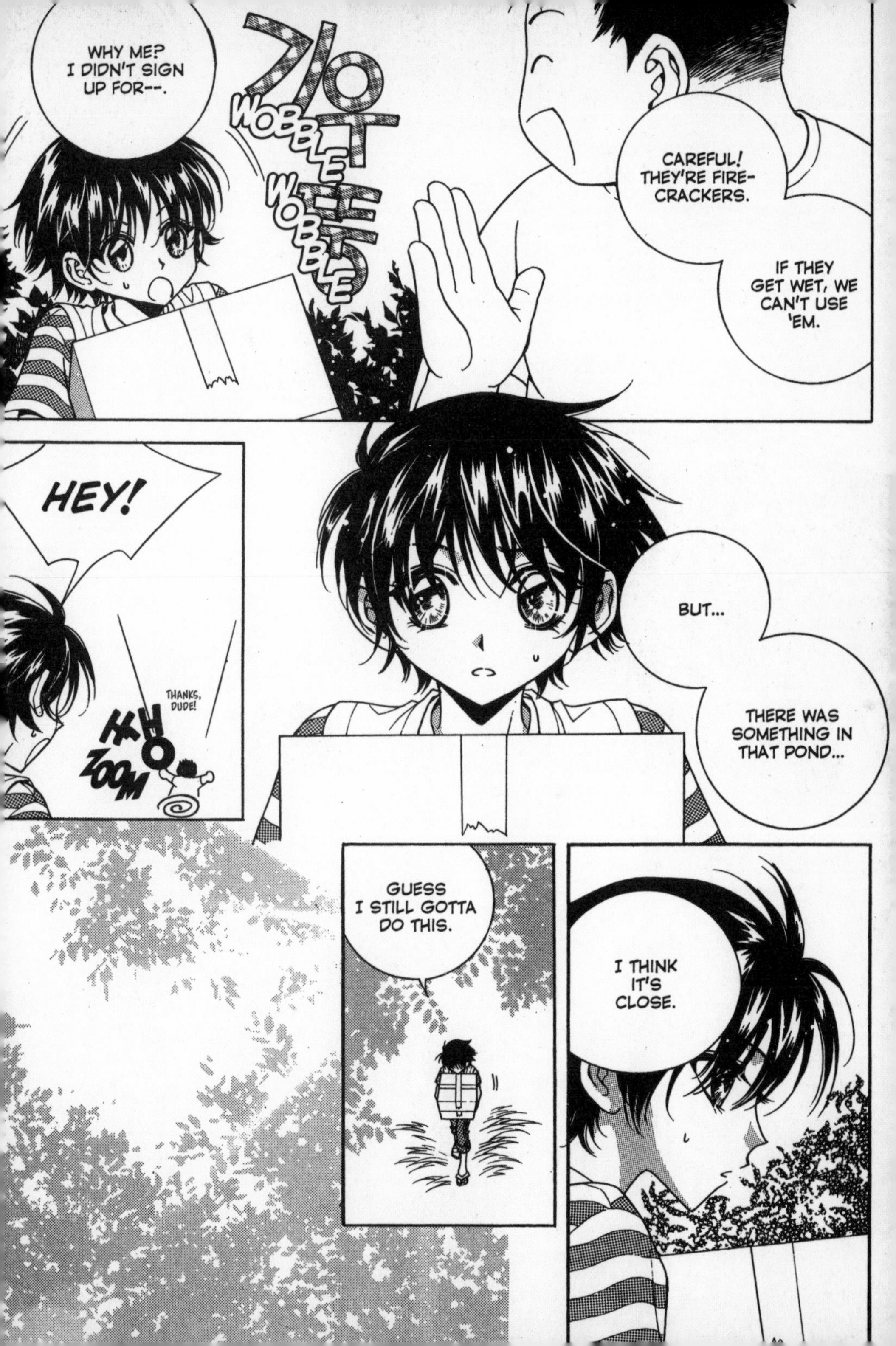
WHY ME? I DIDN'T SIGN UP FOR--.
기우뚱
WOBBLE WOBBLE
CAREFUL! THEY'RE FIRE-CRACKERS.
IF THEY GET WET, WE CAN'T USE 'EM.
HEY!
THANKS, DUDE!
ZOOM
BUT...
THERE WAS SOMETHING IN THAT POND...
GUESS I STILL GOTTA DO THIS.
I THINK IT'S CLOSE.

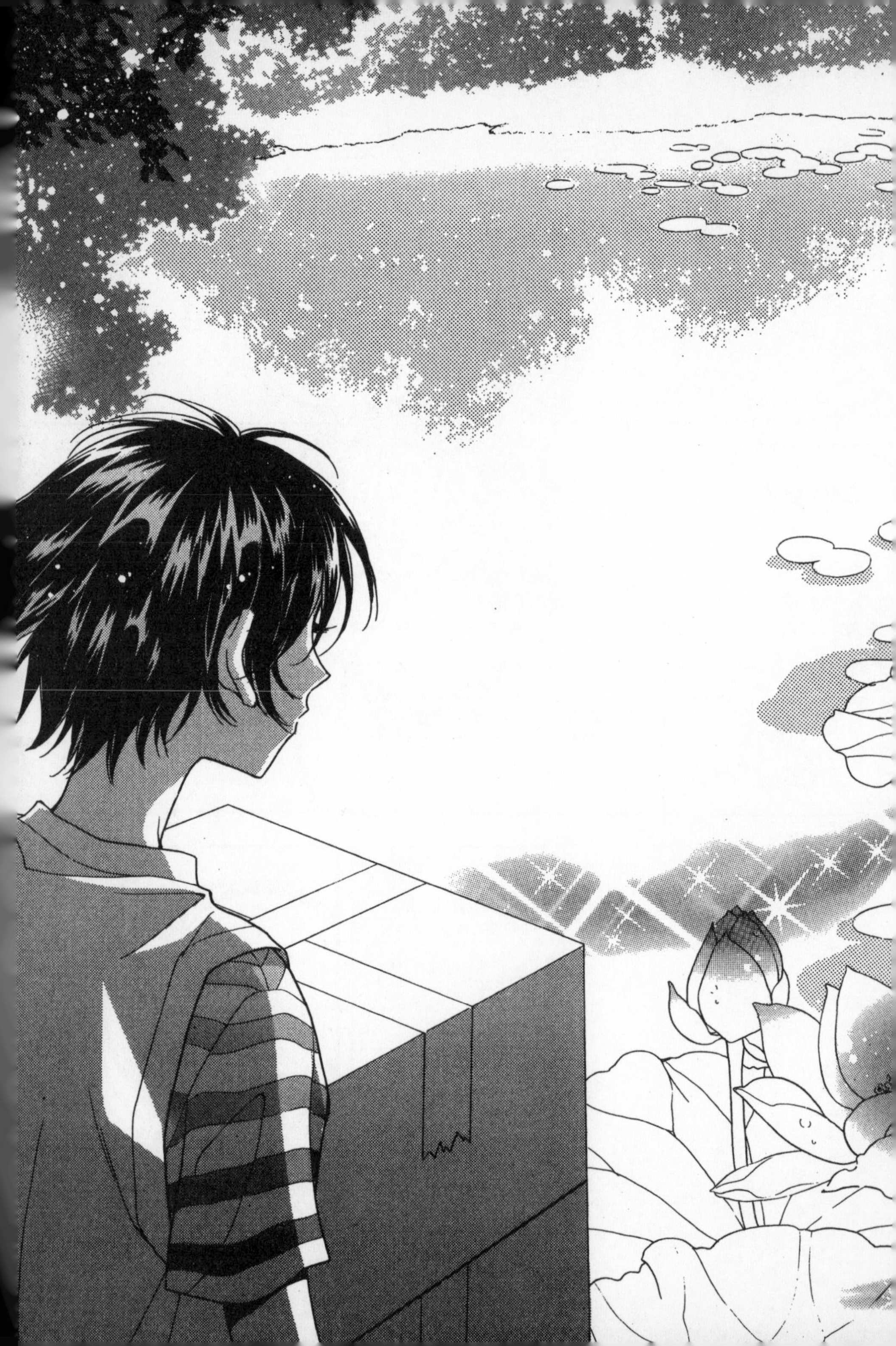

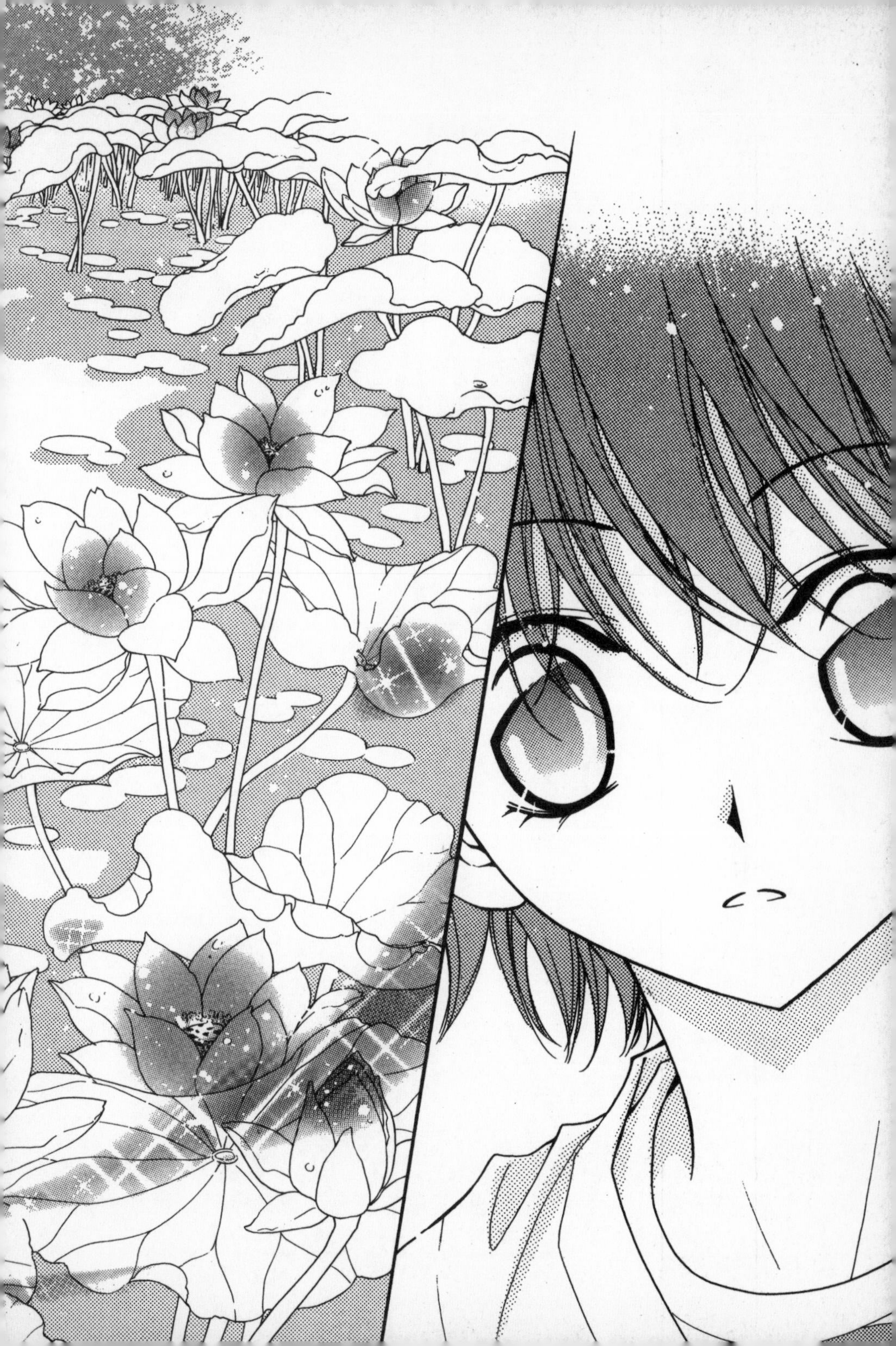

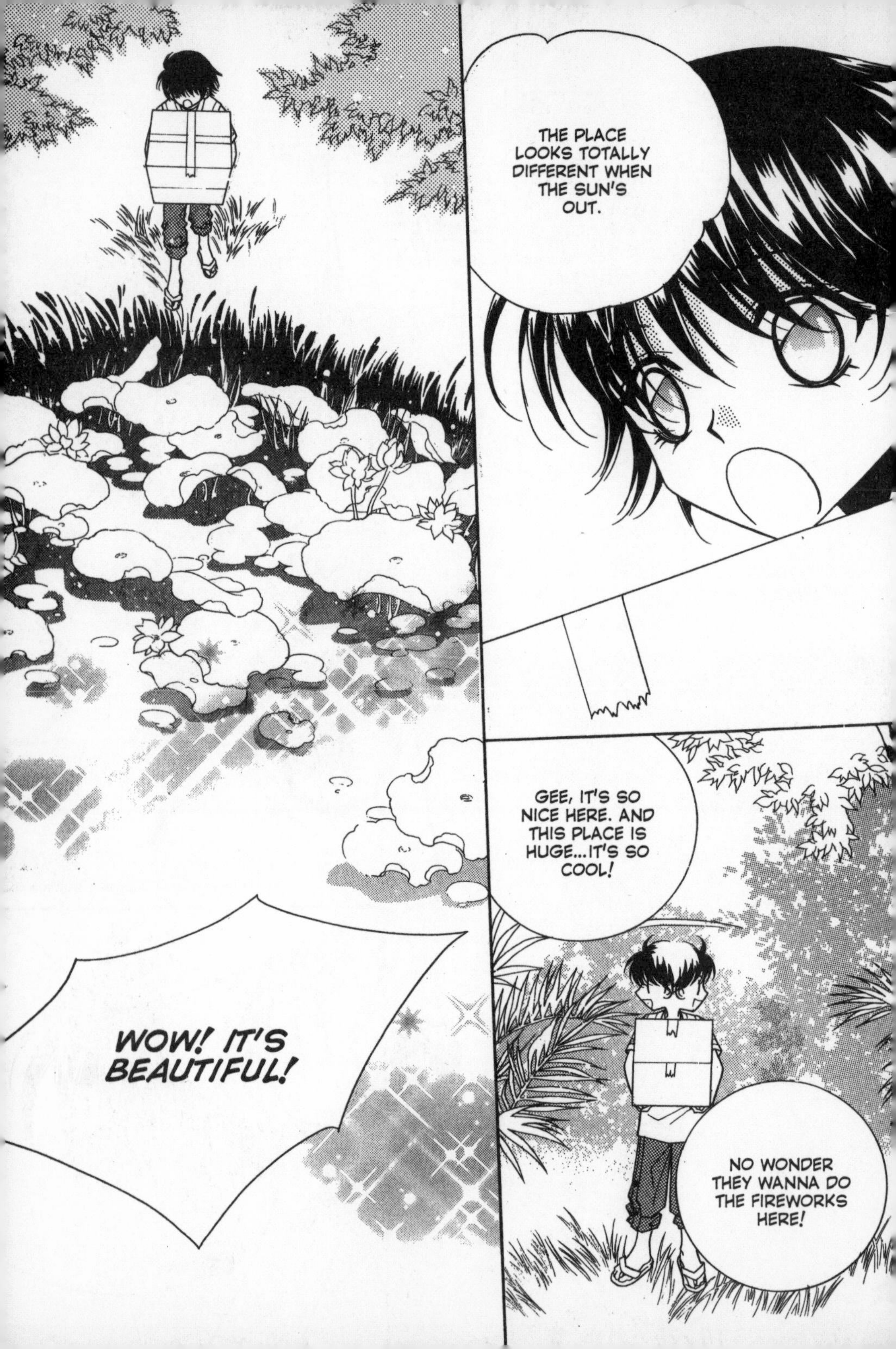
WOW! IT'S BEAUTIFUL!
THE PLACE LOOKS TOTALLY DIFFERENT WHEN THE SUN'S OUT.
GEE, IT'S SO NICE HERE. AND THIS PLACE IS HUGE...IT'S SO COOL!
NO WONDER THEY WANNA DO THE FIREWORKS HERE!

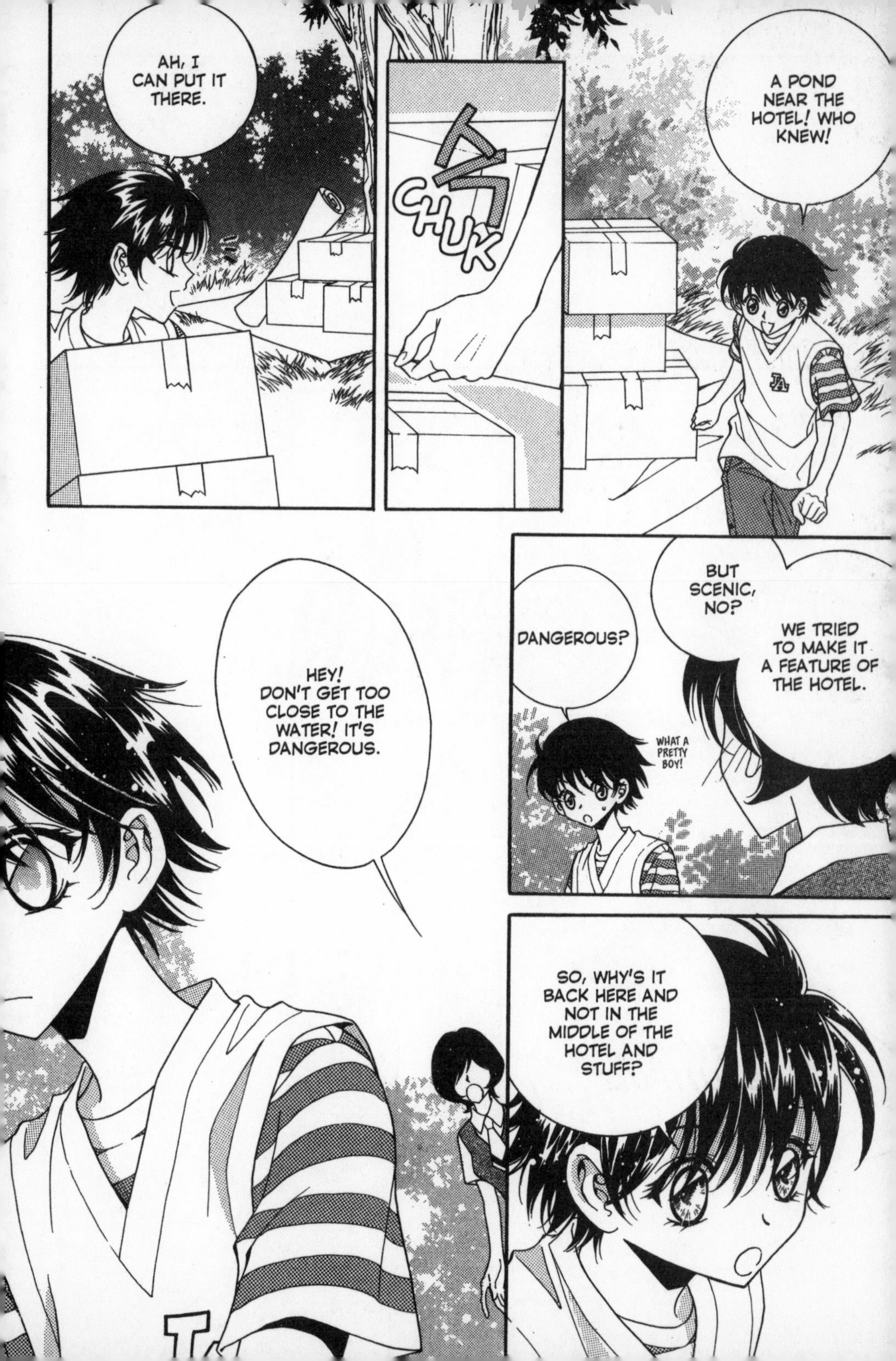
AH, I CAN PUT IT THERE.
CHUK
A POND NEAR THE HOTEL! WHO KNEW!
HEY! DON'T GET TOO CLOSE TO THE WATER! IT'S DANGEROUS.
DANGEROUS?
WHAT A PRETTY BOY!
BUT SCENIC, NO?
WE TRIED TO MAKE IT A FEATURE OF THE HOTEL.
SO, WHY'S IT BACK HERE AND NOT IN THE MIDDLE OF THE HOTEL AND STUFF?

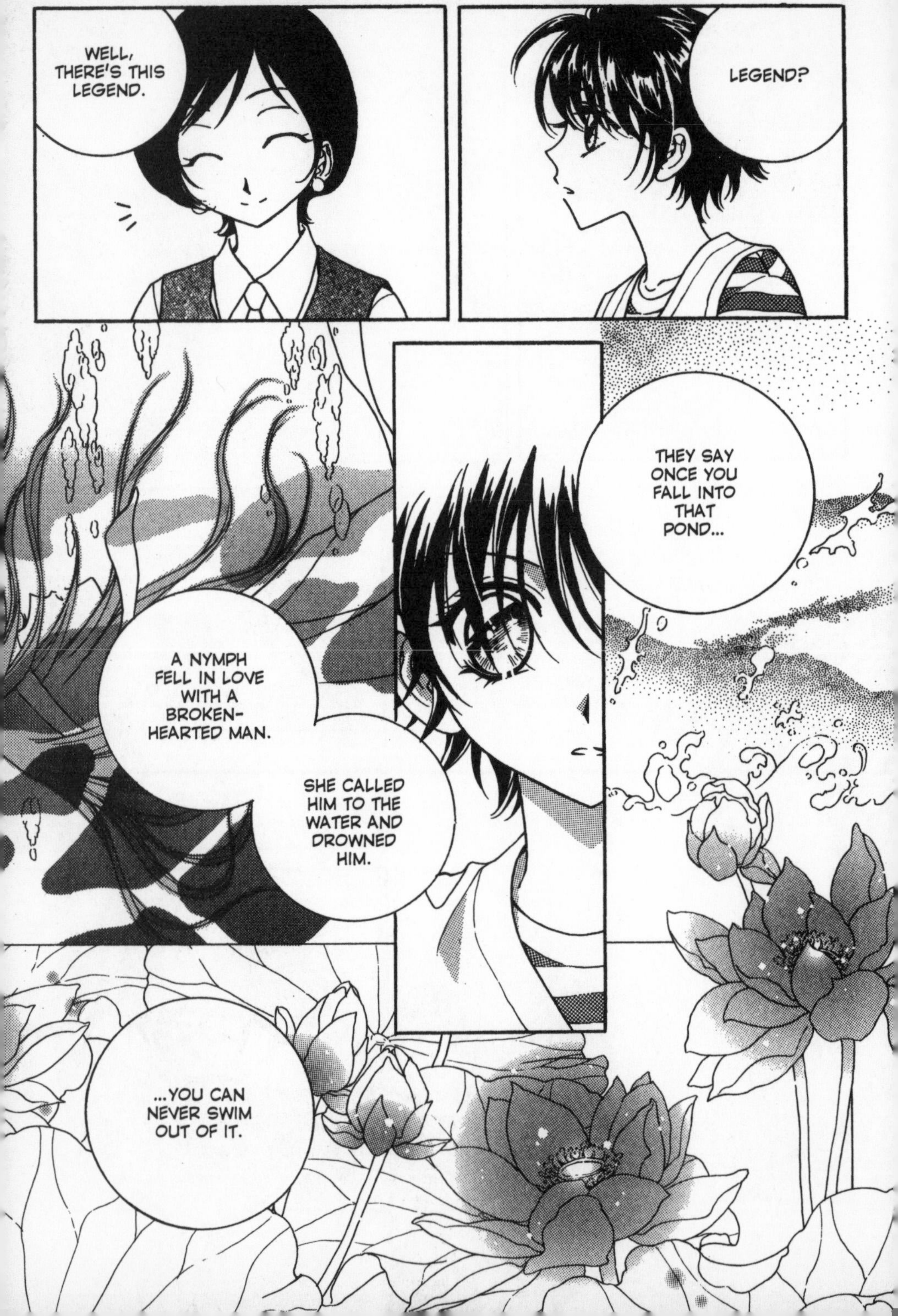
WELL, THERE'S THIS LEGEND.
LEGEND?
THEY SAY ONCE YOU FALL INTO THAT POND...
A NYMPH FELL IN LOVE WITH A BROKEN-HEARTED MAN.
SHE CALLED HIM TO THE WATER AND DROWNED HIM.
...YOU CAN NEVER SWIM OUT OF IT.

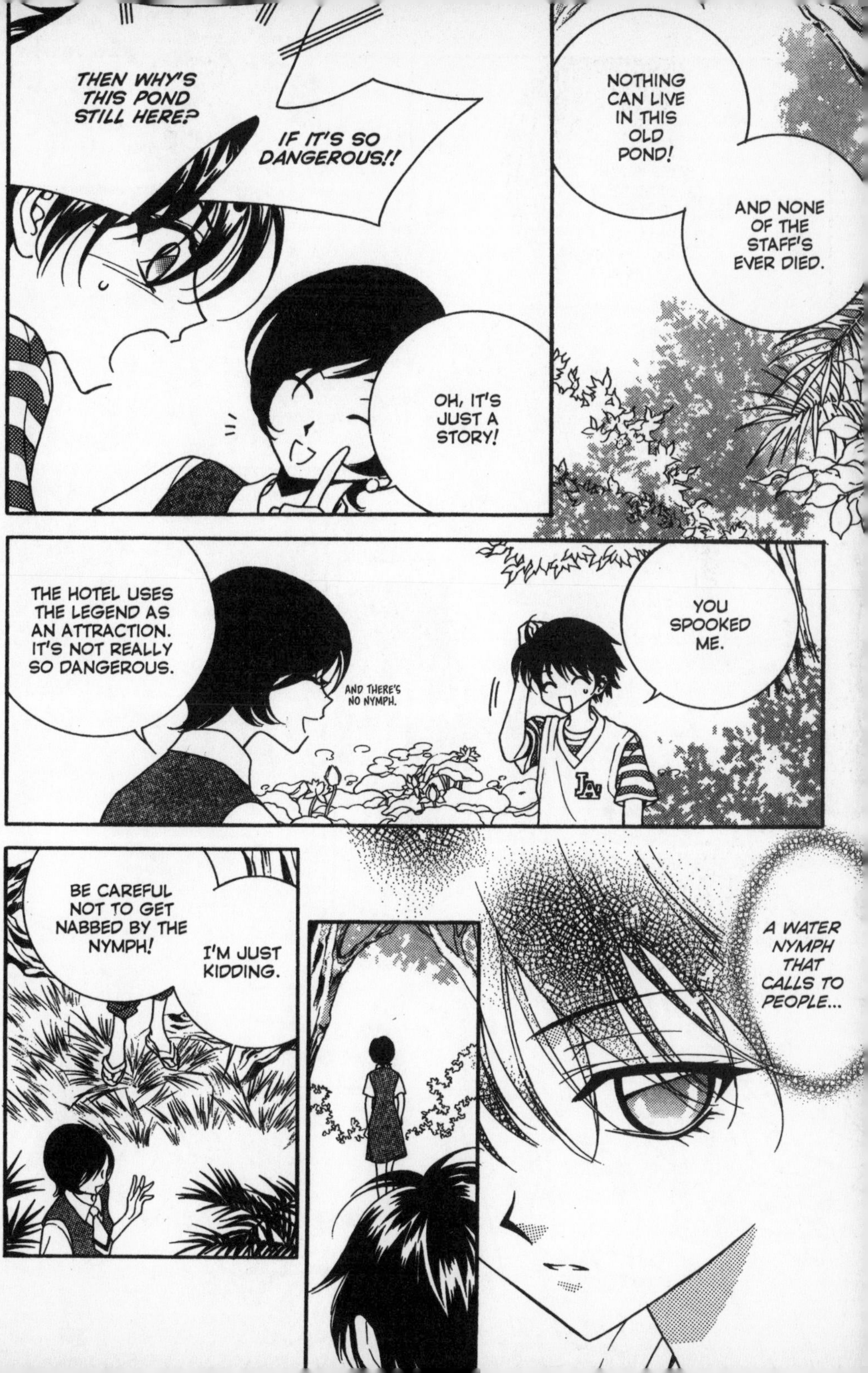
THEN WHY'S THIS POND STILL HERE?
IF IT'S SO DANGEROUS!!
OH, IT'S JUST A STORY!
NOTHING CAN LIVE IN THIS OLD POND!
AND NONE OF THE STAFF'S EVER DIED.
THE HOTEL USES THE LEGEND AS AN ATTRACTION. IT'S NOT REALLY SO DANGEROUS.
AND THERE'S NO NYMPH.
YOU SPOOKED ME.
BE CAREFUL NOT TO GET NABBED BY THE NYMPH!
I'M JUST KIDDING.
A WATER NYMPH THAT CALLS TO PEOPLE...

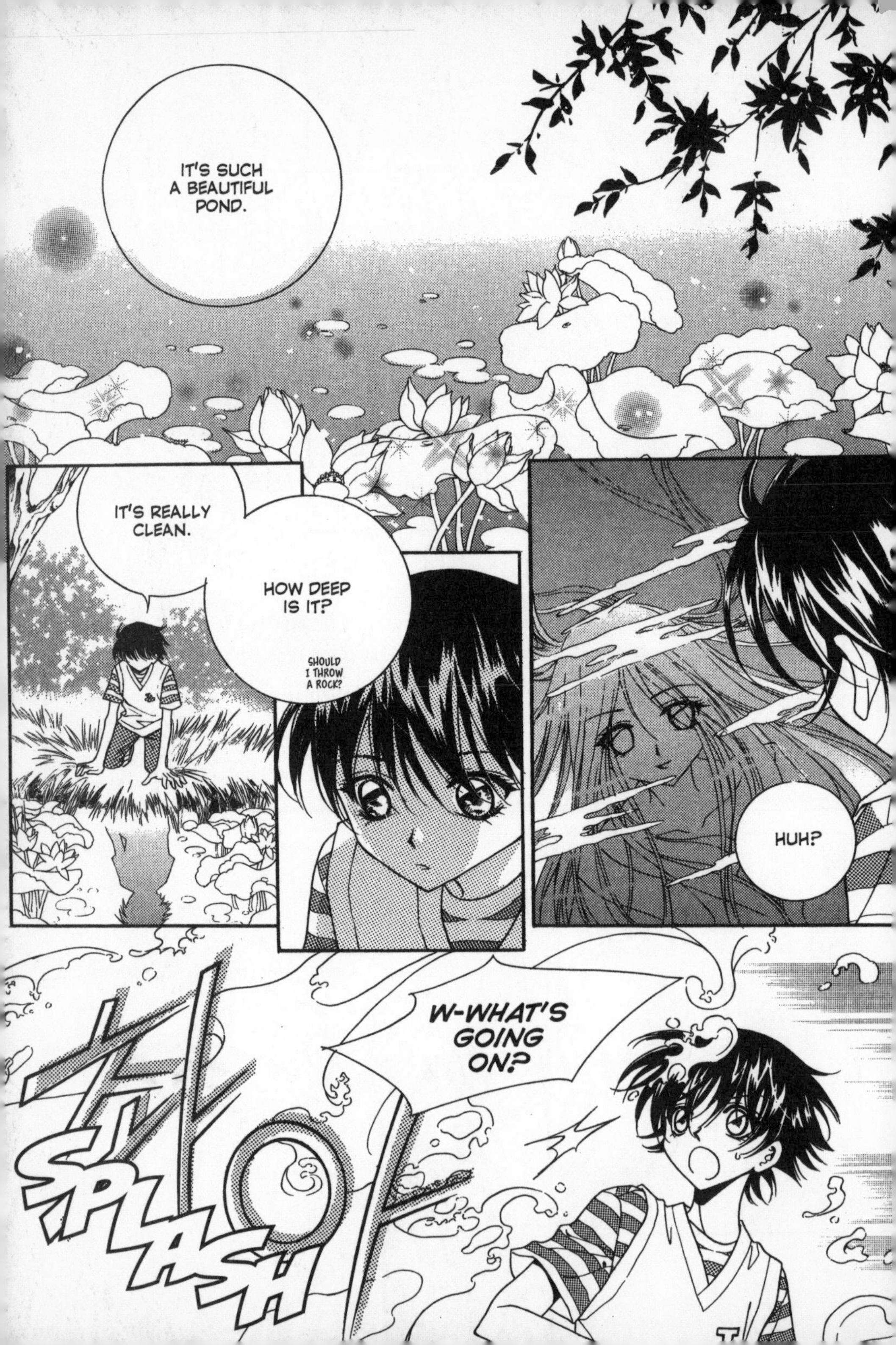
IT'S SUCH A BEAUTIFUL POND.
IT'S REALLY CLEAN.
HOW DEEP IS IT?
SHOULD I THROW A ROCK?
HUH?
SPLASH
W-WHAT'S GOING ON?

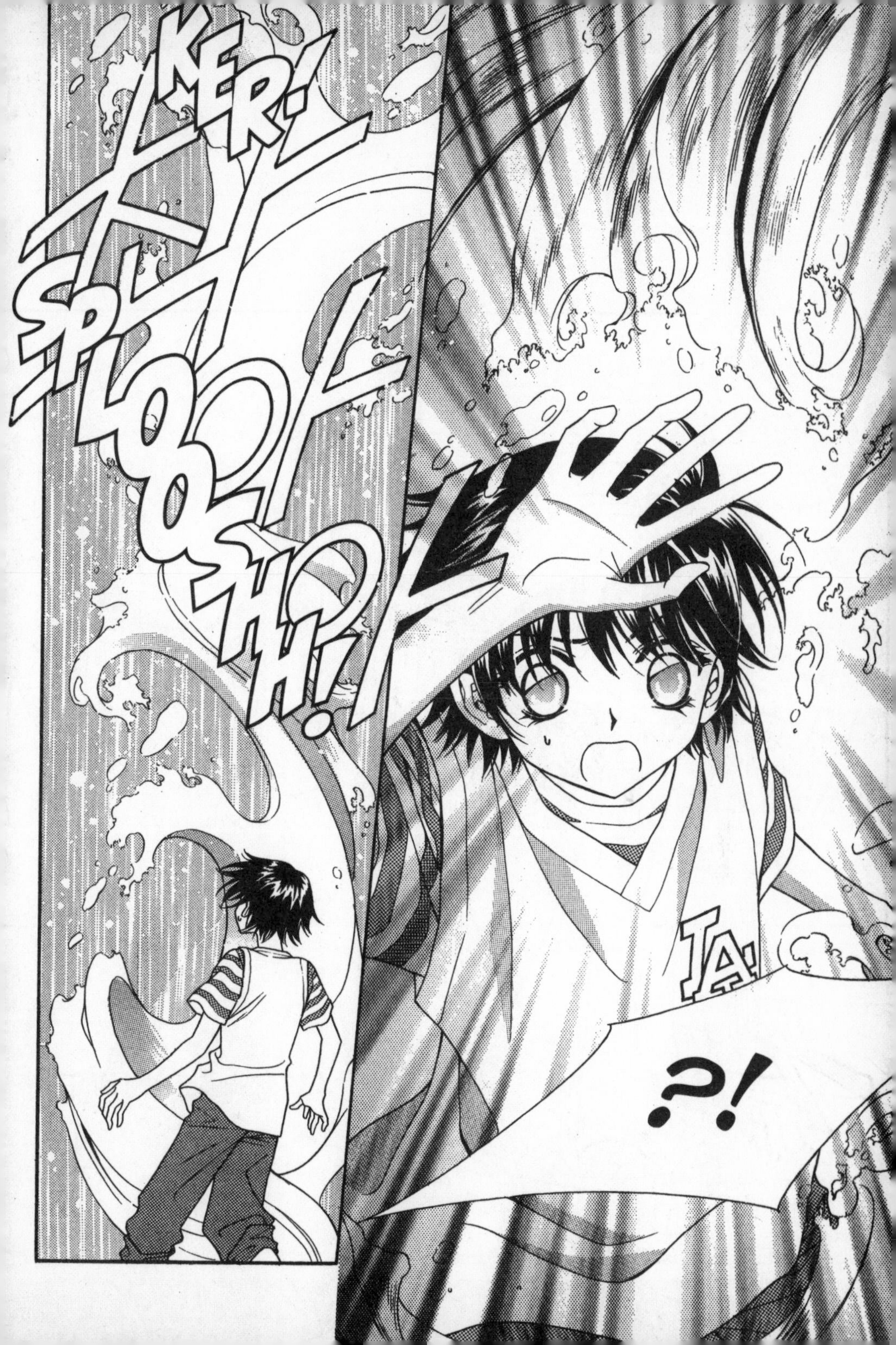
KER-SPLOOSH!
?!

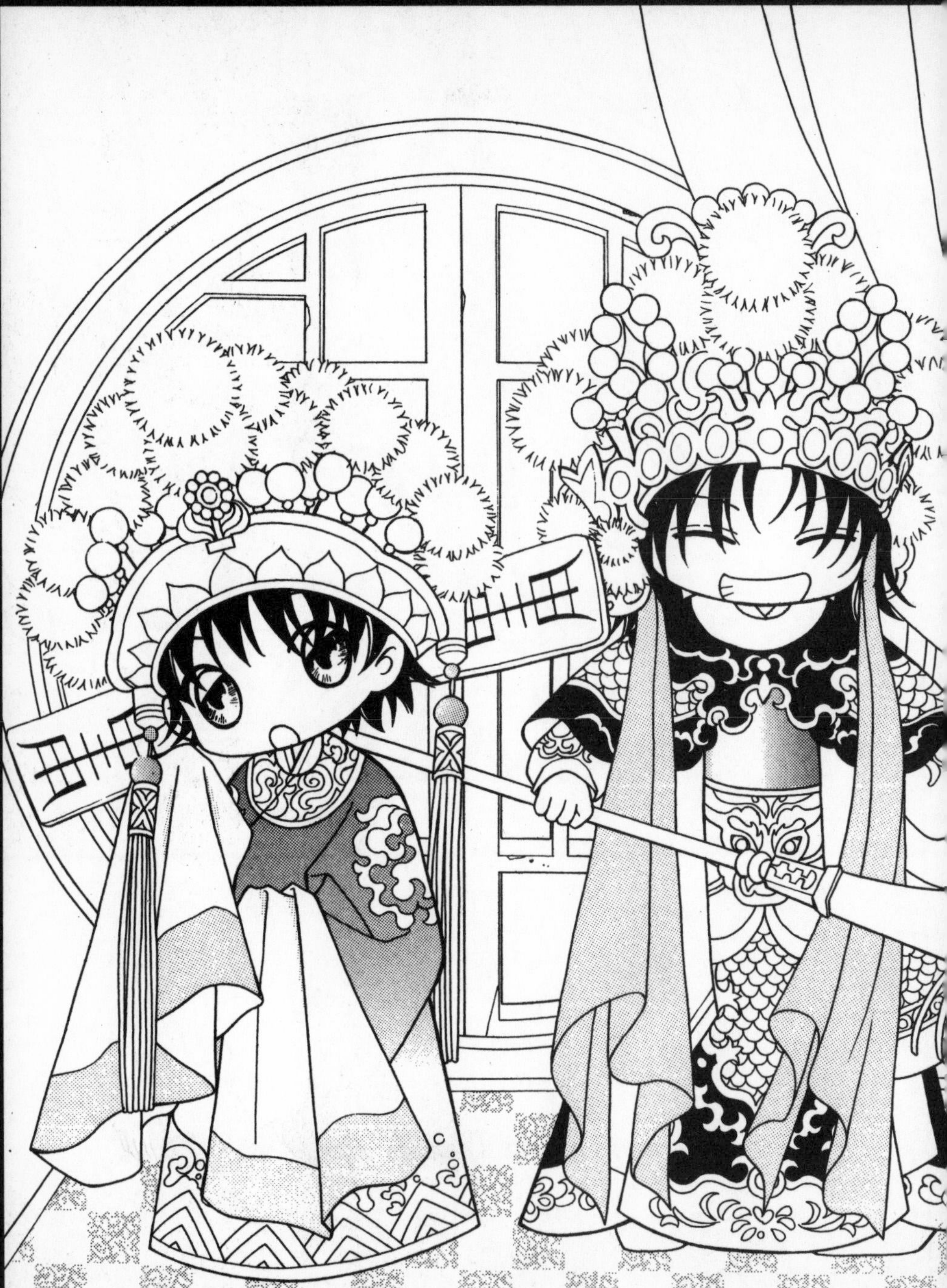

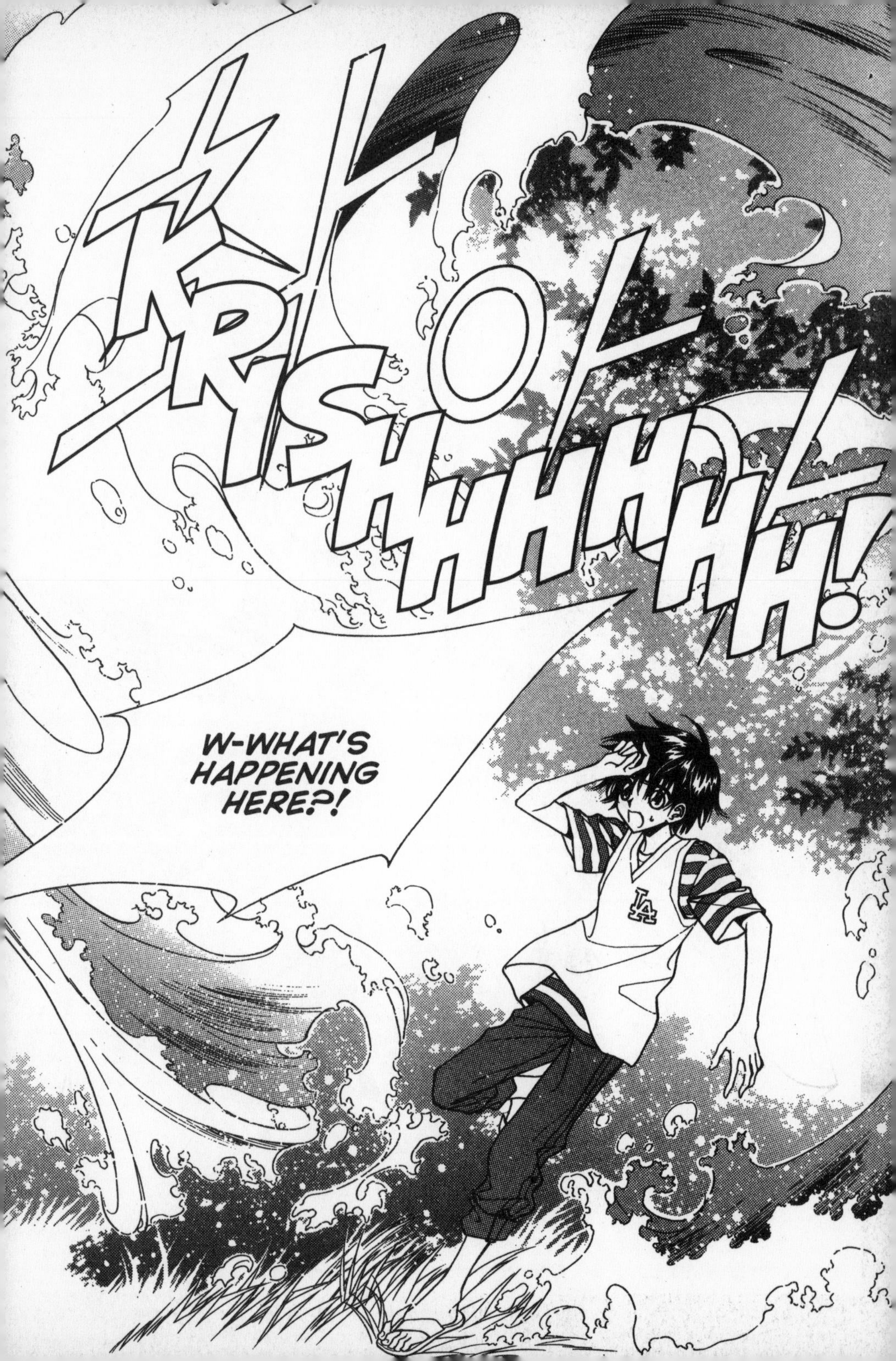
KRISSHHHHHH!
W-WHAT'S HAPPENING HERE?!

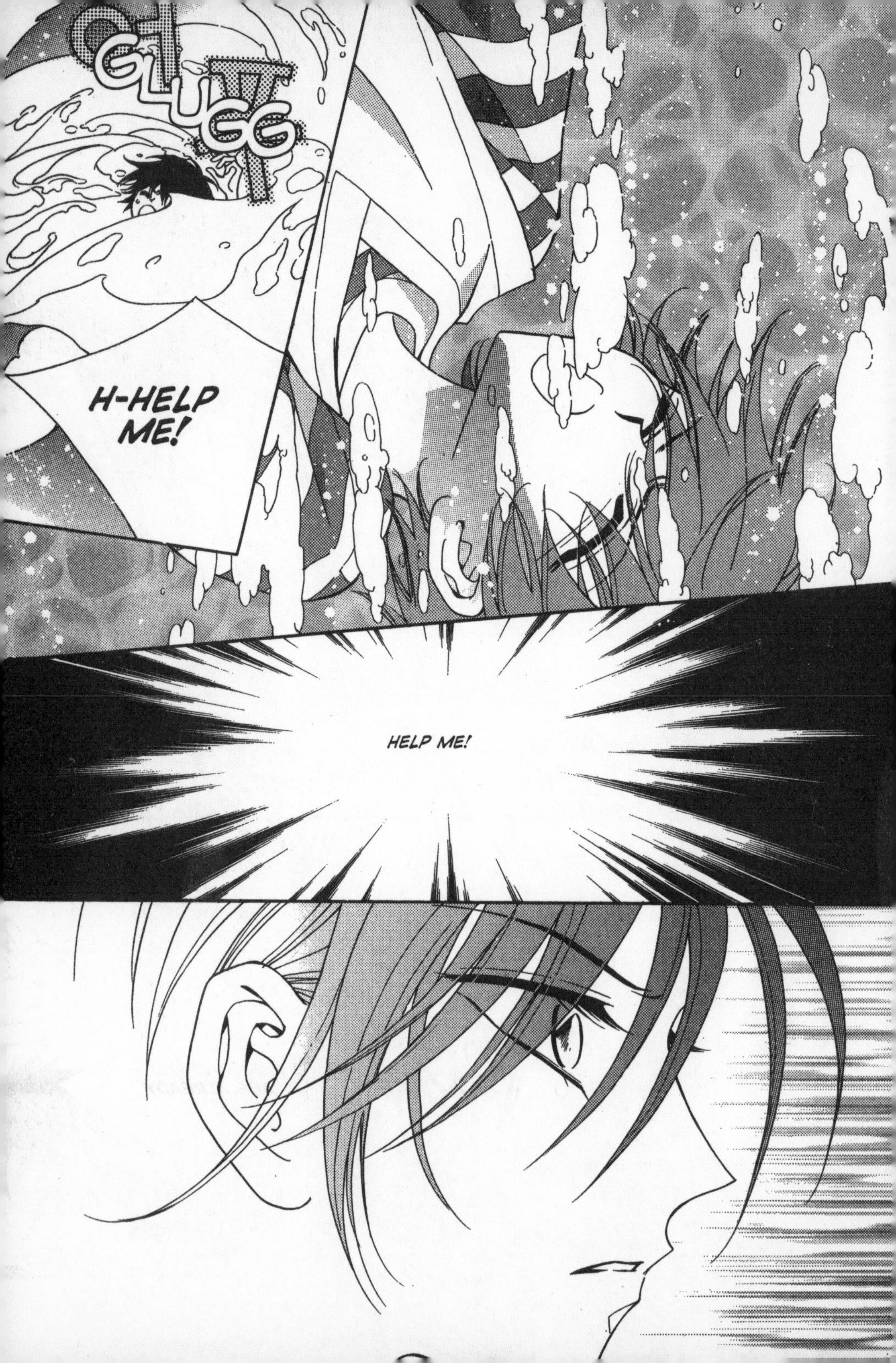
GLUGG
H-HELP ME!
HELP ME!

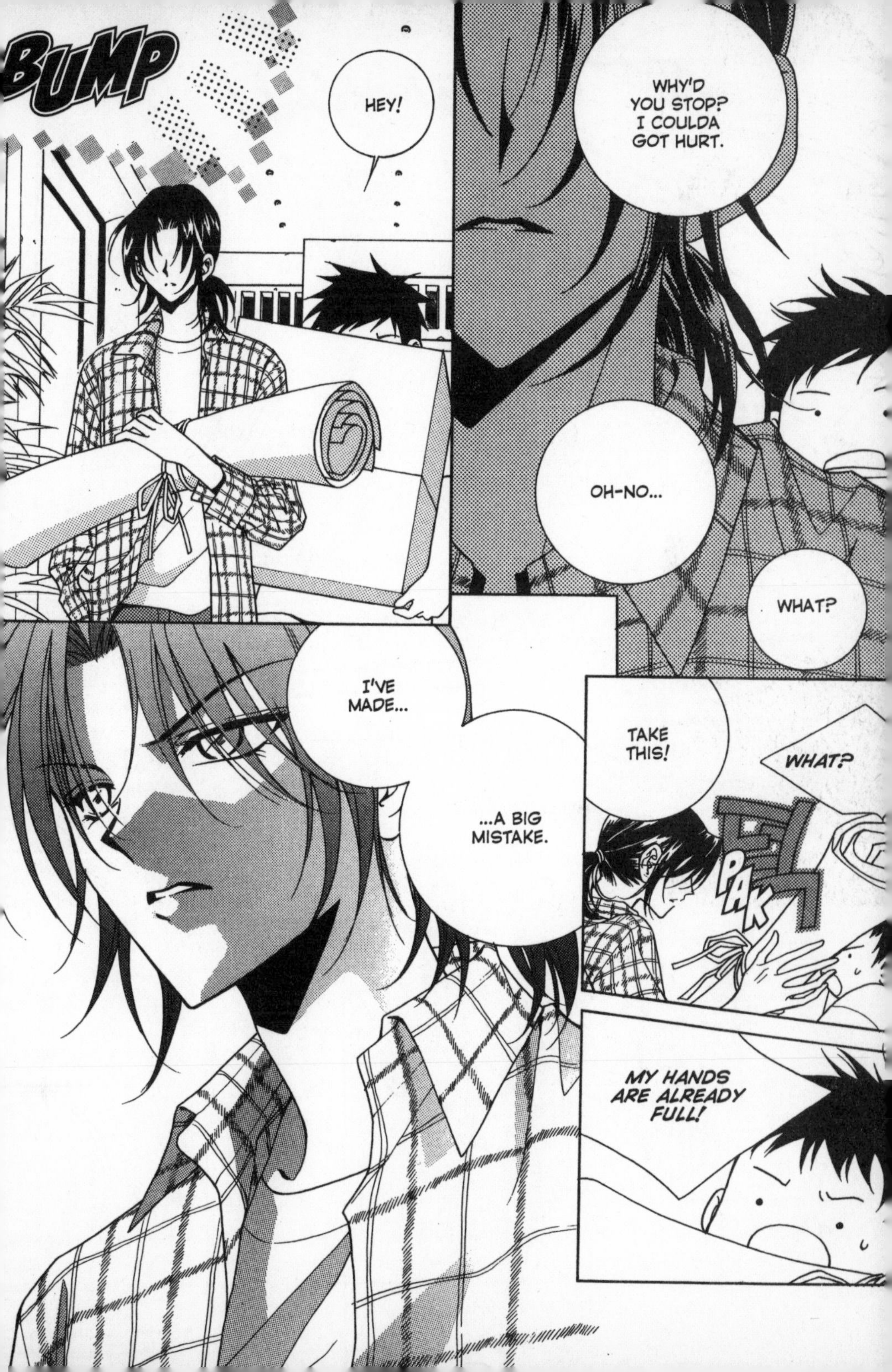
BUMP
HEY!
WHY'D YOU STOP? I COULDA GOT HURT.
OH-NO...
WHAT?
I'VE MADE...
...A BIG MISTAKE.
TAKE THIS!
WHAT?
PAK
MY HANDS ARE ALREADY FULL!

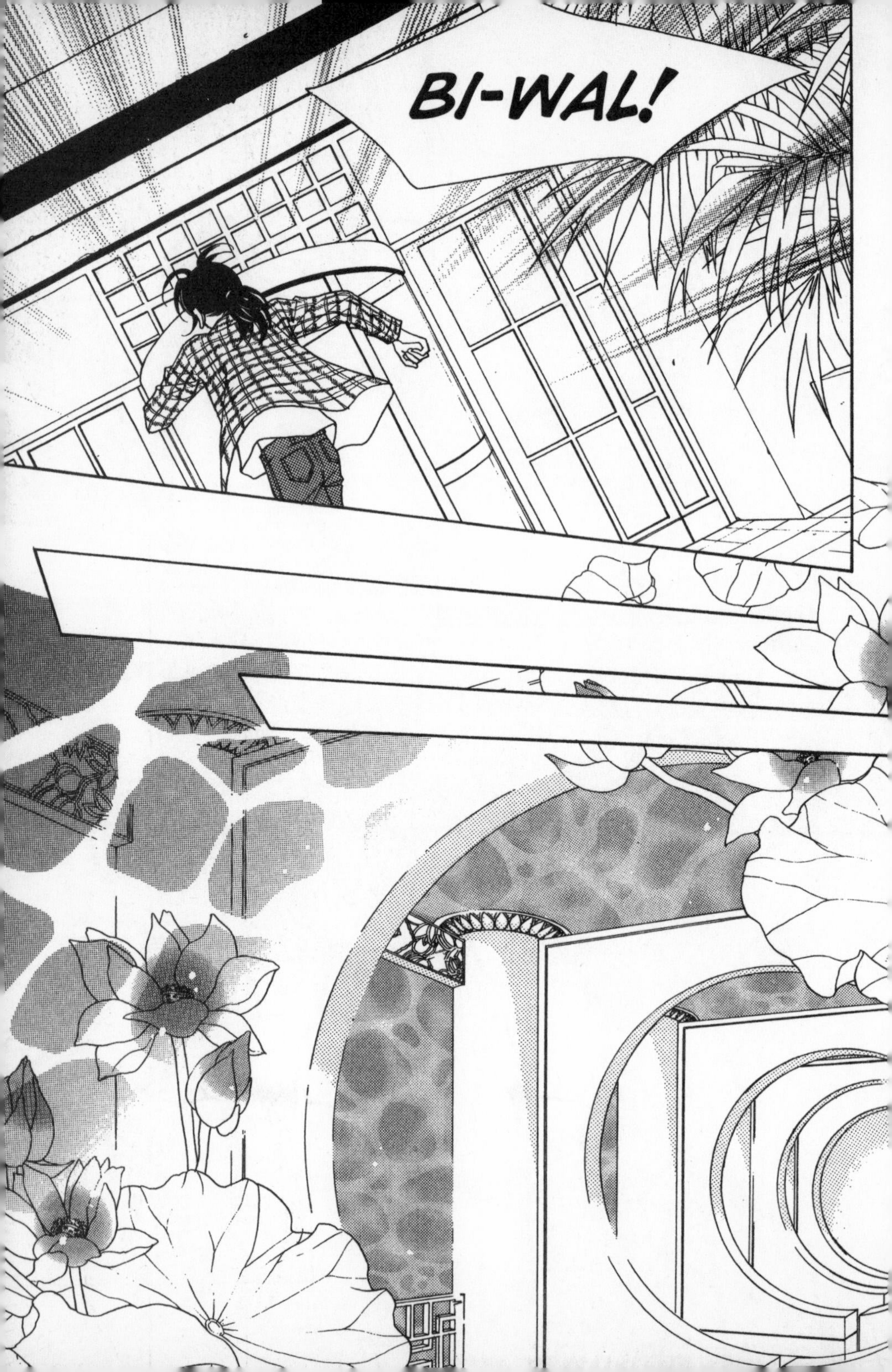
BI-WAL!

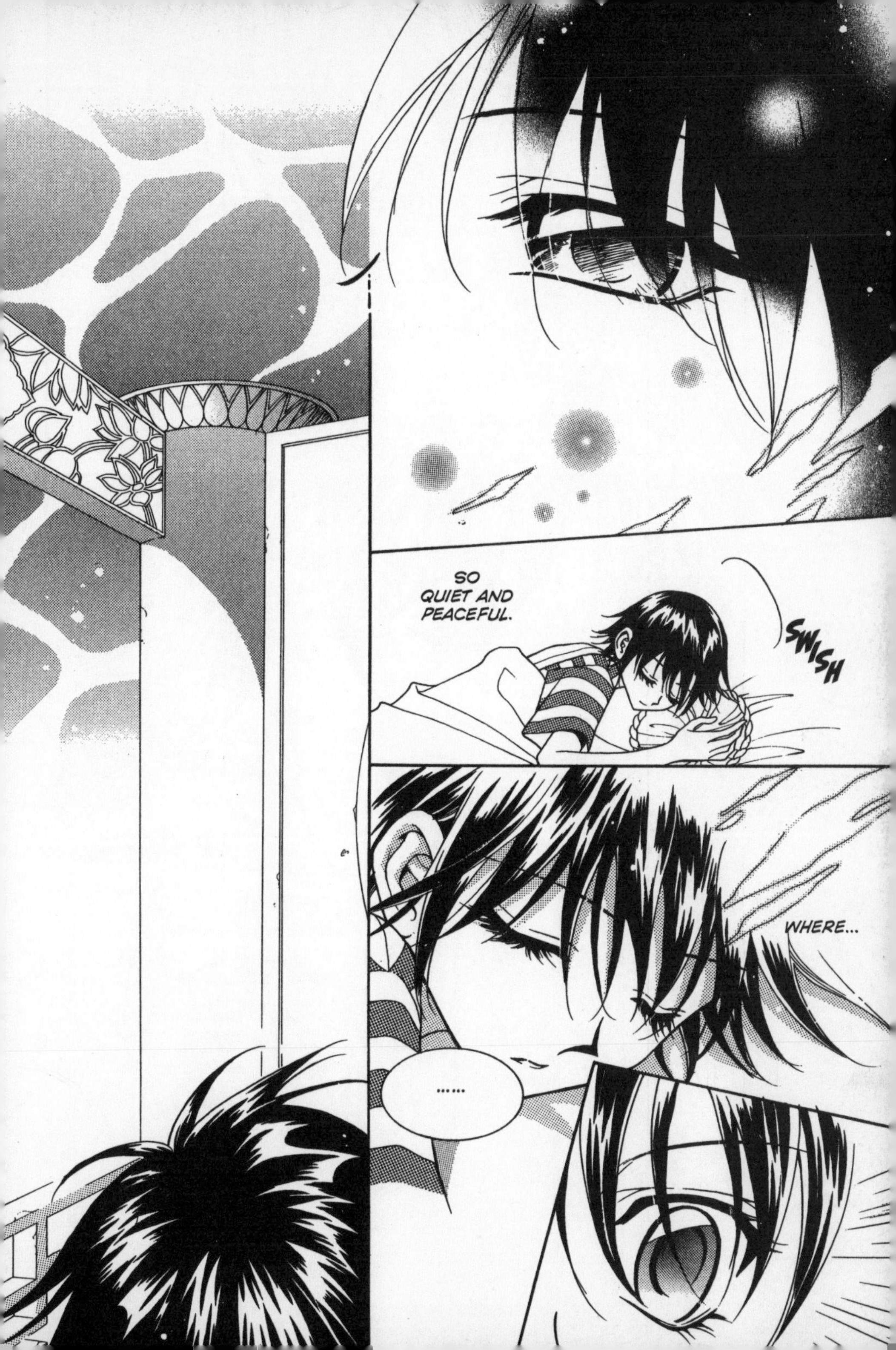
SO QUIET AND PEACEFUL.
SWISH
WHERE...
......

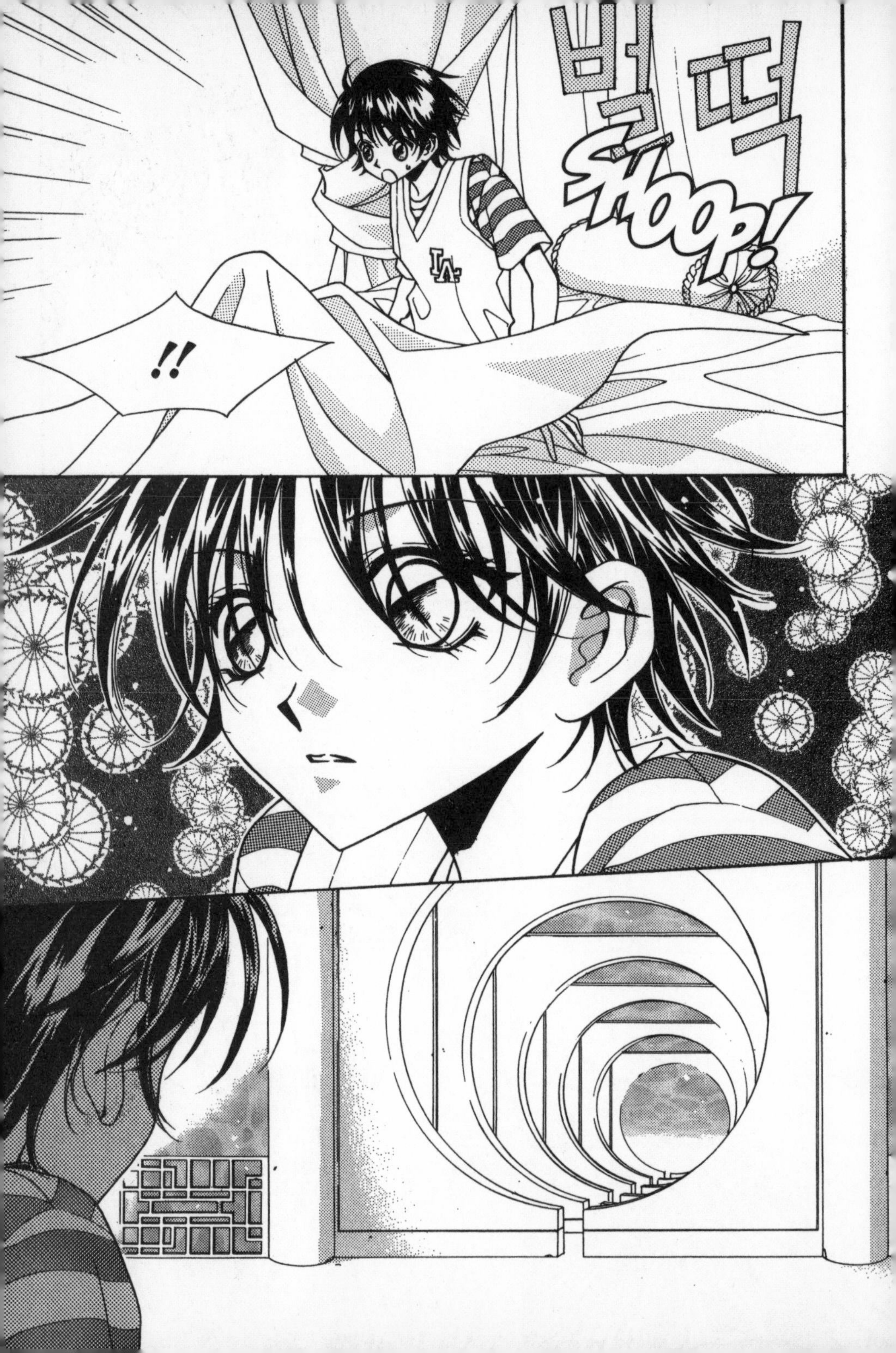
벌떡
SHOOP!
!!

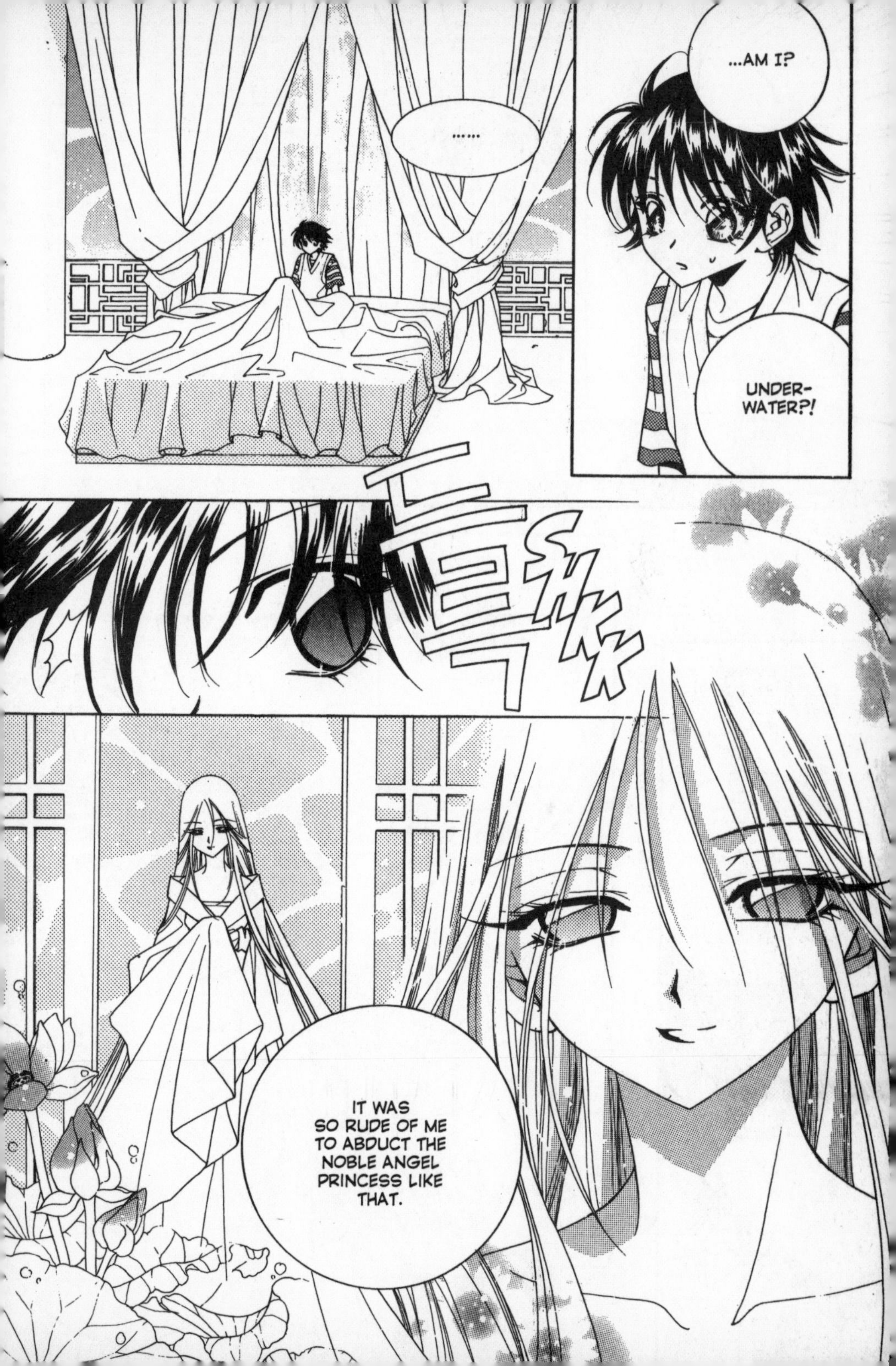
......
...AM I?
UNDER-WATER?!
SHKK
IT WAS SO RUDE OF ME TO ABDUCT THE NOBLE ANGEL PRINCESS LIKE THAT.

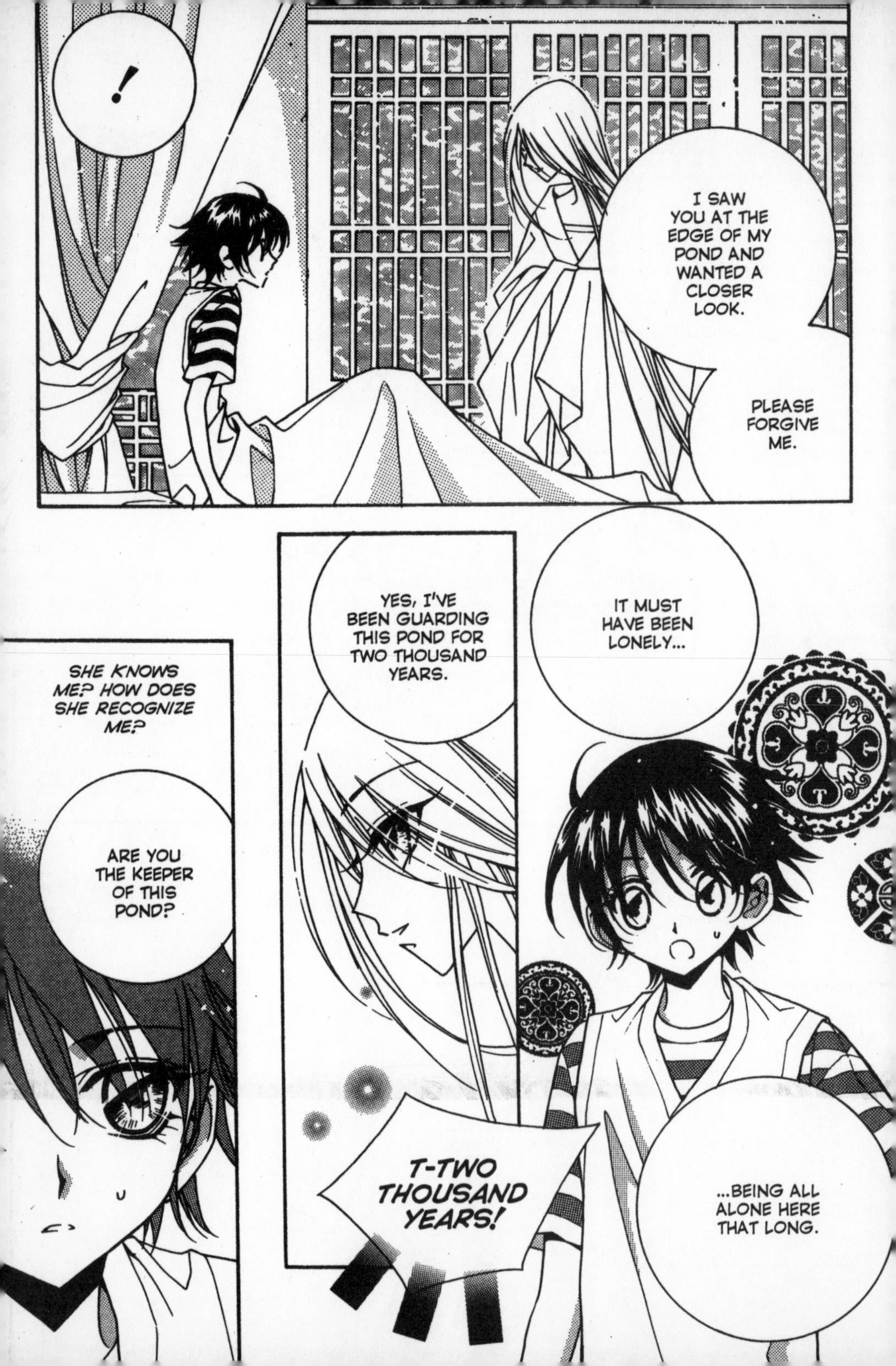
!
I SAW YOU AT THE EDGE OF MY POND AND WANTED A CLOSER LOOK.
PLEASE FORGIVE ME.
SHE KNOWS ME? HOW DOES SHE RECOGNIZE ME?
ARE YOU THE KEEPER OF THIS POND?
YES, I'VE BEEN GUARDING THIS POND FOR TWO THOUSAND YEARS.
T-TWO THOUSAND YEARS!
IT MUST HAVE BEEN LONELY...
...BEING ALL ALONE HERE THAT LONG.

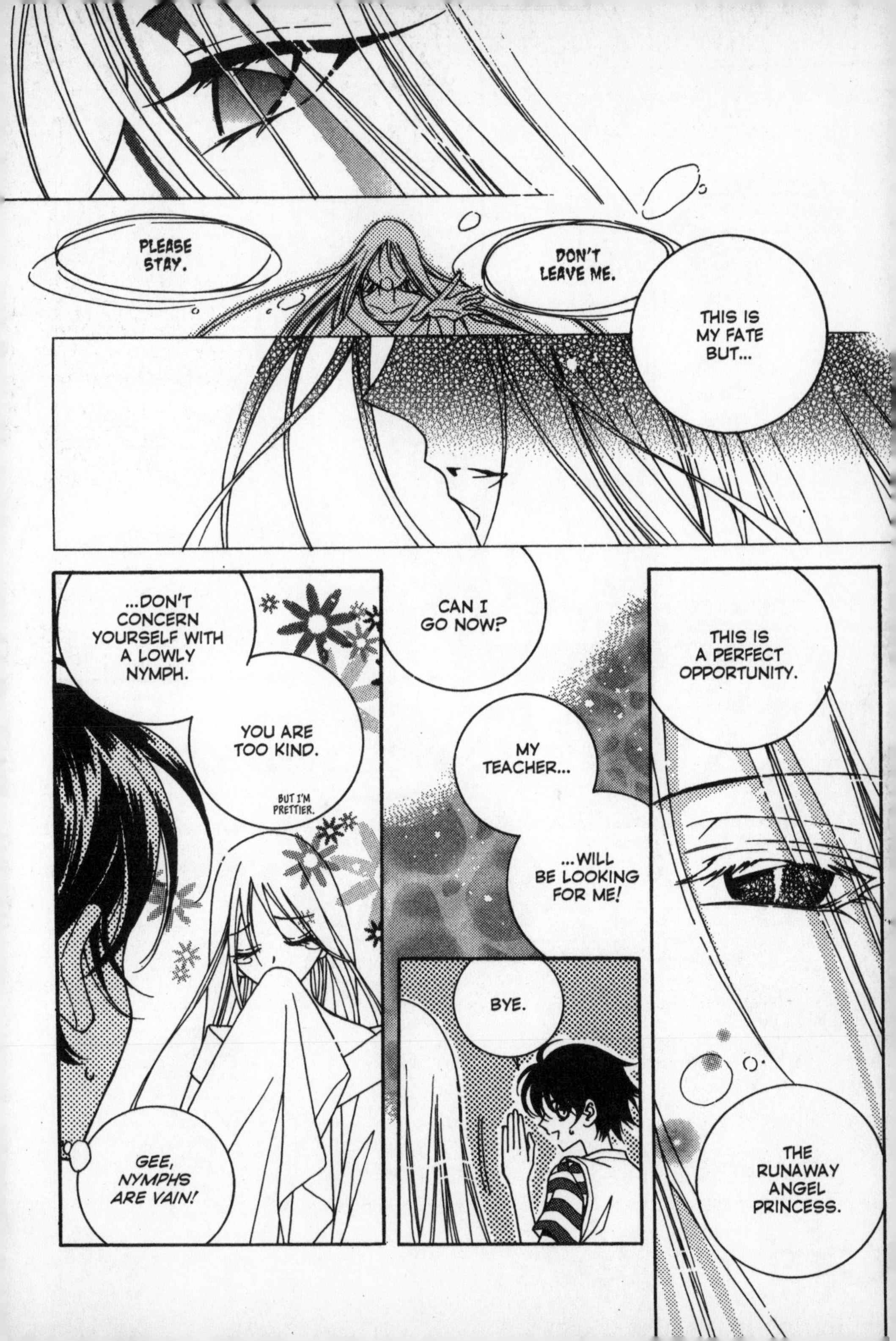
PLEASE STAY.
DON'T LEAVE ME.
THIS IS MY FATE BUT...
...DON'T CONCERN YOURSELF WITH A LOWLY NYMPH.
YOU ARE TOO KIND.
BUT I'M PRETTIER.
GEE, NYMPHS ARE VAIN!
CAN I GO NOW?
MY TEACHER...
...WILL BE LOOKING FOR ME!
BYE.
THIS IS A PERFECT OPPORTUNITY.
THE RUNAWAY ANGEL PRINCESS.

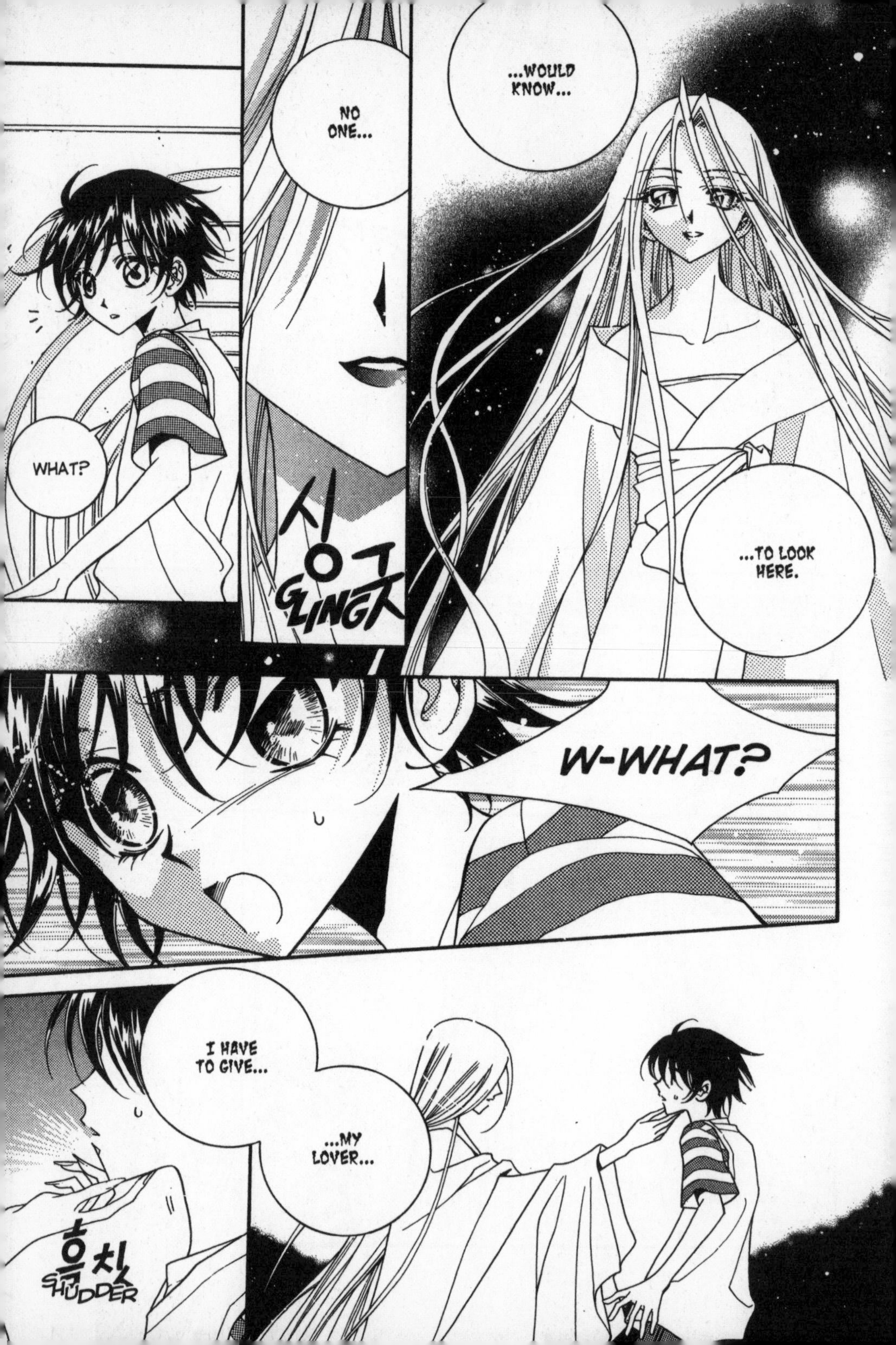
WHAT?
NO ONE...
시잉
GLING
...WOULD KNOW...
...TO LOOK HERE.
W-WHAT?
흐칫
SHUDDER
I HAVE TO GIVE...
...MY LOVER...

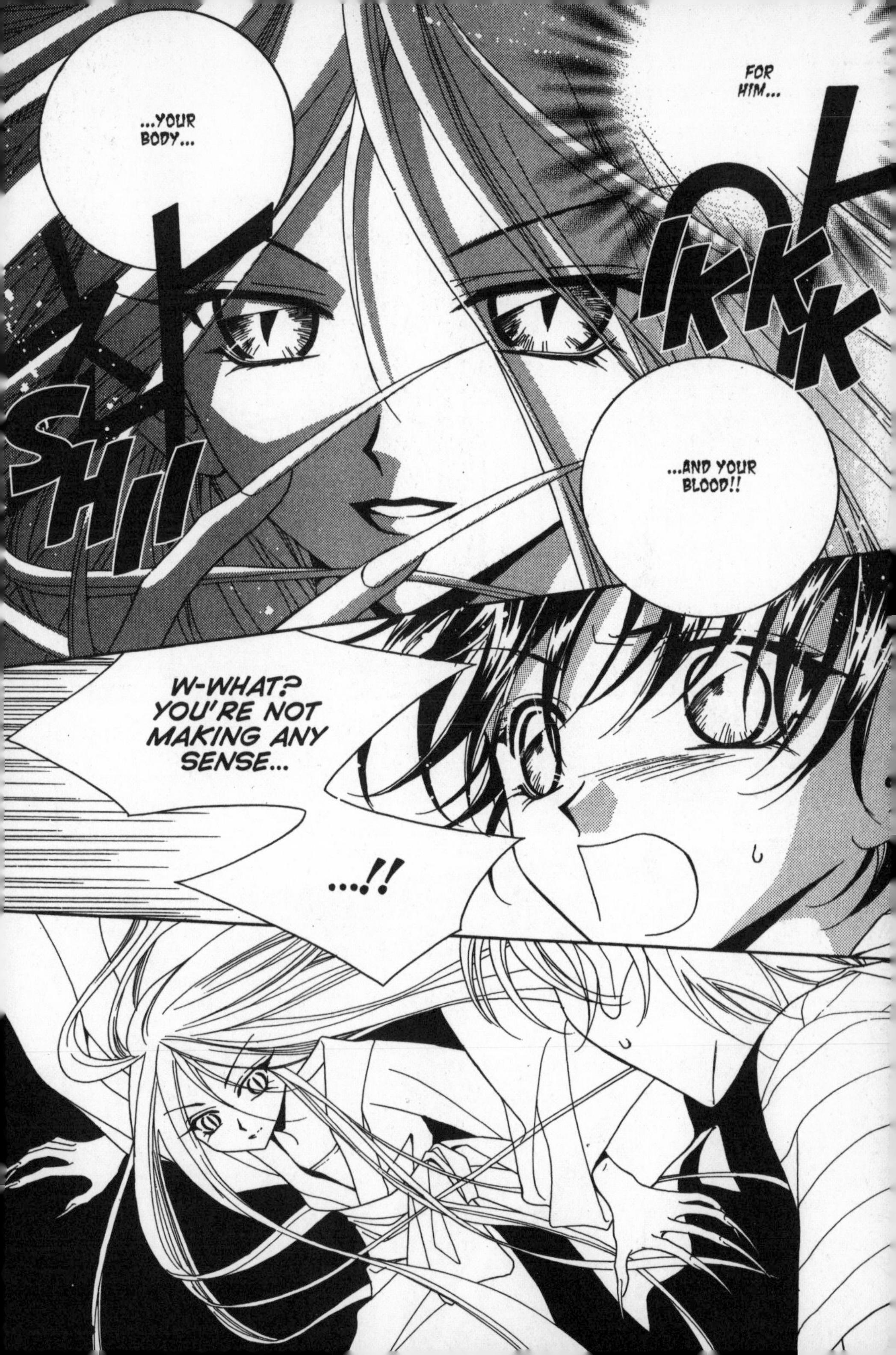
...YOUR BODY...
FOR HIM...
...AND YOUR BLOOD!!
W-WHAT? YOU'RE NOT MAKING ANY SENSE...
...!!

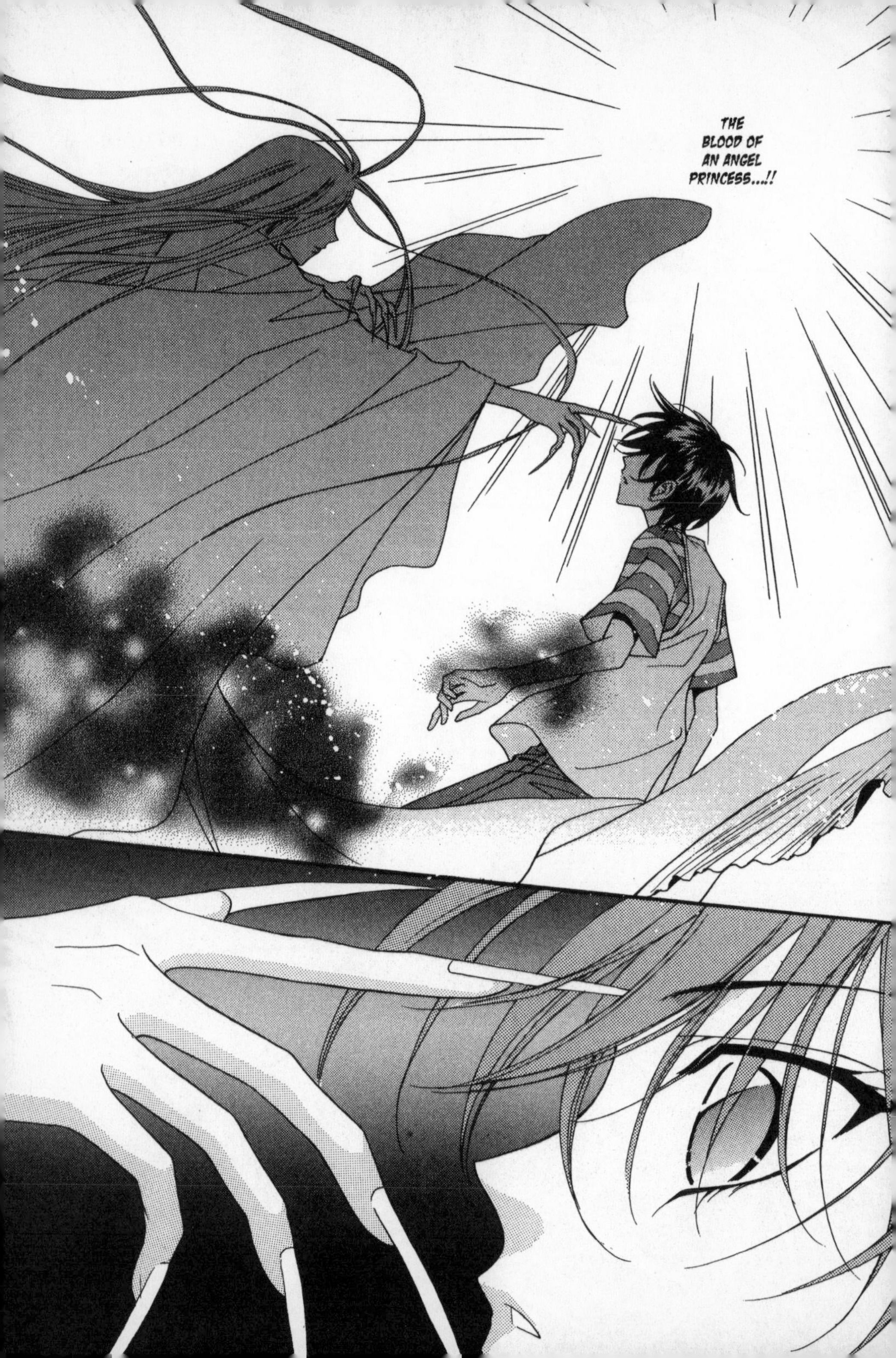
THE BLOOD OF AN ANGEL PRINCESS...!!

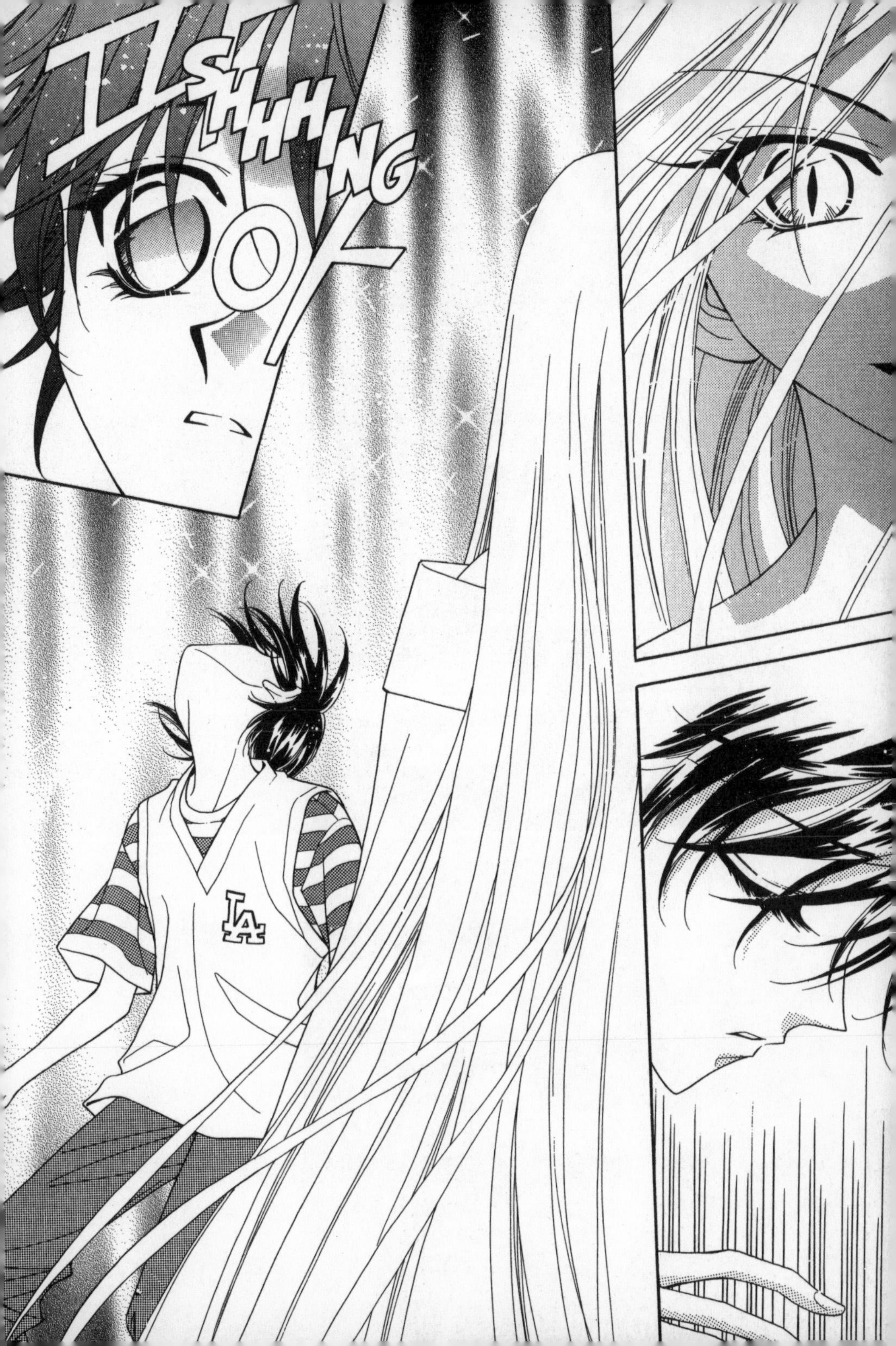
SHHHHING

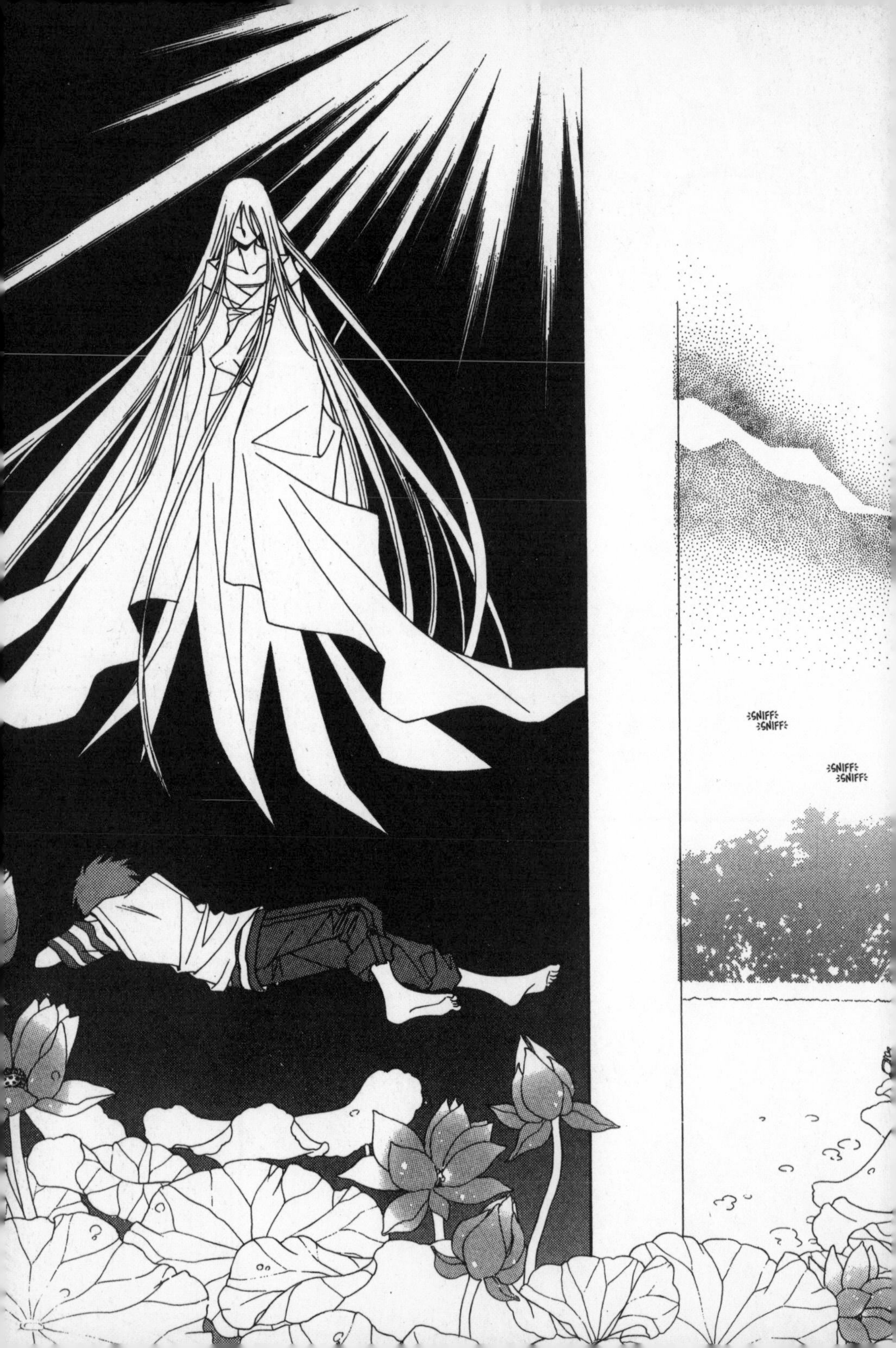
SNIFF SNIFF
SNIFF SNIFF

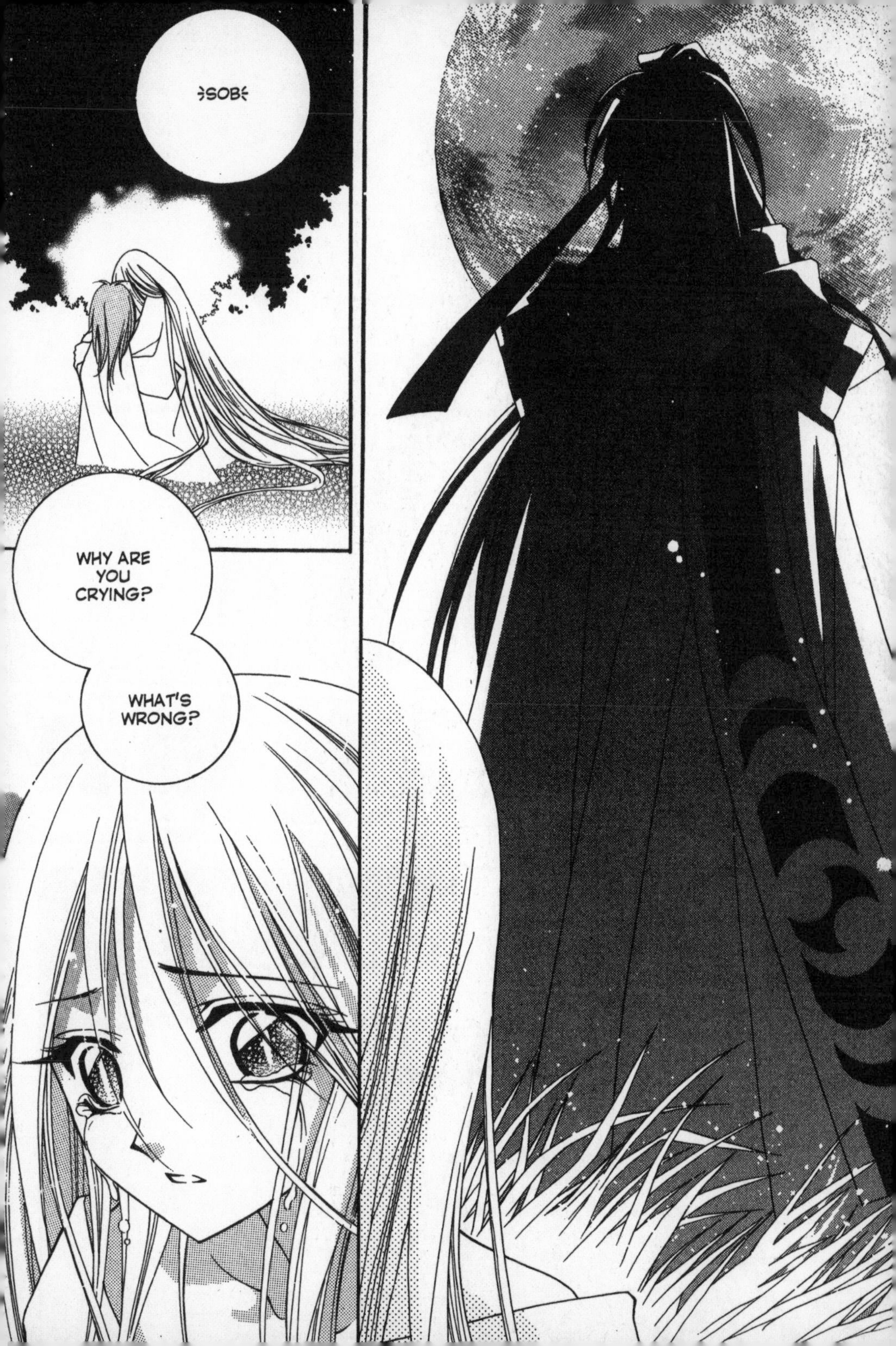
SOB
WHY ARE YOU CRYING?
WHAT'S WRONG?

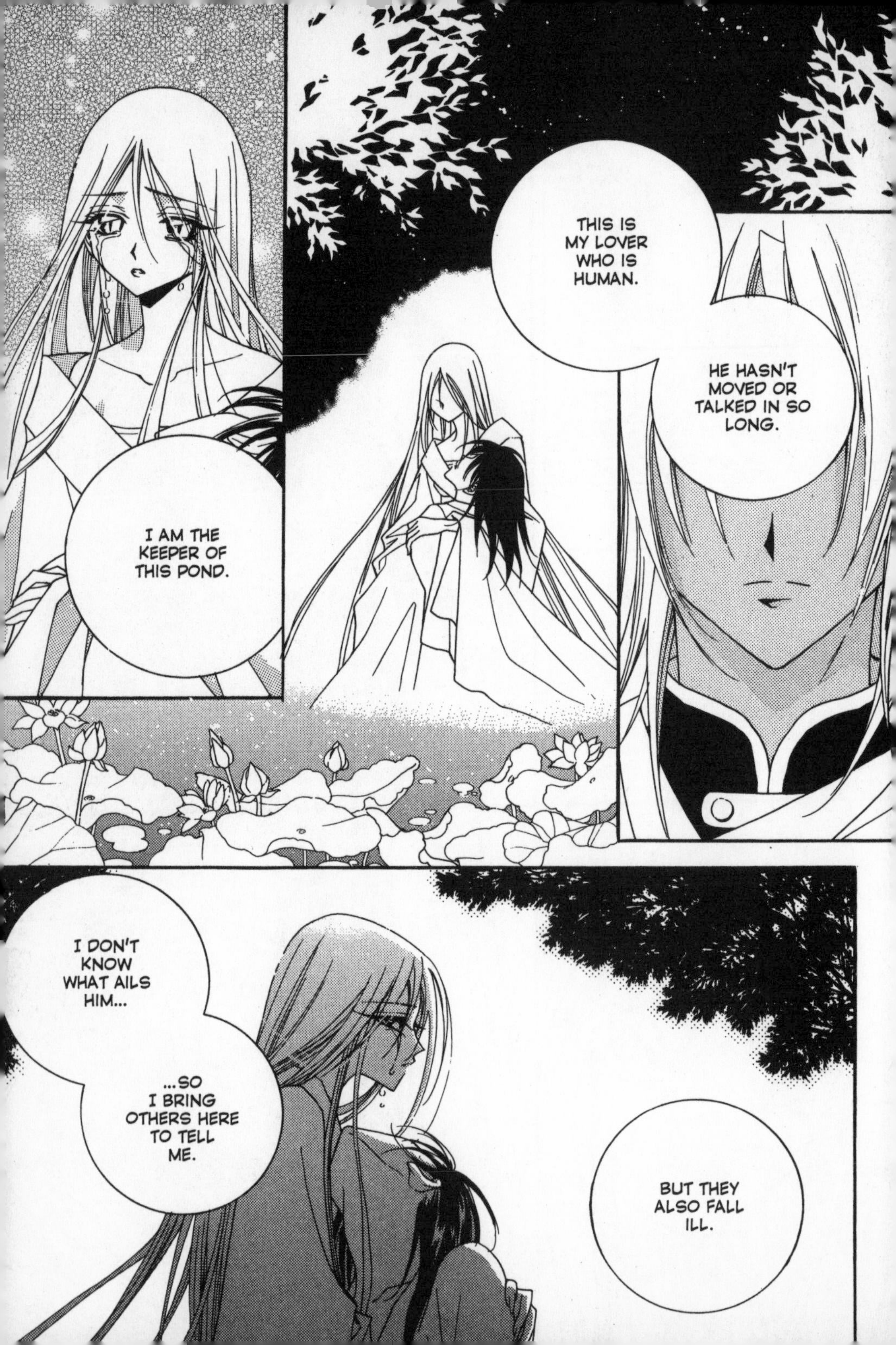
I AM THE KEEPER OF THIS POND.
THIS IS MY LOVER WHO IS HUMAN.
HE HASN'T MOVED OR TALKED IN SO LONG.
I DON'T KNOW WHAT AILS HIM...
...SO I BRING OTHERS HERE TO TELL ME.
BUT THEY ALSO FALL ILL.

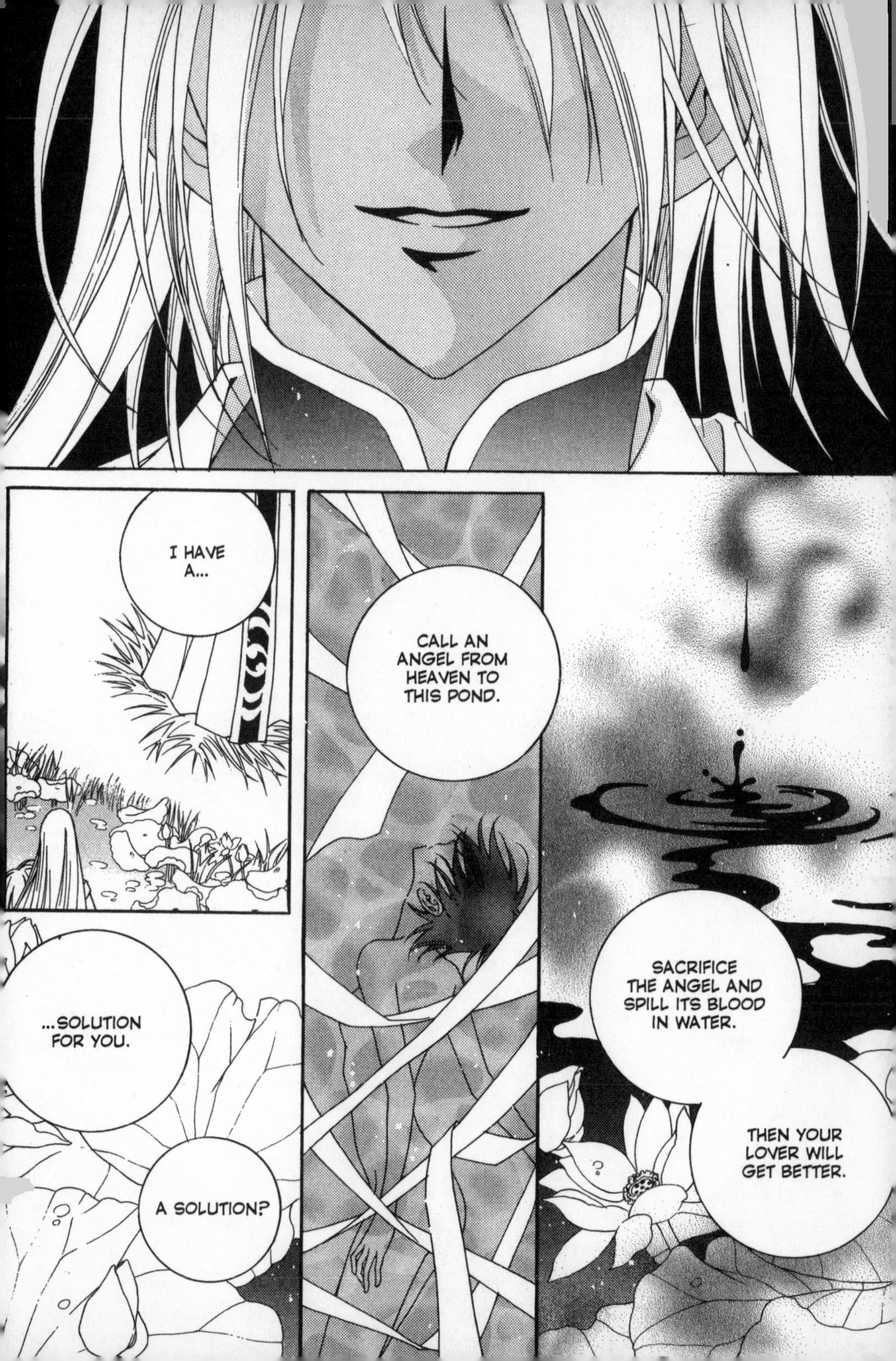
I HAVE A...
...SOLUTION FOR YOU.
A SOLUTION?
CALL AN ANGEL FROM HEAVEN TO THIS POND.
SACRIFICE THE ANGEL AND SPILL ITS BLOOD IN WATER.
THEN YOUR LOVER WILL GET BETTER.

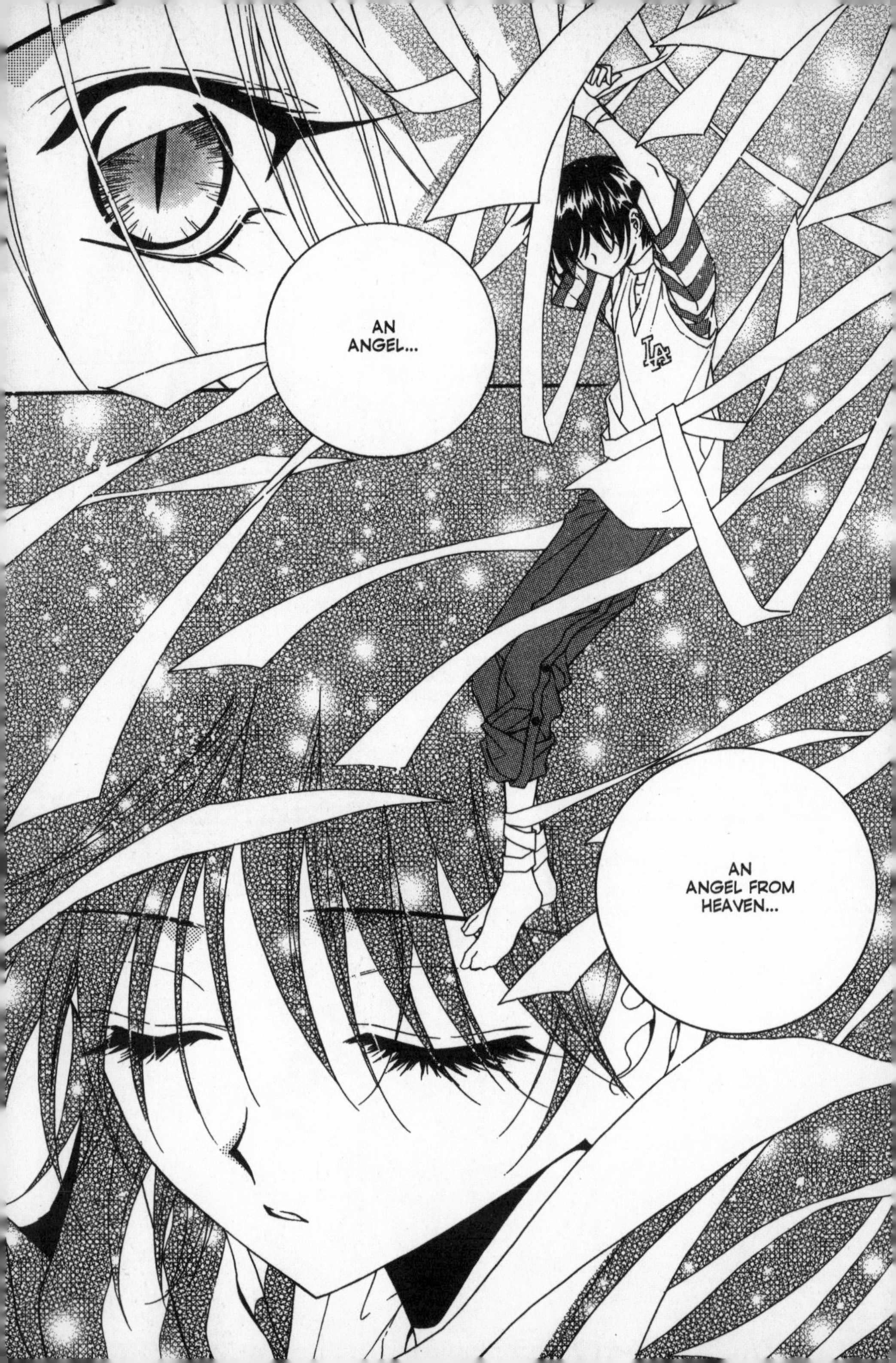
AN ANGEL...
AN ANGEL FROM HEAVEN...

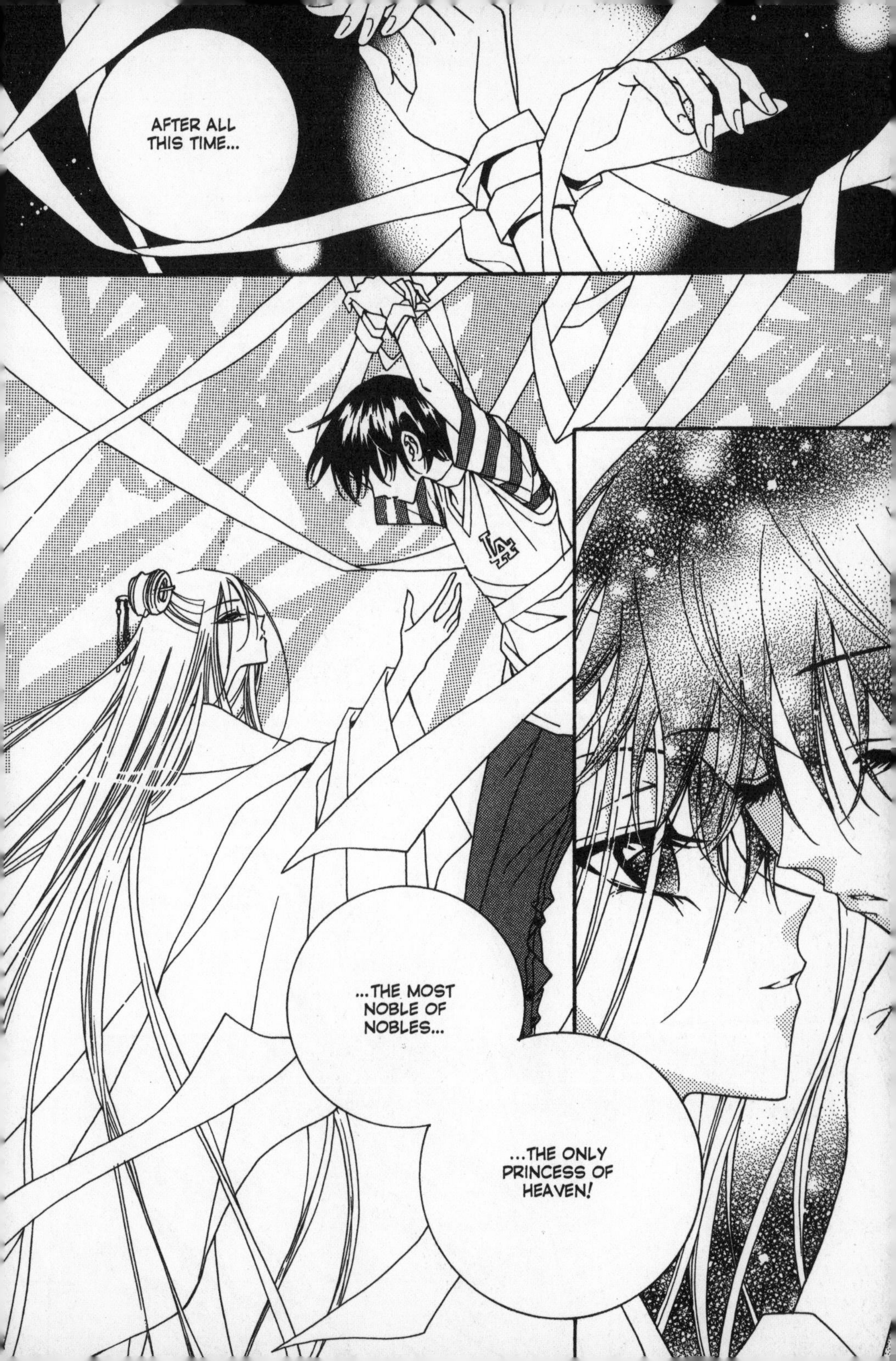
AFTER ALL THIS TIME...
...THE MOST NOBLE OF NOBLES...
...THE ONLY PRINCESS OF HEAVEN!

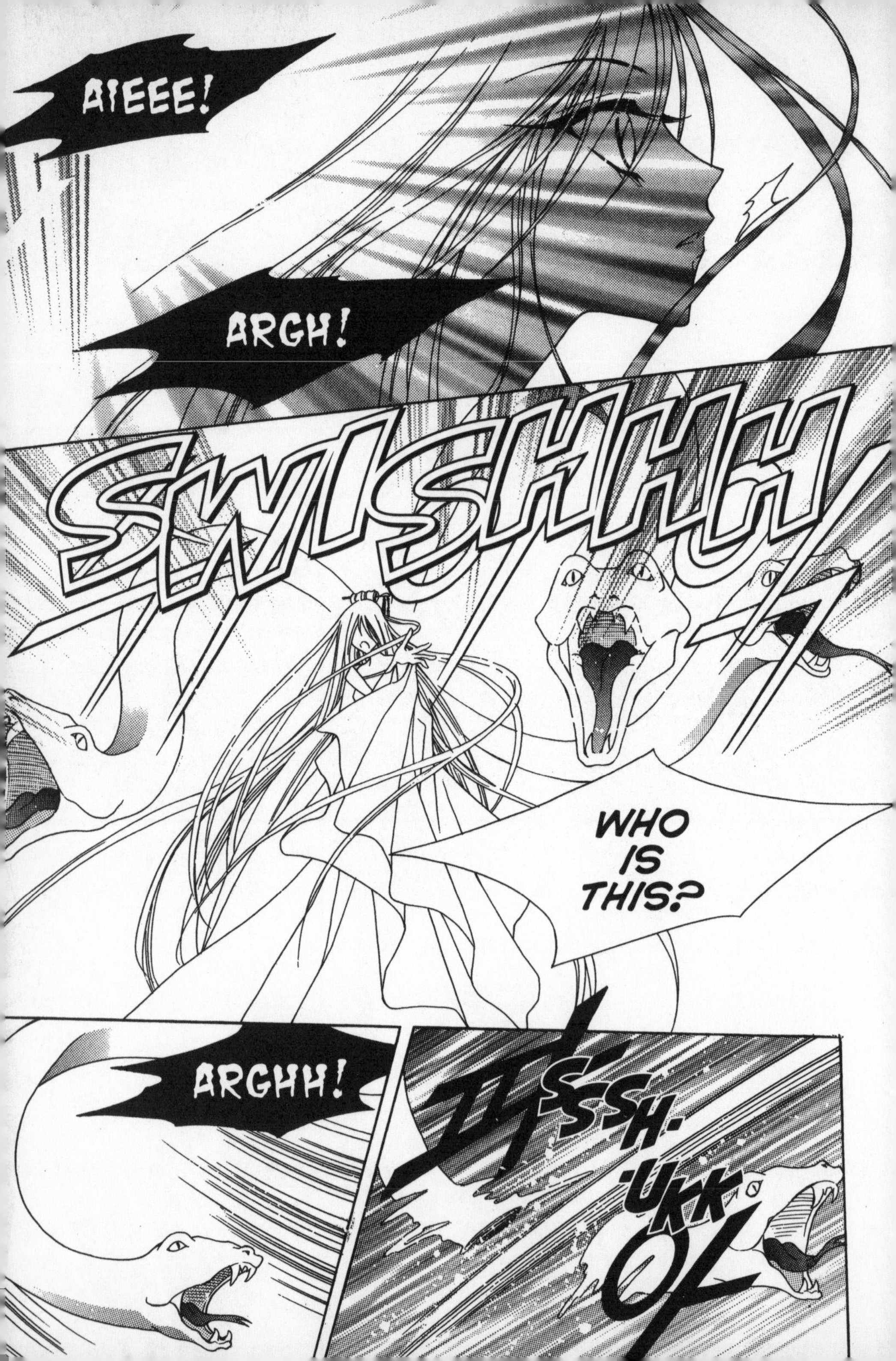
AIEEE!
ARGH!
SWISHHH
WHO IS THIS?
ARGHH!
SSH-
-UKK

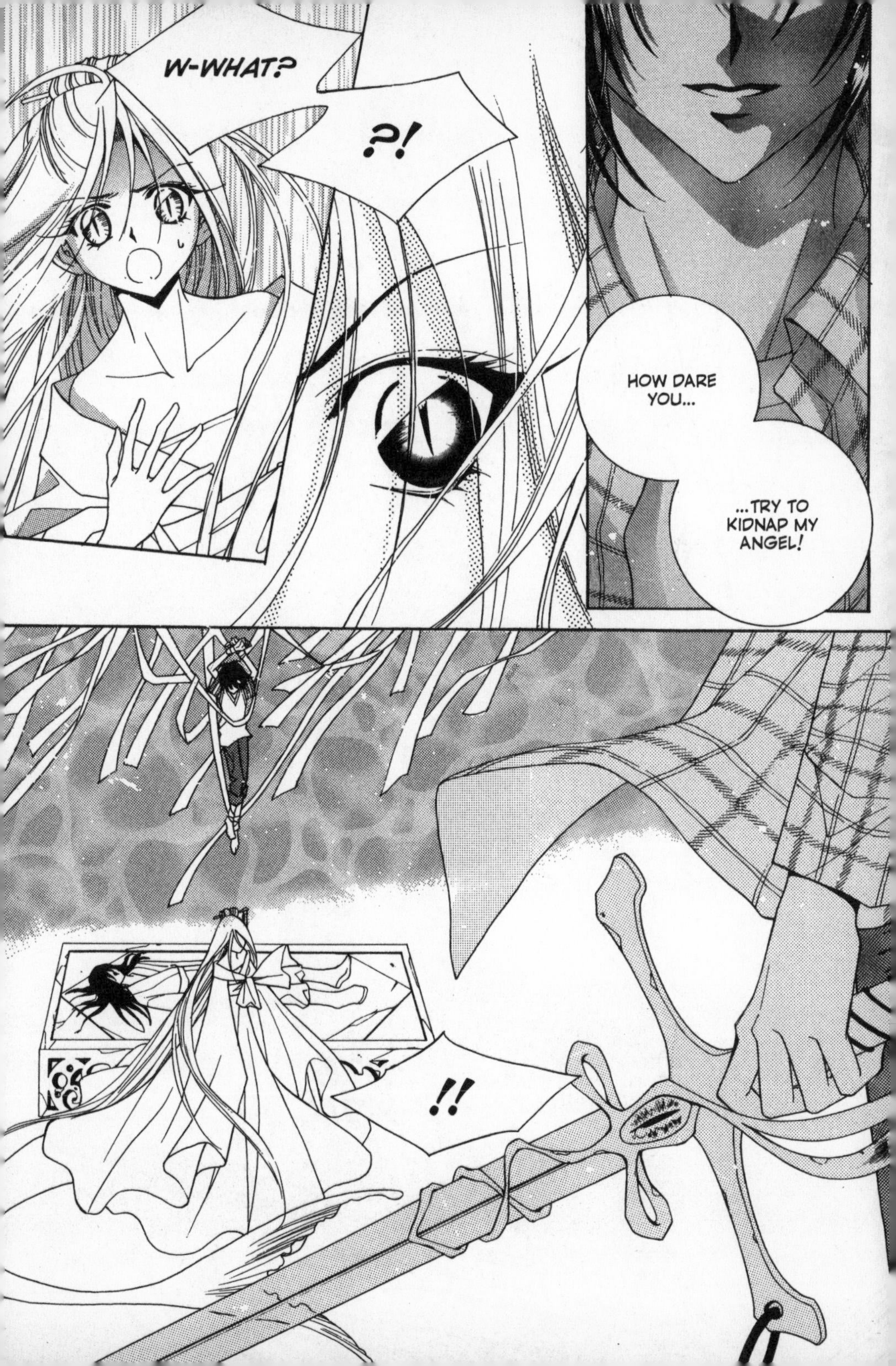
W-WHAT?
?!
HOW DARE YOU...
...TRY TO KIDNAP MY ANGEL!
!!

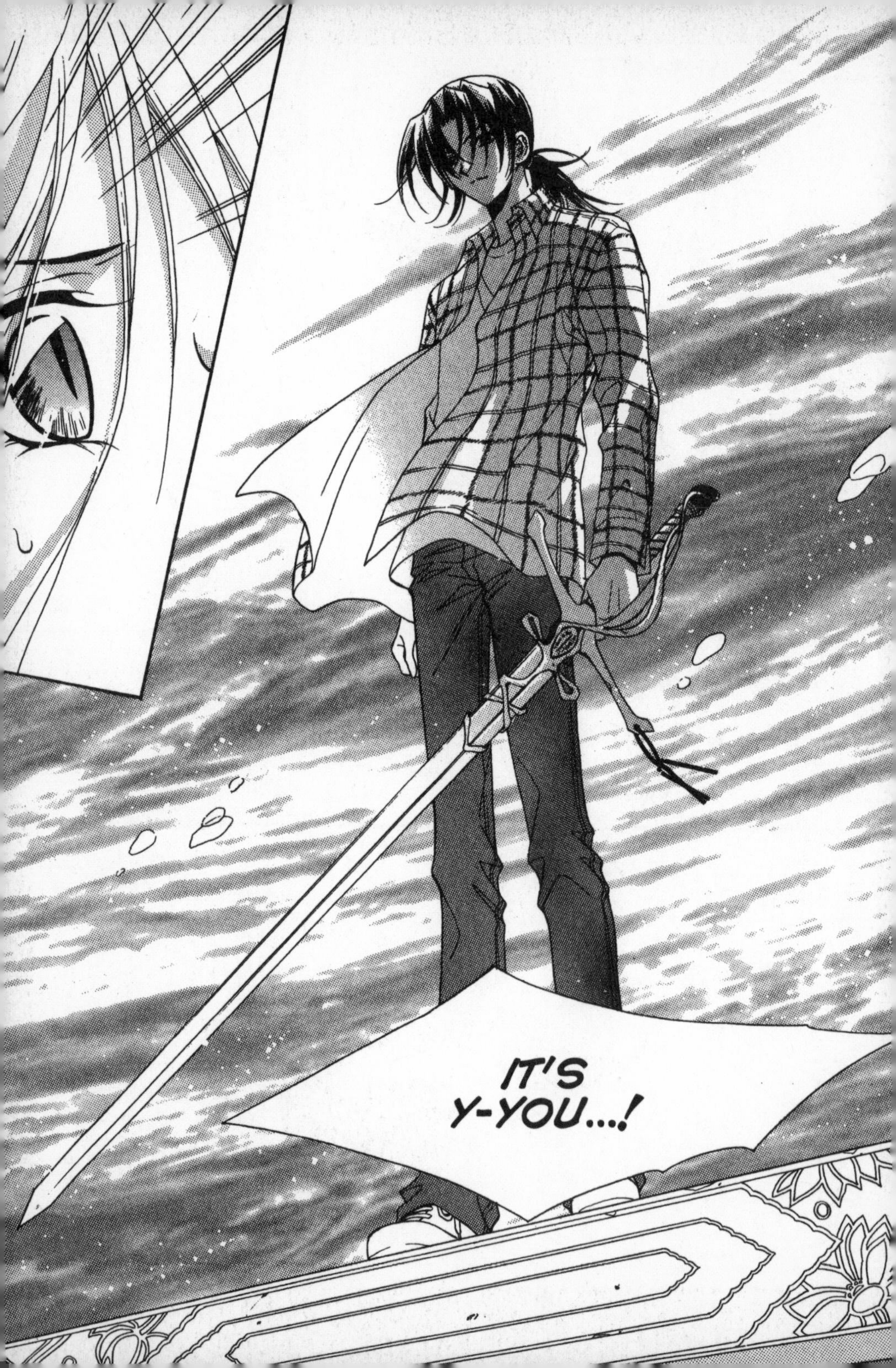
IT'S Y-YOU...!

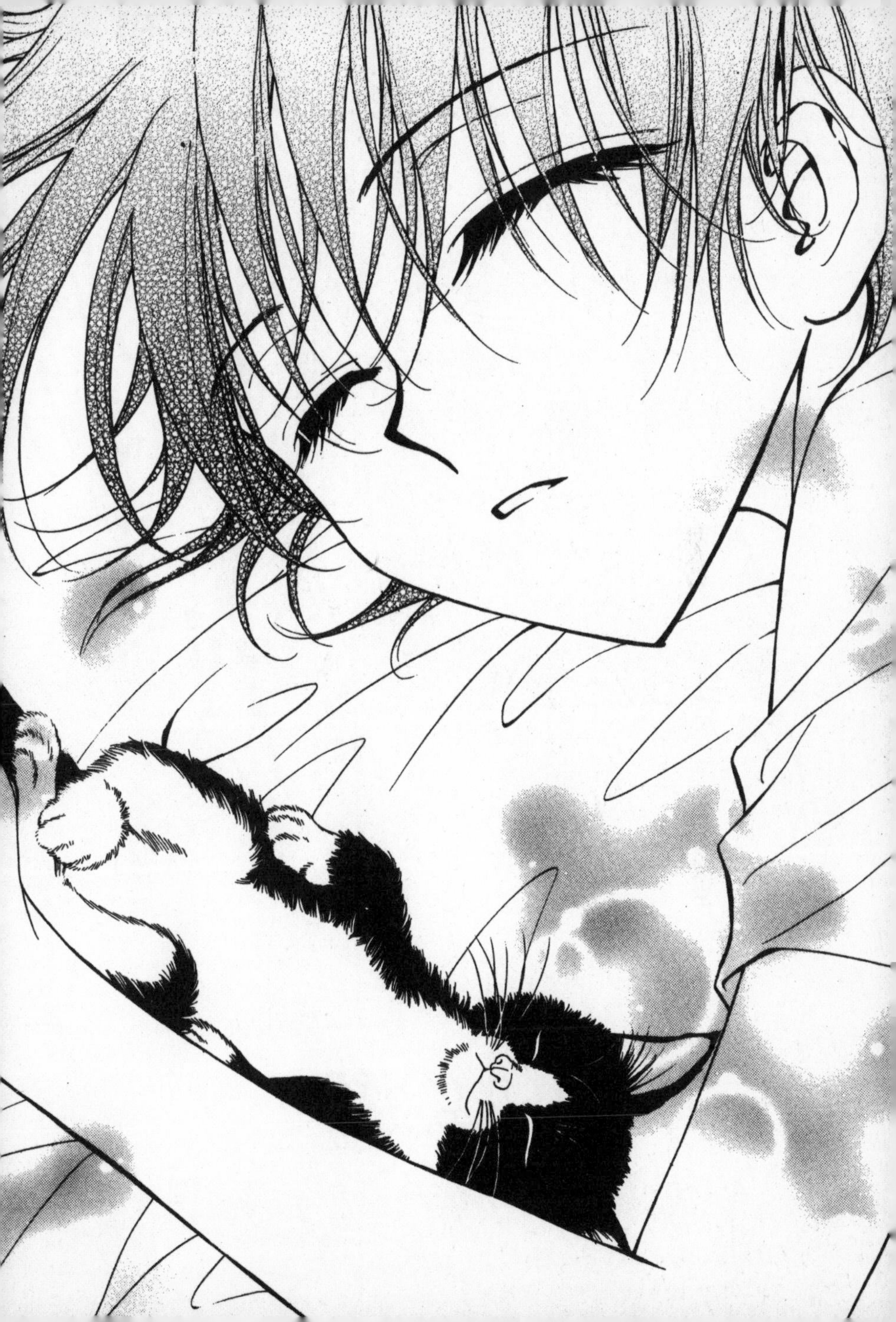

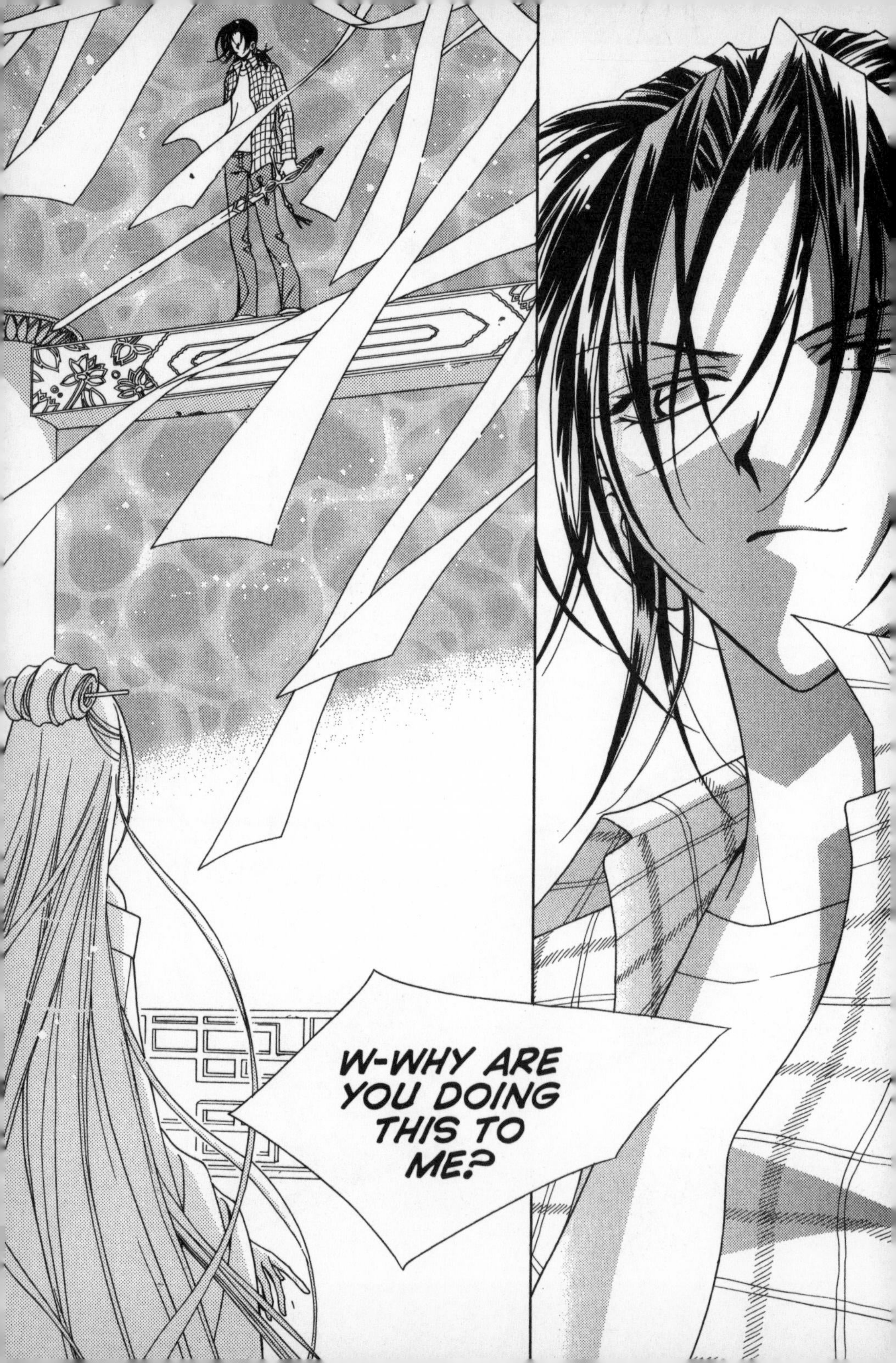
W-WHY ARE YOU DOING THIS TO ME?

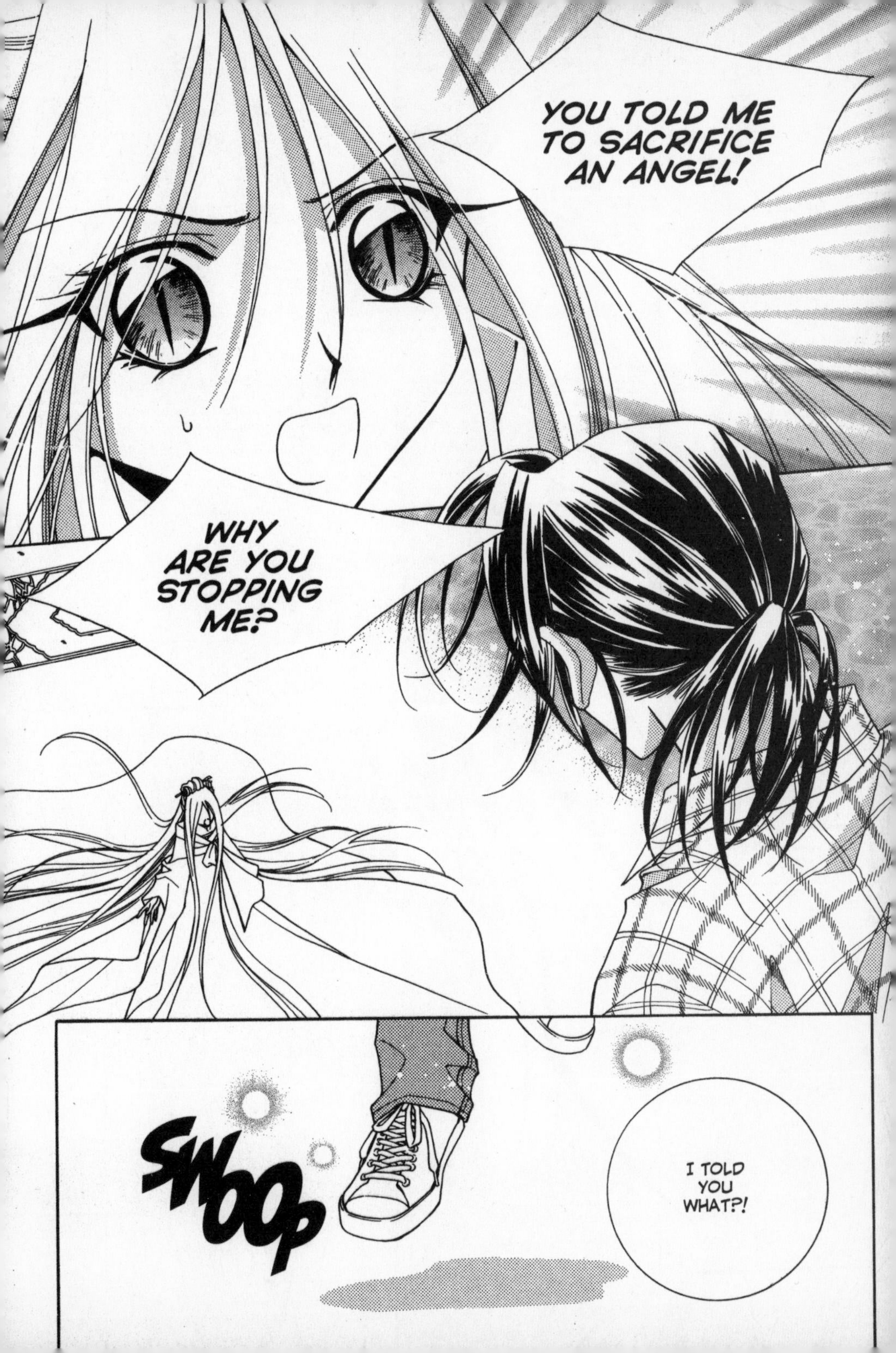
YOU TOLD ME TO SACRIFICE AN ANGEL!
WHY ARE YOU STOPPING ME?
SWOOP
I TOLD YOU WHAT?!

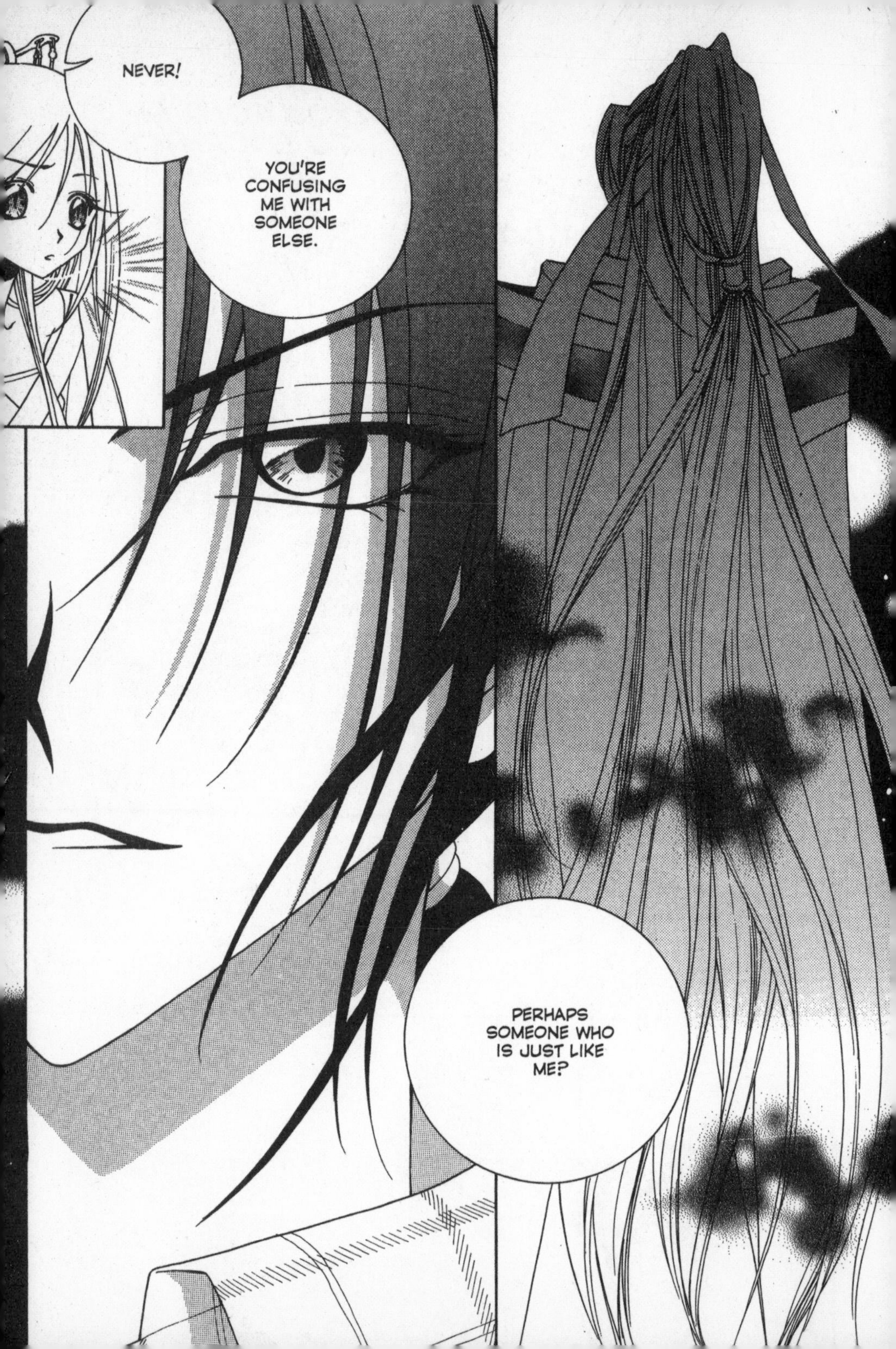
NEVER!
YOU'RE CONFUSING ME WITH SOMEONE ELSE.
PERHAPS SOMEONE WHO IS JUST LIKE ME?

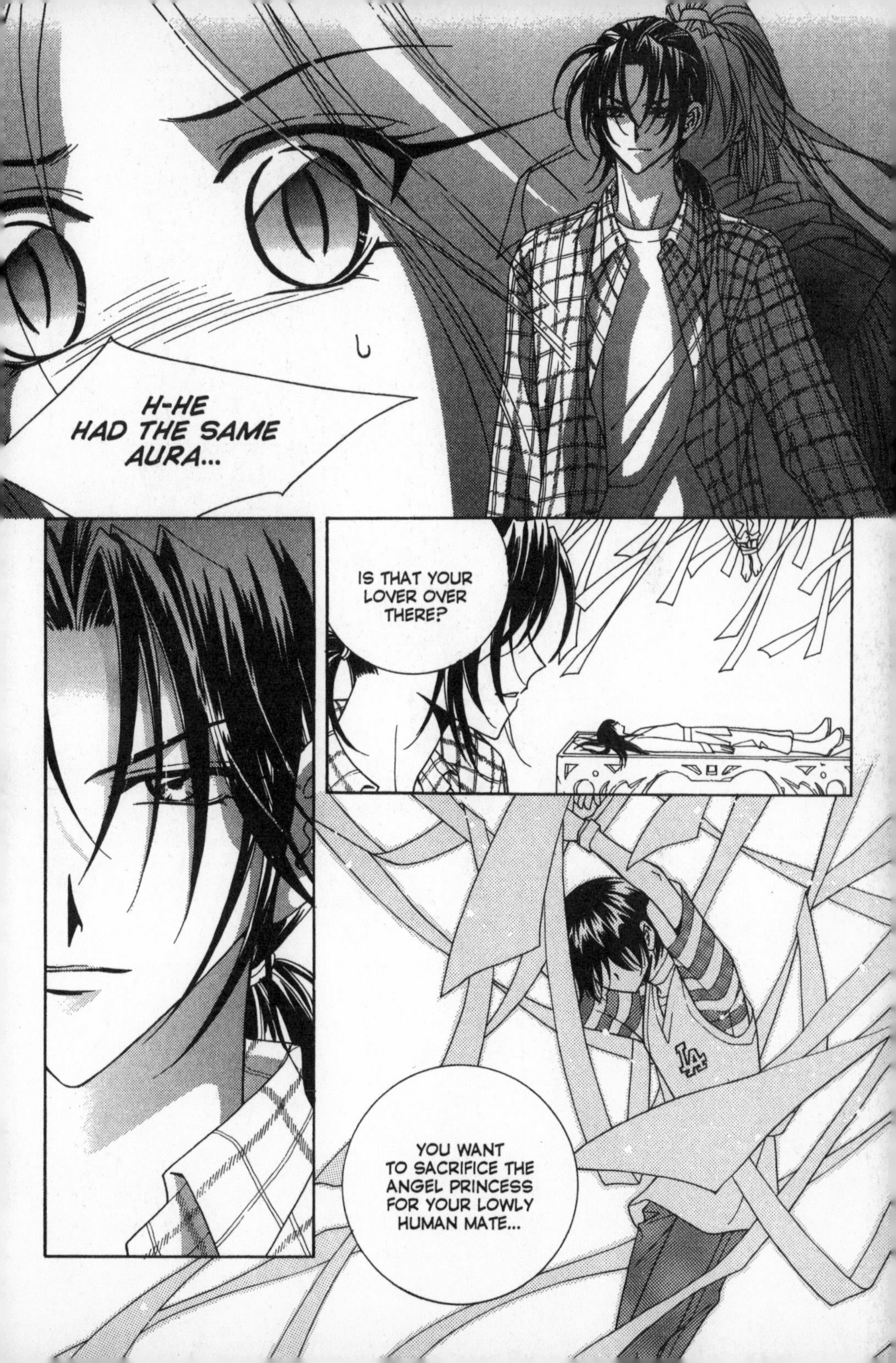
H-HE
HAD THE SAME
AURA...
IS THAT YOUR
LOVER OVER
THERE?
YOU WANT
TO SACRIFICE THE
ANGEL PRINCESS
FOR YOUR LOWLY
HUMAN MATE...

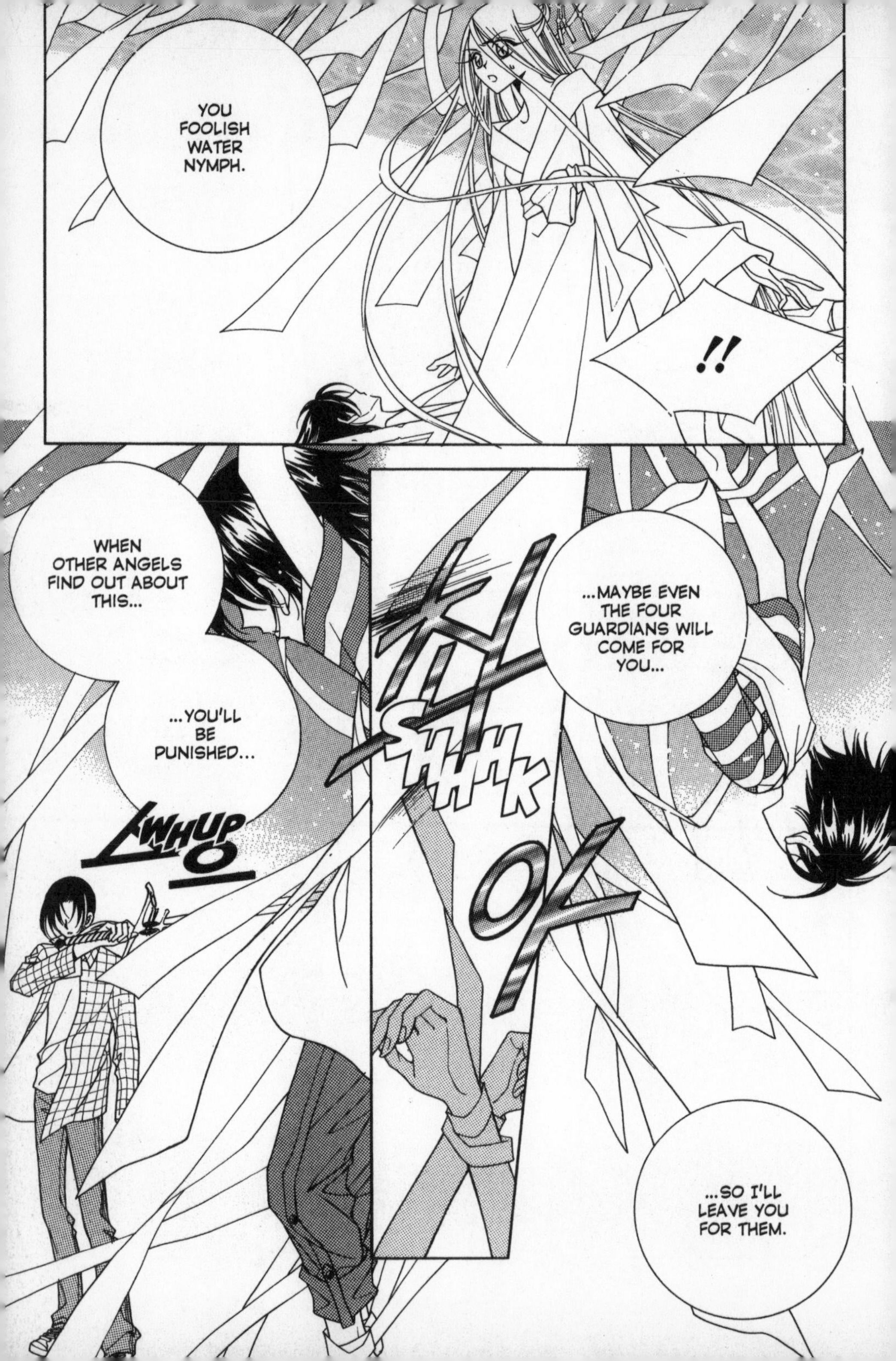
YOU FOOLISH WATER NYMPH.
!!
WHEN OTHER ANGELS FIND OUT ABOUT THIS...
...YOU'LL BE PUNISHED...
WHUP
SHHHK
...MAYBE EVEN THE FOUR GUARDIANS WILL COME FOR YOU...
...SO I'LL LEAVE YOU FOR THEM.

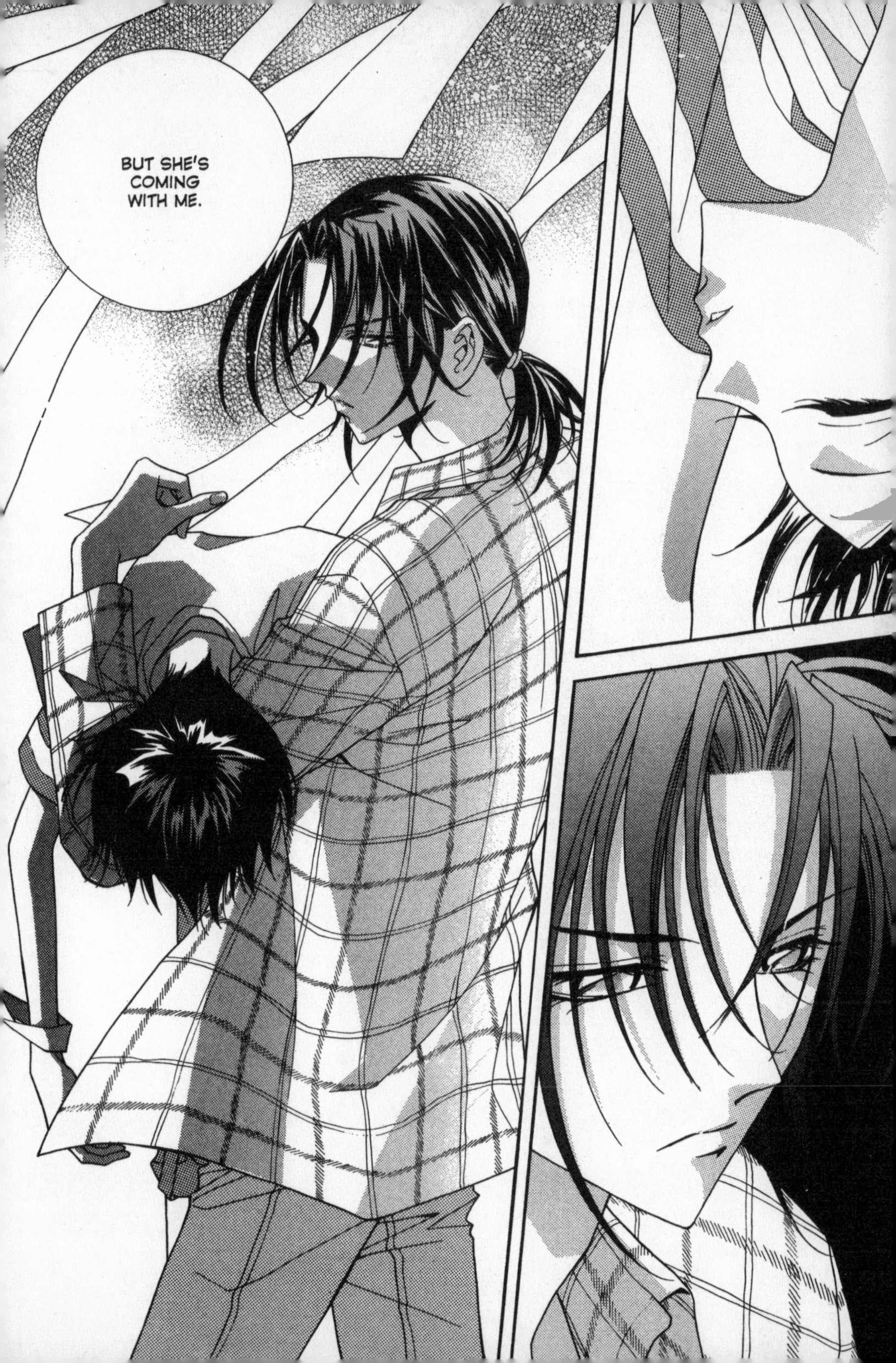
BUT SHE'S COMING WITH ME.

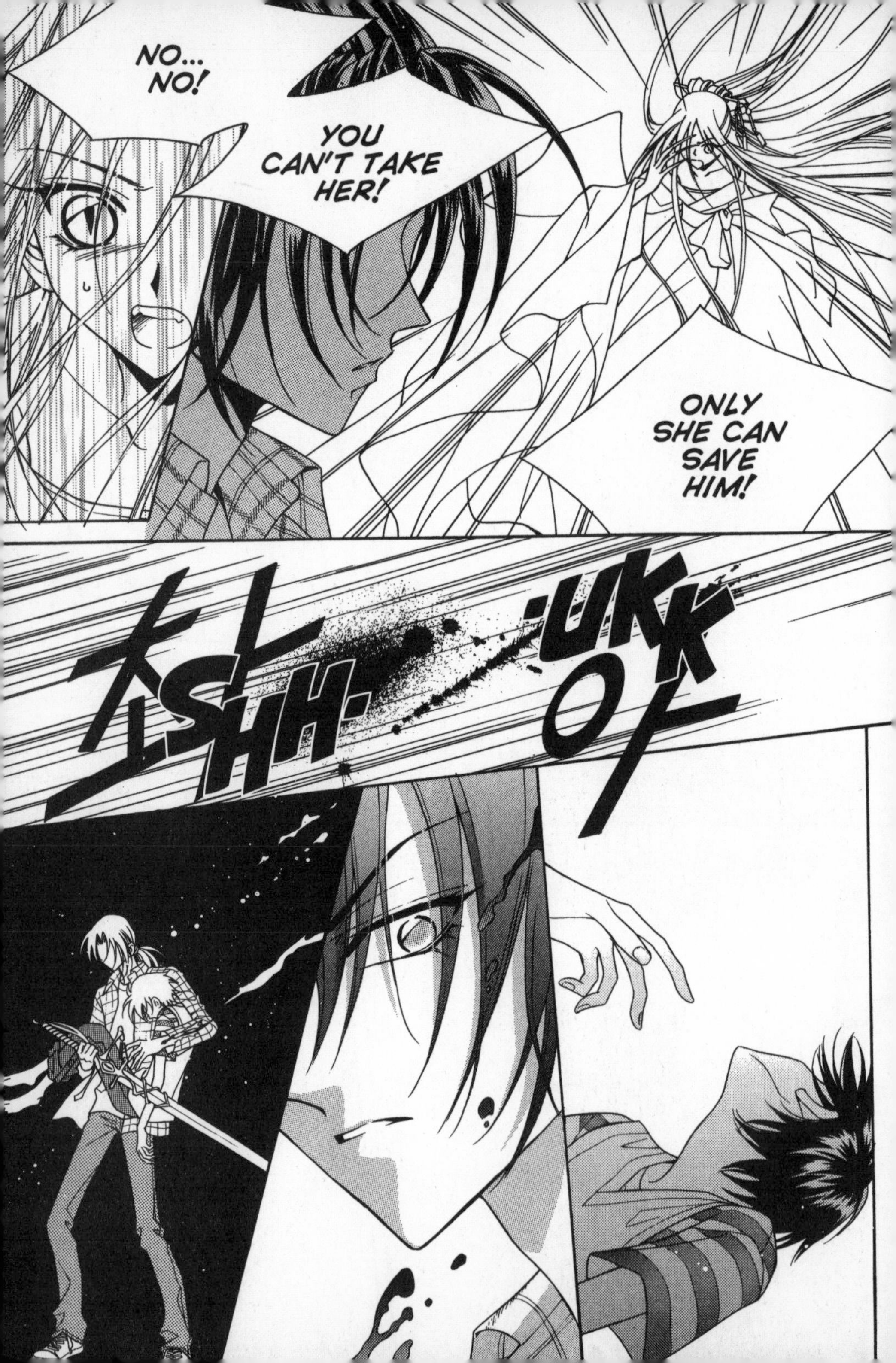
NO... NO!
YOU CAN'T TAKE HER!
ONLY SHE CAN SAVE HIM!
SHH-
-UKK

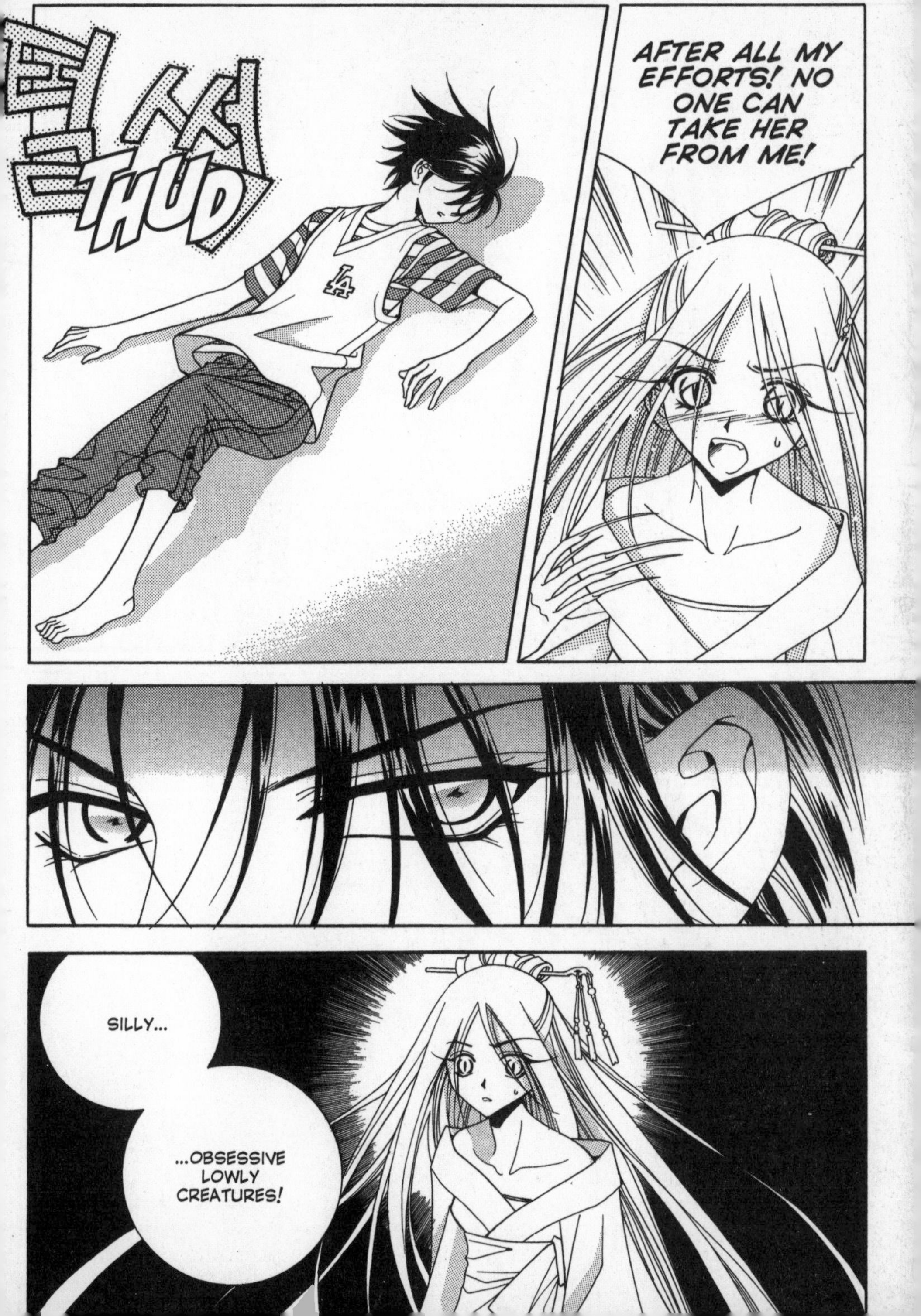
THUD
AFTER ALL MY EFFORTS! NO ONE CAN TAKE HER FROM ME!
SILLY...
...OBSESSIVE LOWLY CREATURES!

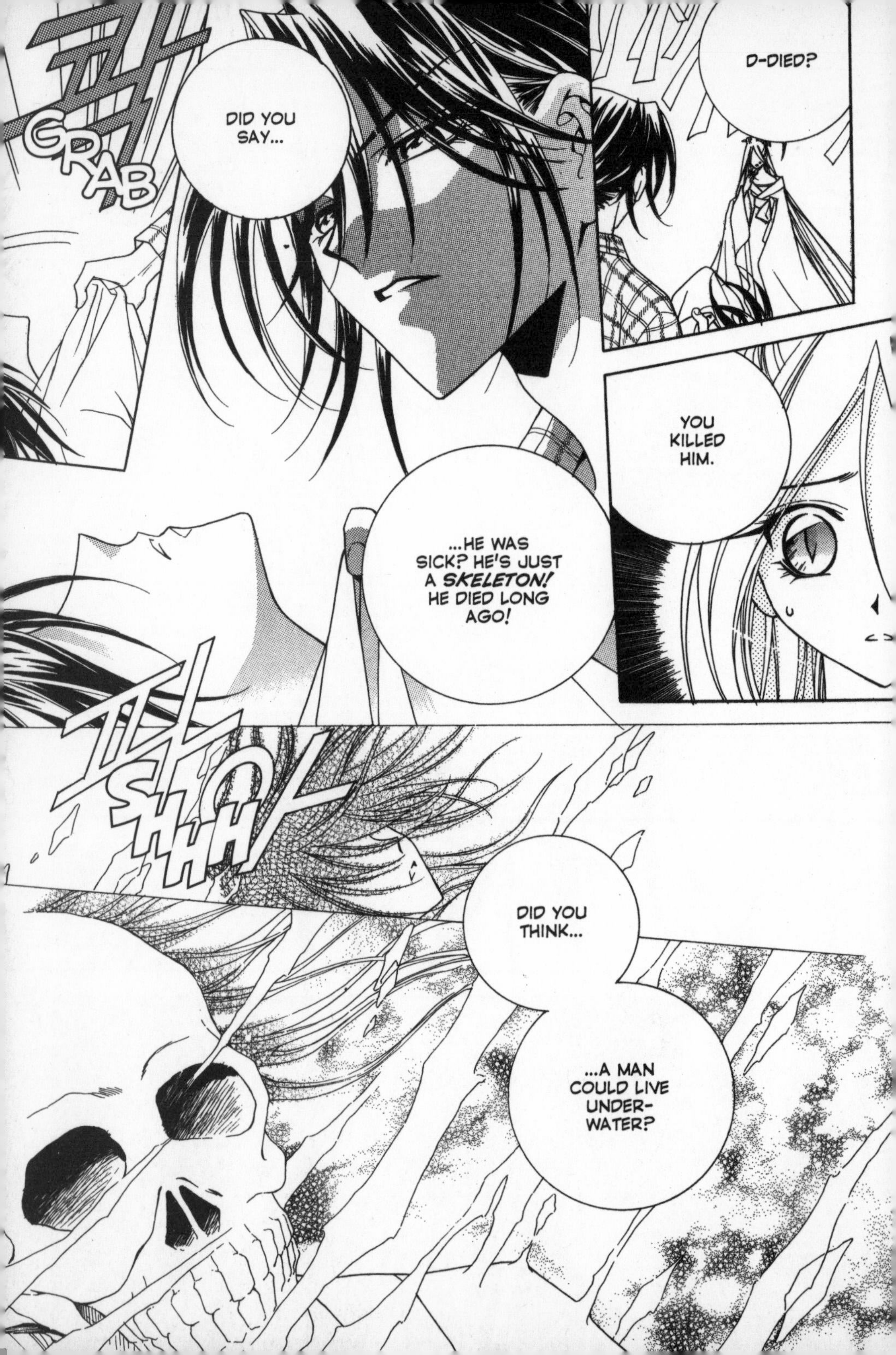
GRAB
DID YOU SAY...
D-DIED?
YOU KILLED HIM.
...HE WAS SICK? HE'S JUST A SKELETON! HE DIED LONG AGO!
SHHHH
DID YOU THINK...
...A MAN COULD LIVE UNDER-WATER?

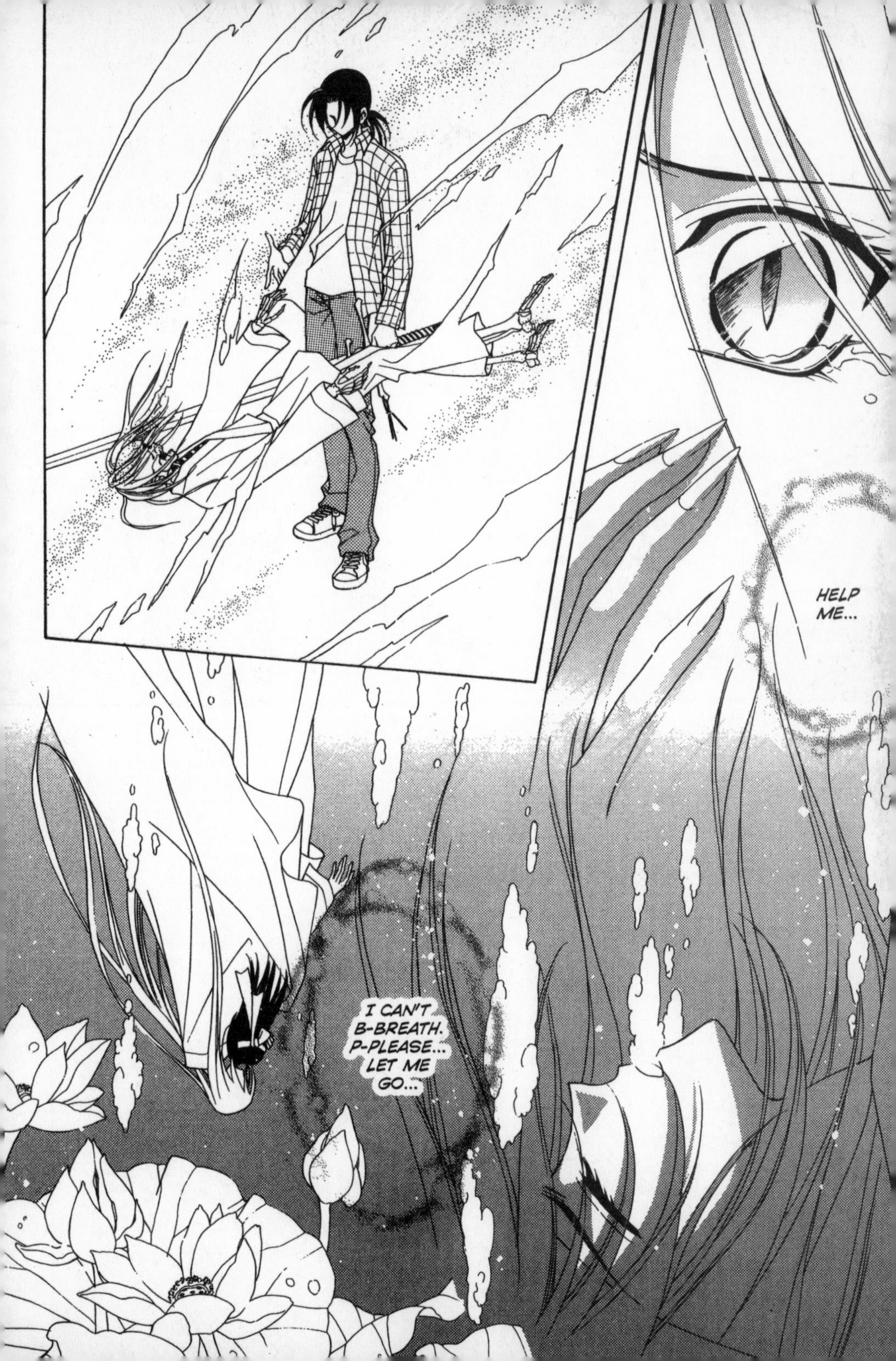
HELP ME...
I CAN'T B-BREATH. P-PLEASE... LET ME GO...

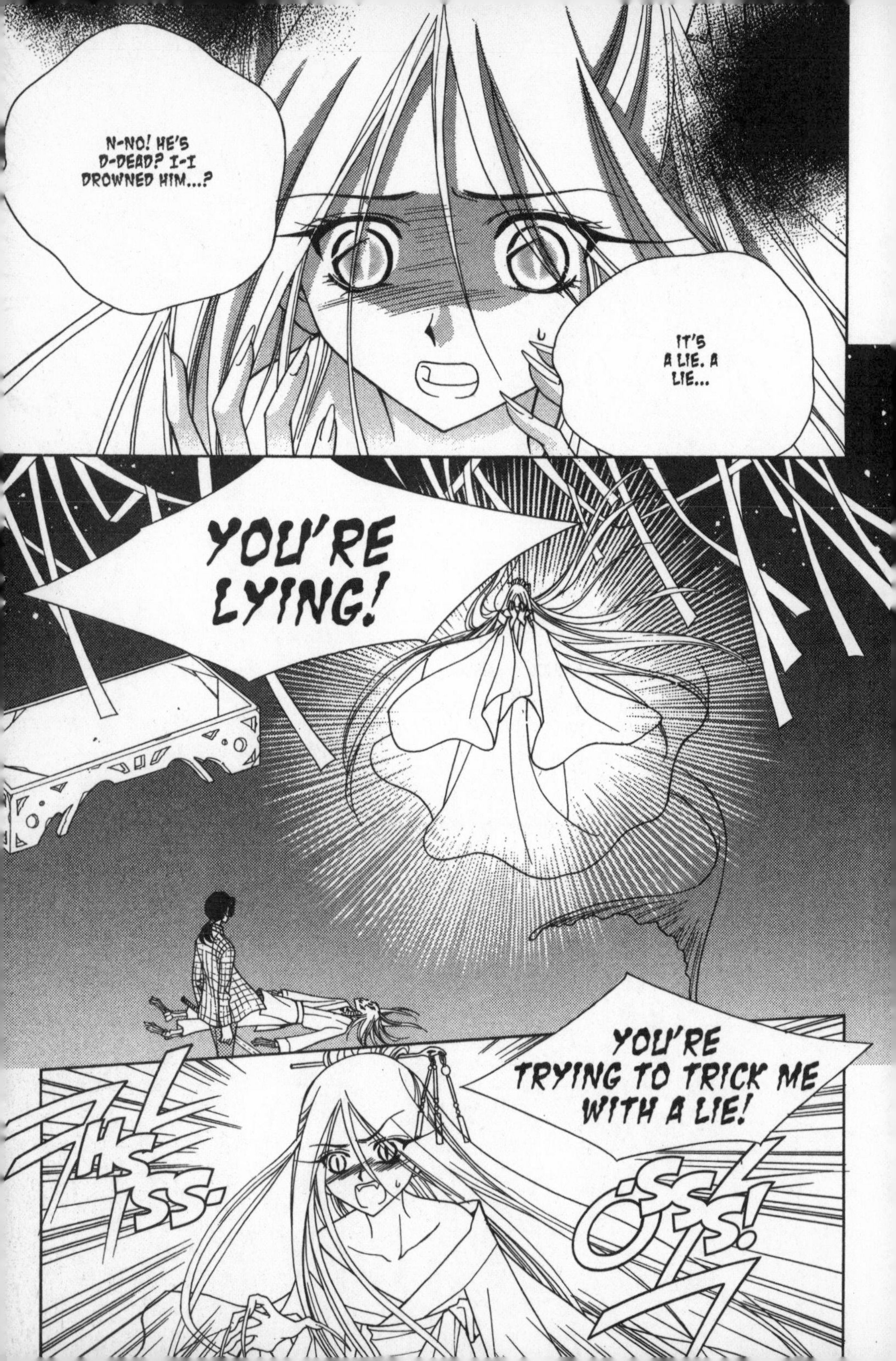
N-NO! HE'S D-DEAD? I-I DROWNED HIM...?
IT'S A LIE. A LIE...
YOU'RE LYING!
YOU'RE TRYING TO TRICK ME WITH A LIE!

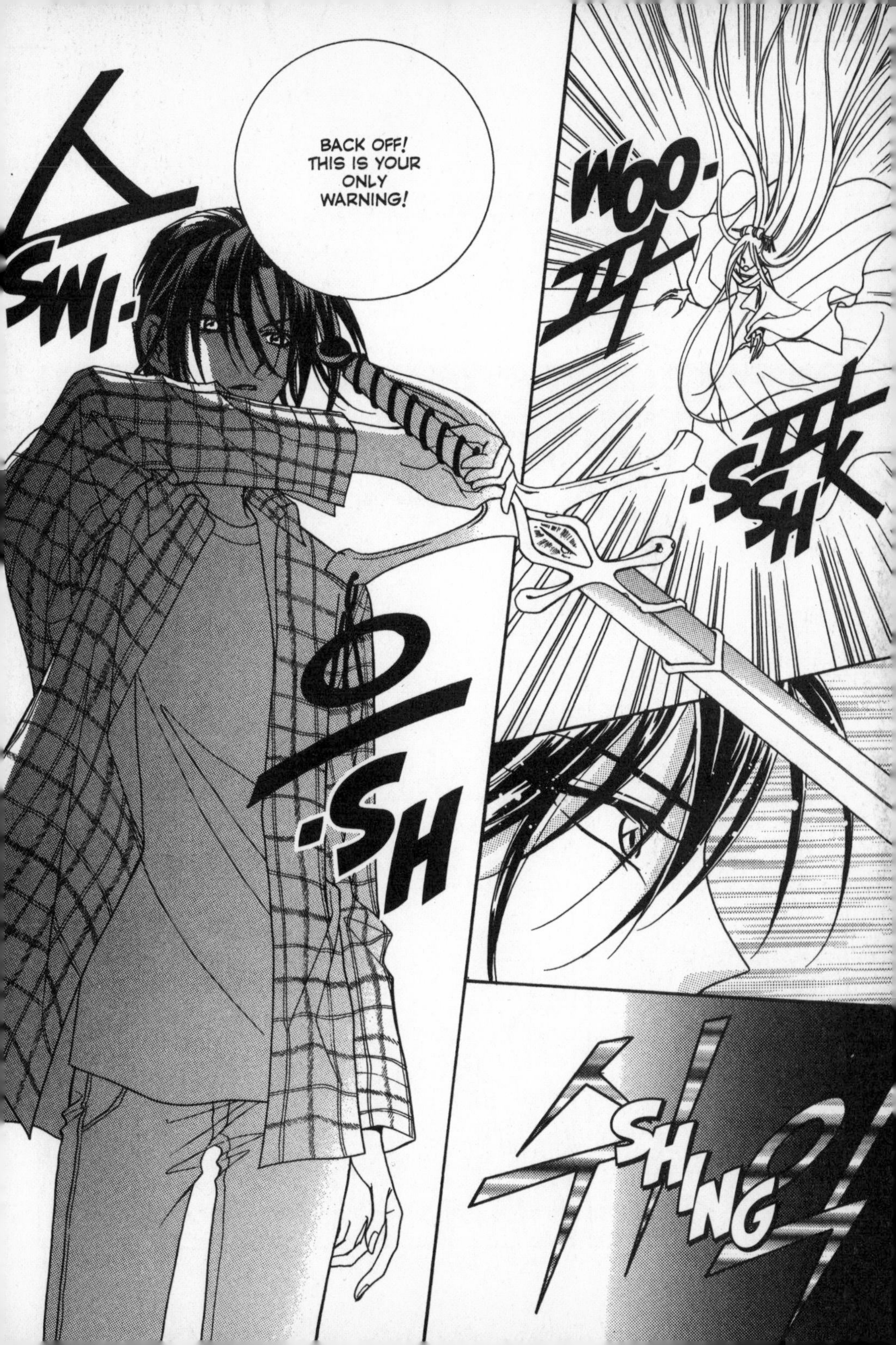
SWI-
BACK OFF! THIS IS YOUR ONLY WARNING!
-SH
WOO-
-SSH
SHING

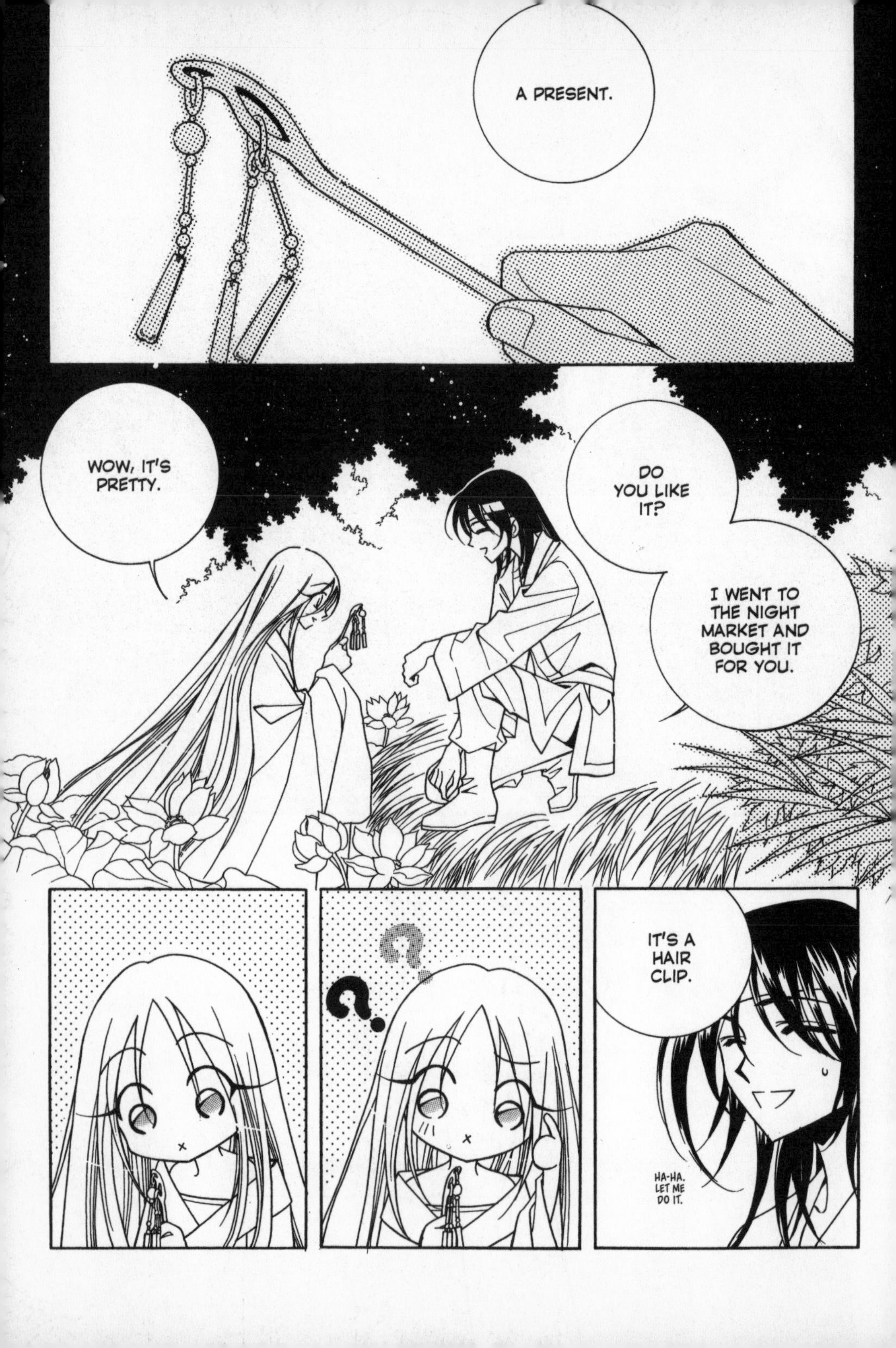
A PRESENT.
WOW, IT'S PRETTY.
DO YOU LIKE IT?
I WENT TO THE NIGHT MARKET AND BOUGHT IT FOR YOU.
?
?
IT'S A HAIR CLIP.
HA-HA. LET ME DO IT.

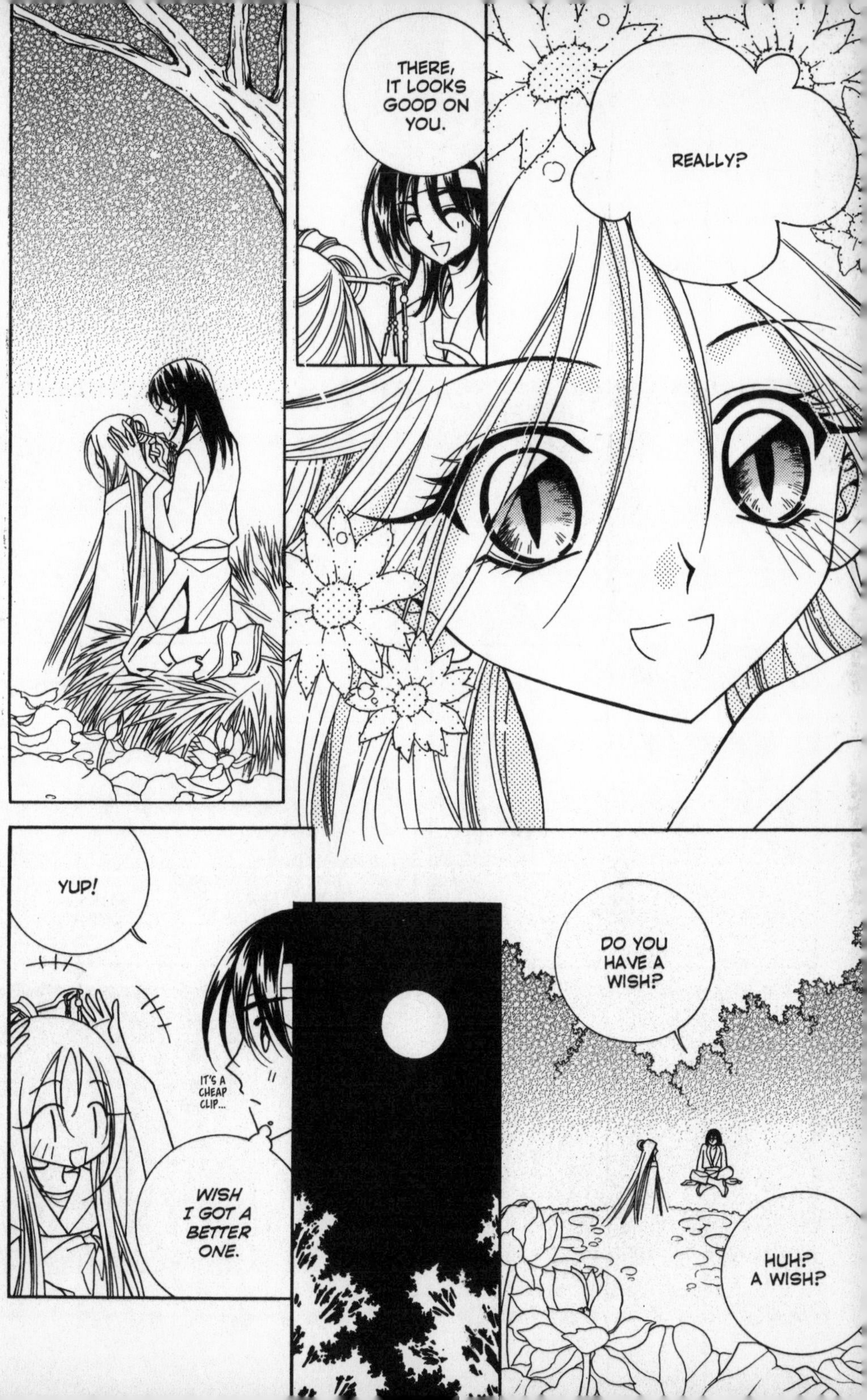
THERE, IT LOOKS GOOD ON YOU.
REALLY?
YUP!
IT'S A CHEAP CLIP...
WISH I GOT A BETTER ONE.
DO YOU HAVE A WISH?
HUH? A WISH?

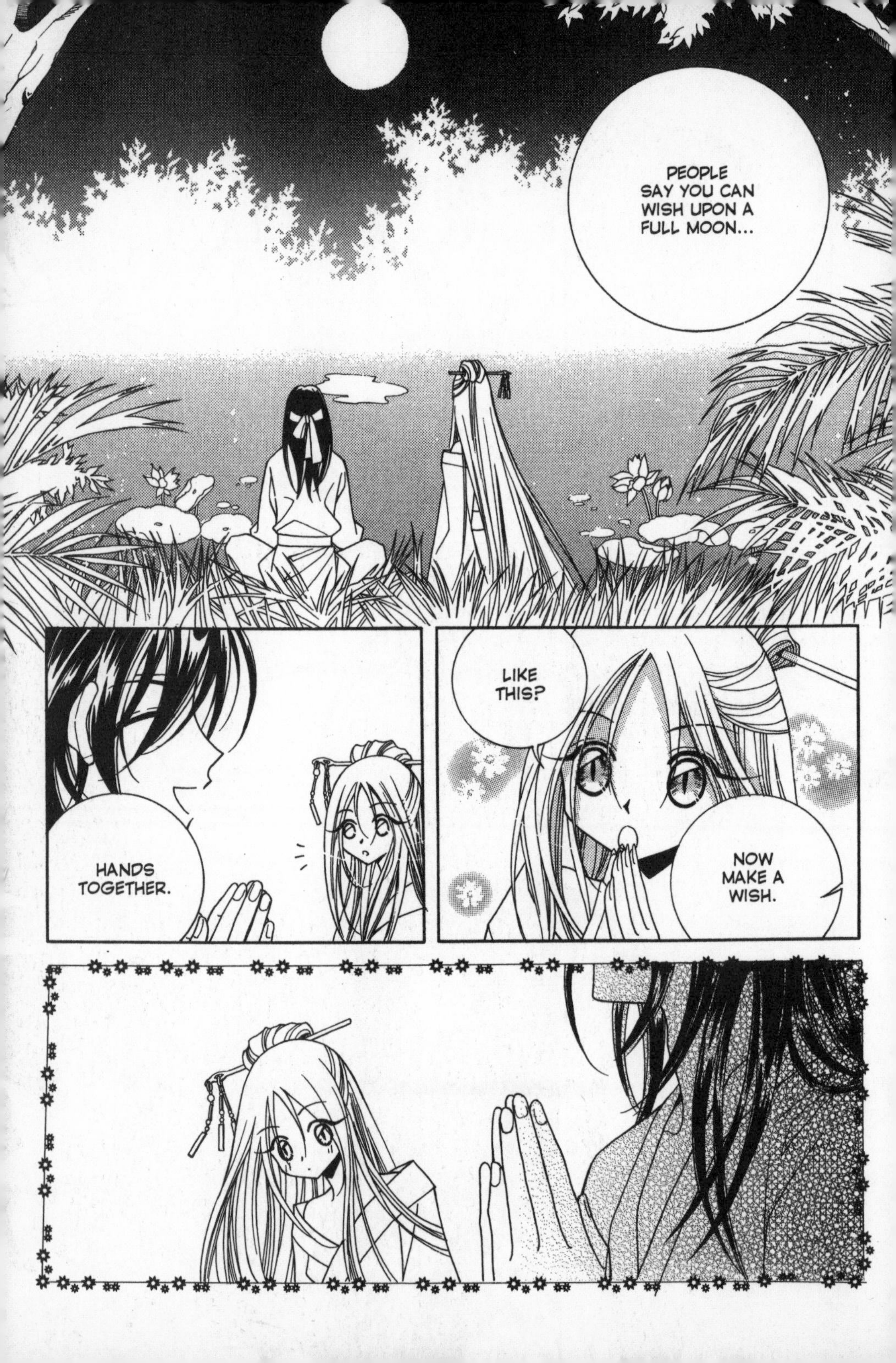
PEOPLE SAY YOU CAN WISH UPON A FULL MOON...
HANDS TOGETHER.
LIKE THIS?
NOW MAKE A WISH.

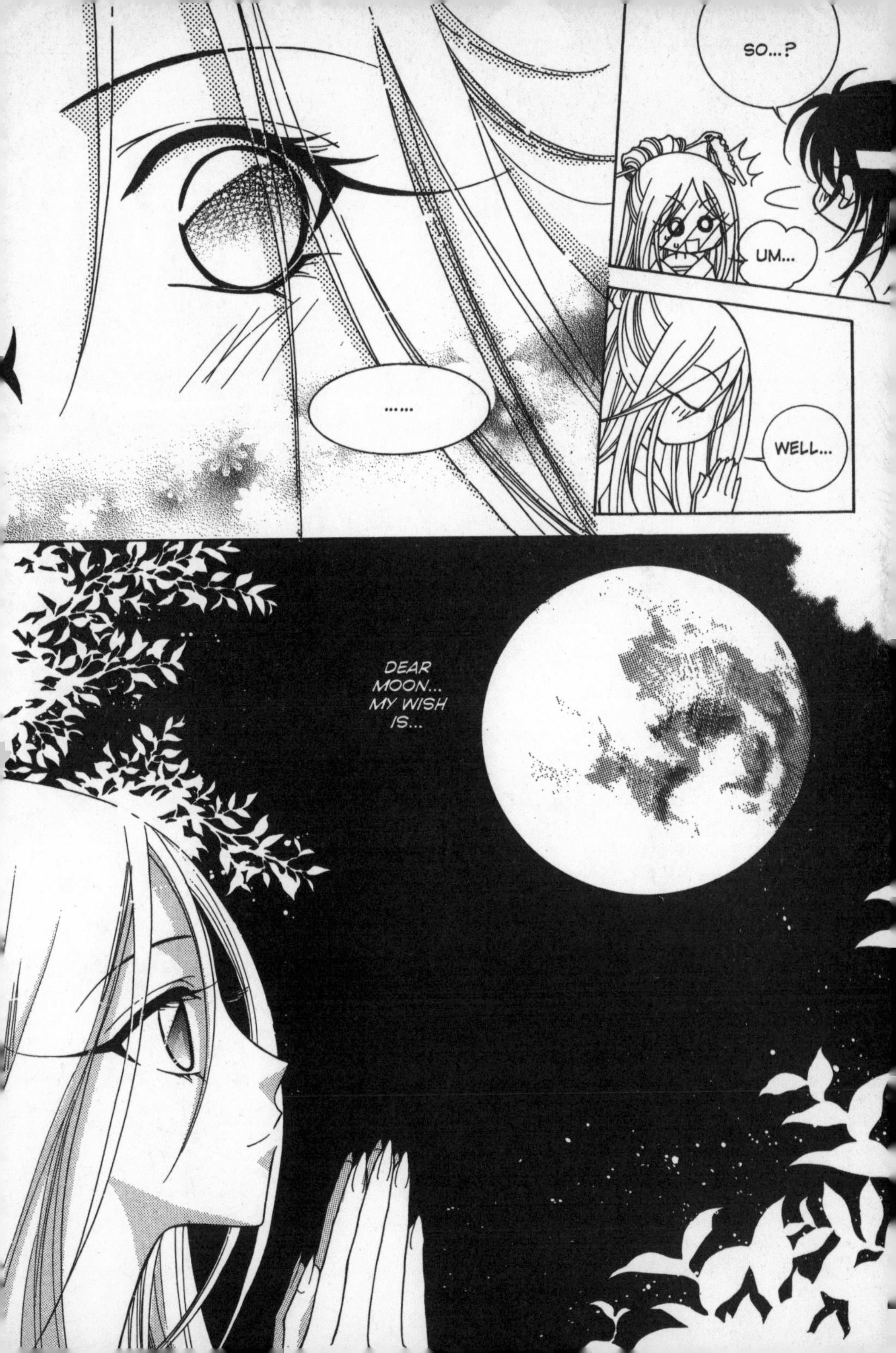
……
SO...?
UM...
WELL...
DEAR MOON... MY WISH IS...

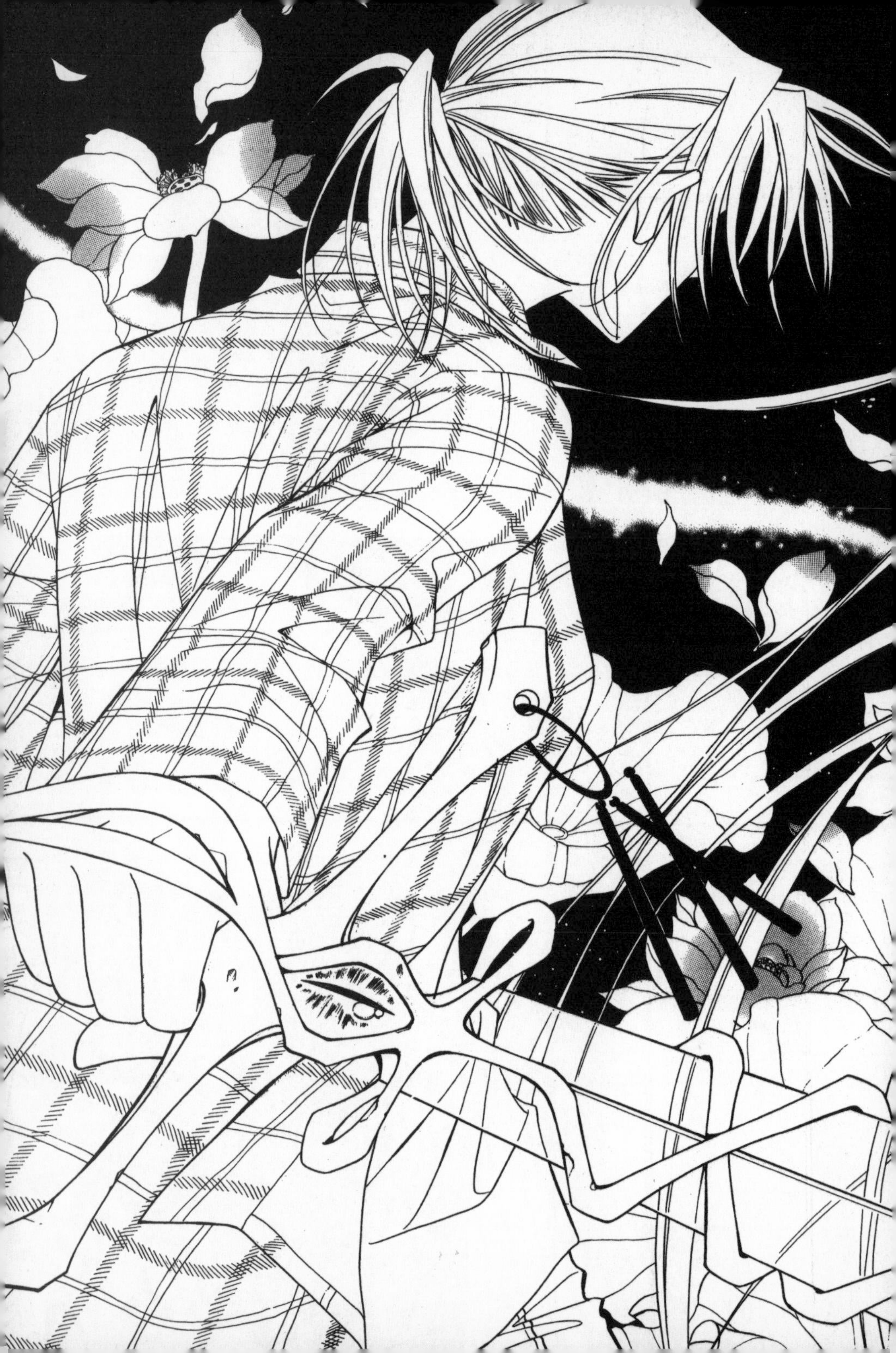

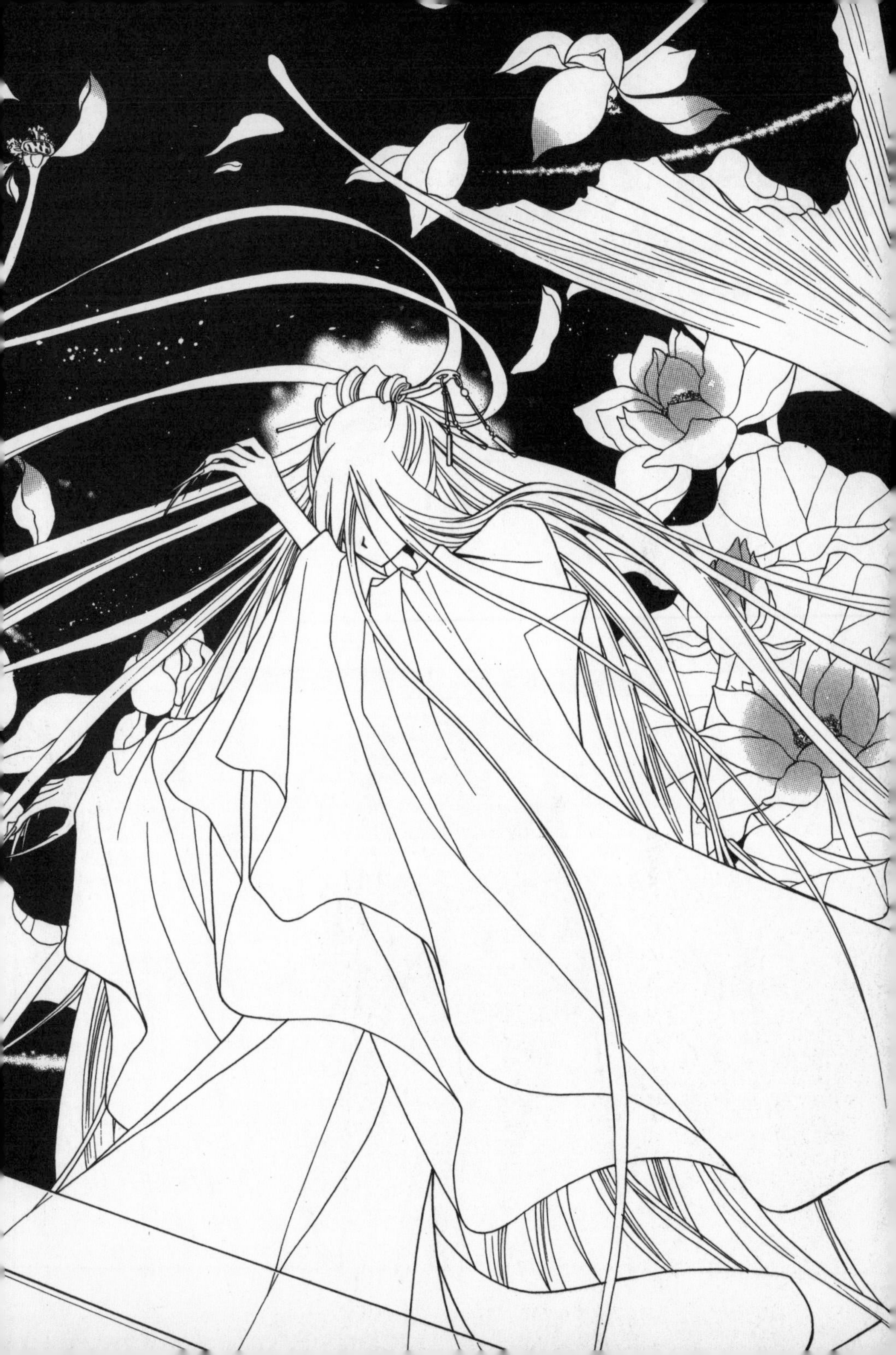

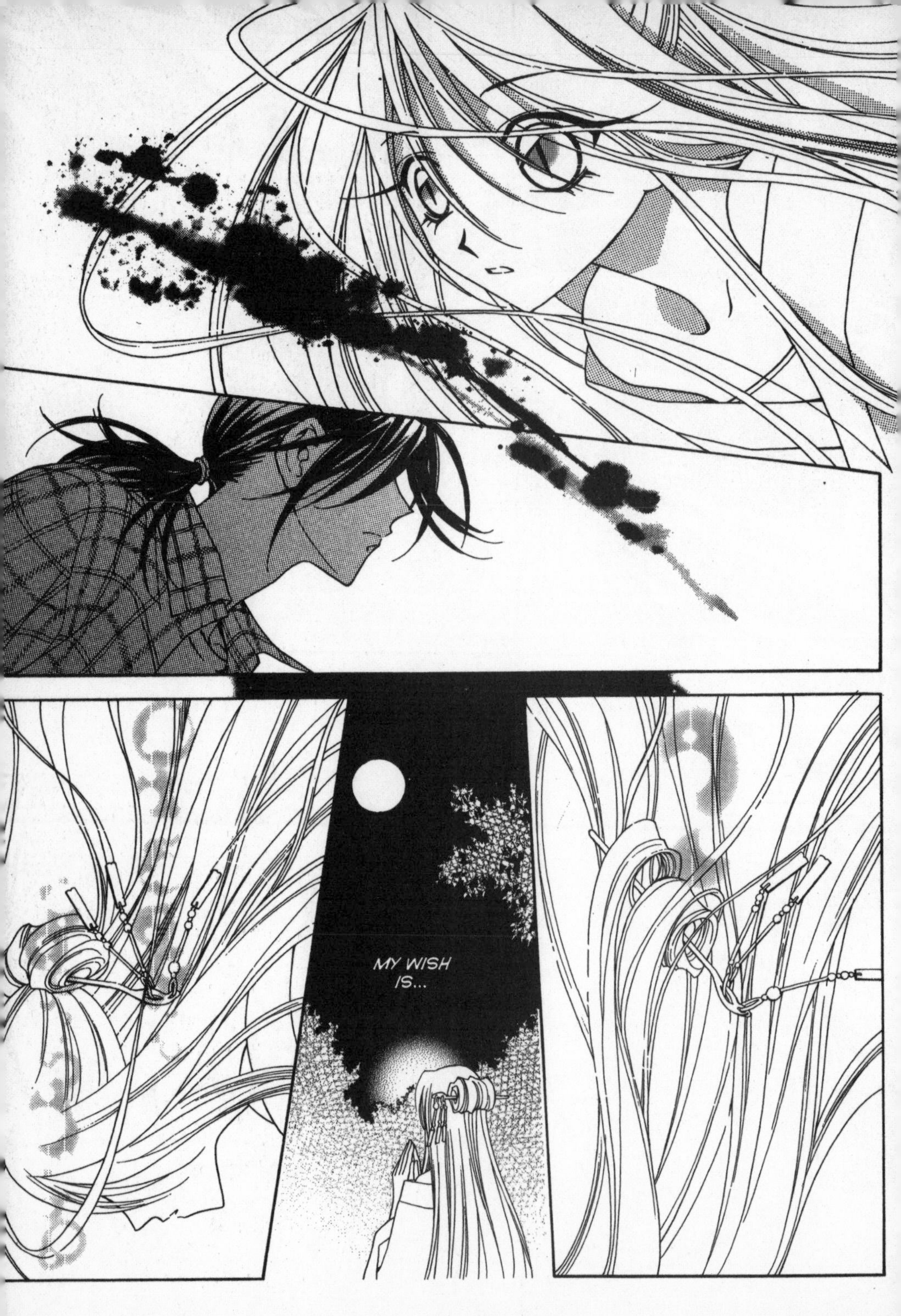
MY WISH
IS...

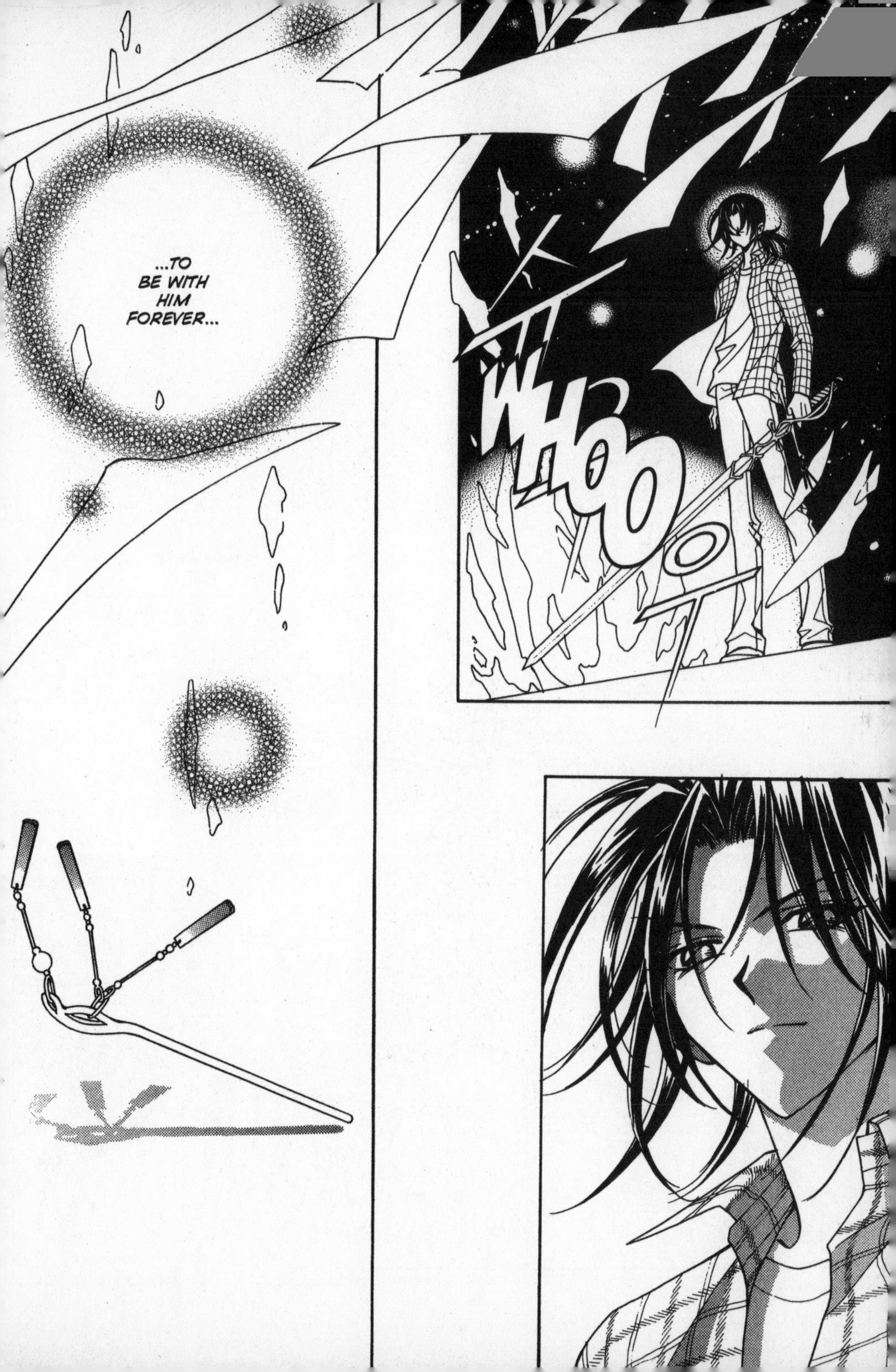
...TO
BE WITH
HIM
FOREVER...
WHOOOT

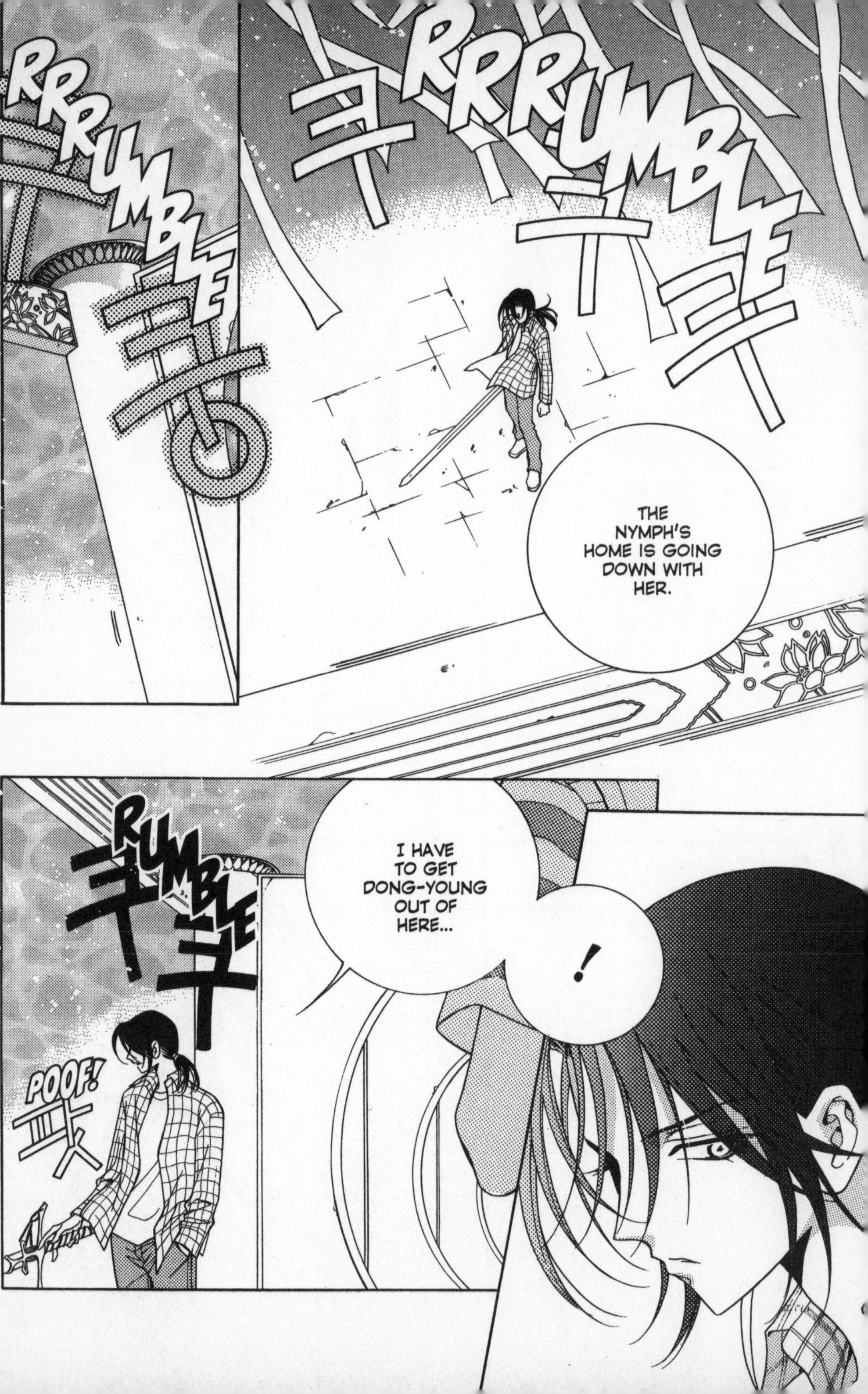
RRRUMBLE
RRRUMBLE
THE NYMPH'S HOME IS GOING DOWN WITH HER.
RUMBLE
POOF!
I HAVE TO GET DONG-YOUNG OUT OF HERE...
!

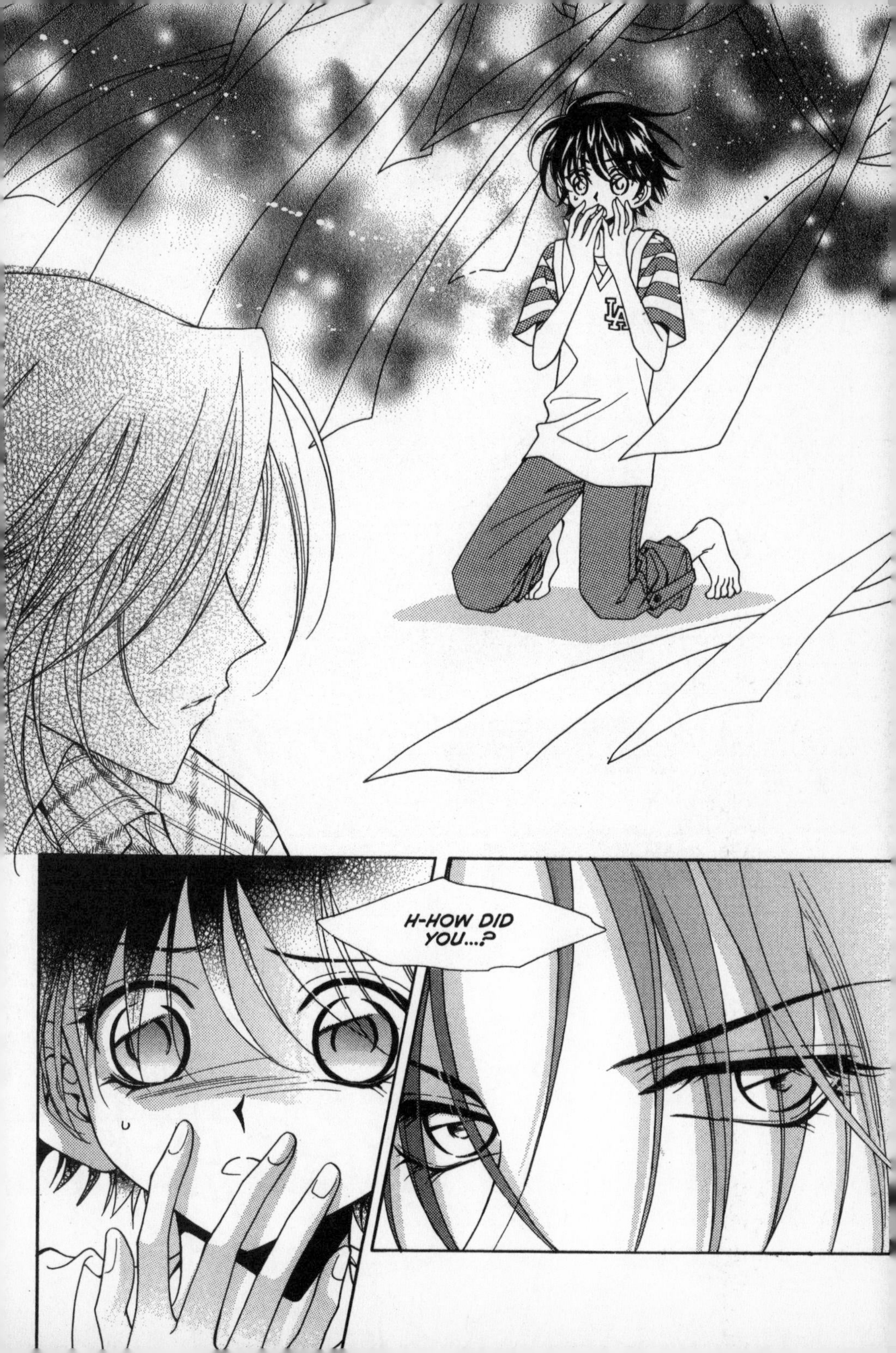
H-HOW DID YOU...?

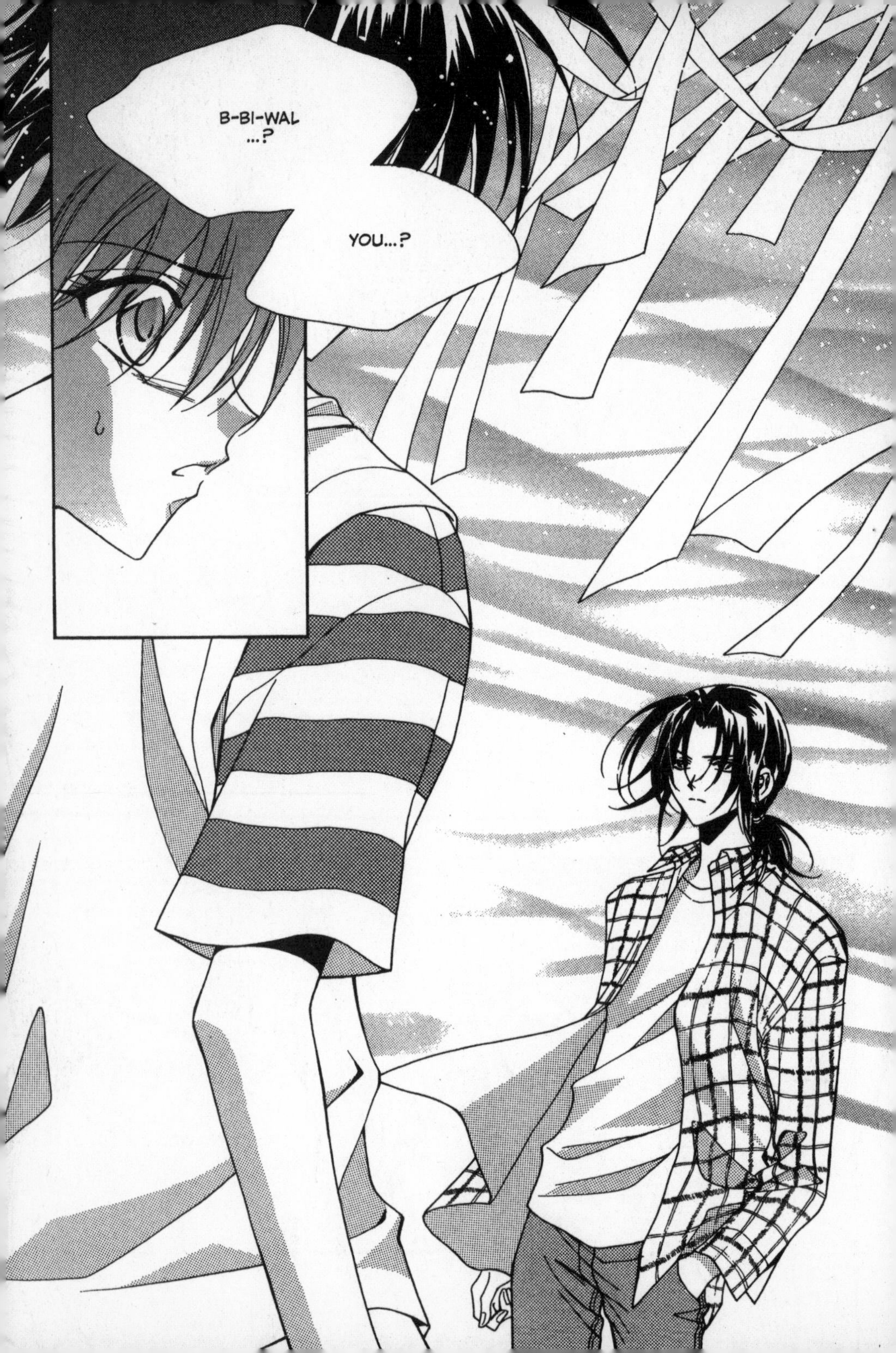
B-BI-WAL
...?
YOU...?

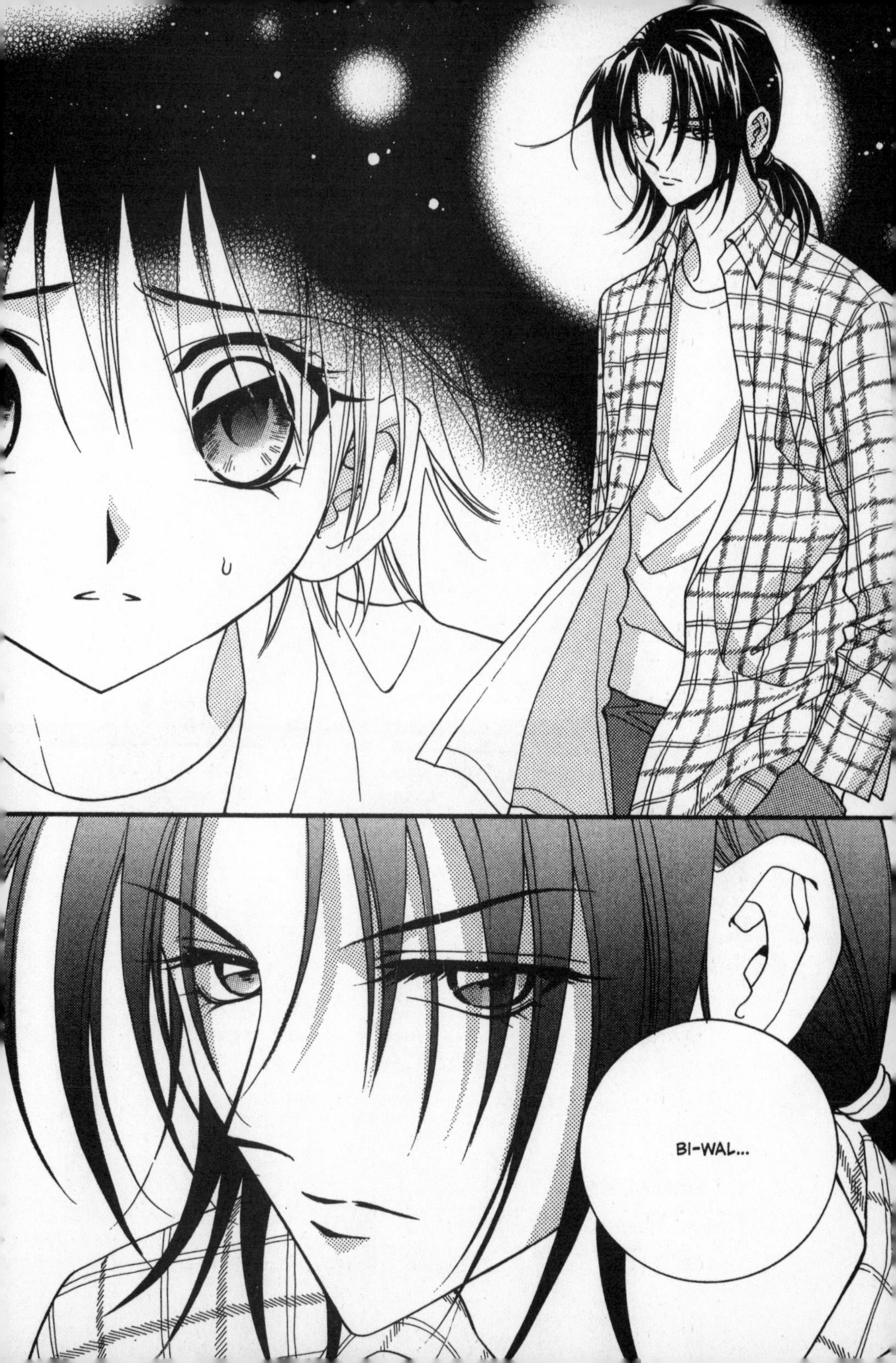
BI-WAL...

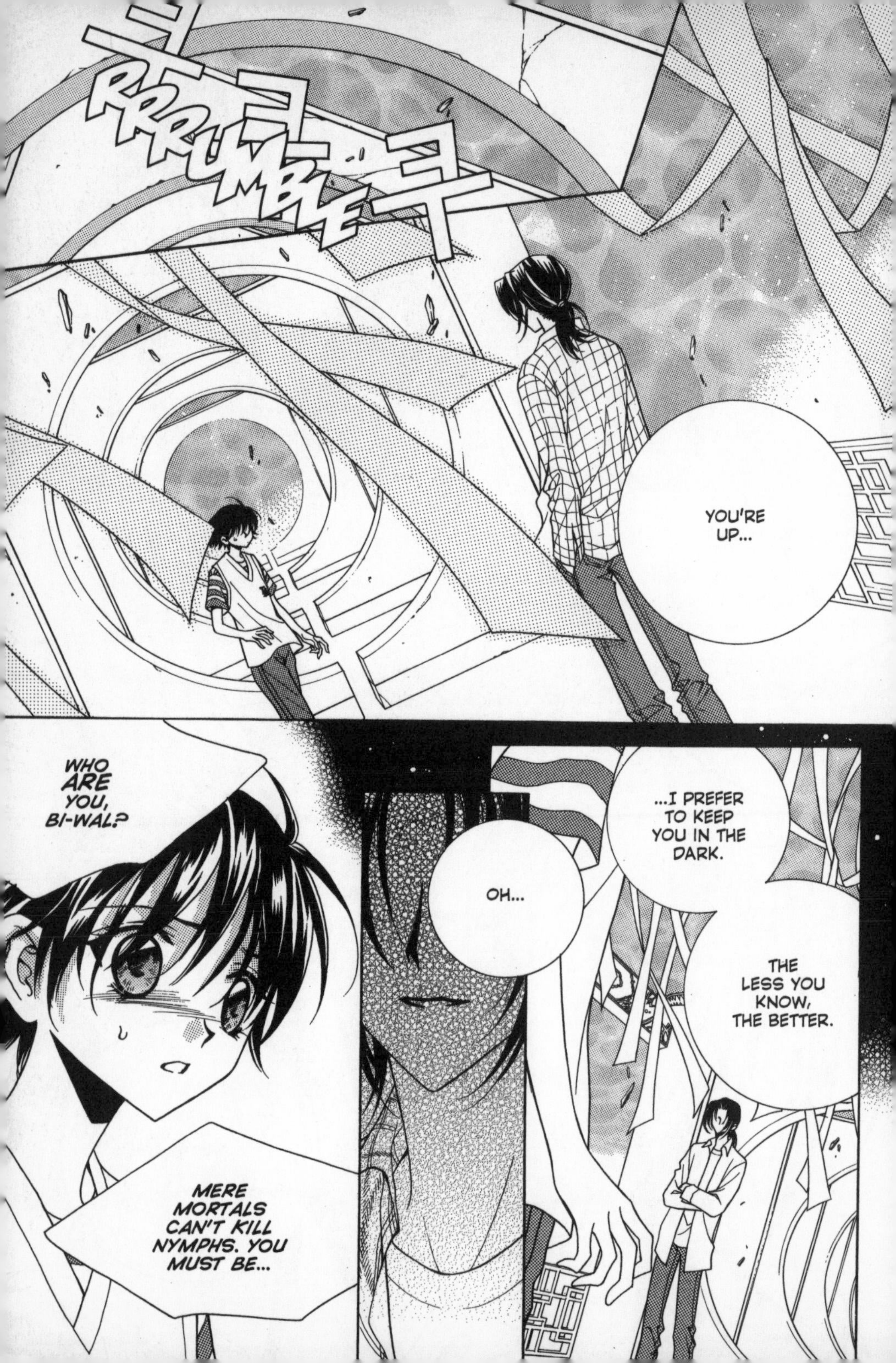

RRRUMBLE
YOU'RE UP...
WHO ARE YOU, BI-WAL?
MERE MORTALS CAN'T KILL NYMPHS. YOU MUST BE...
OH...
...I PREFER TO KEEP YOU IN THE DARK.
THE LESS YOU KNOW, THE BETTER.

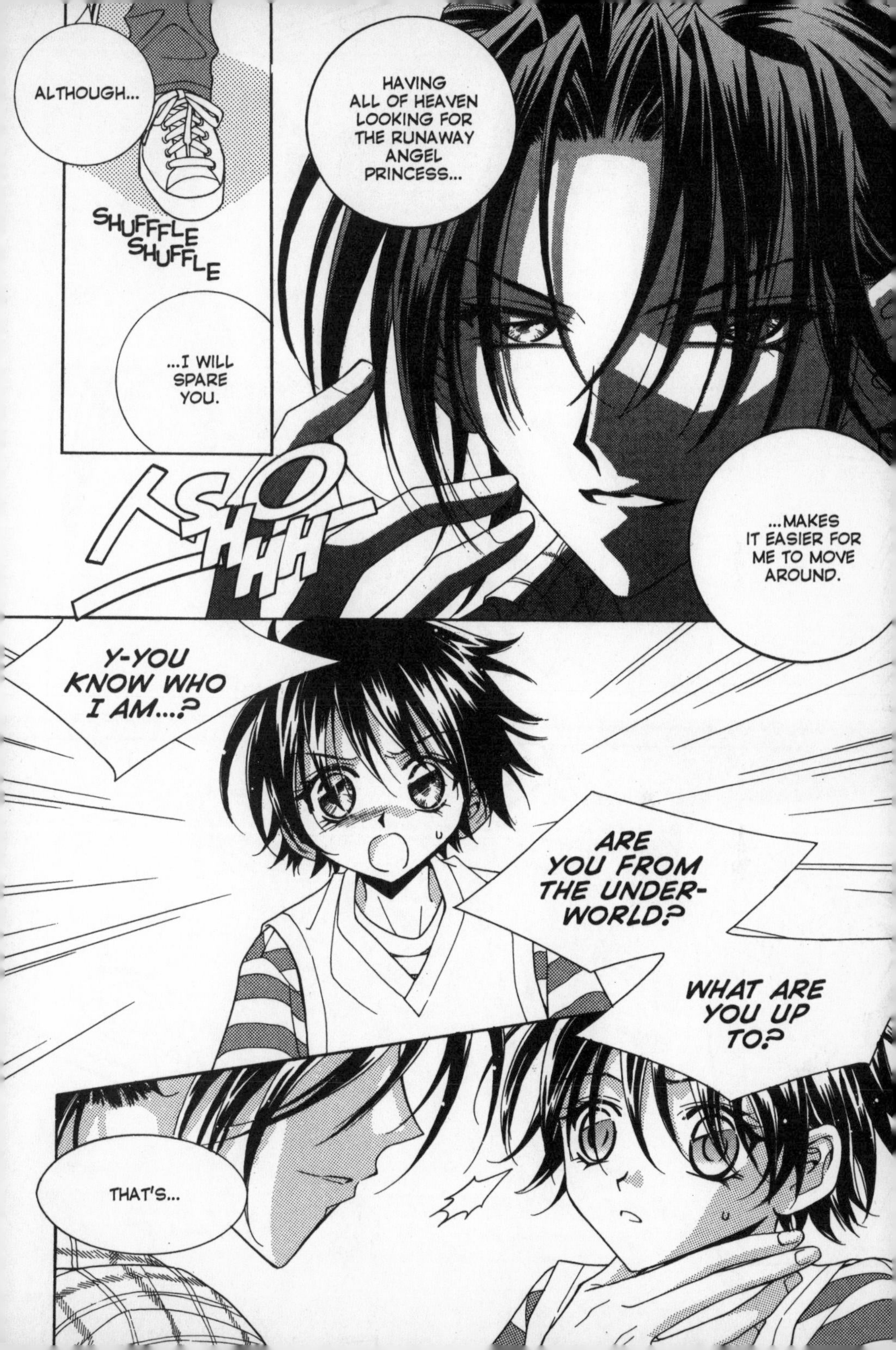
ALTHOUGH...
SHUFFFLE SHUFFLE
...I WILL SPARE YOU.
HAVING ALL OF HEAVEN LOOKING FOR THE RUNAWAY ANGEL PRINCESS...
SHHHH
...MAKES IT EASIER FOR ME TO MOVE AROUND.
Y-YOU KNOW WHO I AM...?
ARE YOU FROM THE UNDER-WORLD?
WHAT ARE YOU UP TO?
THAT'S...

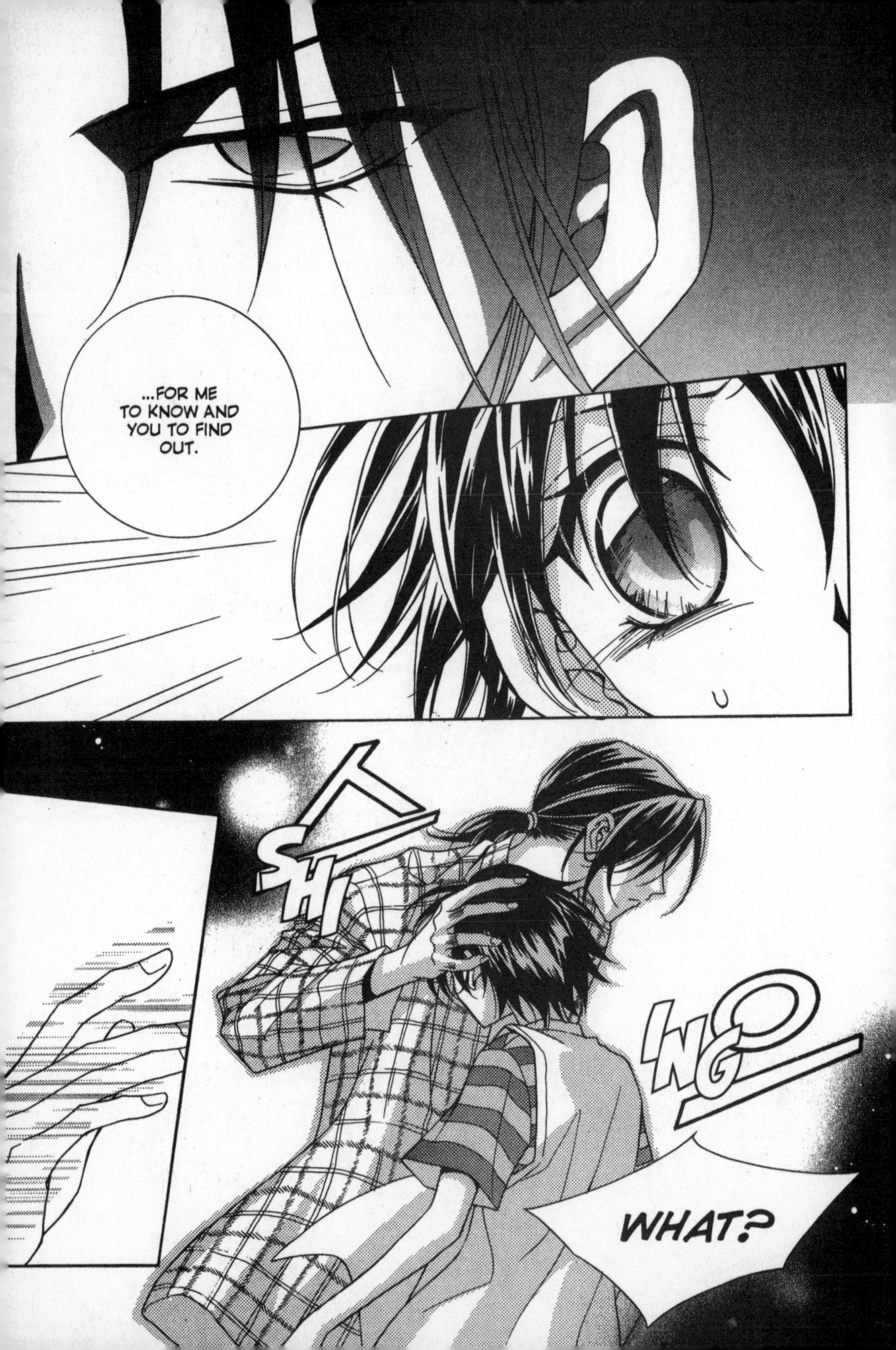
...FOR ME TO KNOW AND YOU TO FIND OUT.
SHING?
WHAT?

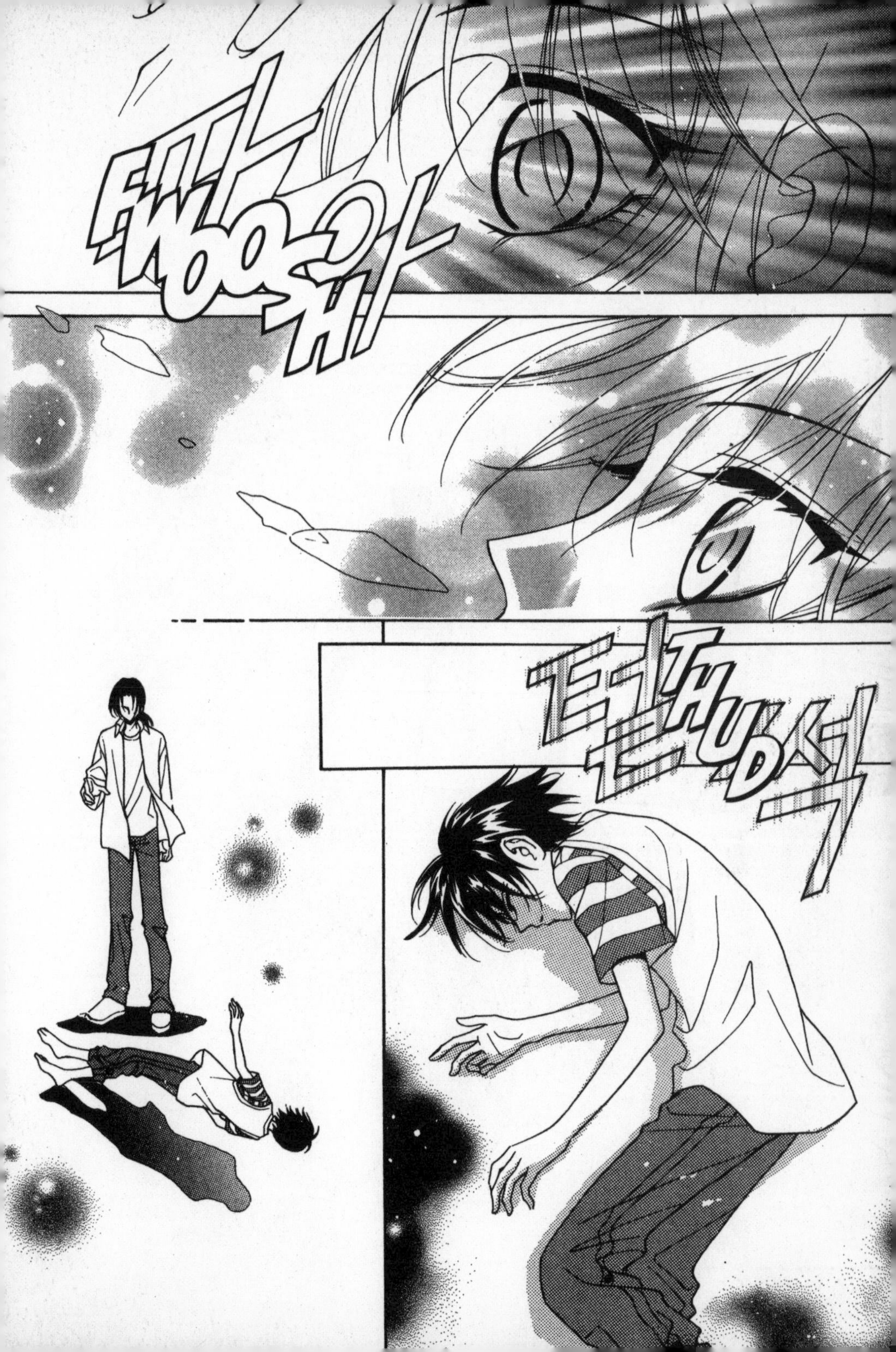
WOOSH!
THUD
털썩

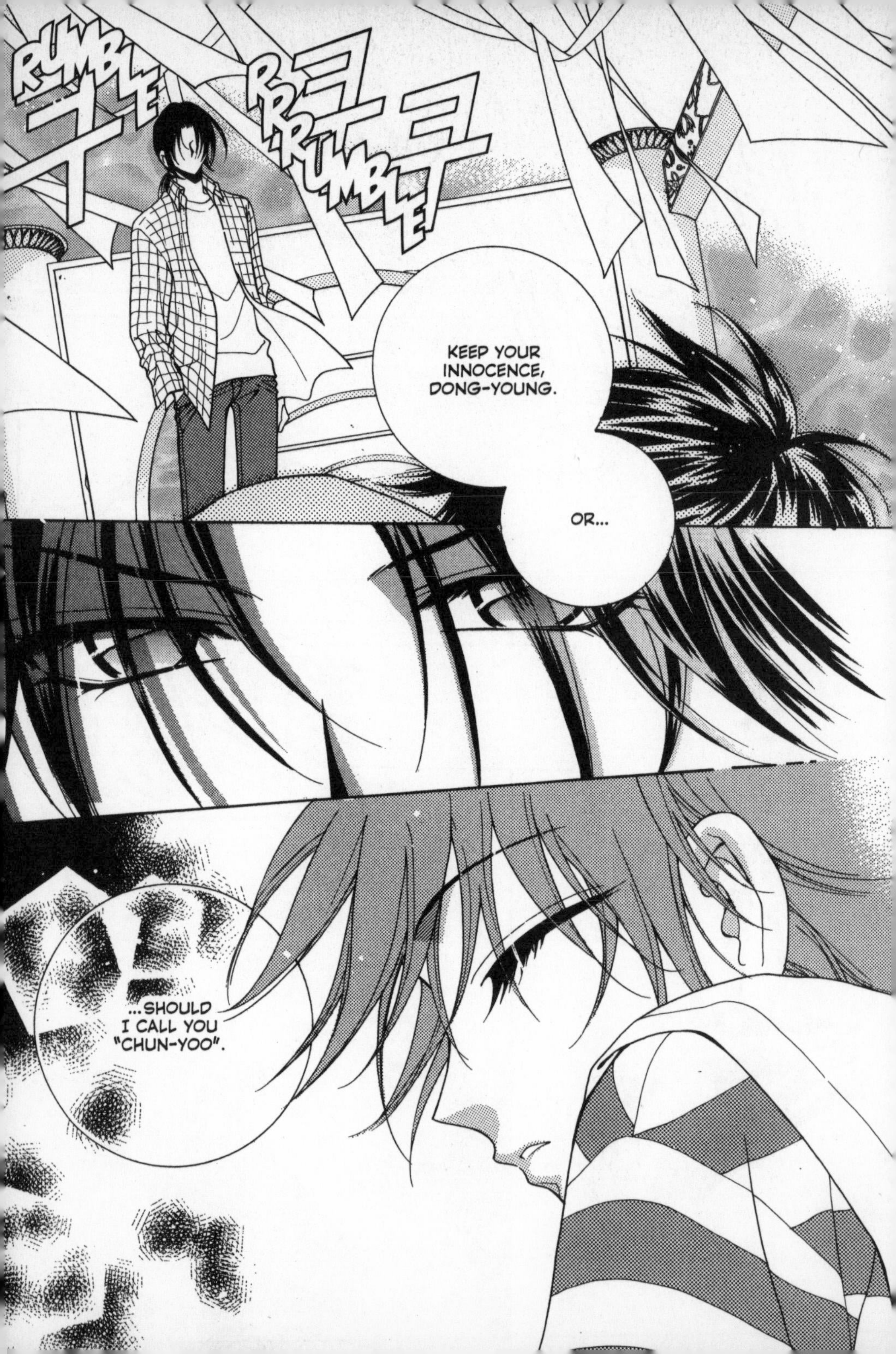
RUMBLE
RRRUMBLE
KEEP YOUR INNOCENCE, DONG-YOUNG.
OR...
...SHOULD I CALL YOU "CHUN-YOO".

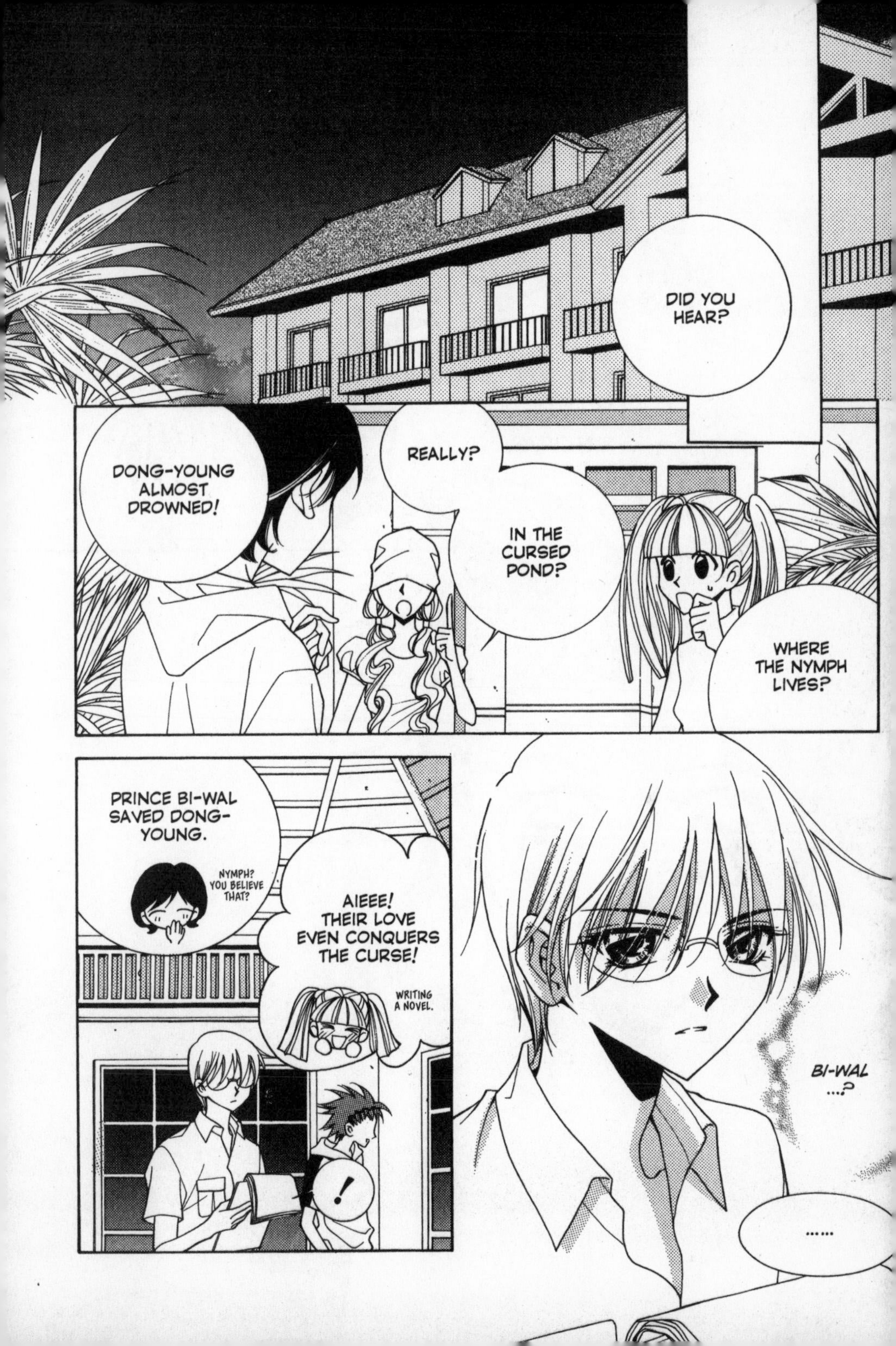
DID YOU HEAR?
DONG-YOUNG ALMOST DROWNED!
REALLY?
IN THE CURSED POND?
WHERE THE NYMPH LIVES?
PRINCE BI-WAL SAVED DONG-YOUNG.
NYMPH? YOU BELIEVE THAT?
AIEEE! THEIR LOVE EVEN CONQUERS THE CURSE!
WRITING A NOVEL.
!
BI-WAL ...?
......

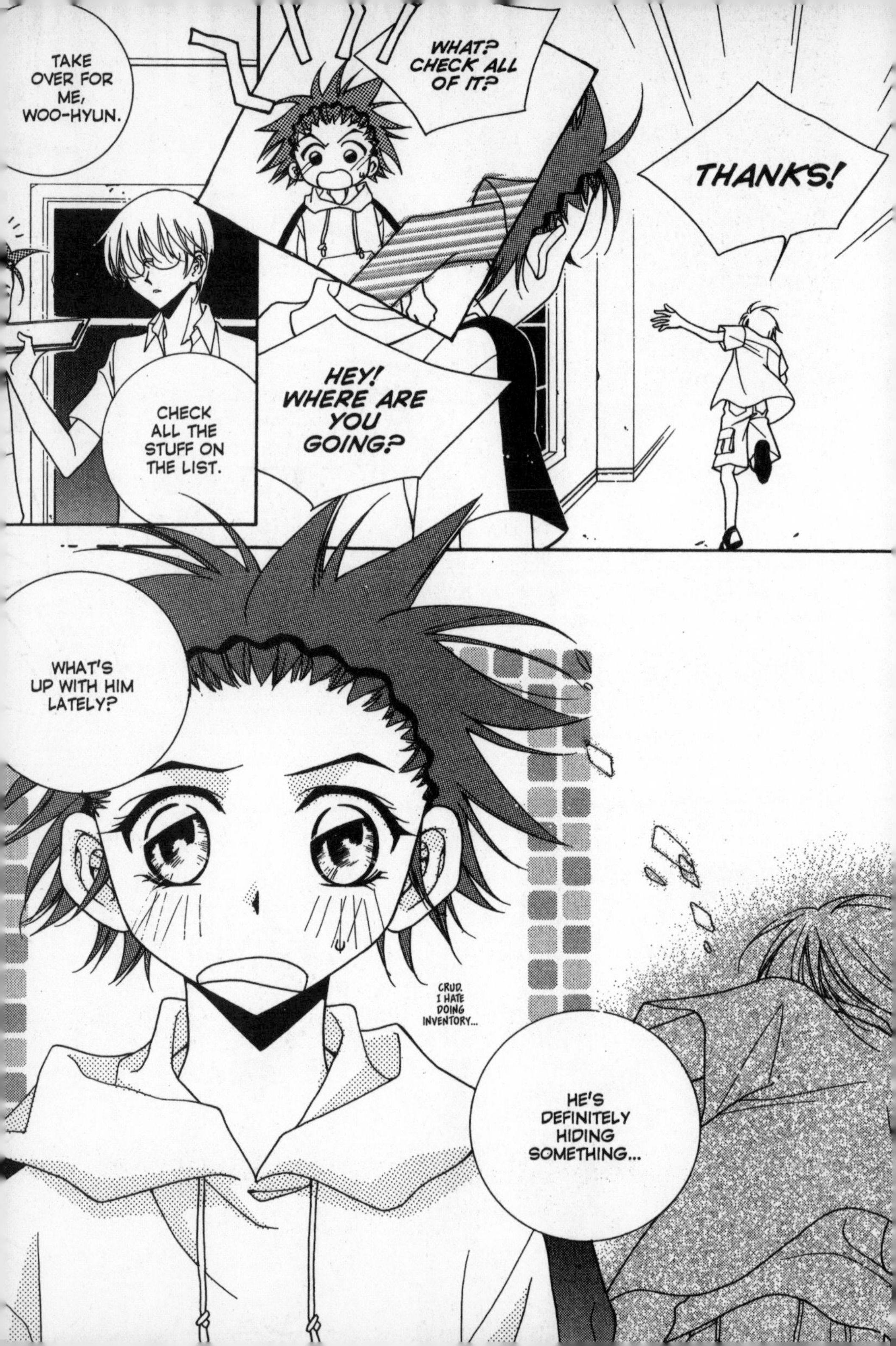
TAKE OVER FOR ME, WOO-HYUN.
CHECK ALL THE STUFF ON THE LIST.
WHAT? CHECK ALL OF IT?
HEY! WHERE ARE YOU GOING?
THANKS!
WHAT'S UP WITH HIM LATELY?
CRUD. I HATE DOING INVENTORY...
HE'S DEFINITELY HIDING SOMETHING...

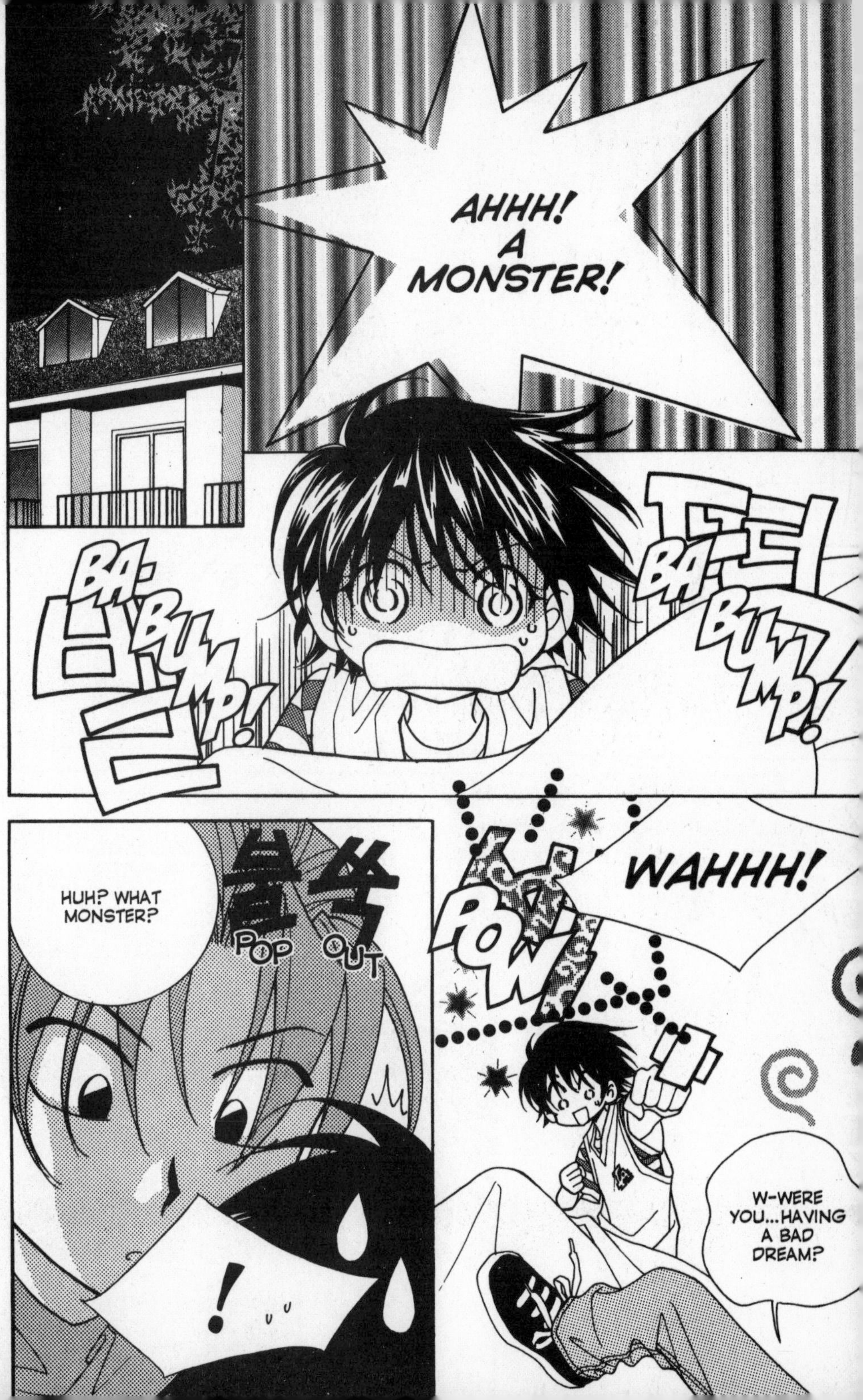
AHHH! A MONSTER!
BA-BUMP!
BA-BUMP!
HUH? WHAT MONSTER?
POP OUT
!
WAHHH!
POW!
W-WERE YOU...HAVING A BAD DREAM?

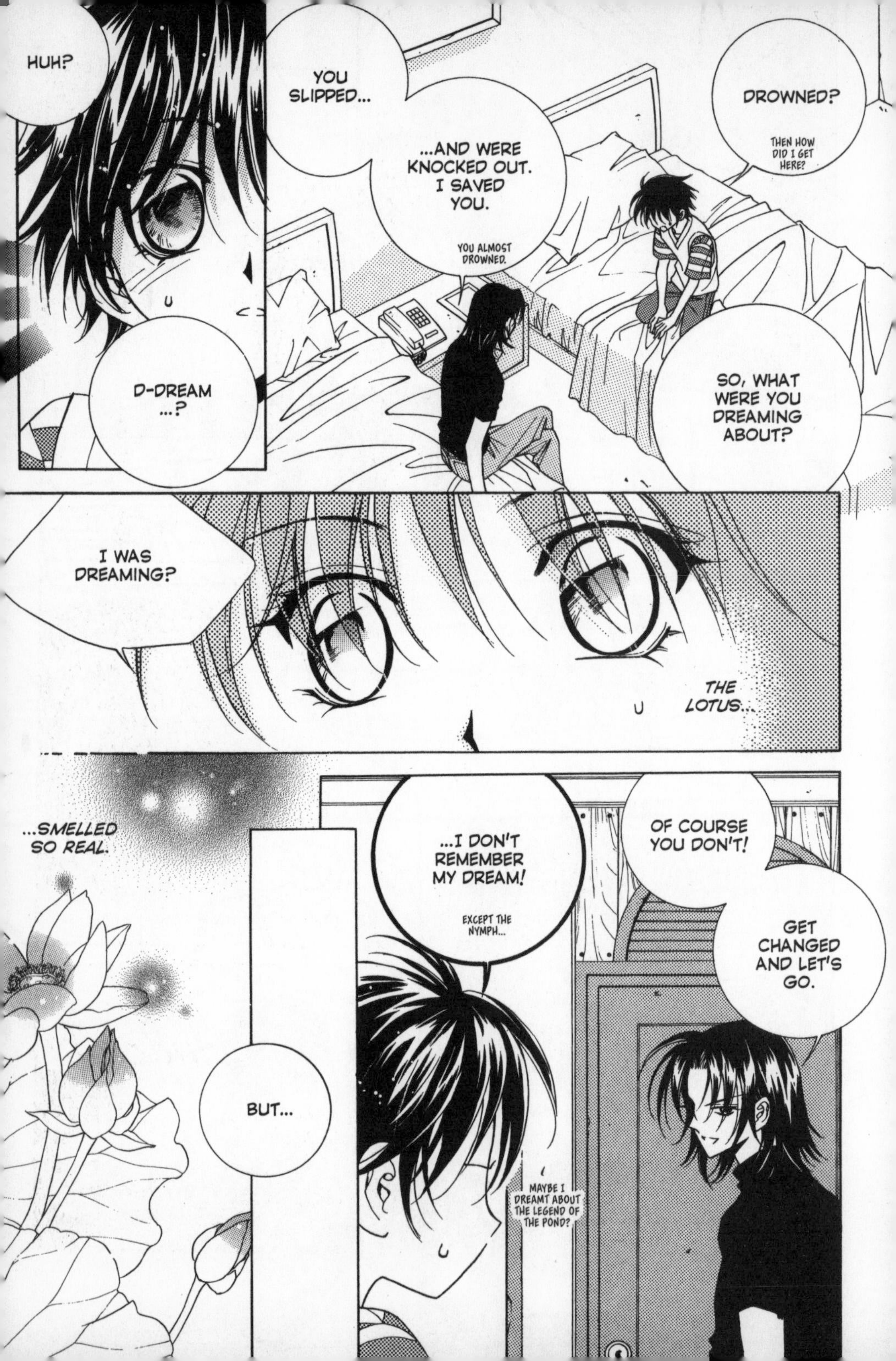
HUH?
D-DREAM ...?
YOU SLIPPED...
...AND WERE KNOCKED OUT. I SAVED YOU.
YOU ALMOST DROWNED.
DROWNED?
THEN HOW DID I GET HERE?
SO, WHAT WERE YOU DREAMING ABOUT?
I WAS DREAMING?
THE LOTUS...
...SMELLED SO REAL.
BUT...
...I DON'T REMEMBER MY DREAM!
EXCEPT THE NYMPH...
MAYBE I DREAMT ABOUT THE LEGEND OF THE POND?
OF COURSE YOU DON'T!
GET CHANGED AND LET'S GO.

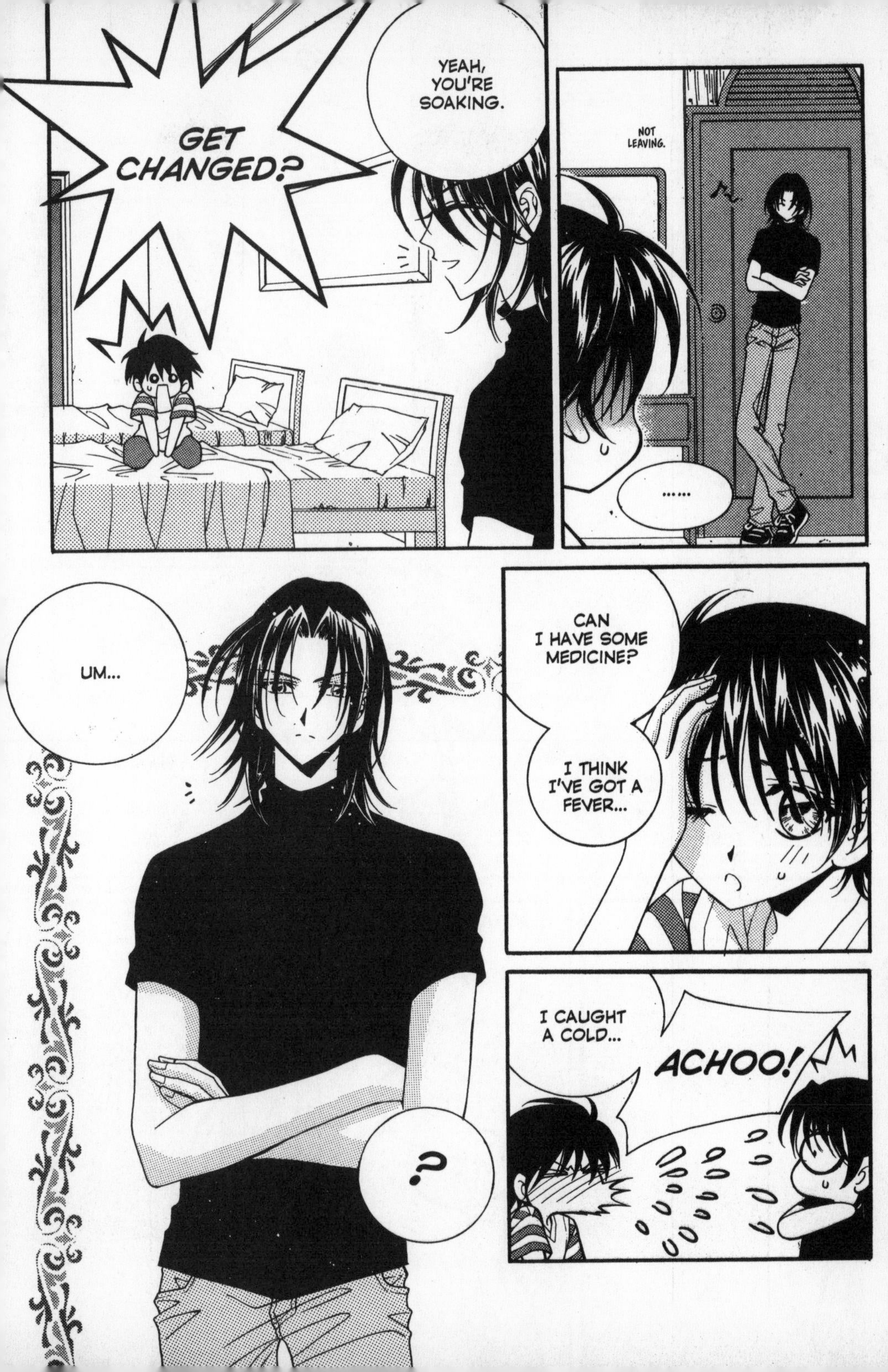
GET CHANGED?
YEAH, YOU'RE SOAKING.
NOT LEAVING.
......
UM...
?
CAN I HAVE SOME MEDICINE?
I THINK I'VE GOT A FEVER...
I CAUGHT A COLD...
ACHOO!

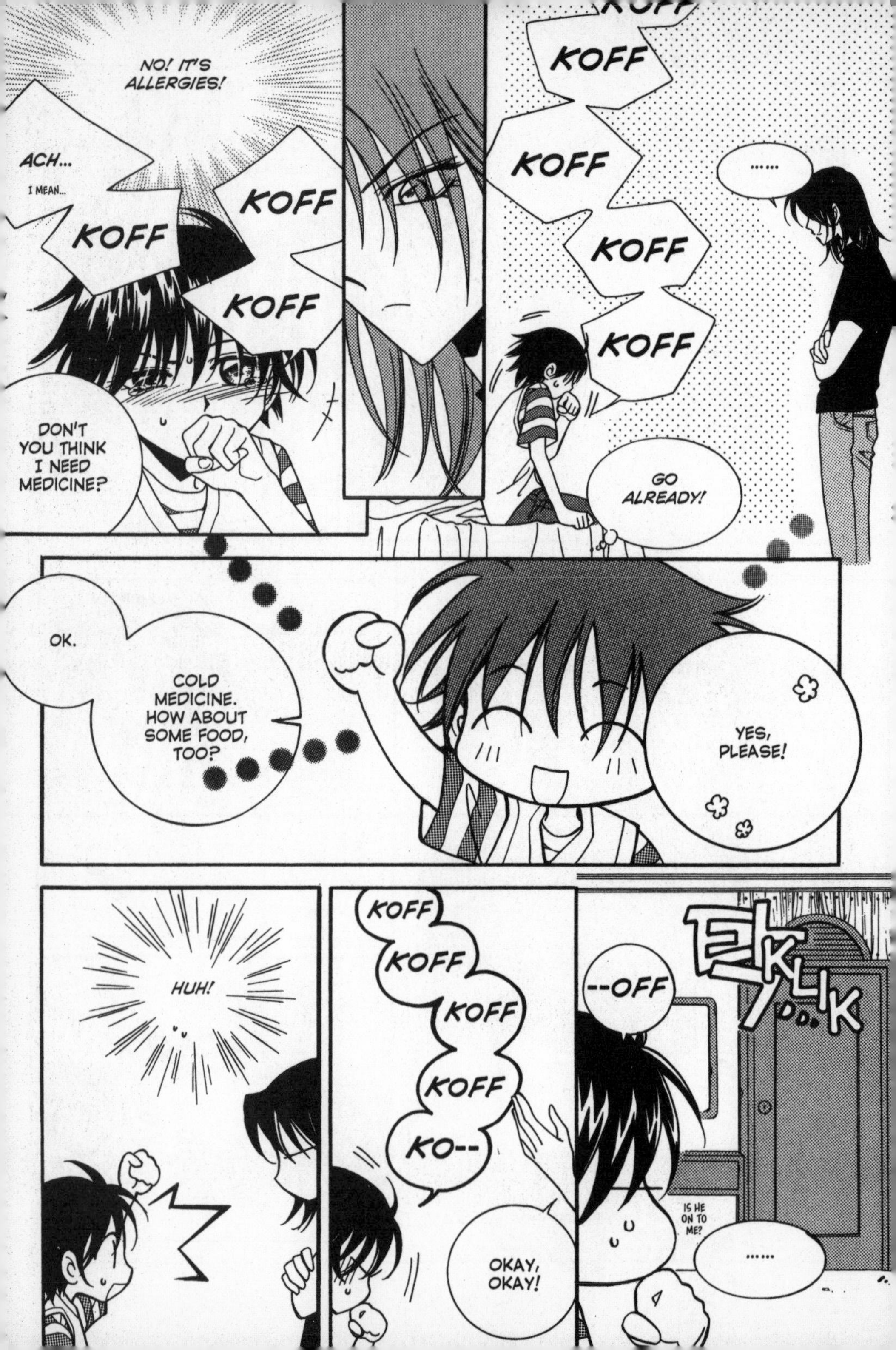
NO! IT'S ALLERGIES!
ACH...
I MEAN...
KOFF
KOFF
KOFF
DON'T YOU THINK I NEED MEDICINE?
KOFF
KOFF
KOFF
KOFF
......
GO ALREADY!
OK.
COLD MEDICINE. HOW ABOUT SOME FOOD, TOO?
YES, PLEASE!
HUH!
KOFF
KOFF
KOFF
KOFF
KO--
OKAY, OKAY!
KLIK
--OFF
IS HE ON TO ME?
......

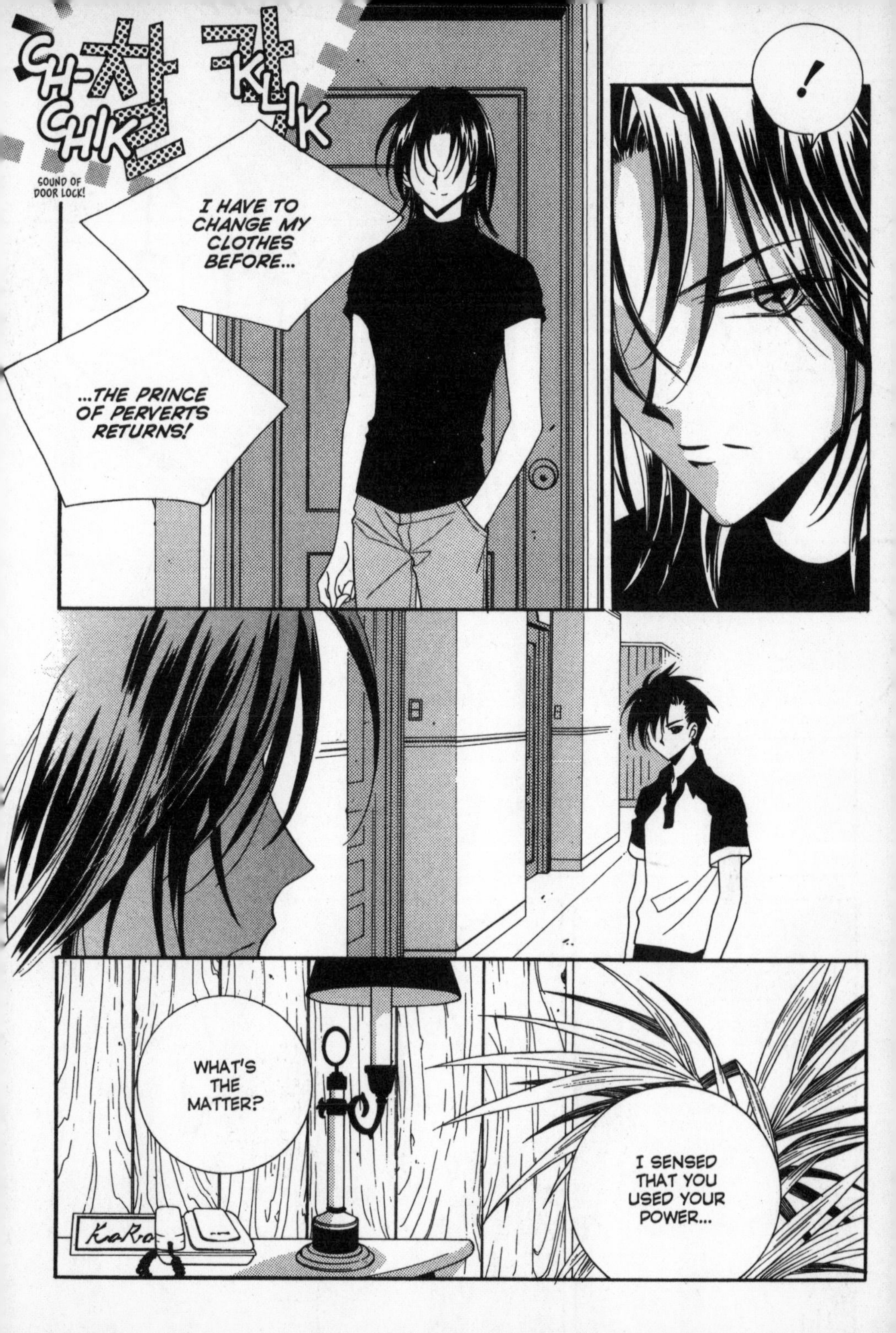
CH-CHIK 찰
칵 KLIK
SOUND OF DOOR LOCK!
I HAVE TO CHANGE MY CLOTHES BEFORE...
...THE PRINCE OF PERVERTS RETURNS!
!
WHAT'S THE MATTER?
KaRo
I SENSED THAT YOU USED YOUR POWER...

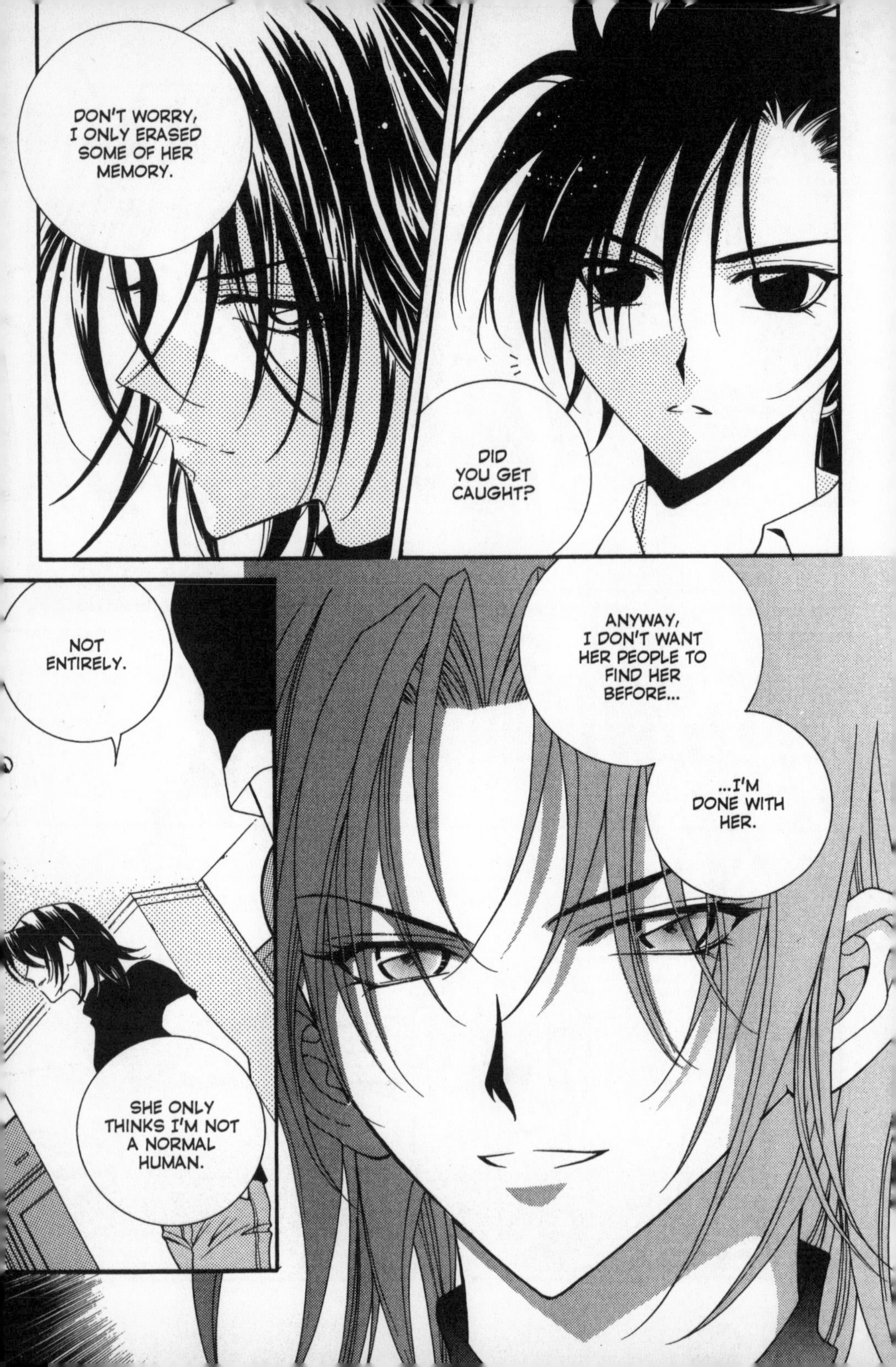
DON'T WORRY, I ONLY ERASED SOME OF HER MEMORY.
DID YOU GET CAUGHT?
NOT ENTIRELY.
SHE ONLY THINKS I'M NOT A NORMAL HUMAN.
ANYWAY, I DON'T WANT HER PEOPLE TO FIND HER BEFORE...
...I'M DONE WITH HER.

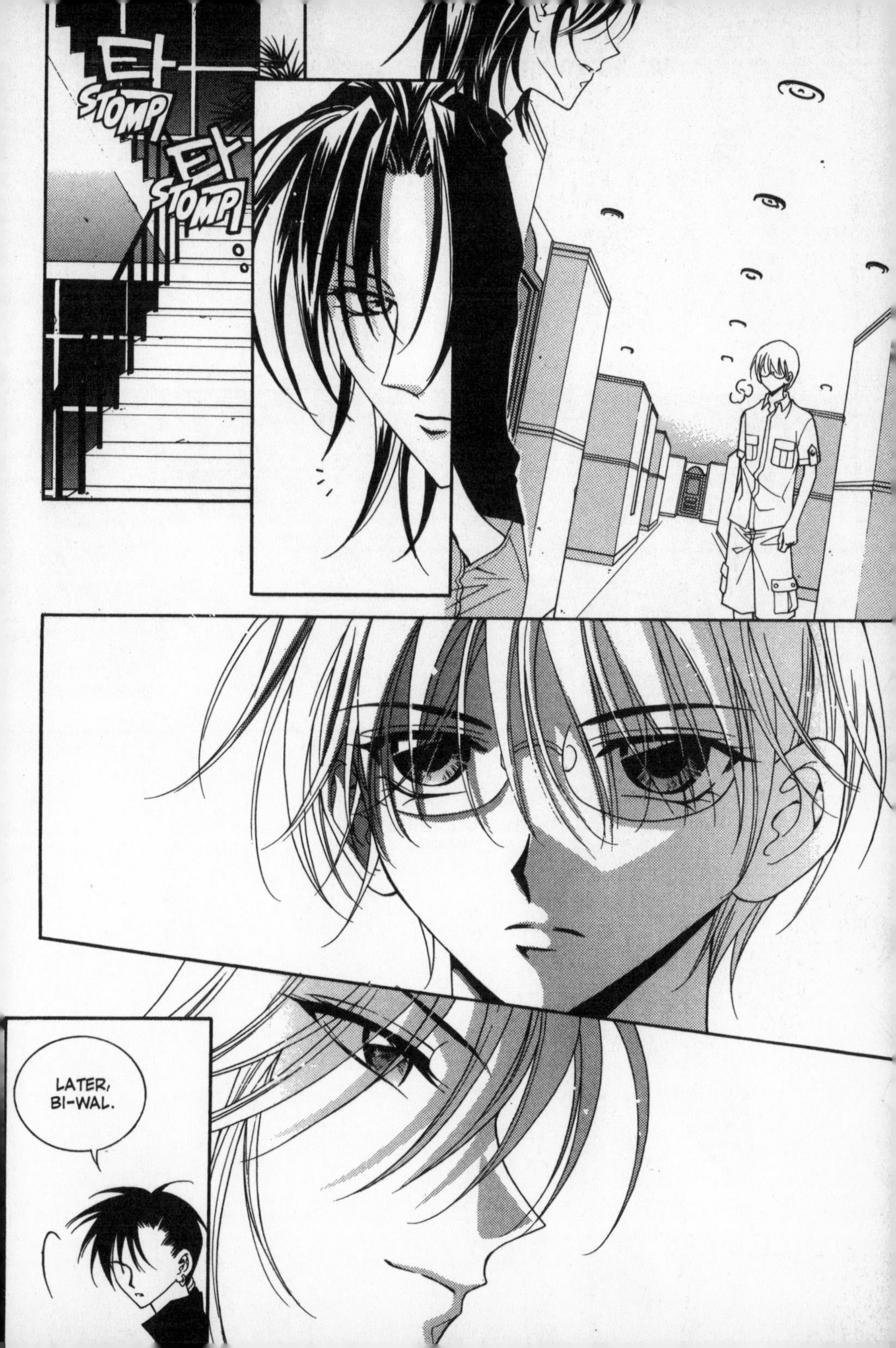

STOMP
STOMP
LATER, BI-WAL.

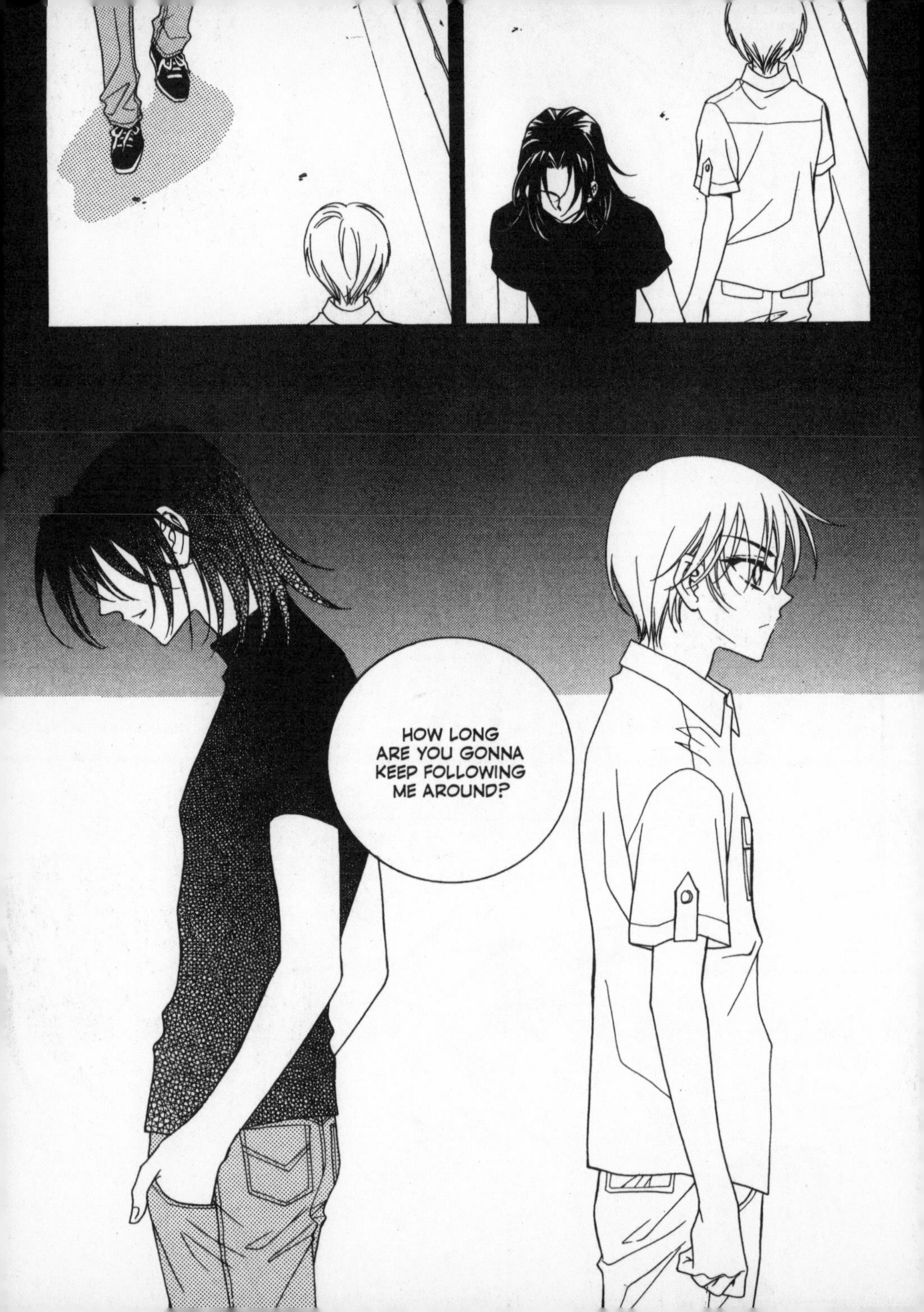
HOW LONG ARE YOU GONNA KEEP FOLLOWING ME AROUND?

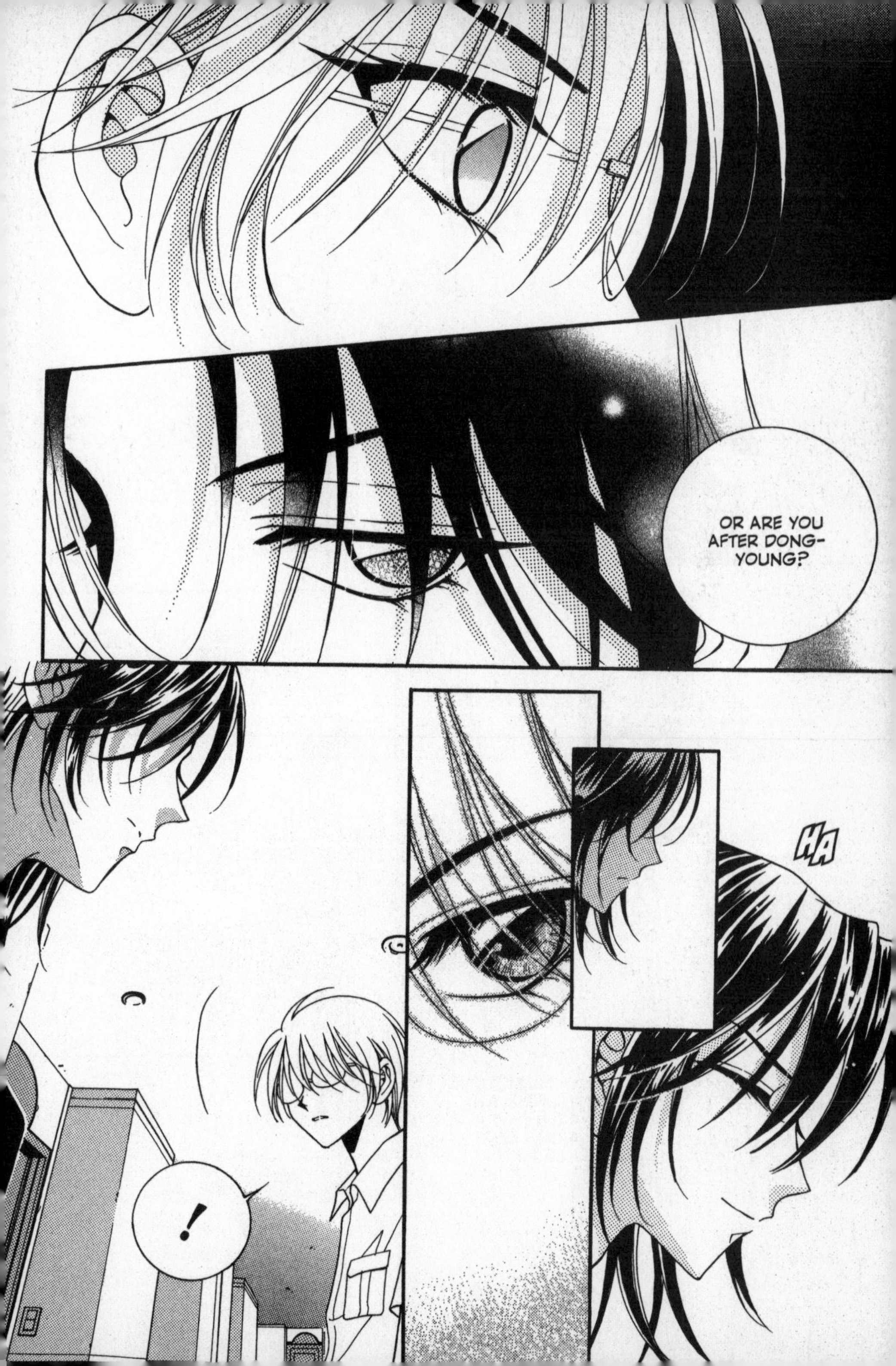
OR ARE YOU AFTER DONG-YOUNG?
!
HA

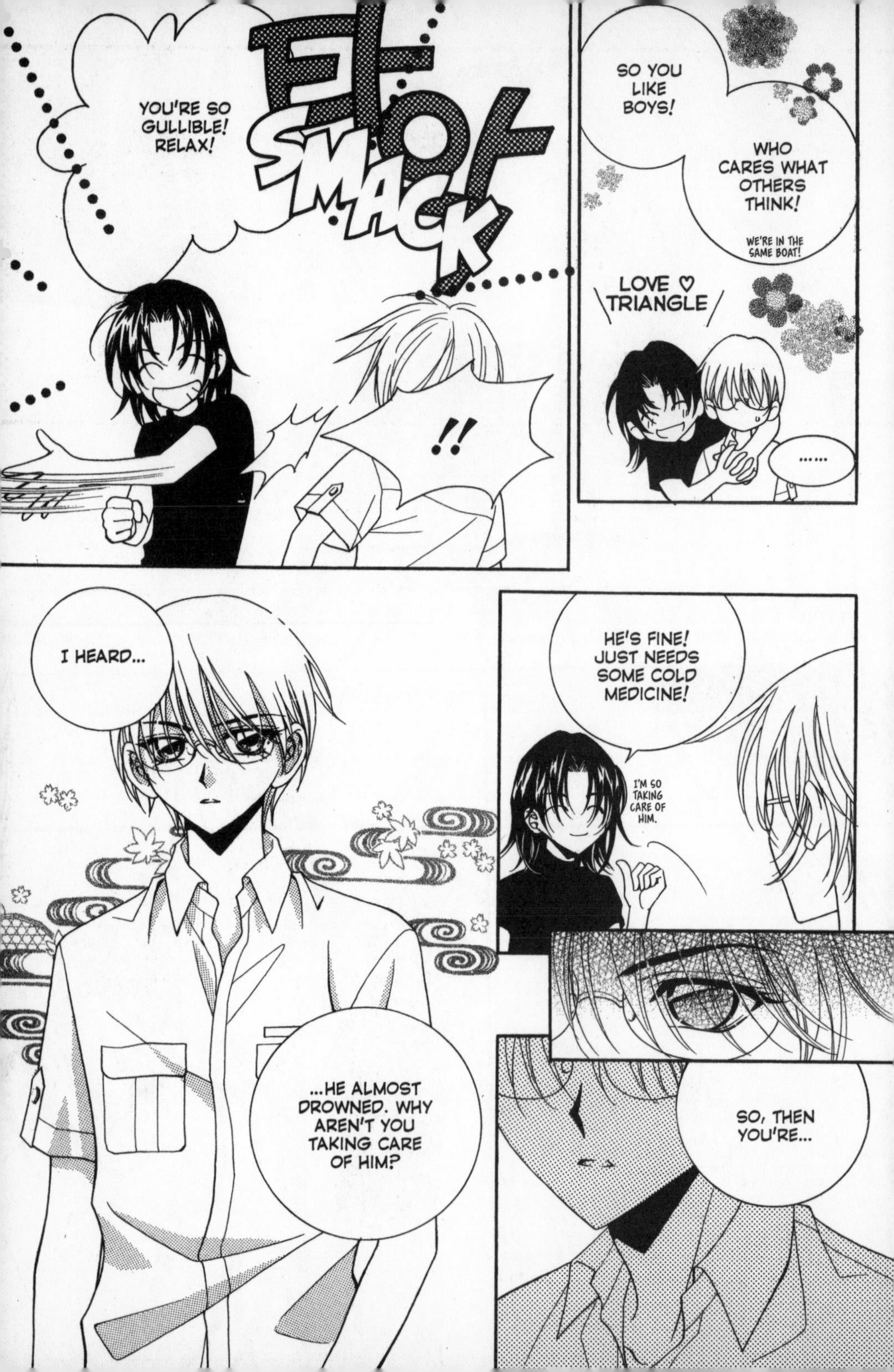
YOU'RE SO GULLIBLE! RELAX!
SMACK!
!!
SO YOU LIKE BOYS!
WHO CARES WHAT OTHERS THINK!
WE'RE IN THE SAME BOAT!
LOVE ♡ TRIANGLE
......
I HEARD...
...HE ALMOST DROWNED. WHY AREN'T YOU TAKING CARE OF HIM?
HE'S FINE! JUST NEEDS SOME COLD MEDICINE!
I'M SO TAKING CARE OF HIM.
SO, THEN YOU'RE...

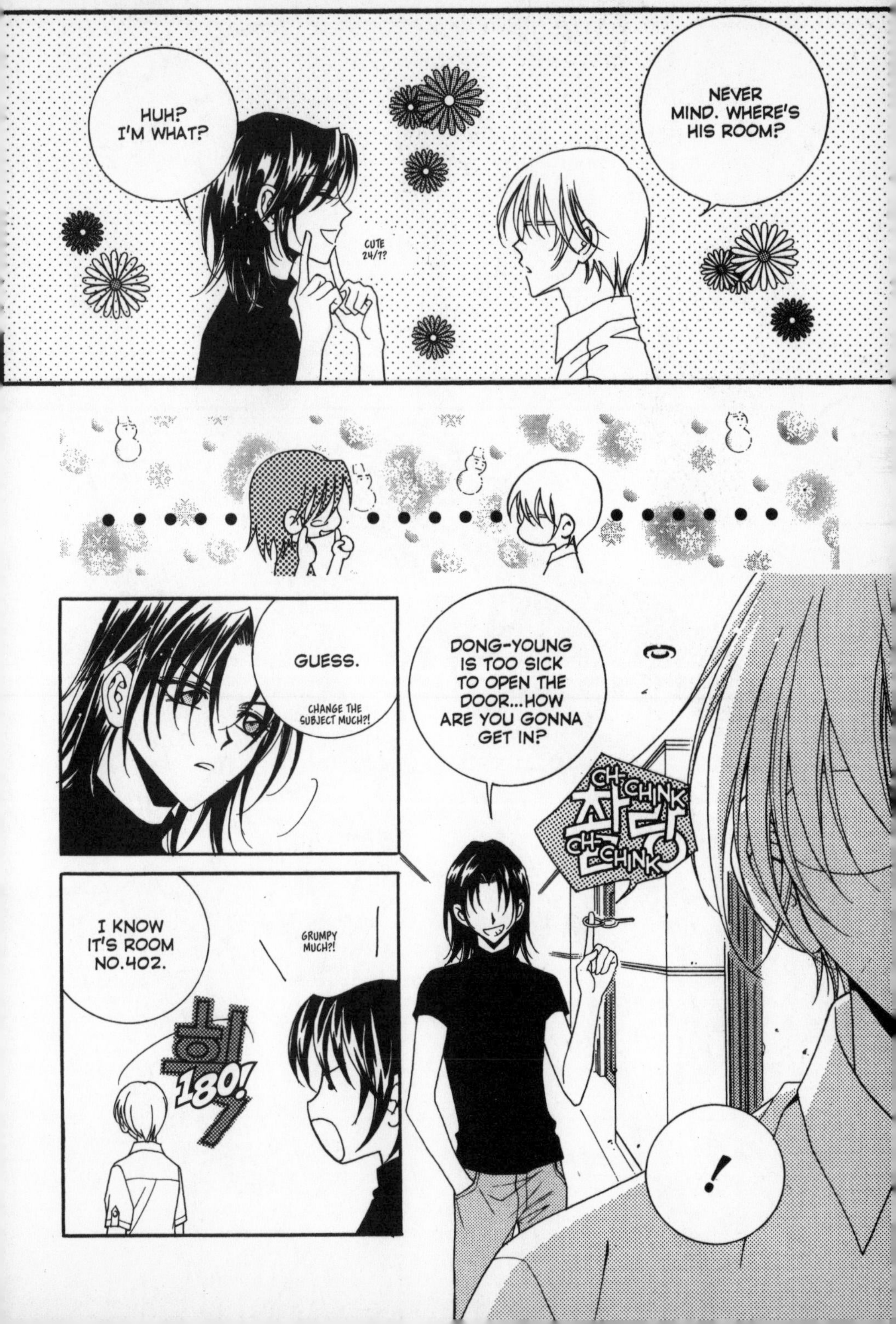
HUH? I'M WHAT?
CUTE 24/7?
NEVER MIND. WHERE'S HIS ROOM?
GUESS.
CHANGE THE SUBJECT MUCH?!
I KNOW IT'S ROOM NO.402.
GRUMPY MUCH?!
180!
DONG-YOUNG IS TOO SICK TO OPEN THE DOOR...HOW ARE YOU GONNA GET IN?
CH-CHINK
CH-CHINK
!

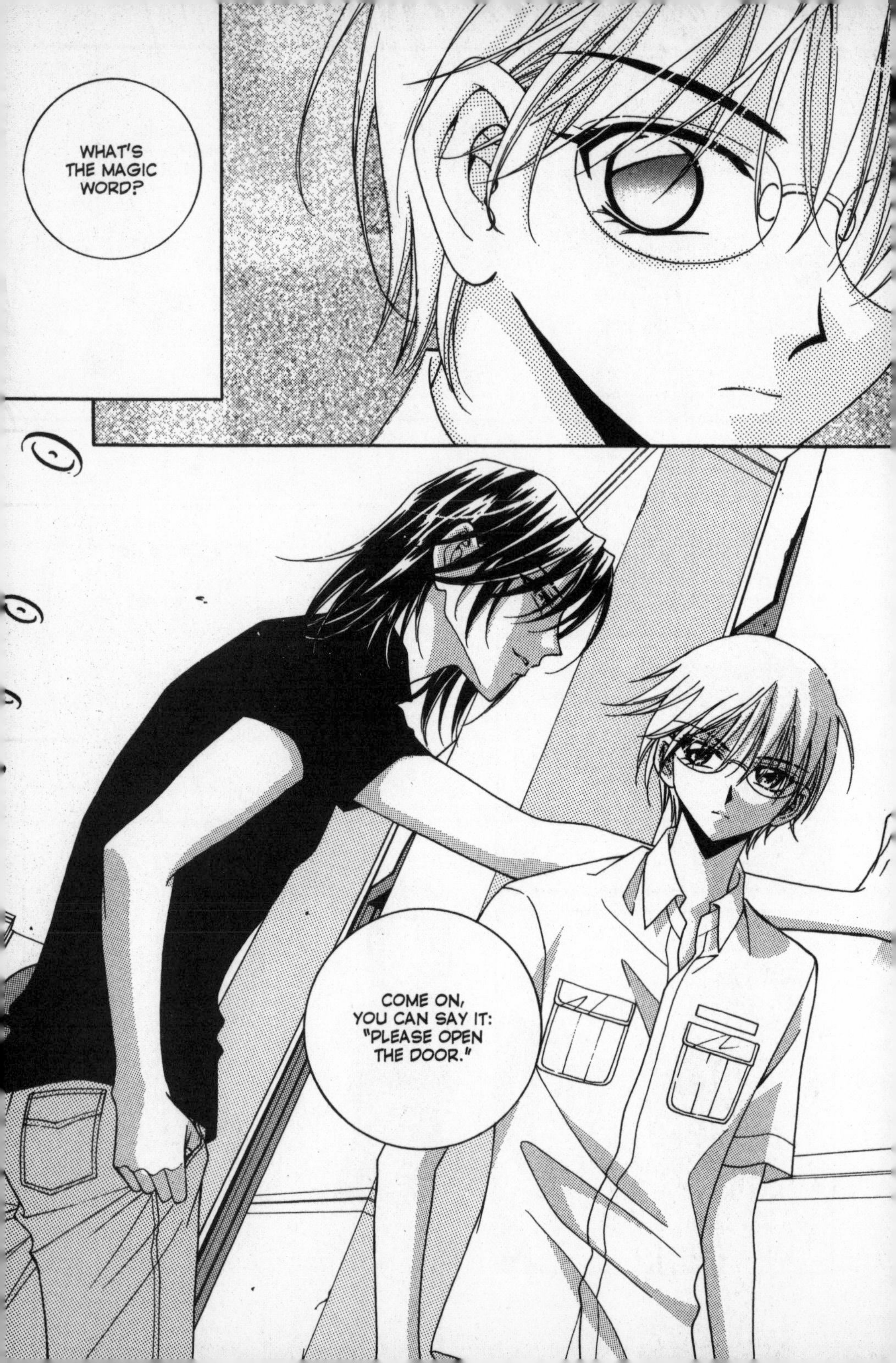
WHAT'S THE MAGIC WORD?
COME ON, YOU CAN SAY IT: "PLEASE OPEN THE DOOR."

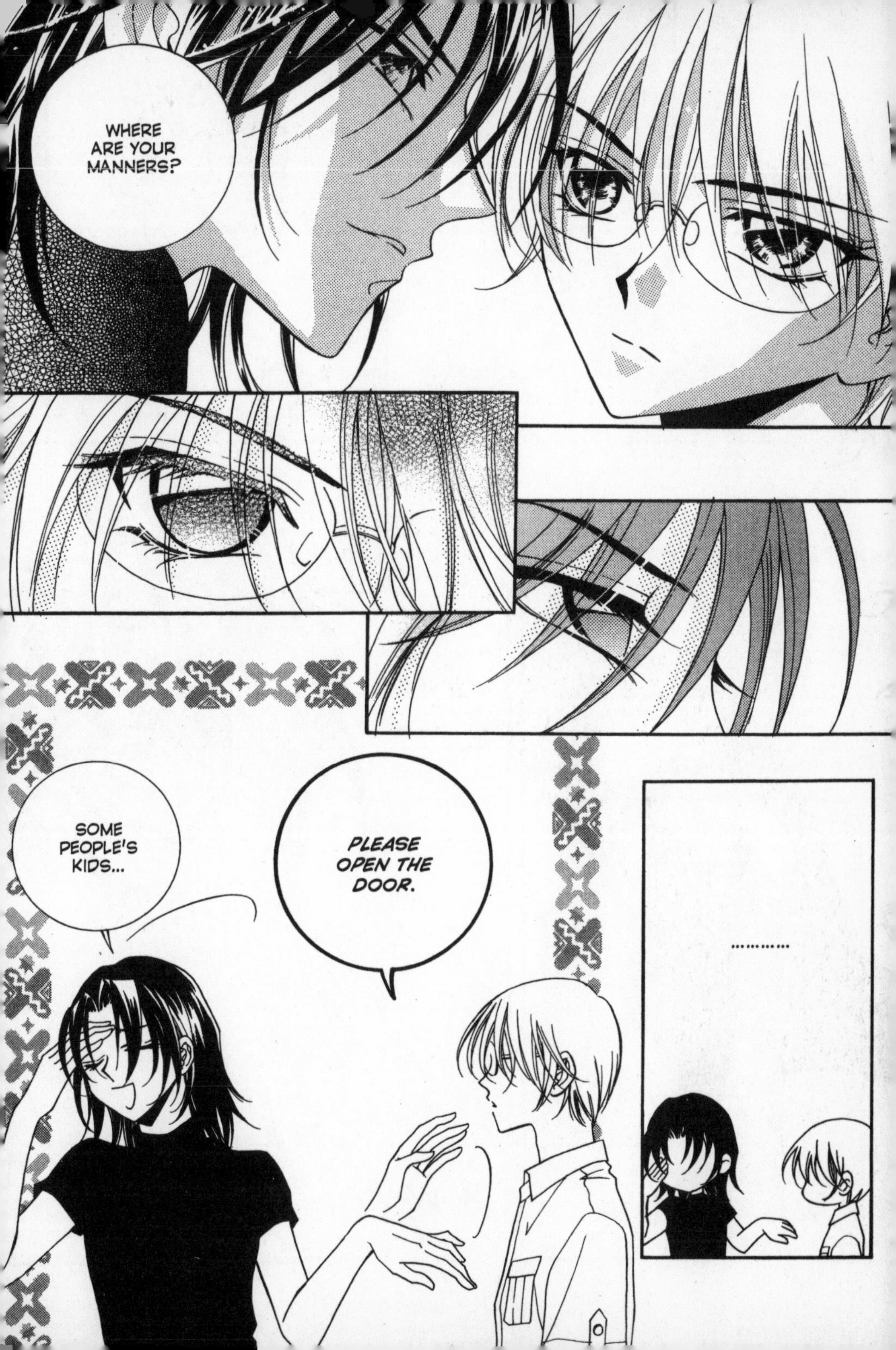
WHERE ARE YOUR MANNERS?
SOME PEOPLE'S KIDS...
PLEASE OPEN THE DOOR.
....

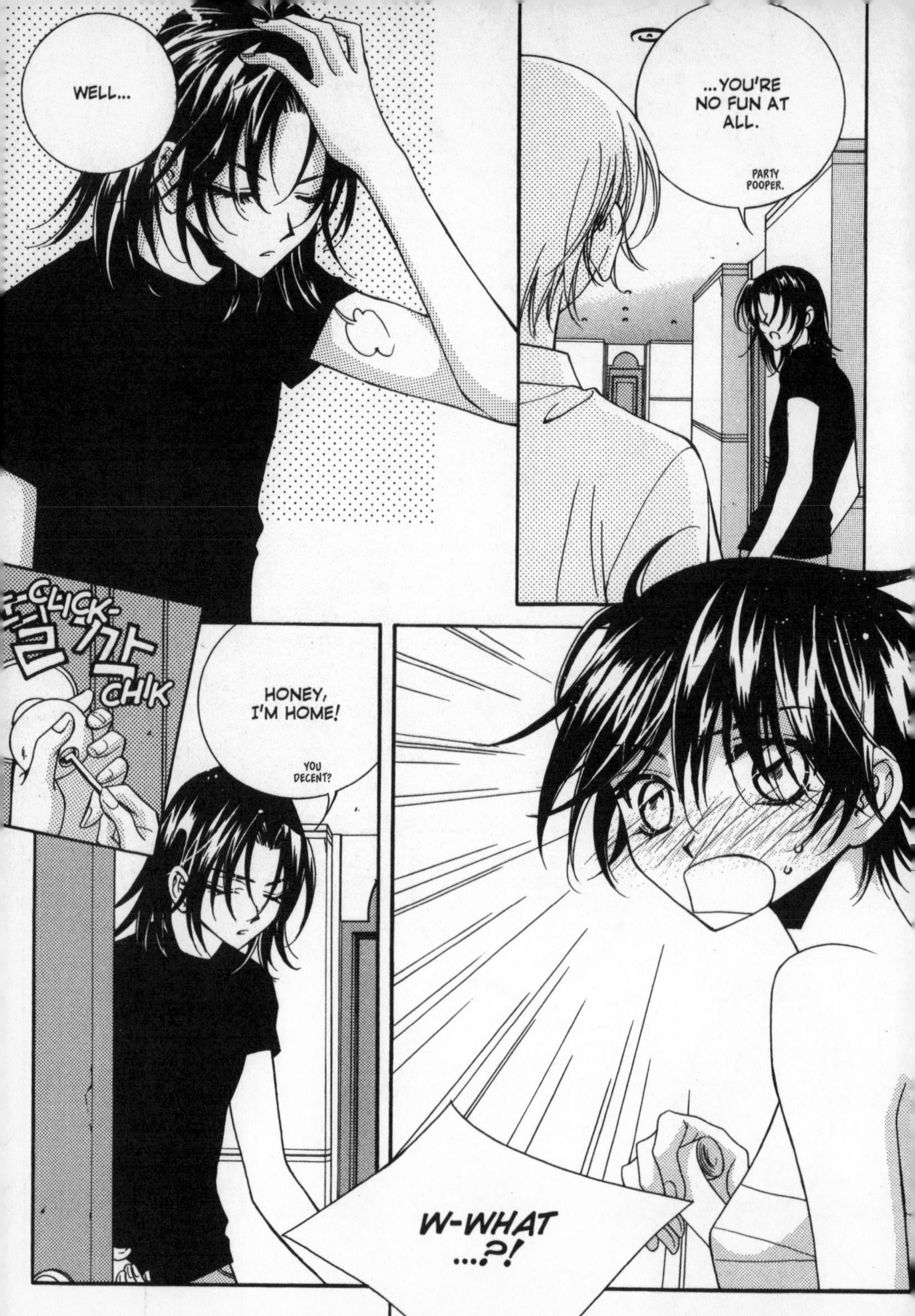

WELL...
...YOU'RE NO FUN AT ALL.
PARTY POOPER.
CLICK-CHIK
HONEY, I'M HOME!
YOU DECENT?
W-WHAT ...?!

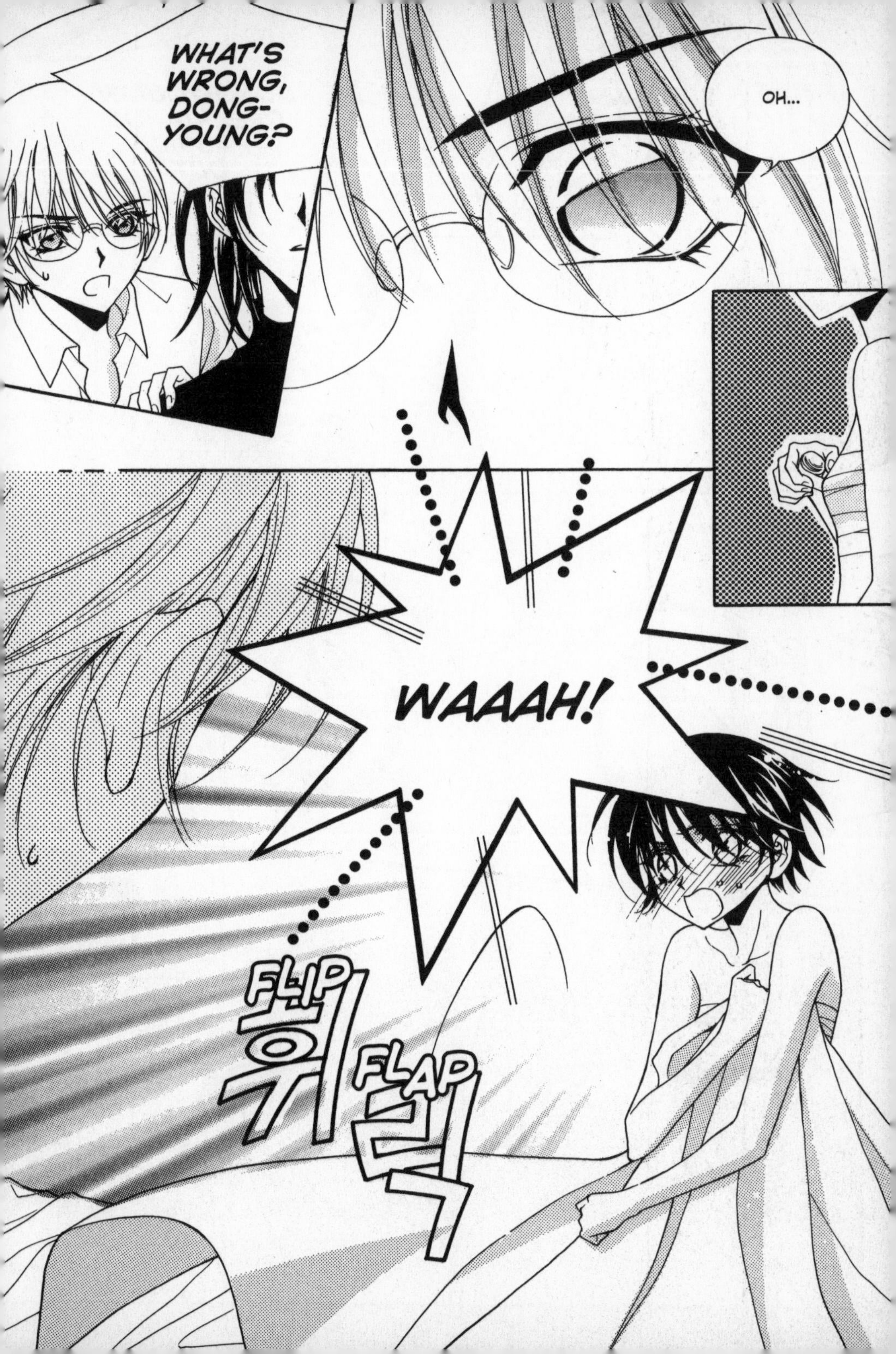
WHAT'S WRONG, DONG-YOUNG?
OH...
WAAAH!
FLIP
휘
FLAP
릭

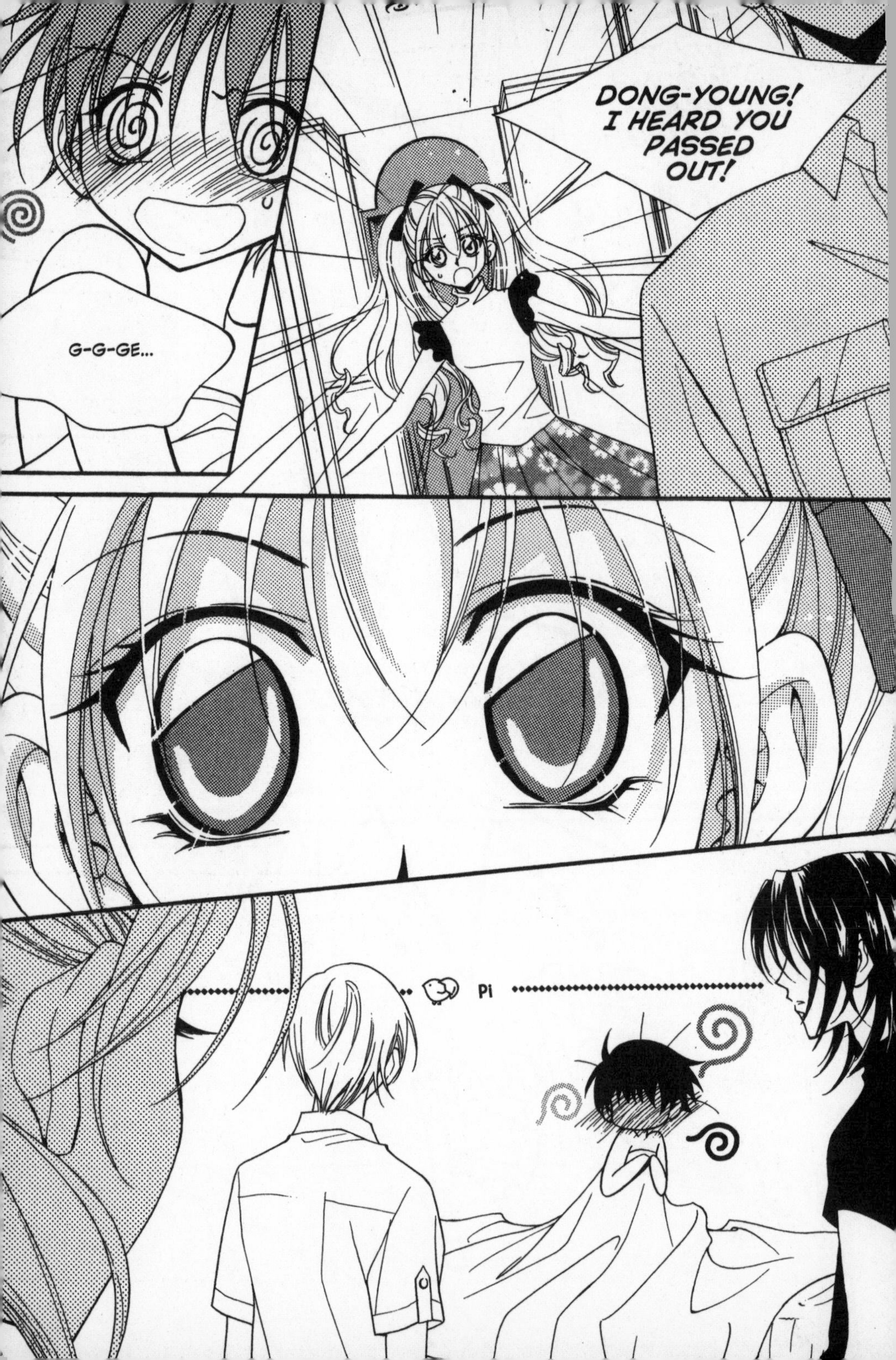
G-G-GE...
DONG-YOUNG! I HEARD YOU PASSED OUT!
Pi

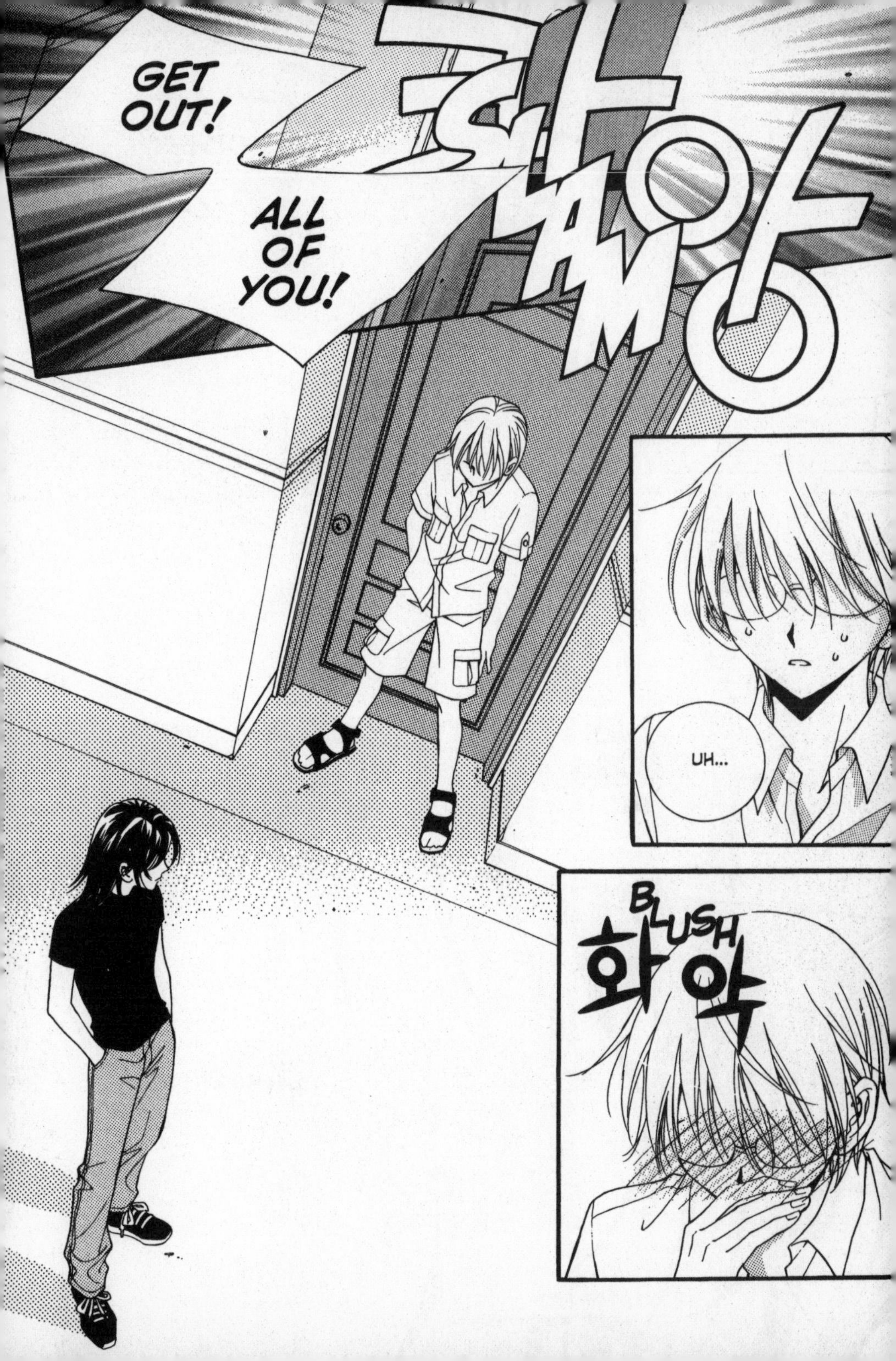
GET OUT!
ALL OF YOU!
SLAM
UH...
BLUSH
화악

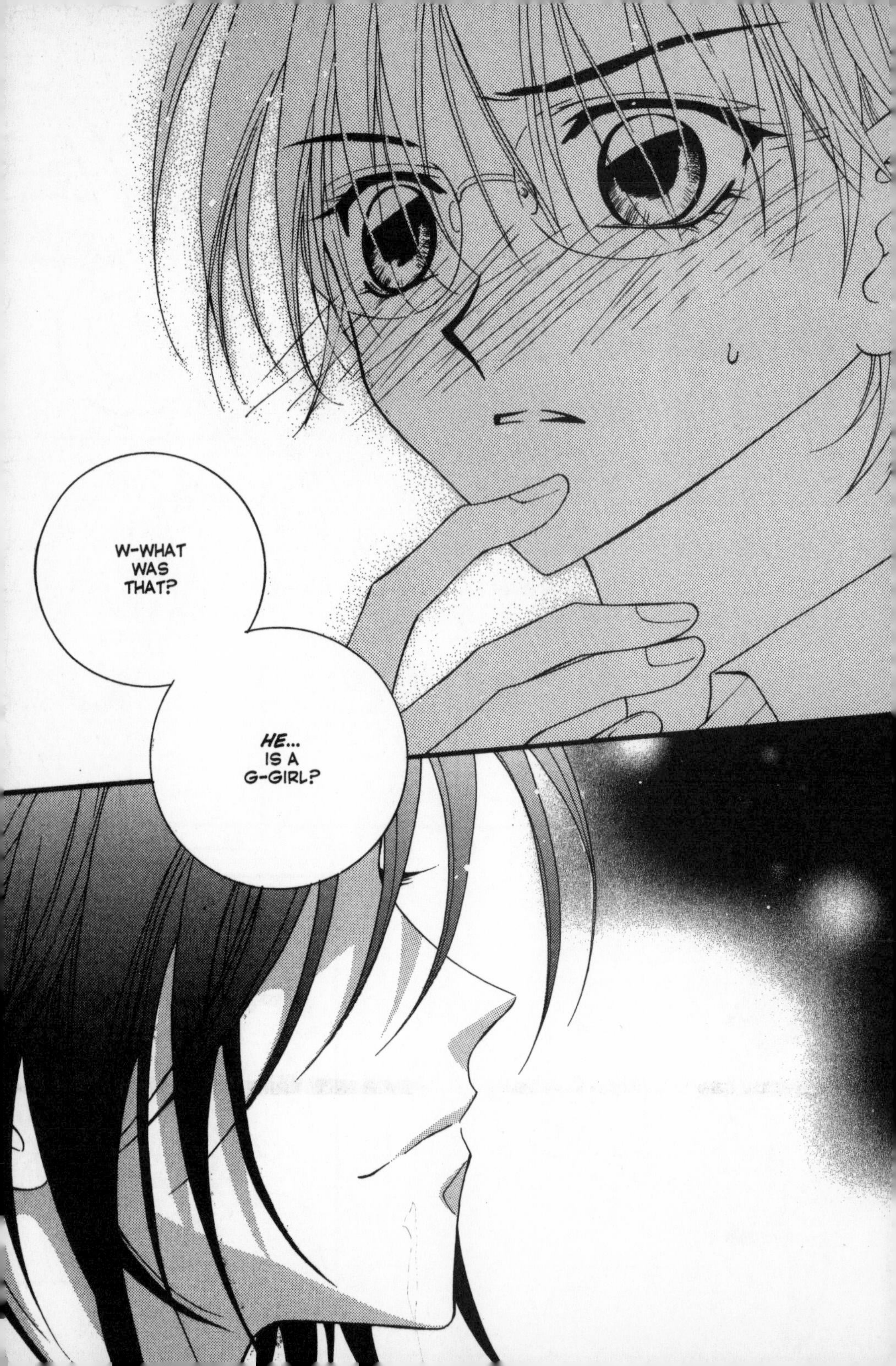
W-WHAT WAS THAT?
HE... IS A G-GIRL?

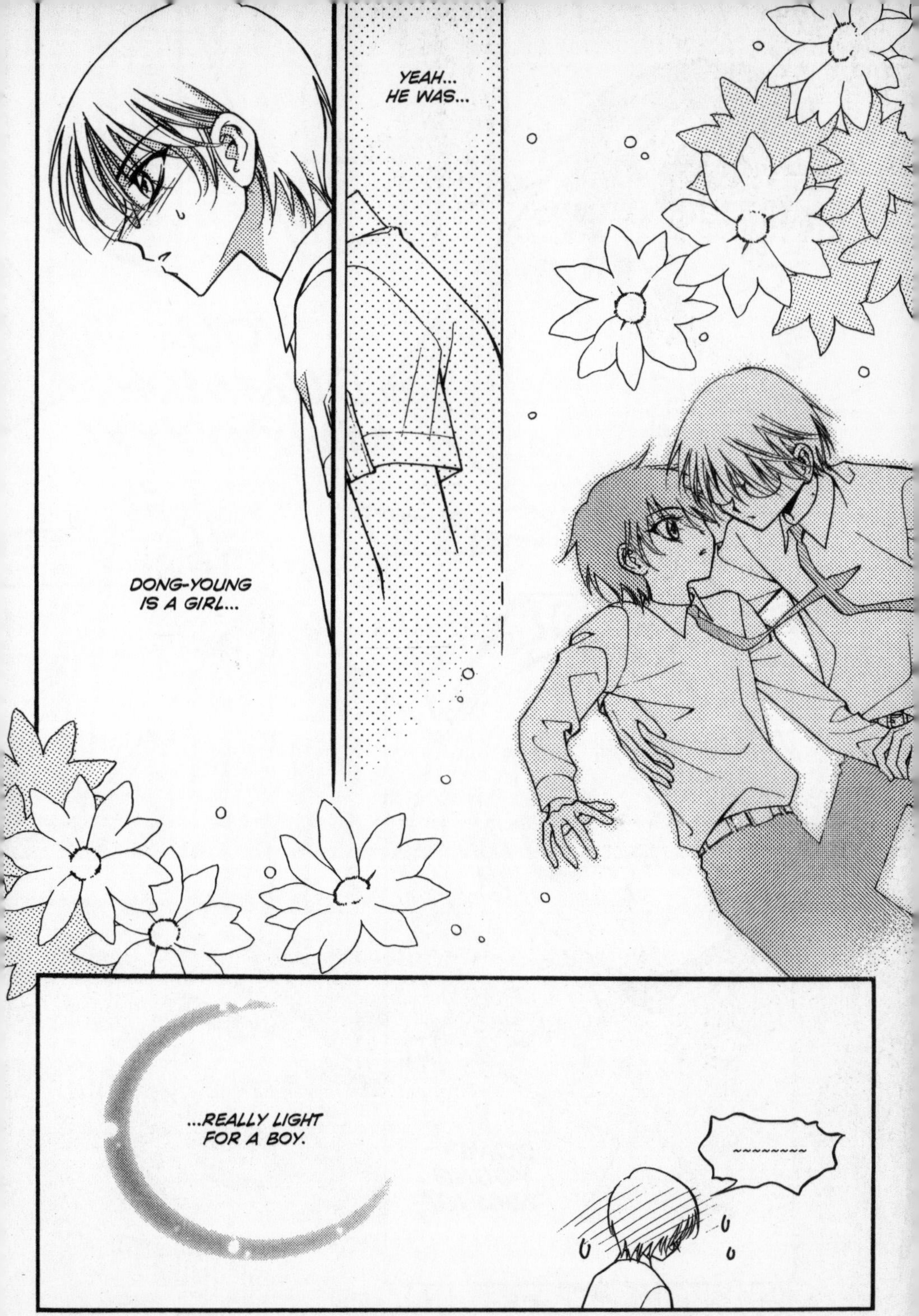
DONG-YOUNG IS A GIRL...
YEAH... HE WAS...
...REALLY LIGHT FOR A BOY.
~~~~~~~~
~~~~~~~~

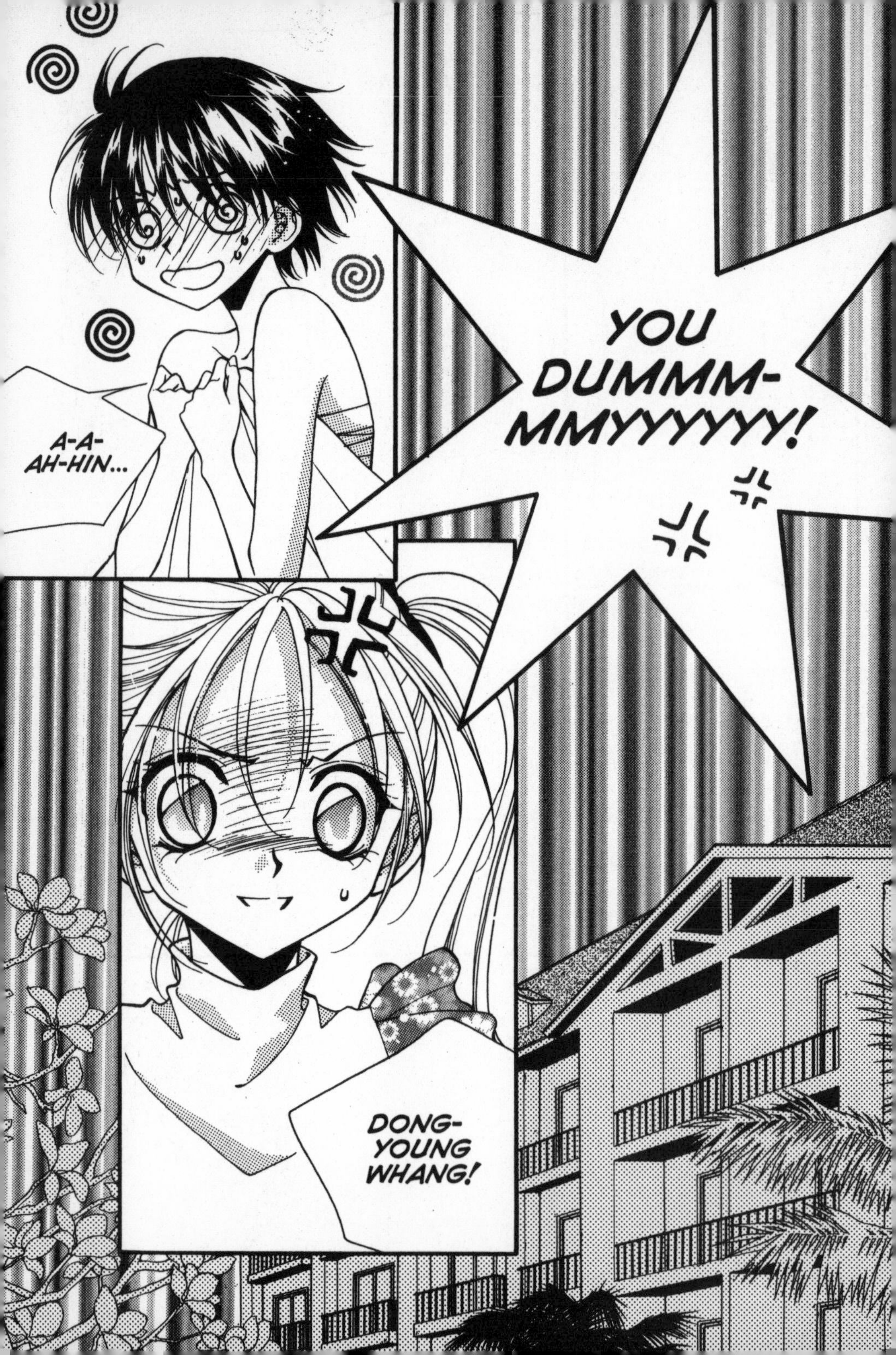
A-A-
AH-HIN...
YOU
DUMMM-
MMYYYYYY!
DONG-
YOUNG
WHANG!

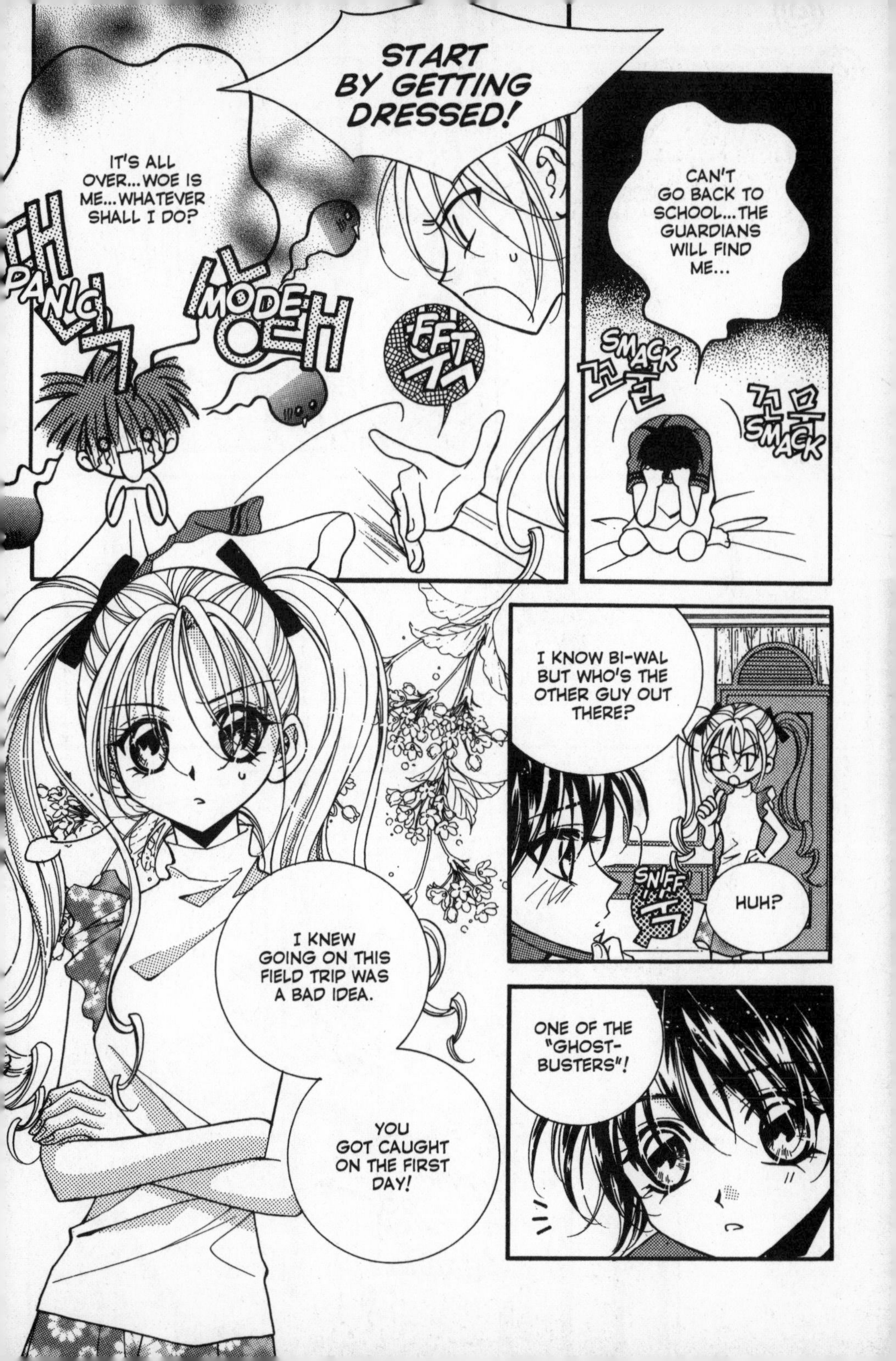
IT'S ALL OVER...WOE IS ME...WHATEVER SHALL I DO?
PANIC MODE
START BY GETTING DRESSED!
FFT
CAN'T GO BACK TO SCHOOL...THE GUARDIANS WILL FIND ME...
SMACK
SMACK
I KNEW GOING ON THIS FIELD TRIP WAS A BAD IDEA.
YOU GOT CAUGHT ON THE FIRST DAY!
I KNOW BI-WAL BUT WHO'S THE OTHER GUY OUT THERE?
SNIFF
HUH?
ONE OF THE "GHOST-BUSTERS"!

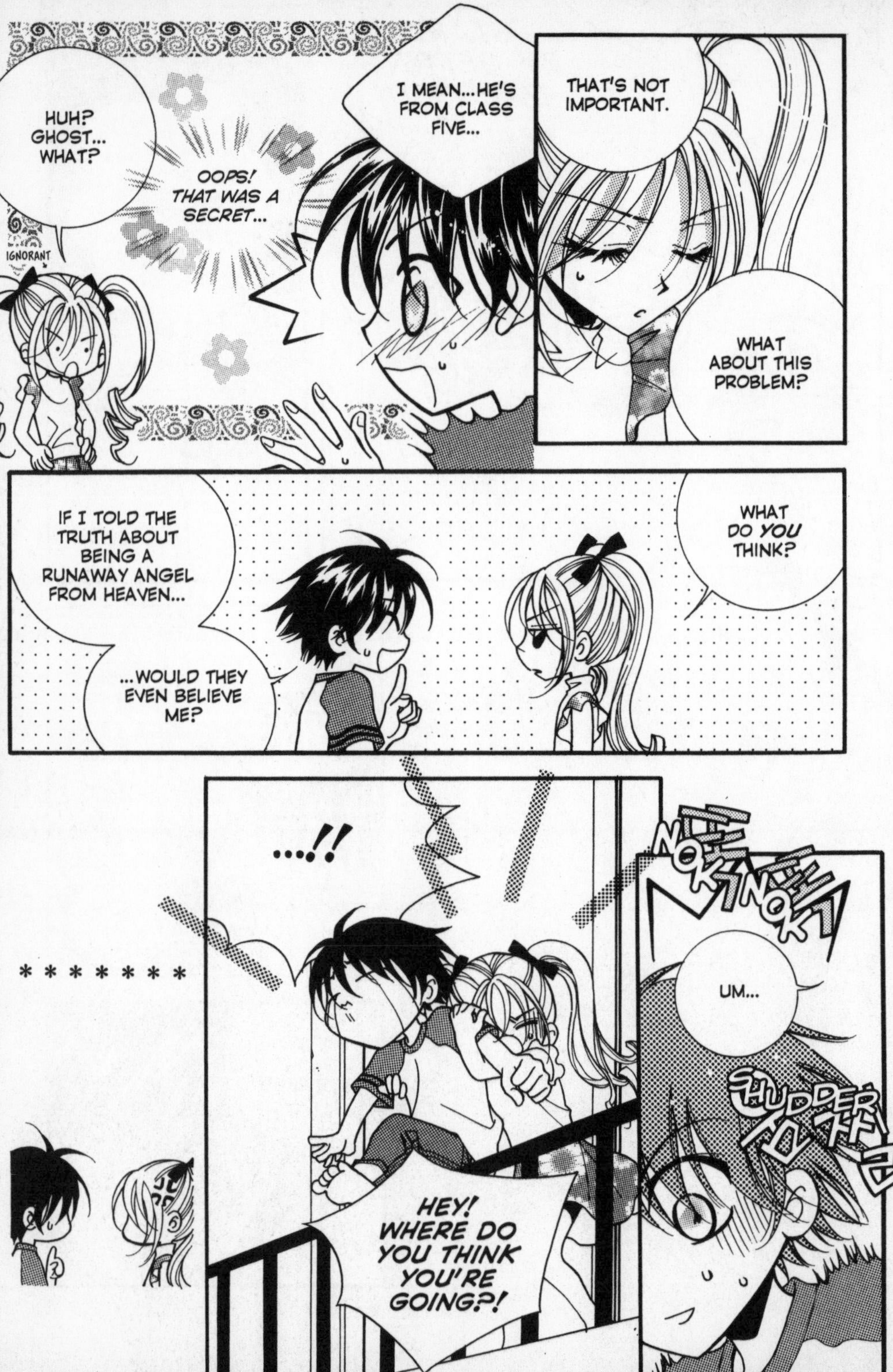
HUH? GHOST... WHAT?
IGNORANT
OOPS! THAT WAS A SECRET...
I MEAN...HE'S FROM CLASS FIVE...
THAT'S NOT IMPORTANT.
WHAT ABOUT THIS PROBLEM?
IF I TOLD THE TRUTH ABOUT BEING A RUNAWAY ANGEL FROM HEAVEN...
...WOULD THEY EVEN BELIEVE ME?
WHAT DO *YOU* THINK?
* * * * * * *
...!!
HEY! WHERE DO YOU THINK YOU'RE GOING?!
NOK NOK
UM...
SHUDDER

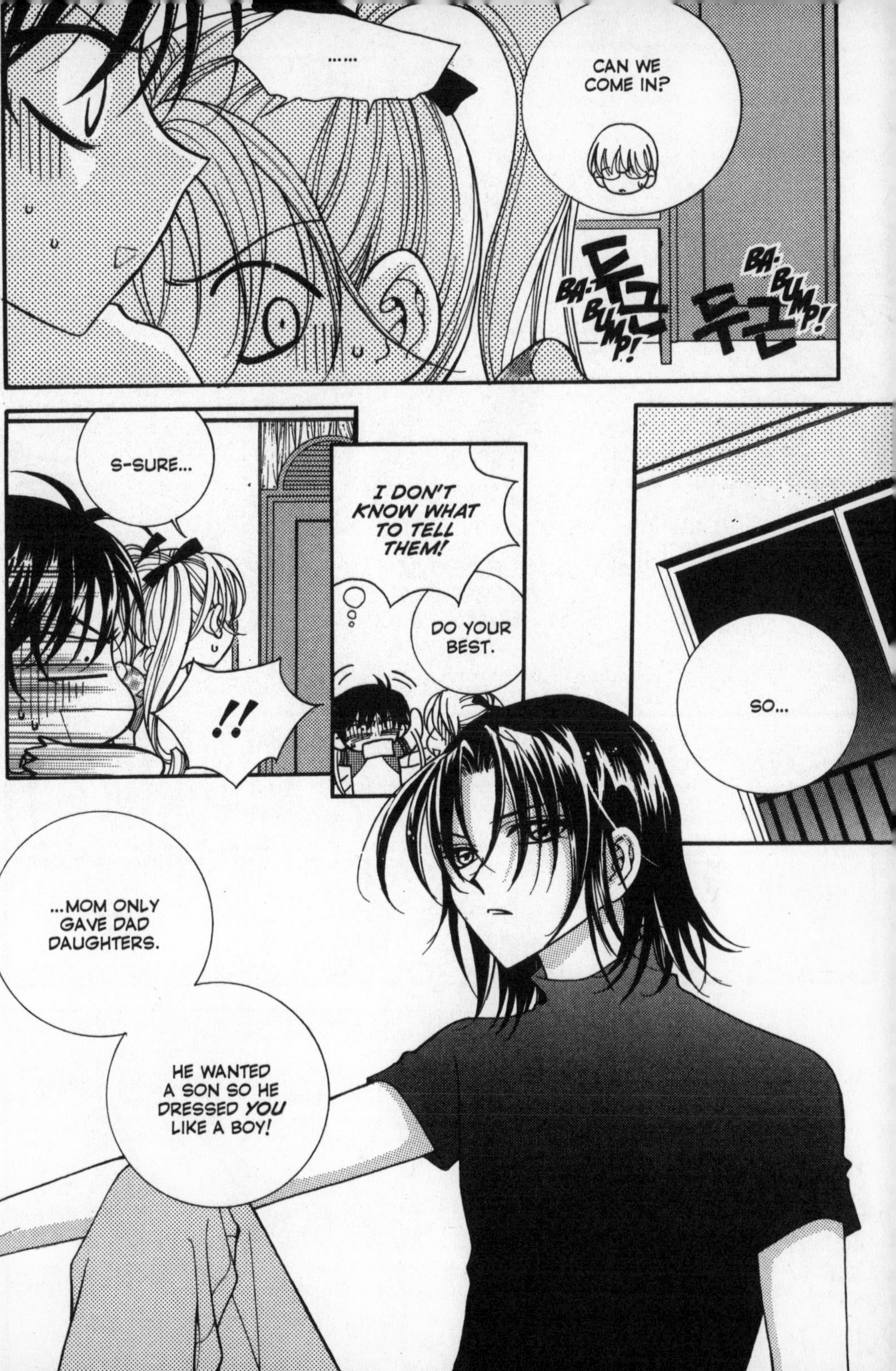
......
CAN WE COME IN?
두근
BA-BUMP!
두근
BA-BUMP!
S-SURE...
!!
I DON'T KNOW WHAT TO TELL THEM!
DO YOUR BEST.
SO...
...MOM ONLY GAVE DAD DAUGHTERS.
HE WANTED A SON SO HE DRESSED *YOU* LIKE A BOY!

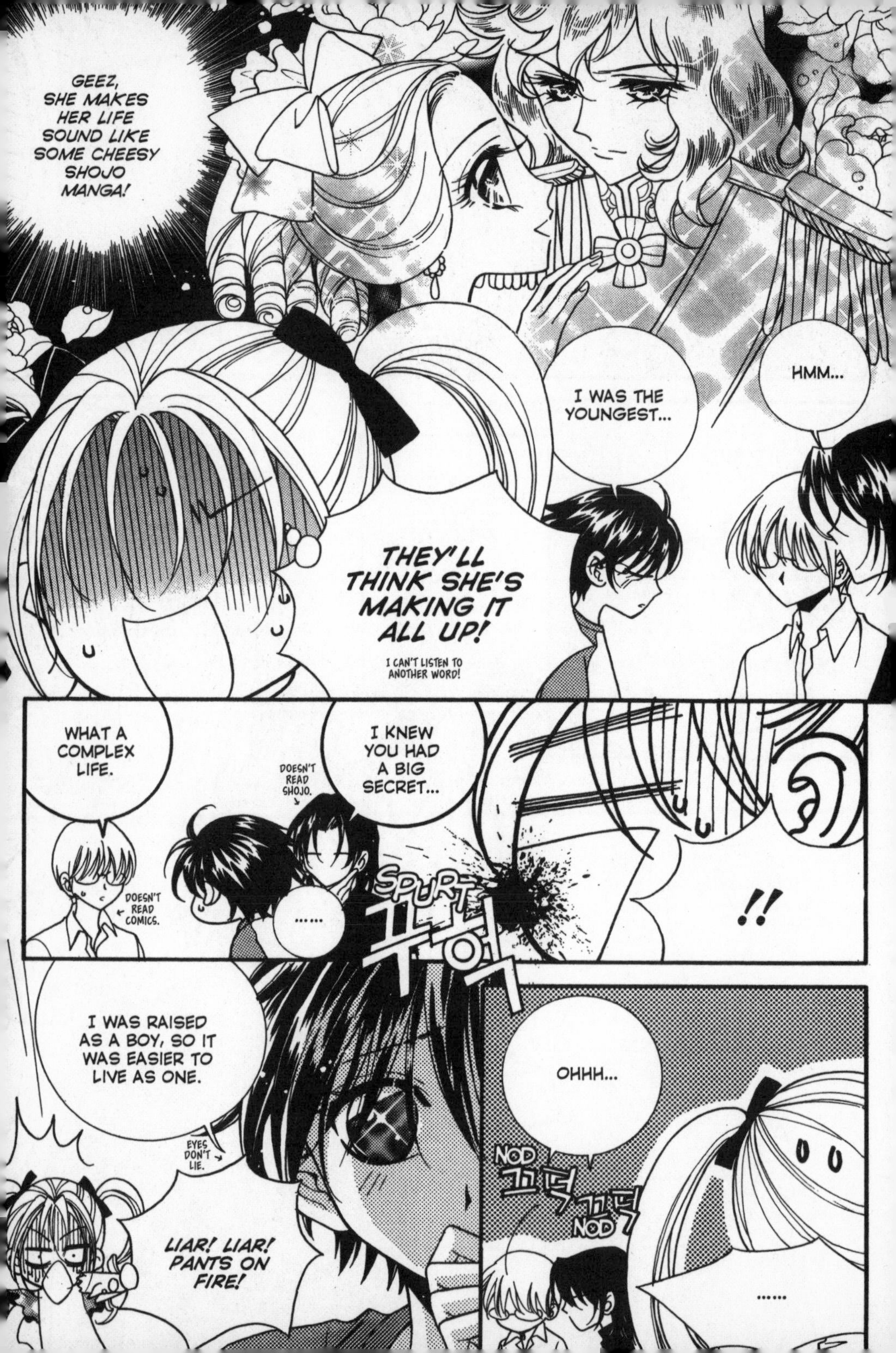
GEEZ, SHE MAKES HER LIFE SOUND LIKE SOME CHEESY SHOJO MANGA!
I WAS THE YOUNGEST...
HMM...
THEY'LL THINK SHE'S MAKING IT ALL UP!
I CAN'T LISTEN TO ANOTHER WORD!
WHAT A COMPLEX LIFE.
DOESN'T READ COMICS.
DOESN'T READ SHOJO.
I KNEW YOU HAD A BIG SECRET...
......
SPURT
!!
I WAS RAISED AS A BOY, SO IT WAS EASIER TO LIVE AS ONE.
EYES DON'T LIE.
LIAR! LIAR! PANTS ON FIRE!
OHHH...
NOD
끄덕
끄덕
NOD
......

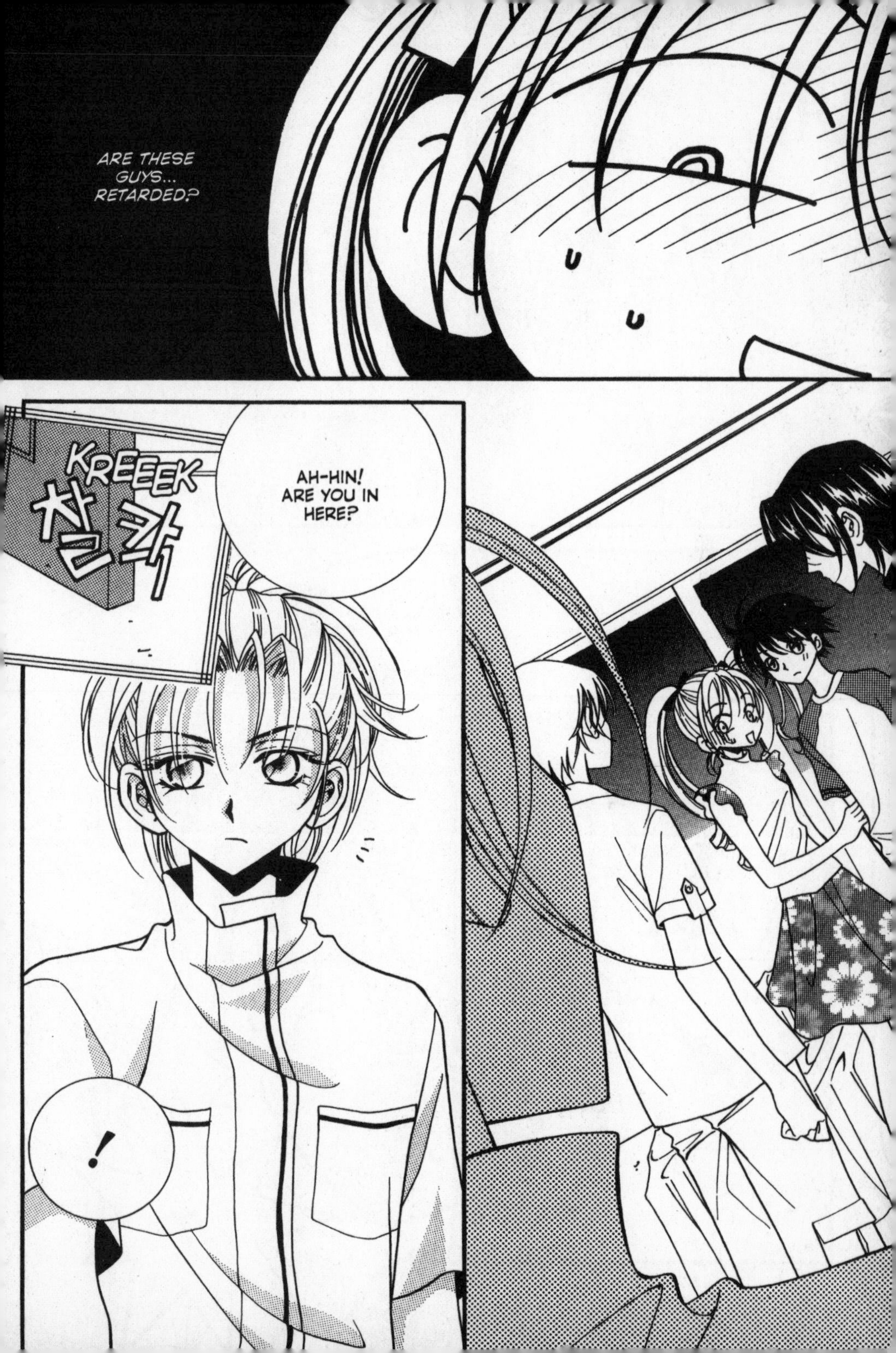
ARE THESE GUYS... RETARDED?
KREEEK
AH-HIN! ARE YOU IN HERE?
!

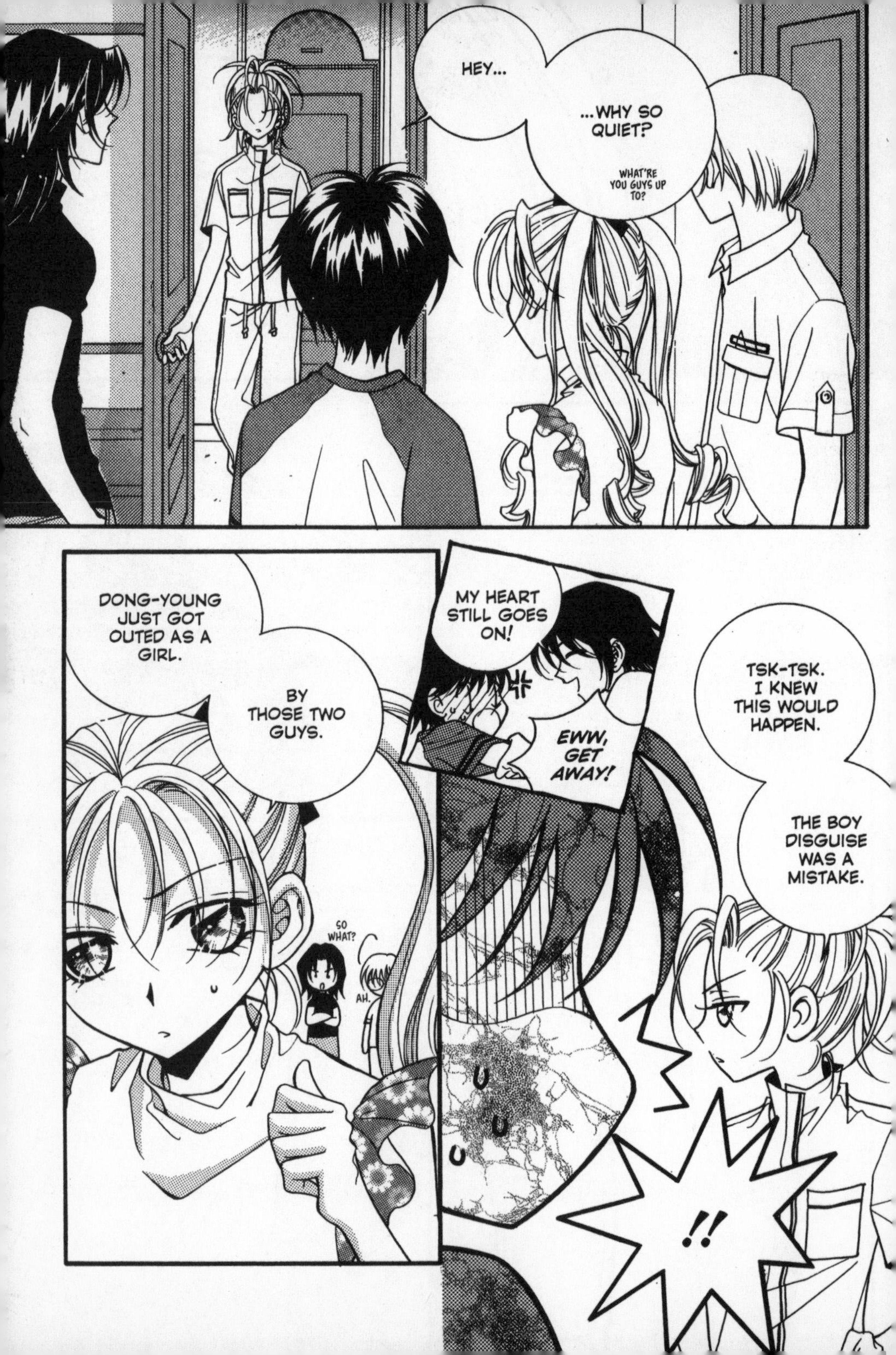
HEY...
...WHY SO QUIET?
WHAT'RE YOU GUYS UP TO?
DONG-YOUNG JUST GOT OUTED AS A GIRL.
BY THOSE TWO GUYS.
SO WHAT?
AH.
MY HEART STILL GOES ON!
EWW, GET AWAY!
TSK-TSK. I KNEW THIS WOULD HAPPEN.
THE BOY DISGUISE WAS A MISTAKE.
!!

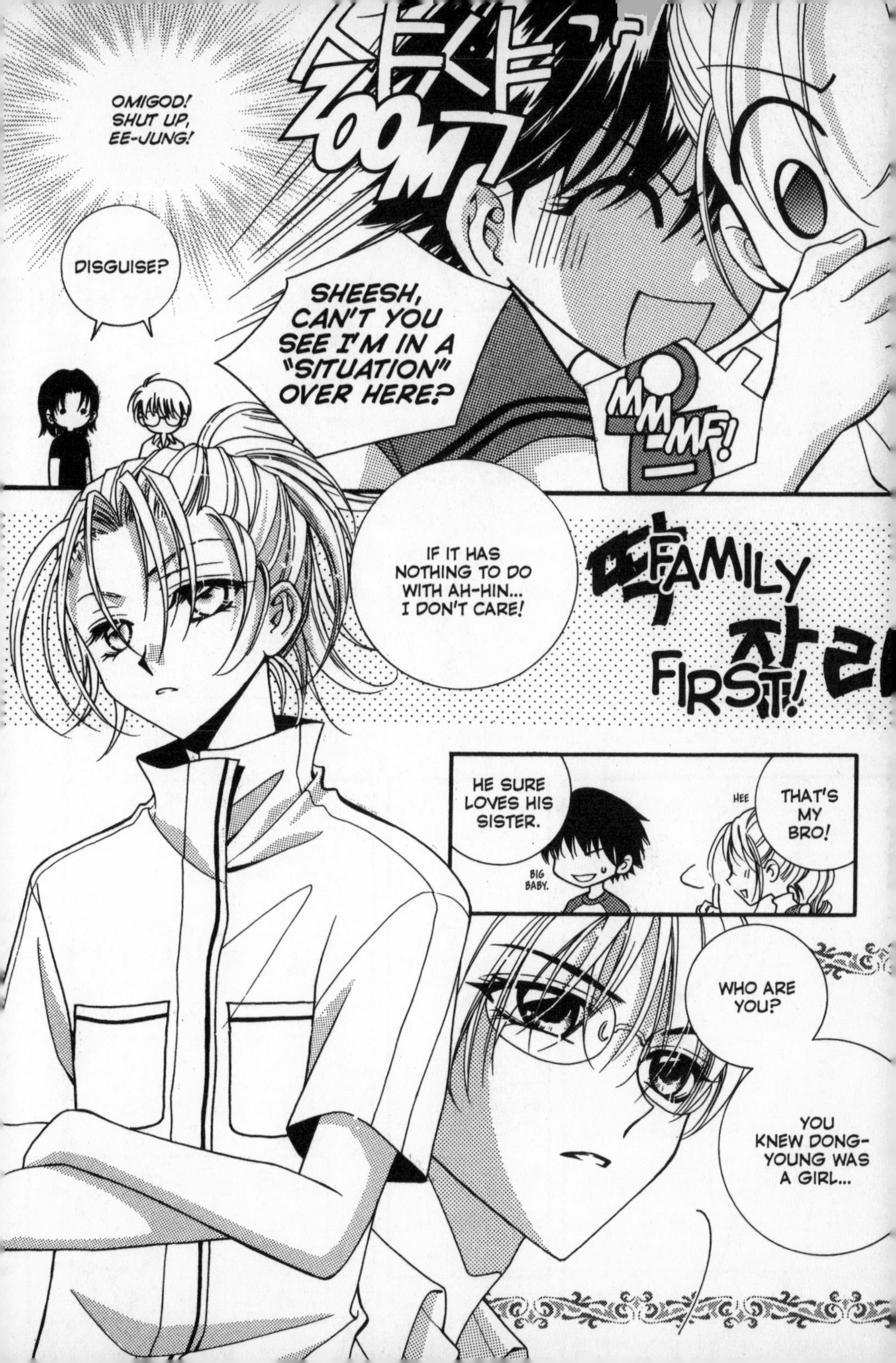
OMIGOD! SHUT UP, EE-JUNG!
ZOOM
DISGUISE?
SHEESH, CAN'T YOU SEE I'M IN A "SITUATION" OVER HERE?
MMMF!
IF IT HAS NOTHING TO DO WITH AH-HIN... I DON'T CARE!
FAMILY FIRST!
HE SURE LOVES HIS SISTER.
BIG BABY.
HEE
THAT'S MY BRO!
WHO ARE YOU?
YOU KNEW DONG-YOUNG WAS A GIRL...

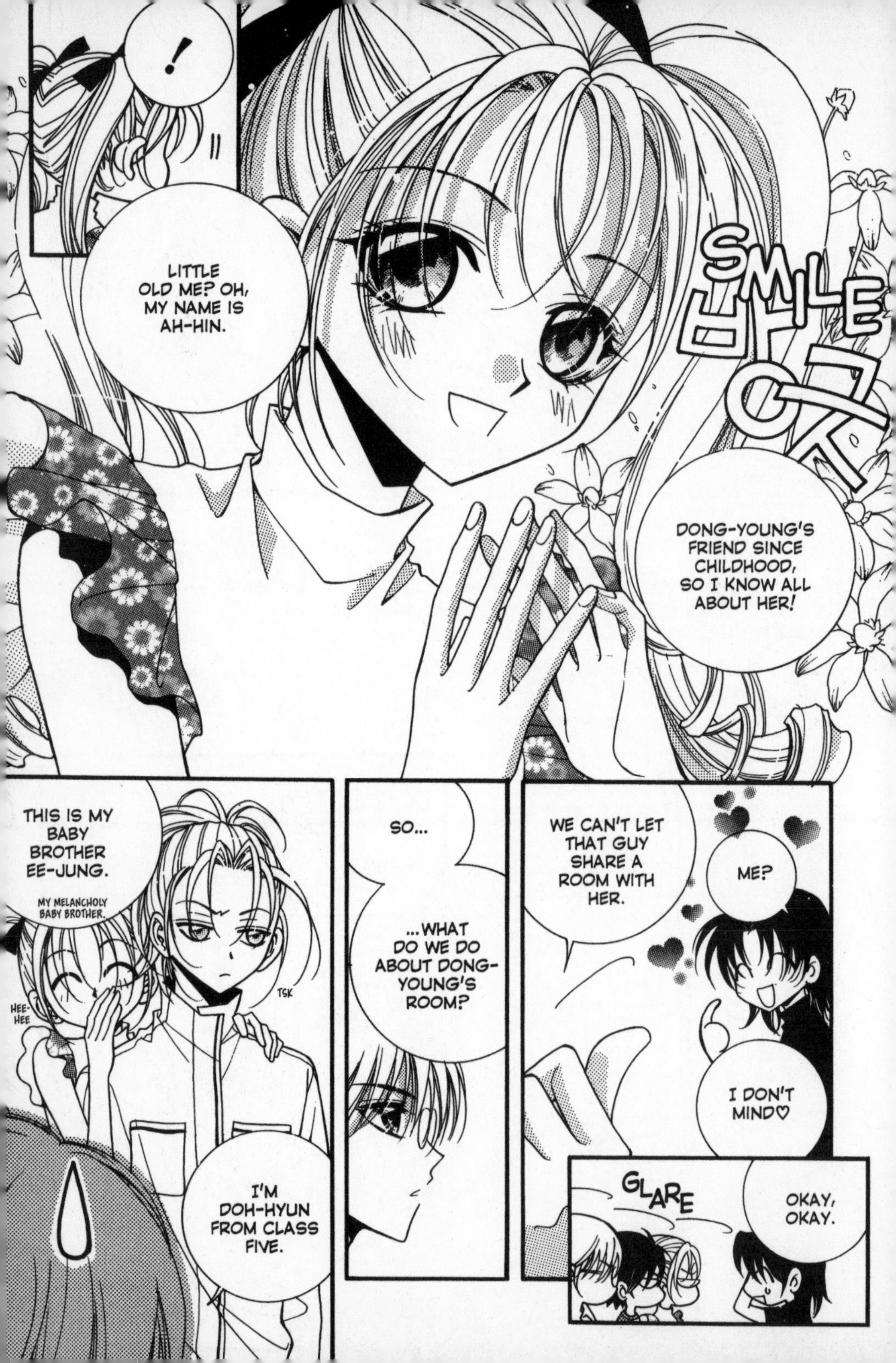
!
LITTLE OLD ME? OH, MY NAME IS AH-HIN.
SMILE
DONG-YOUNG'S FRIEND SINCE CHILDHOOD, SO I KNOW ALL ABOUT HER!
THIS IS MY BABY BROTHER EE-JUNG.
MY MELANCHOLY BABY BROTHER.
HEE-HEE
TSK
I'M DOH-HYUN FROM CLASS FIVE.
SO...
...WHAT DO WE DO ABOUT DONG-YOUNG'S ROOM?
WE CAN'T LET THAT GUY SHARE A ROOM WITH HER.
ME?
I DON'T MIND♡
GLARE
OKAY, OKAY.

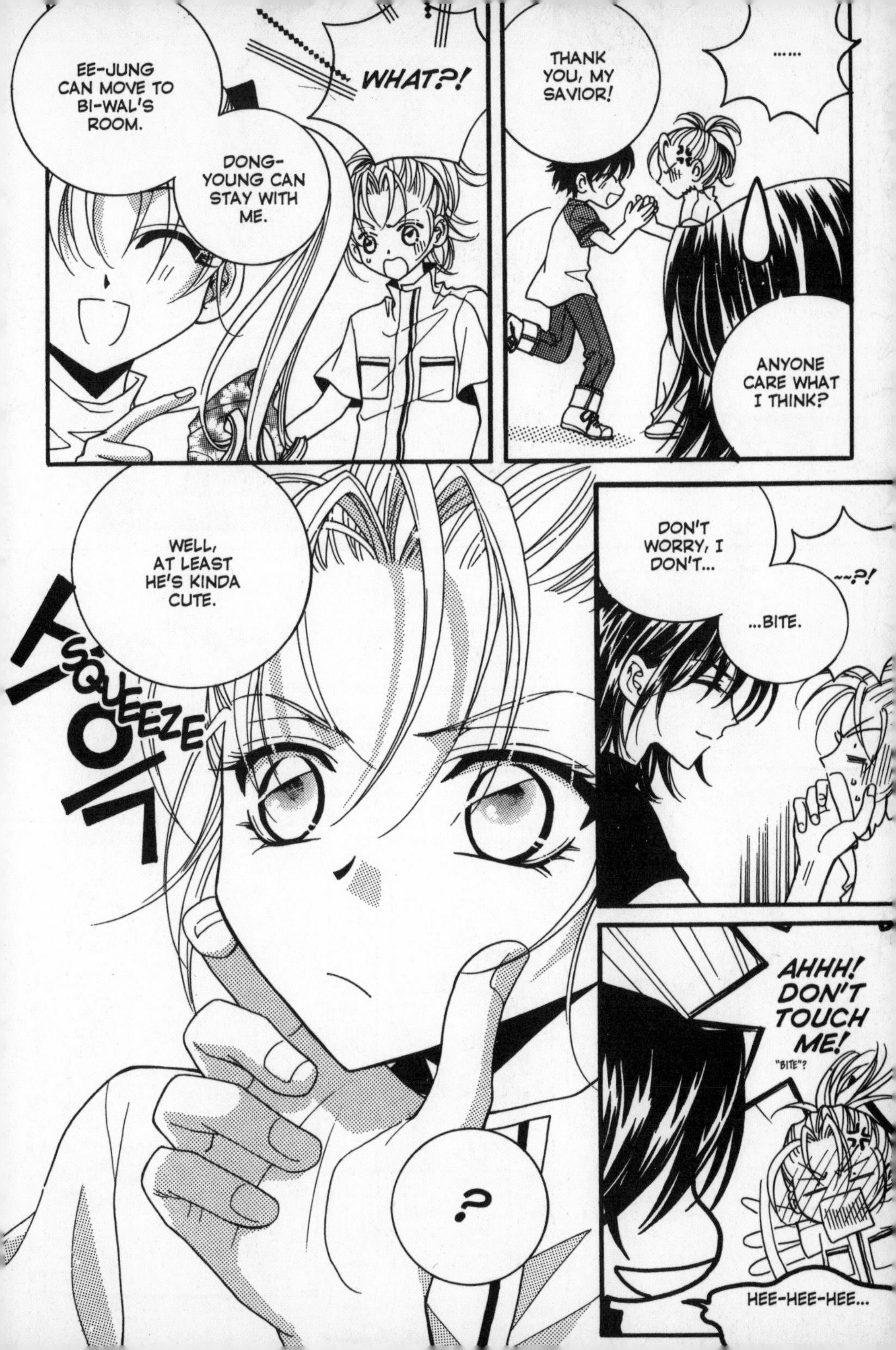
EE-JUNG CAN MOVE TO BI-WAL'S ROOM.
DONG-YOUNG CAN STAY WITH ME.
WHAT?!
THANK YOU, MY SAVIOR!
......
ANYONE CARE WHAT I THINK?
WELL, AT LEAST HE'S KINDA CUTE.
SQUEEZE
?
DON'T WORRY, I DON'T...
~~?!
...BITE.
AHHH! DON'T TOUCH ME!
"BITE"?
HEE-HEE-HEE...

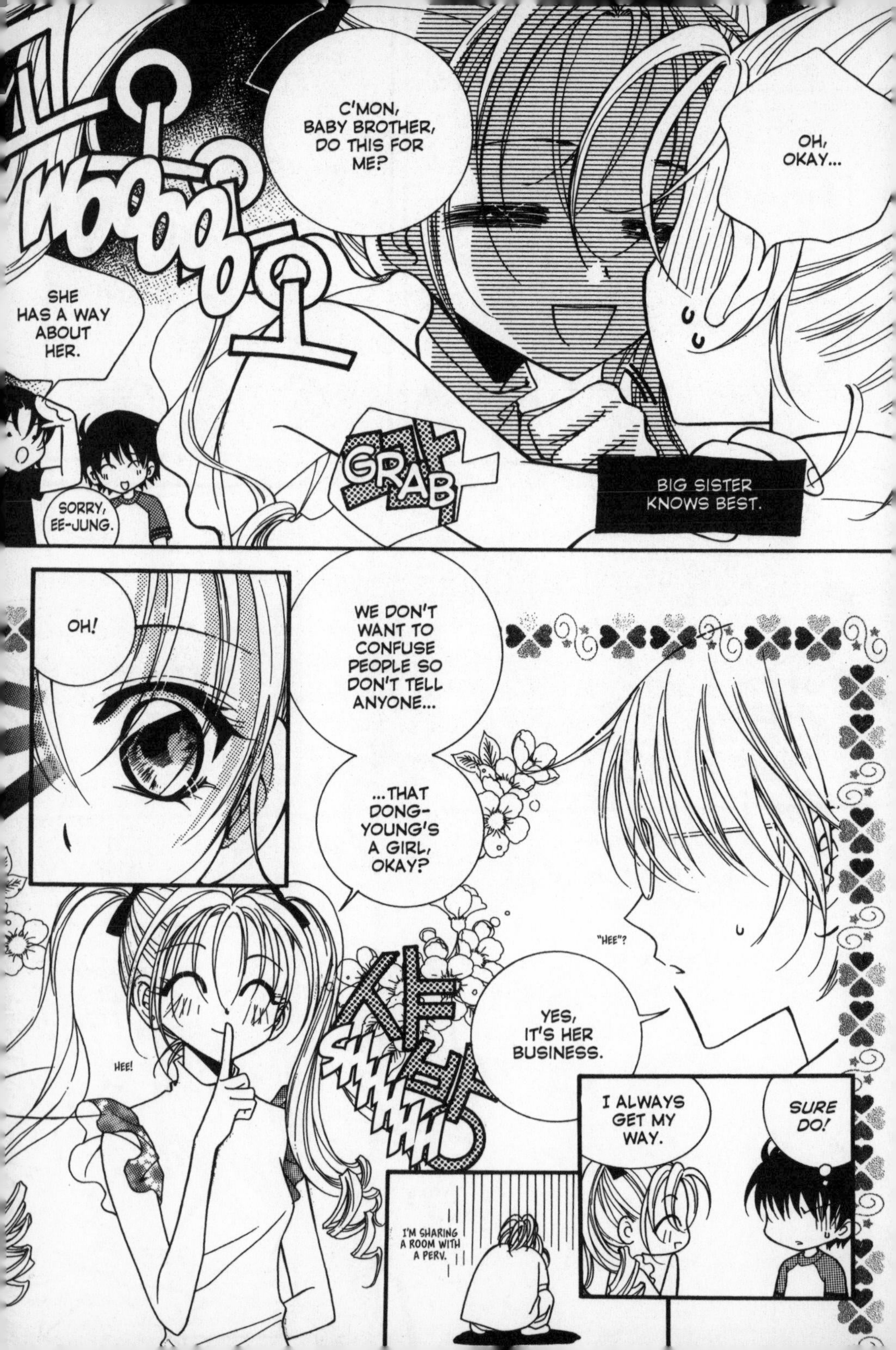
C'MON, BABY BROTHER, DO THIS FOR ME?
OH, OKAY...
SHE HAS A WAY ABOUT HER.
SORRY, EE-JUNG.
GRAB
BIG SISTER KNOWS BEST.
OH!
WE DON'T WANT TO CONFUSE PEOPLE SO DON'T TELL ANYONE...
...THAT DONG-YOUNG'S A GIRL, OKAY?
"HEE"?
HEE!
YES, IT'S HER BUSINESS.
I'M SHARING A ROOM WITH A PERV.
I ALWAYS GET MY WAY.
SURE DO!

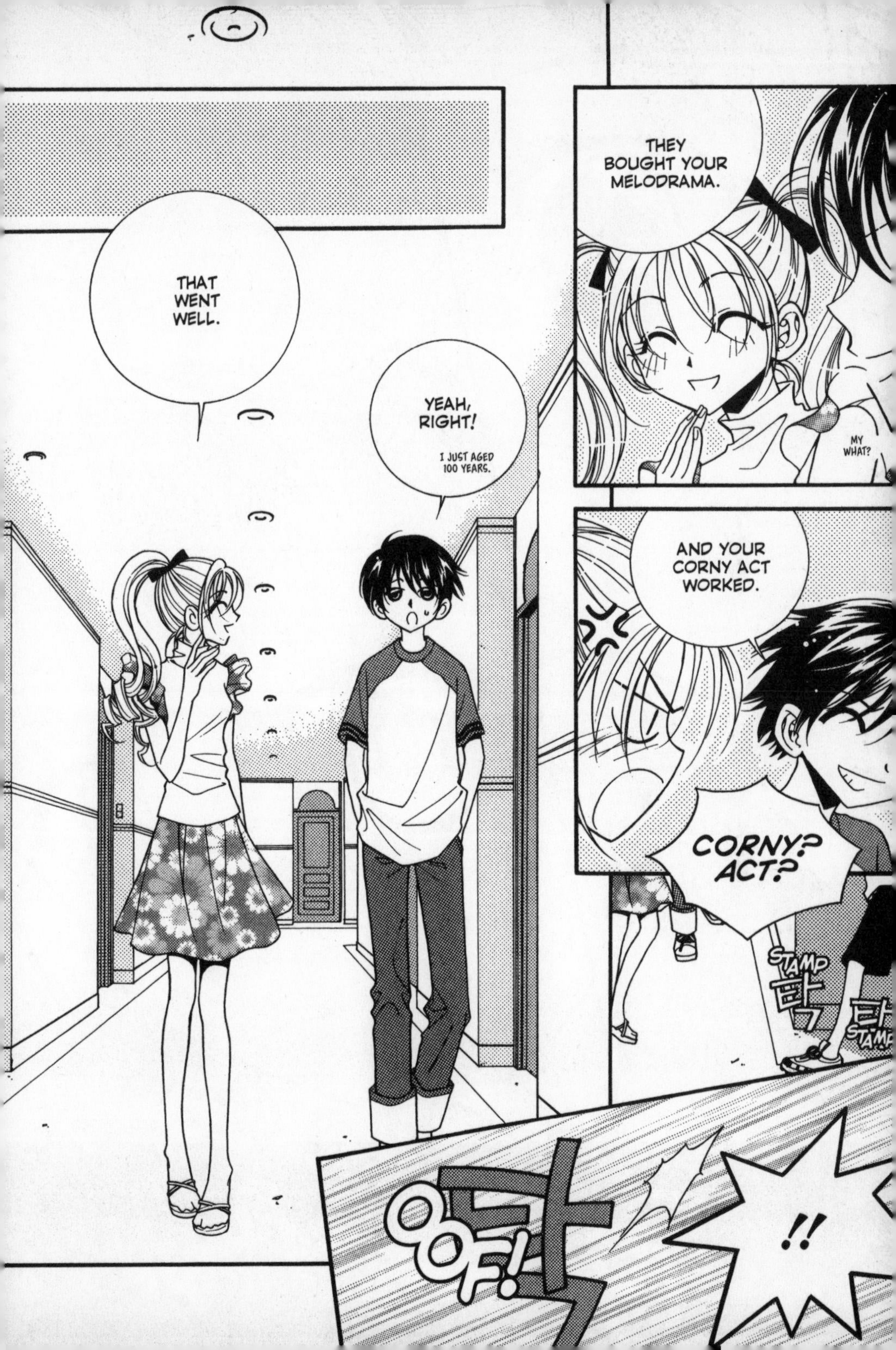
THAT WENT WELL.
YEAH, RIGHT!
I JUST AGED 100 YEARS.
THEY BOUGHT YOUR MELODRAMA.
MY WHAT?
AND YOUR CORNY ACT WORKED.
CORNY? ACT?
STAMP
탁
탁
STAMP
OOF!
!!

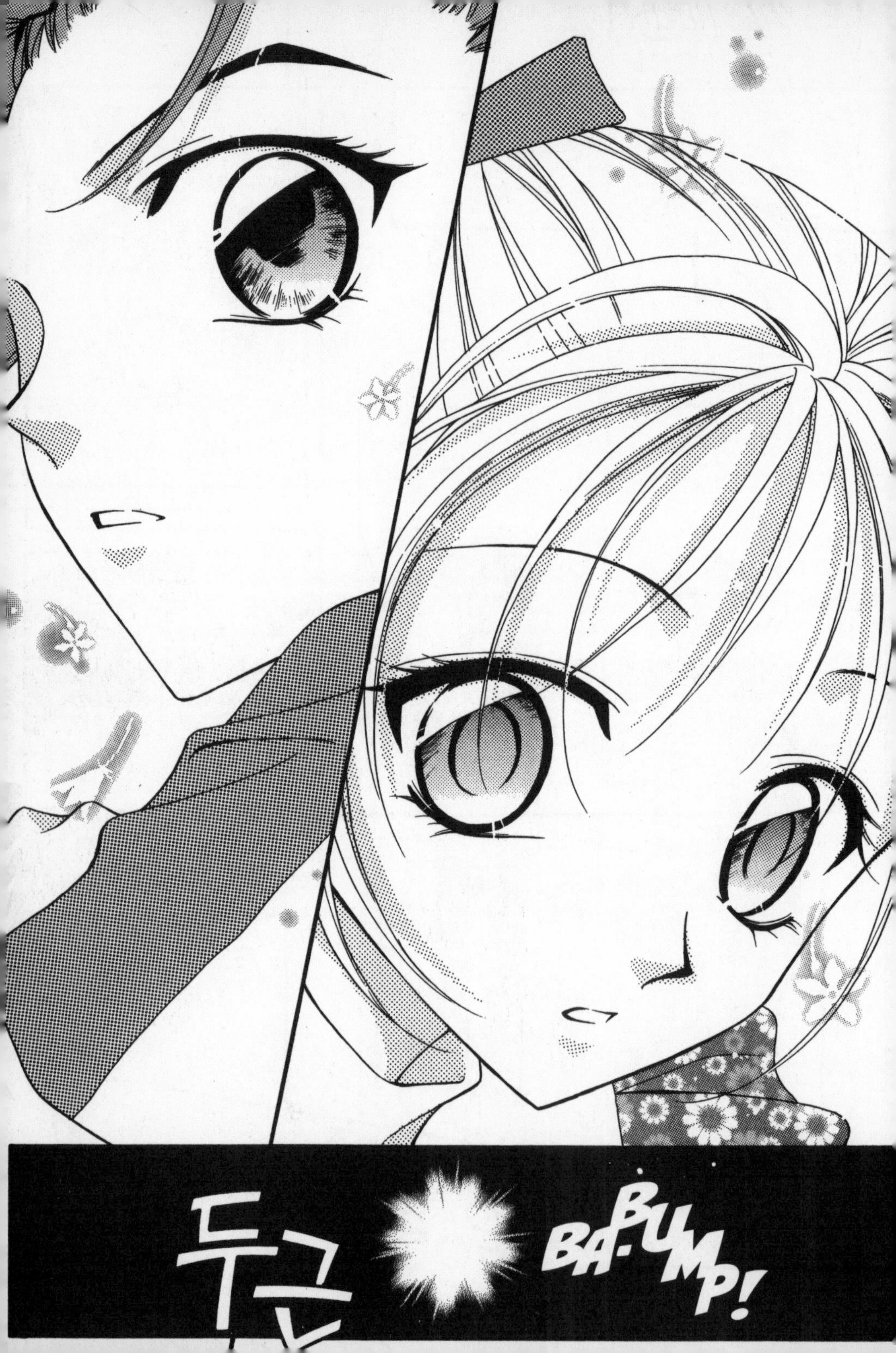
두근
BA-BUMP!

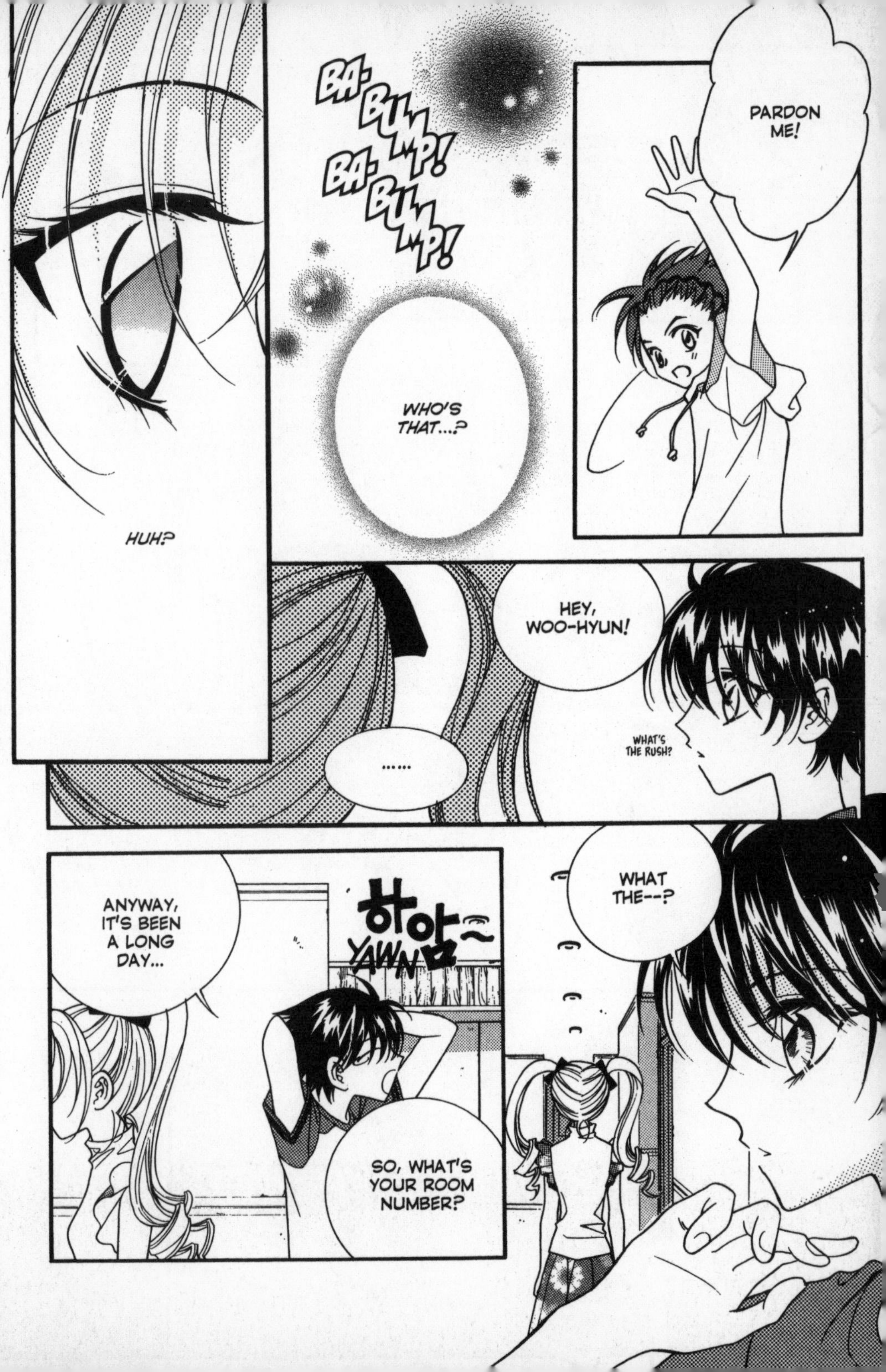
HUH?
BA-BUMP! BA-BUMP!
WHO'S THAT...?
PARDON ME!
......
HEY, WOO-HYUN!
WHAT'S THE RUSH?
ANYWAY, IT'S BEEN A LONG DAY...
하암~
YAWN
SO, WHAT'S YOUR ROOM NUMBER?
WHAT THE--?

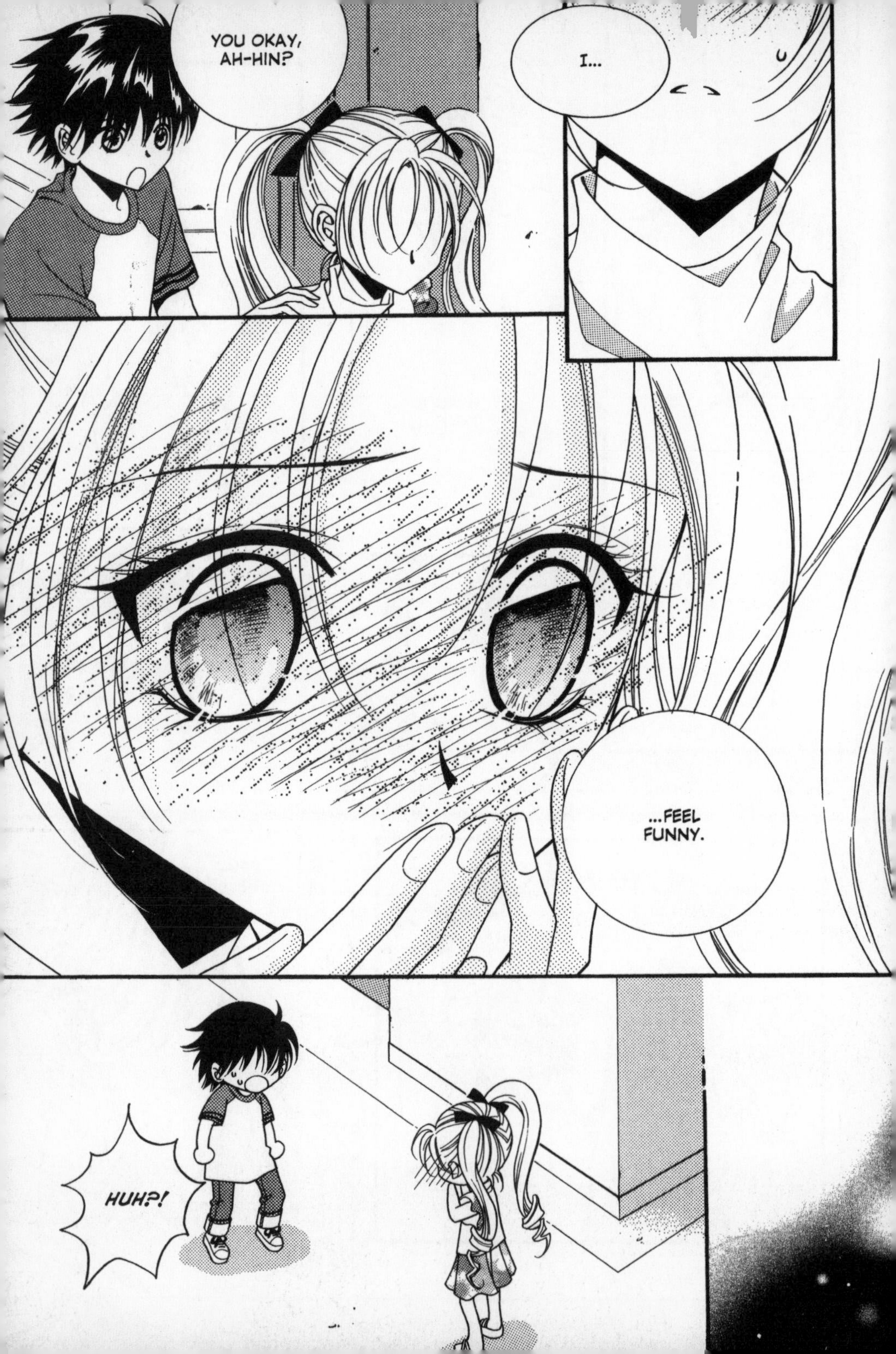

YOU OKAY, AH-HIN?
I...
...FEEL FUNNY.
HUH?!

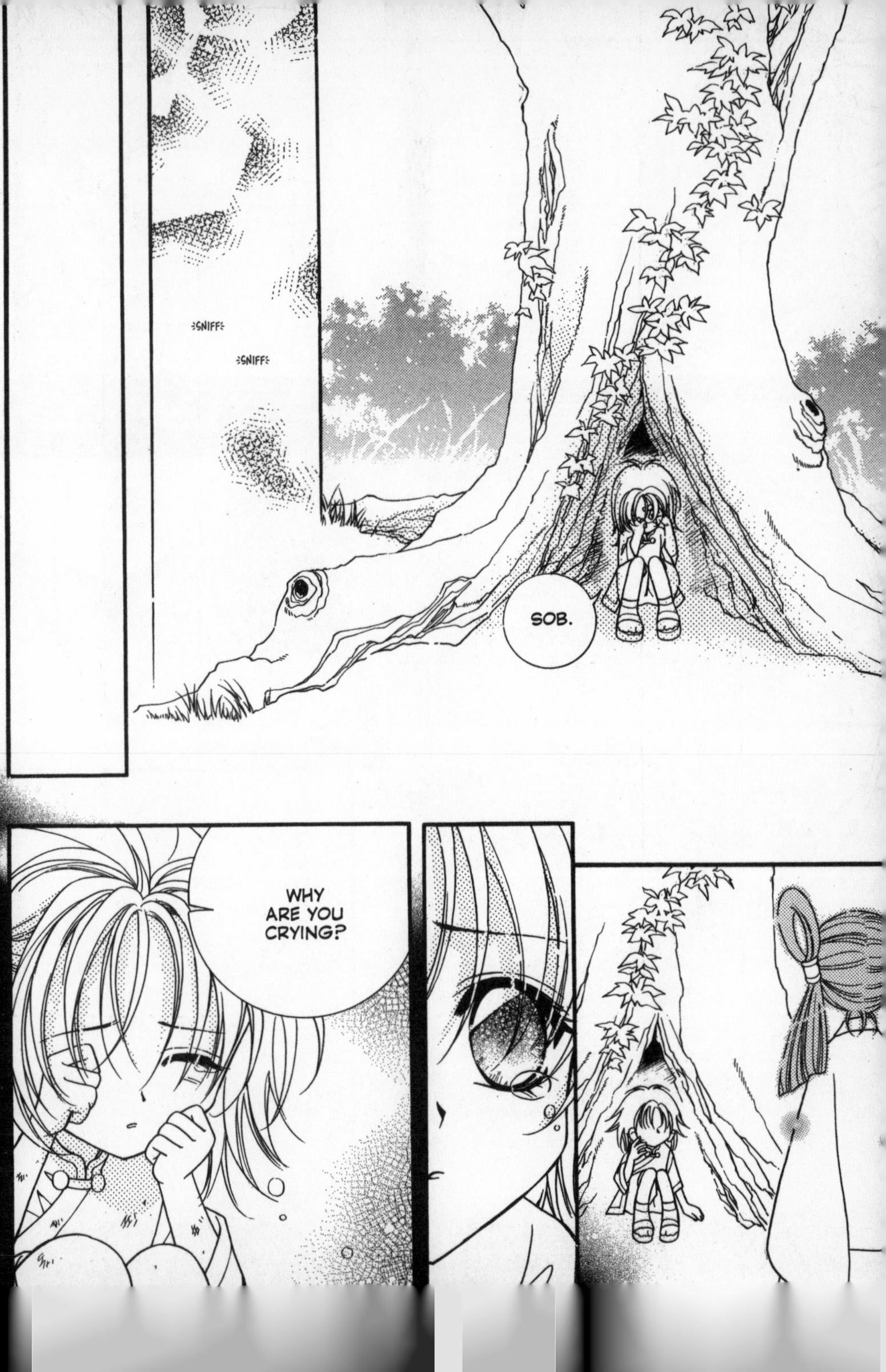
SNIFF
SNIFF
SOB.
WHY ARE YOU CRYING?

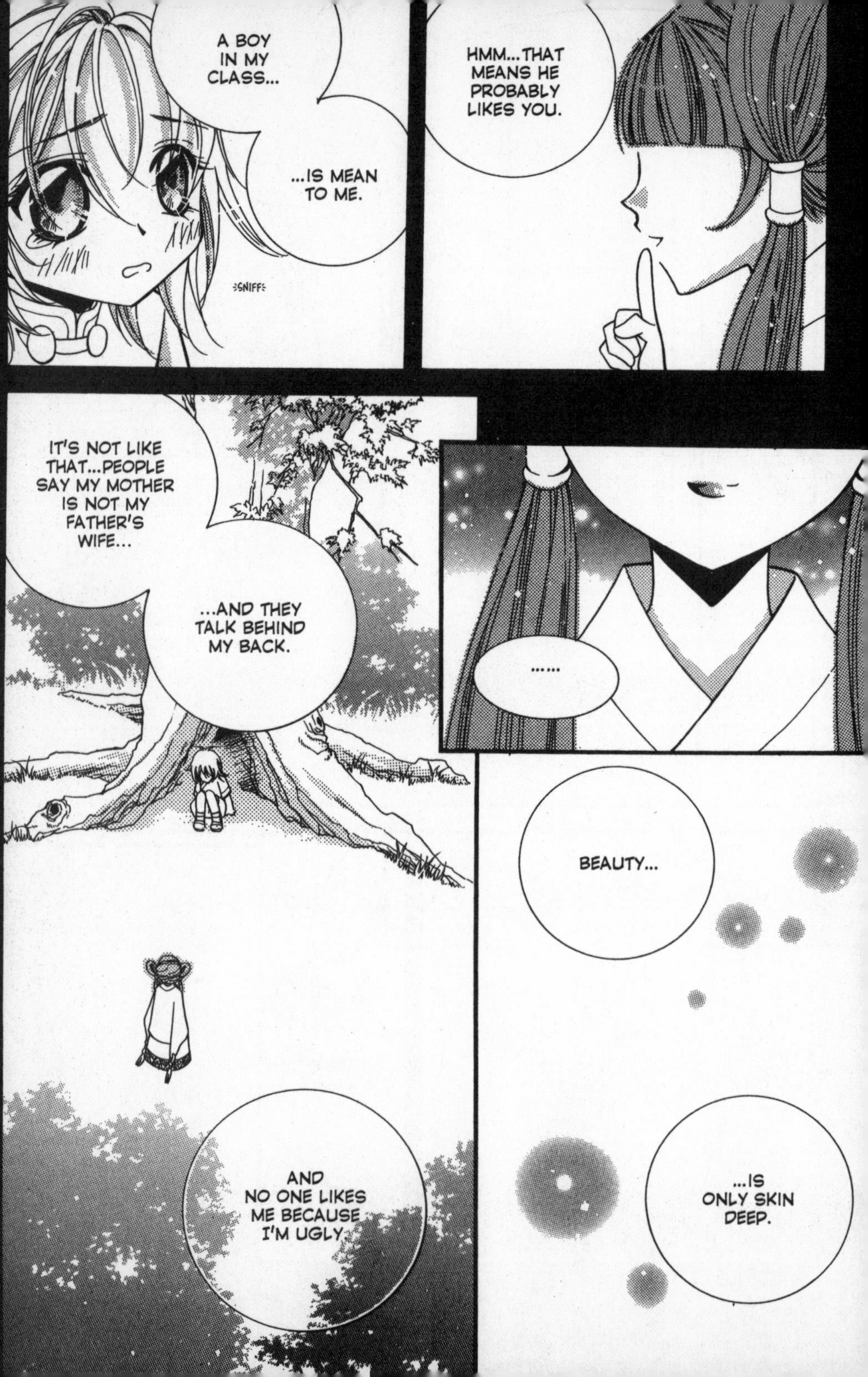
A BOY IN MY CLASS...
...IS MEAN TO ME.
SNIFF
HMM...THAT MEANS HE PROBABLY LIKES YOU.
IT'S NOT LIKE THAT...PEOPLE SAY MY MOTHER IS NOT MY FATHER'S WIFE...
...AND THEY TALK BEHIND MY BACK.
AND NO ONE LIKES ME BECAUSE I'M UGLY.
......
BEAUTY...
...IS ONLY SKIN DEEP.

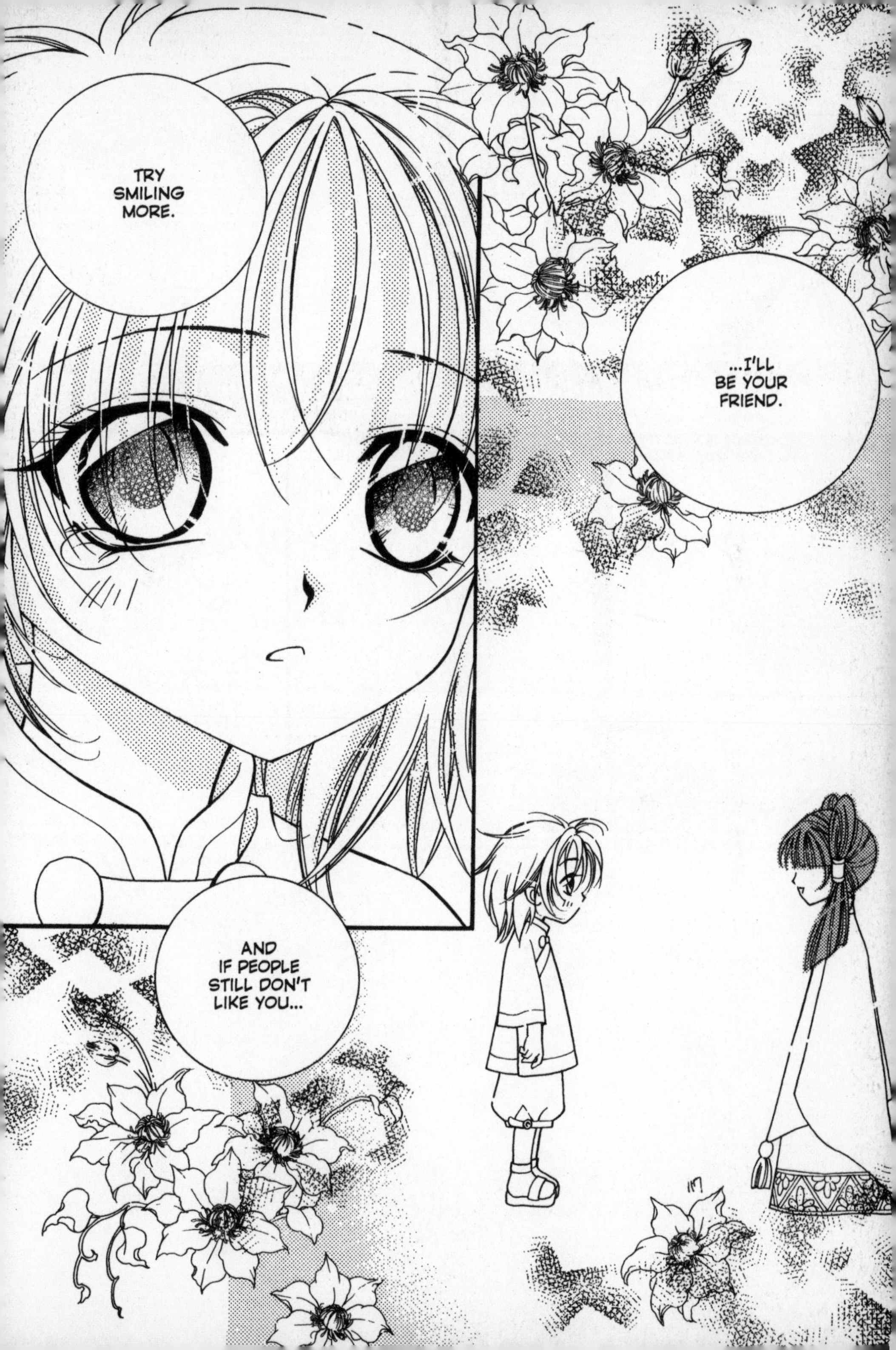
TRY SMILING MORE.
AND IF PEOPLE STILL DON'T LIKE YOU...
...I'LL BE YOUR FRIEND.

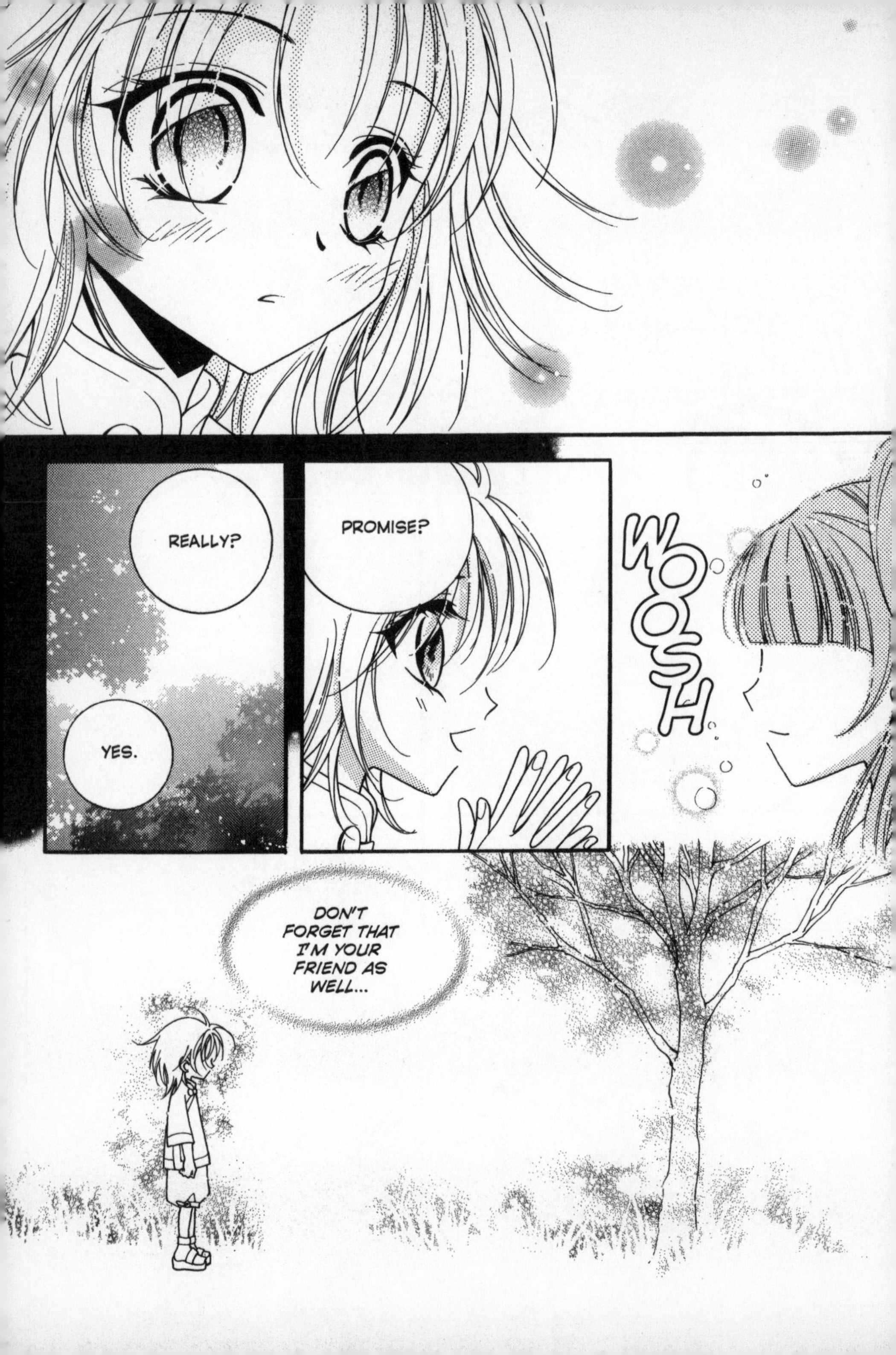

REALLY?
YES.
PROMISE?
WOOSH
DON'T FORGET THAT I'M YOUR FRIEND AS WELL...

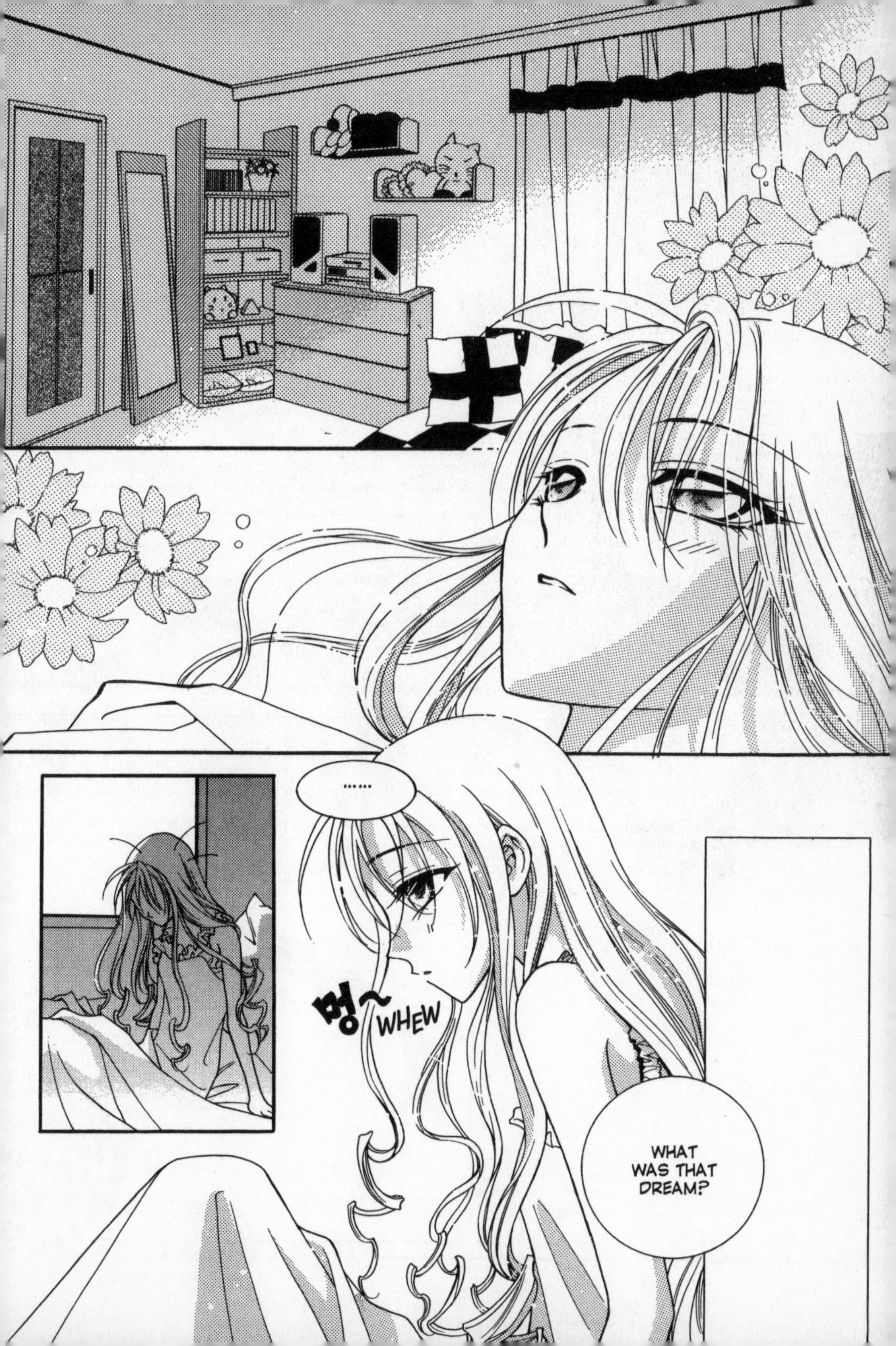

......
멍~
WHEW
WHAT WAS THAT DREAM?

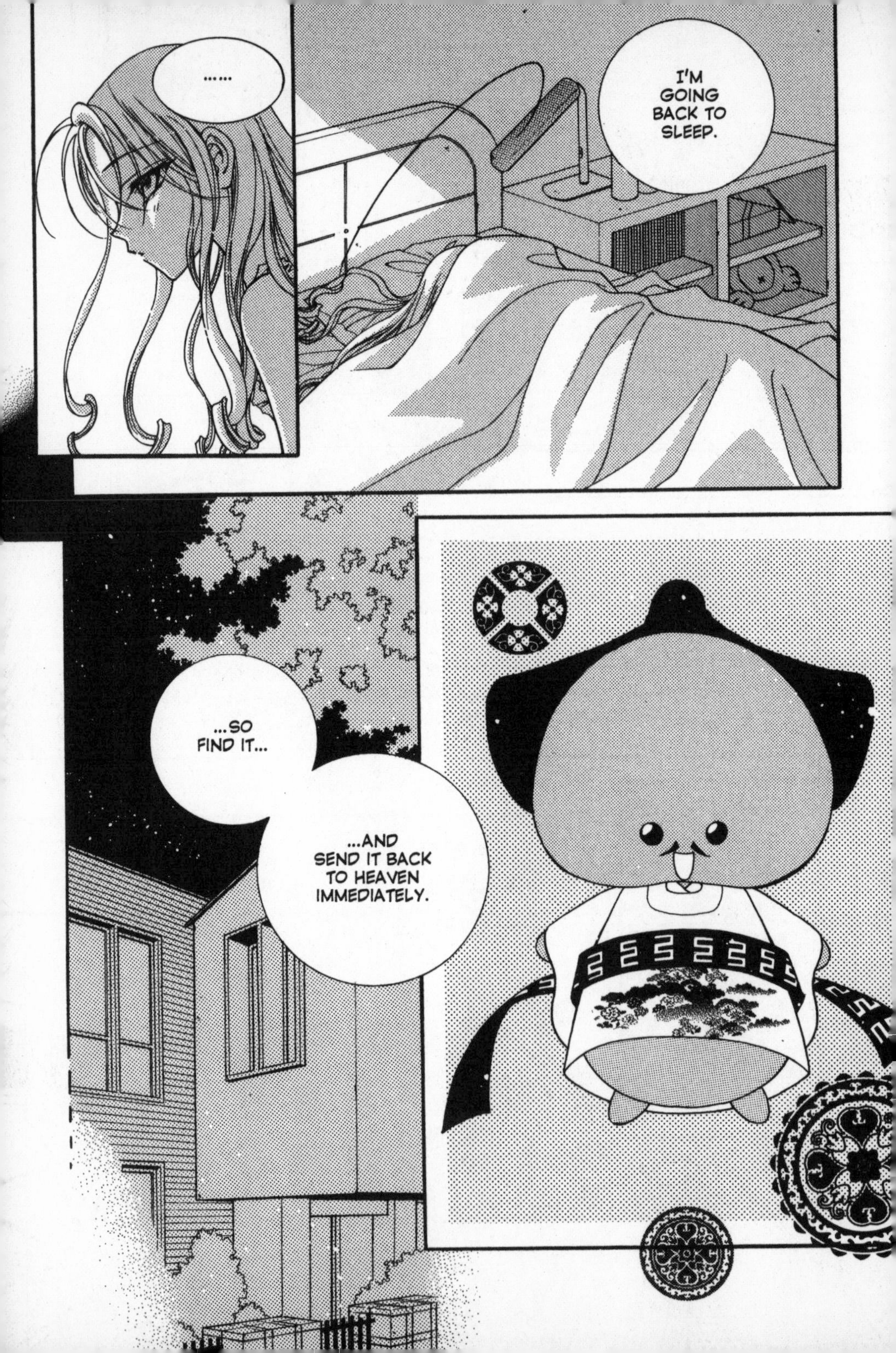
……
I'M GOING BACK TO SLEEP.
...SO FIND IT...
...AND SEND IT BACK TO HEAVEN IMMEDIATELY.

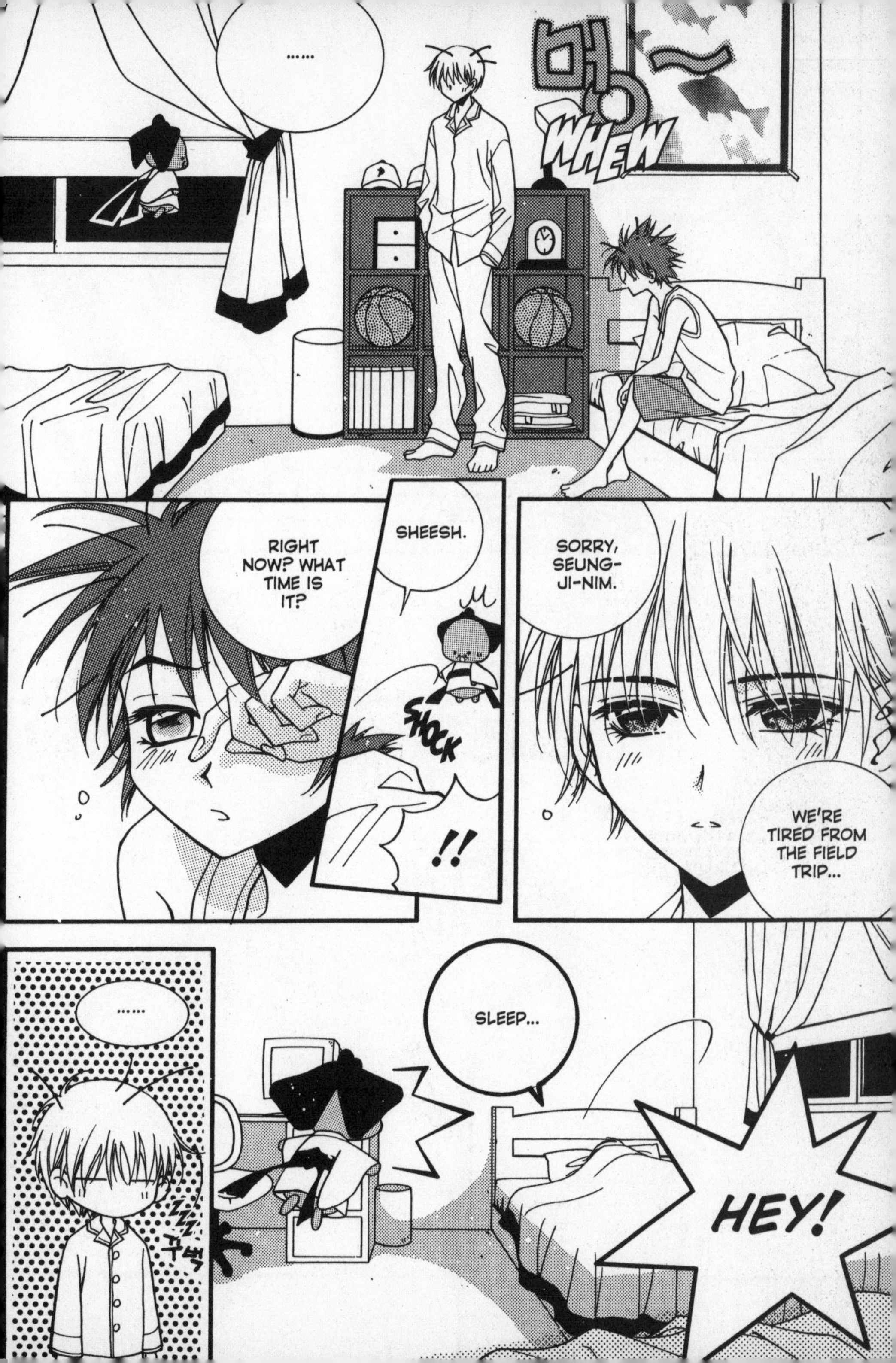
......
WHEW
RIGHT NOW? WHAT TIME IS IT?
SHEESH.
SHOCK
!!
SORRY, SEUNG-JI-NIM.
WE'RE TIRED FROM THE FIELD TRIP...
......
ZZZ
꾸벅
SLEEP...
HEY!

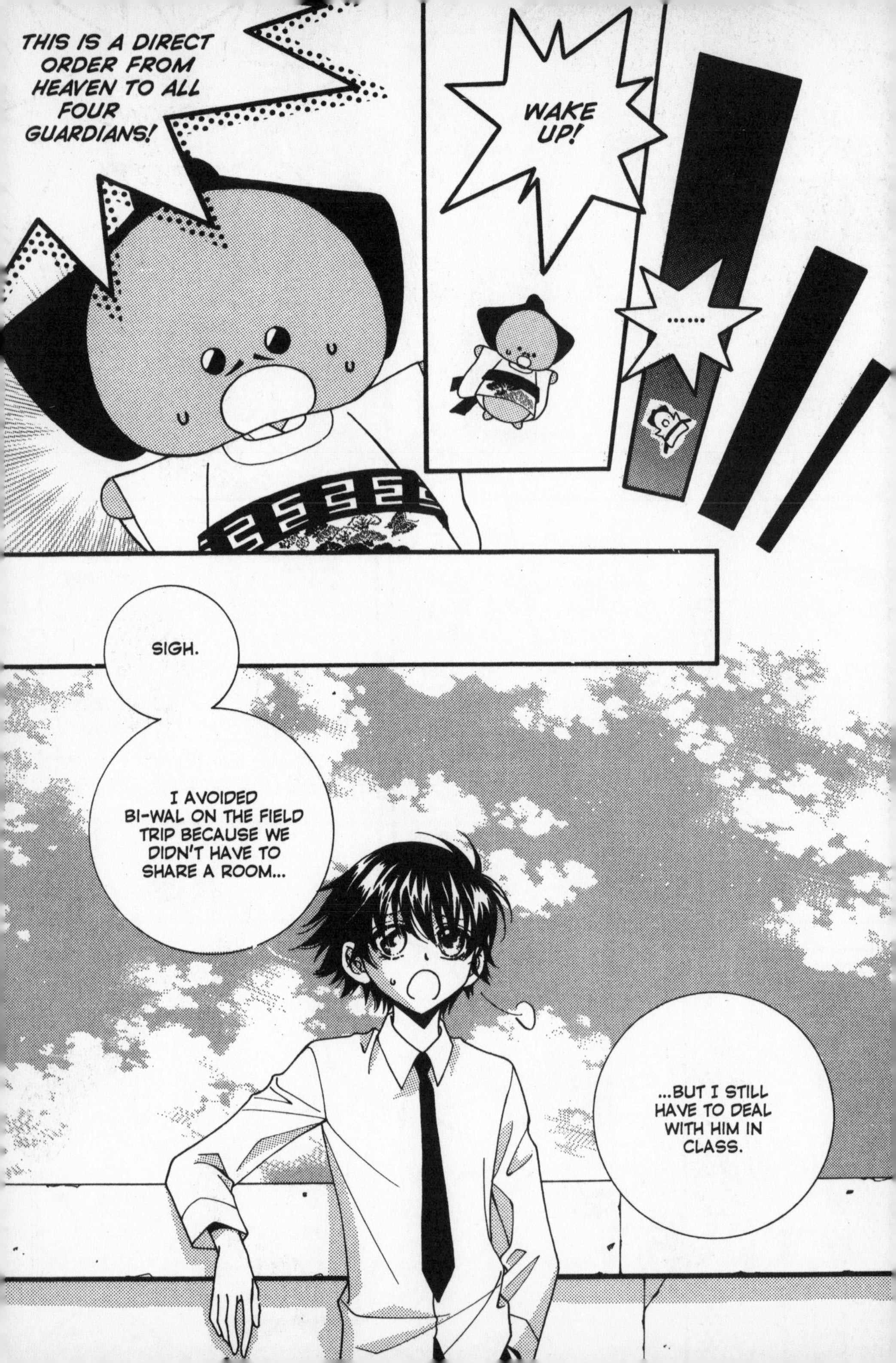
THIS IS A DIRECT ORDER FROM HEAVEN TO ALL FOUR GUARDIANS!
WAKE UP!
......
SIGH.
I AVOIDED BI-WAL ON THE FIELD TRIP BECAUSE WE DIDN'T HAVE TO SHARE A ROOM...
...BUT I STILL HAVE TO DEAL WITH HIM IN CLASS.

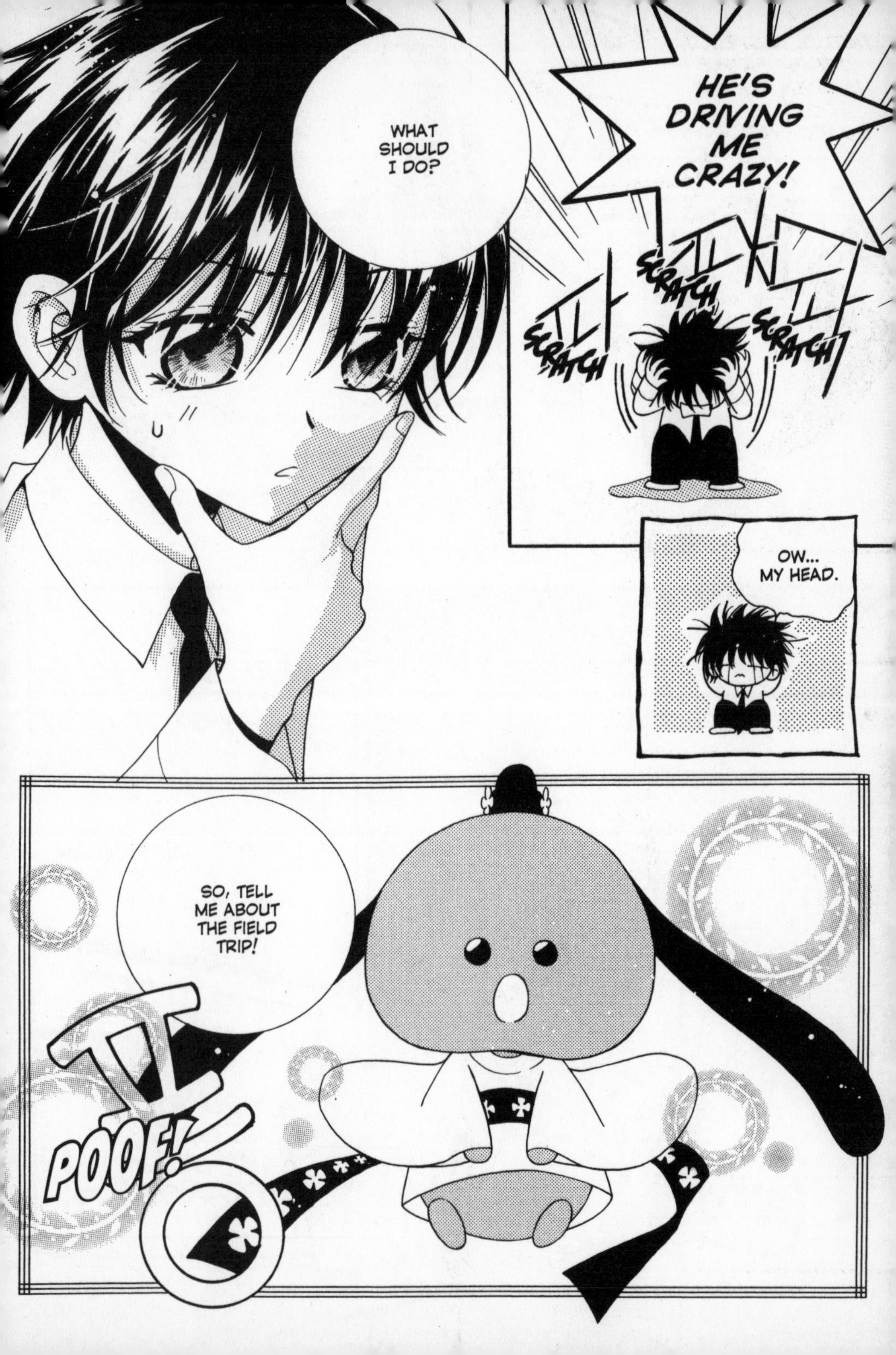
WHAT SHOULD I DO?
HE'S DRIVING ME CRAZY!
SCRATCH SCRATCH SCRATCH SCRATCH
OW... MY HEAD.
SO, TELL ME ABOUT THE FIELD TRIP!
POOF!

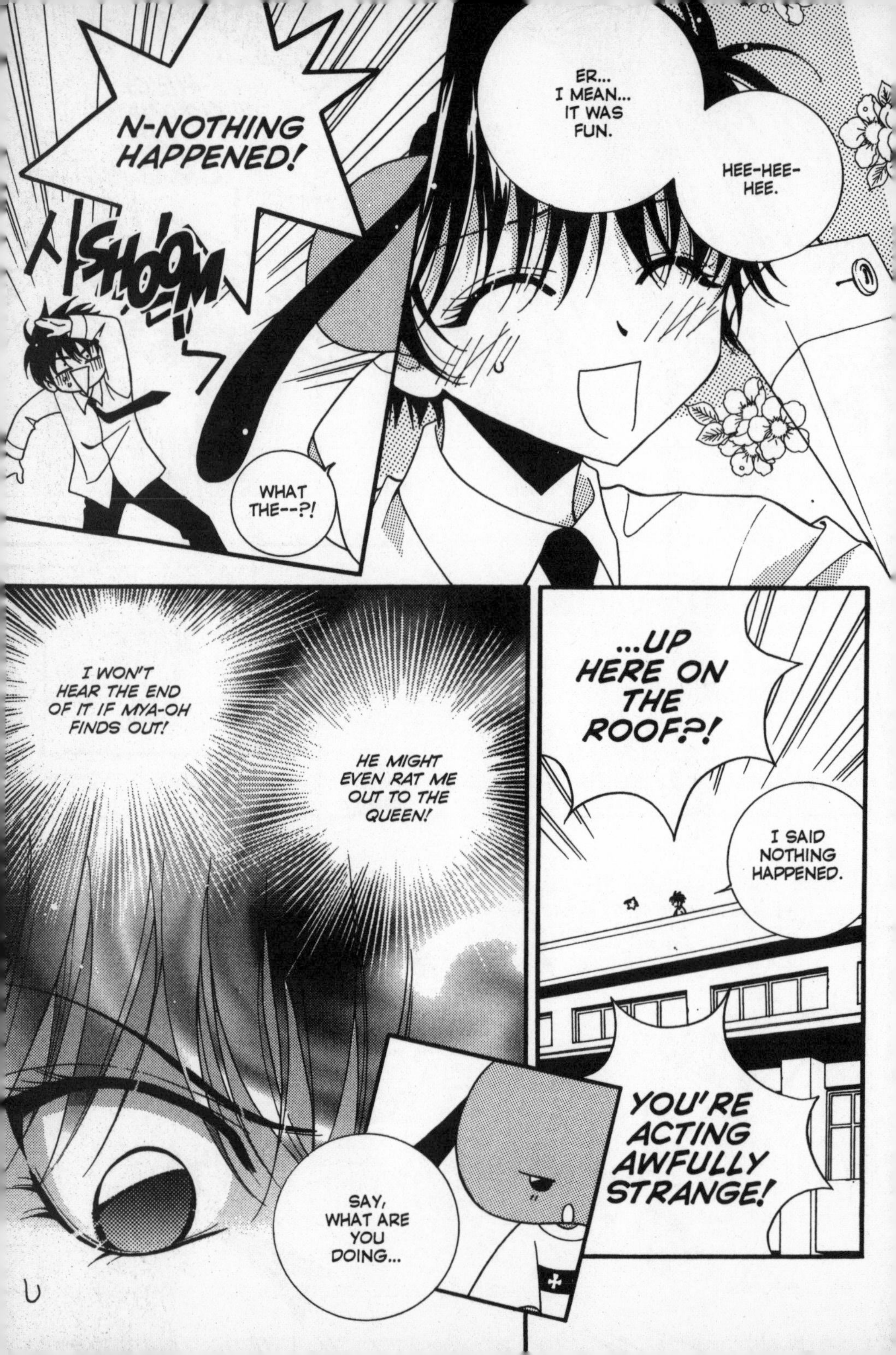
N-NOTHING HAPPENED!
SHOOM
WHAT THE--?!
ER... I MEAN... IT WAS FUN.
HEE-HEE-HEE.
I WON'T HEAR THE END OF IT IF MYA-OH FINDS OUT!
HE MIGHT EVEN RAT ME OUT TO THE QUEEN!
SAY, WHAT ARE YOU DOING...
...UP HERE ON THE ROOF?!
I SAID NOTHING HAPPENED.
YOU'RE ACTING AWFULLY STRANGE!

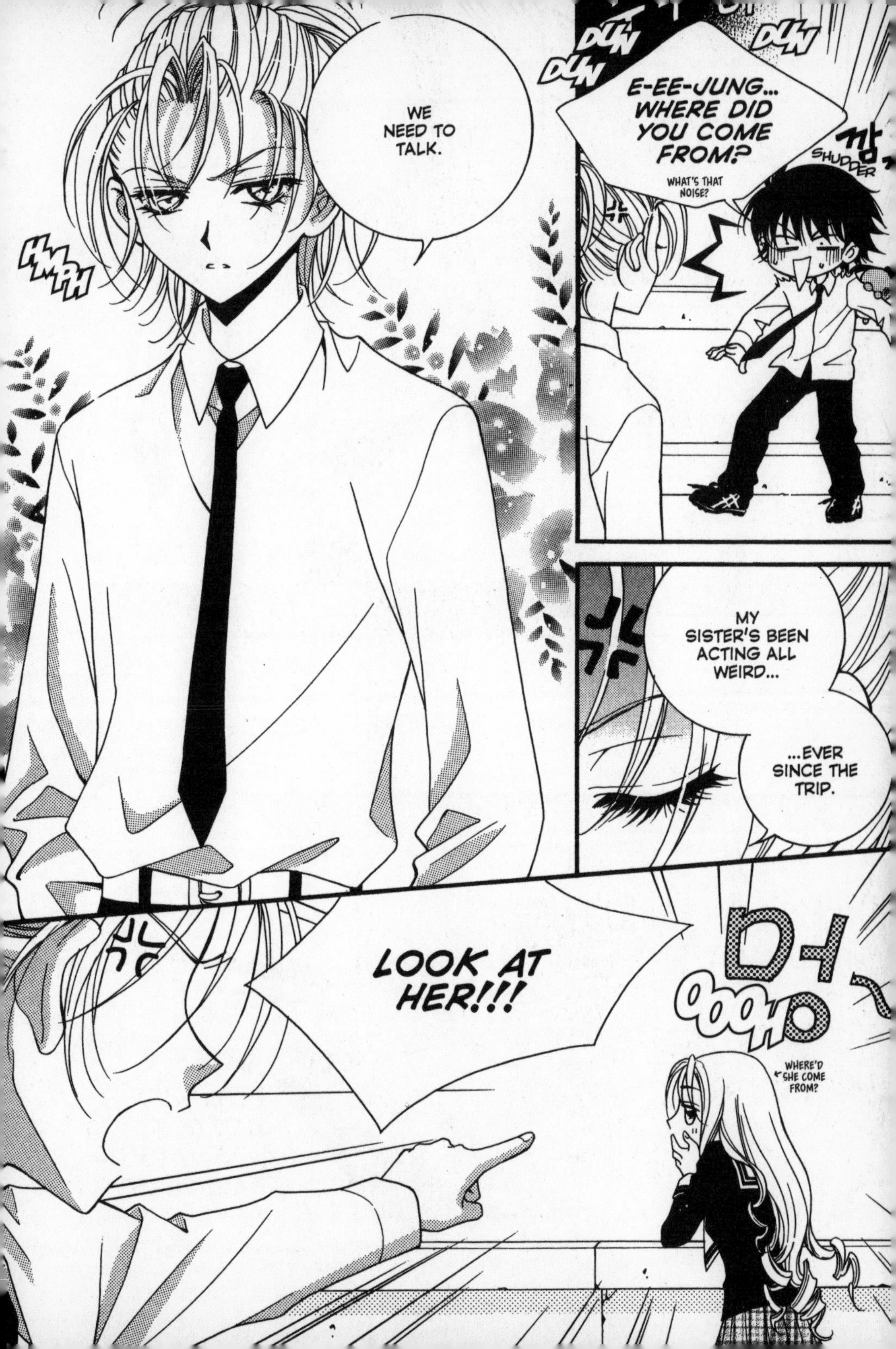
HMPH
WE NEED TO TALK.
DUN DUN DUN
E-EE-JUNG... WHERE DID YOU COME FROM?
WHAT'S THAT NOISE?
깜
SHUDDER
MY SISTER'S BEEN ACTING ALL WEIRD...
...EVER SINCE THE TRIP.
LOOK AT HER!!!
WHERE'D SHE COME FROM?

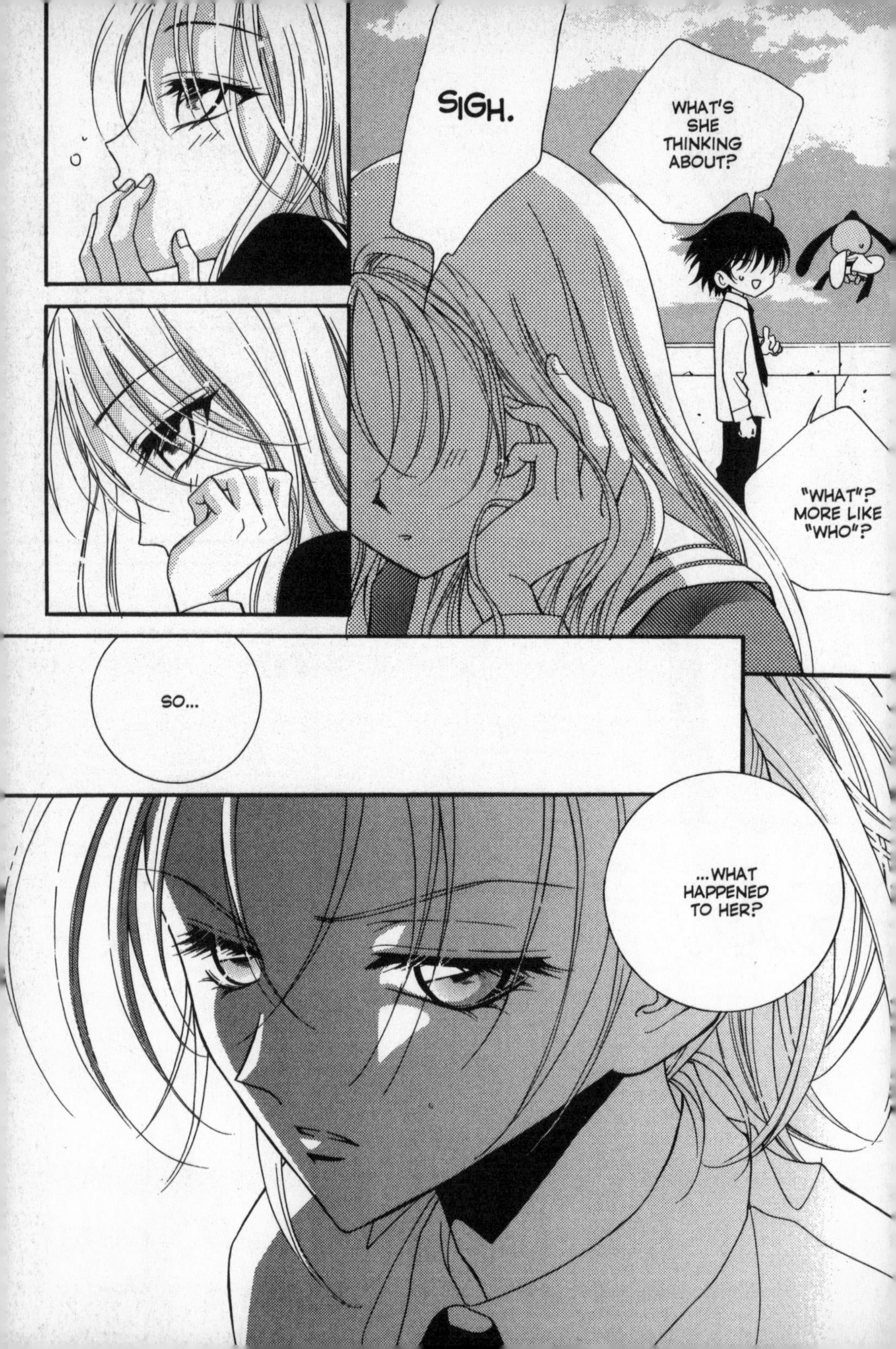
SIGH.
WHAT'S SHE THINKING ABOUT?
"WHAT"? MORE LIKE "WHO"?
SO...
...WHAT HAPPENED TO HER?

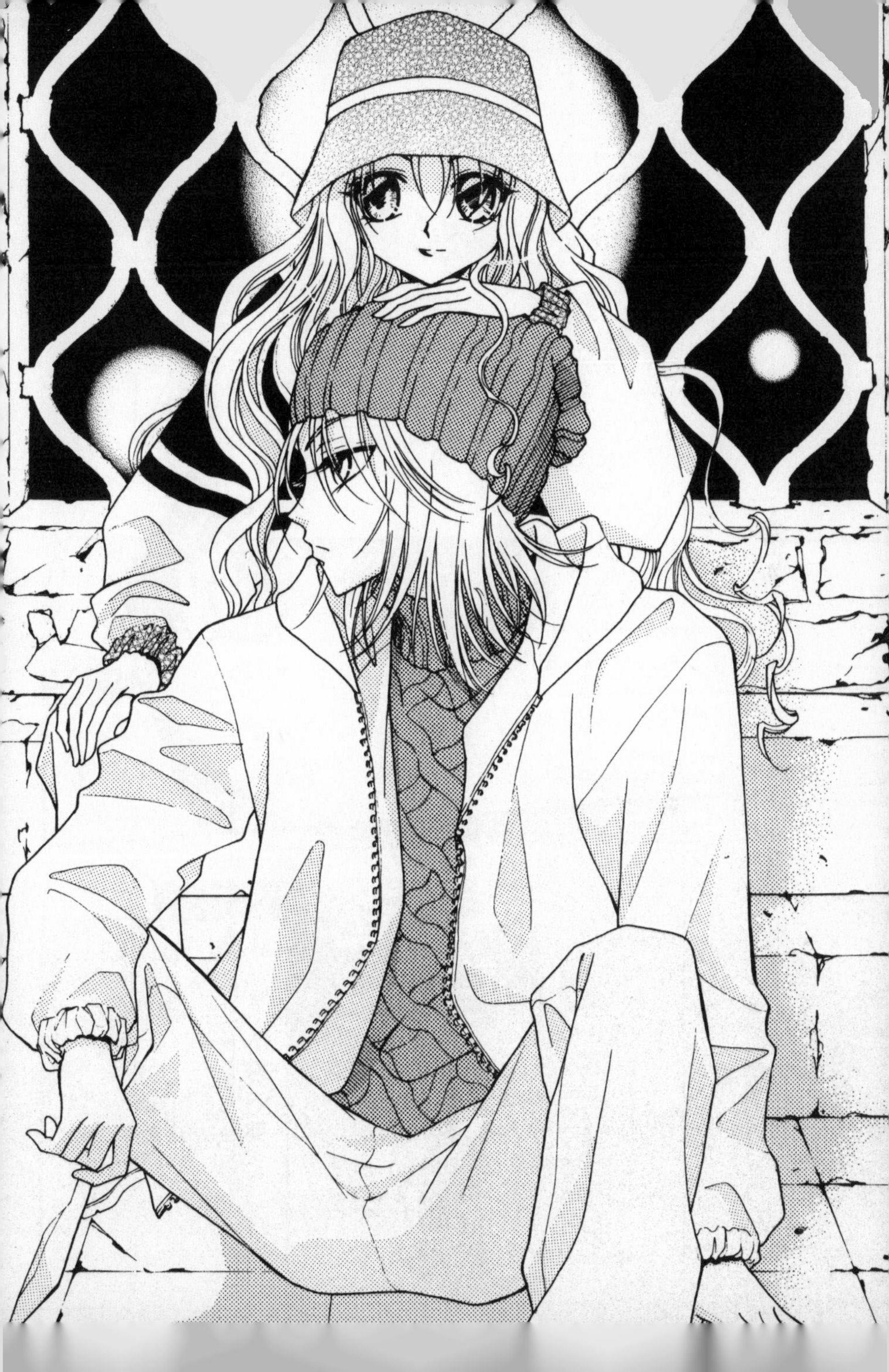

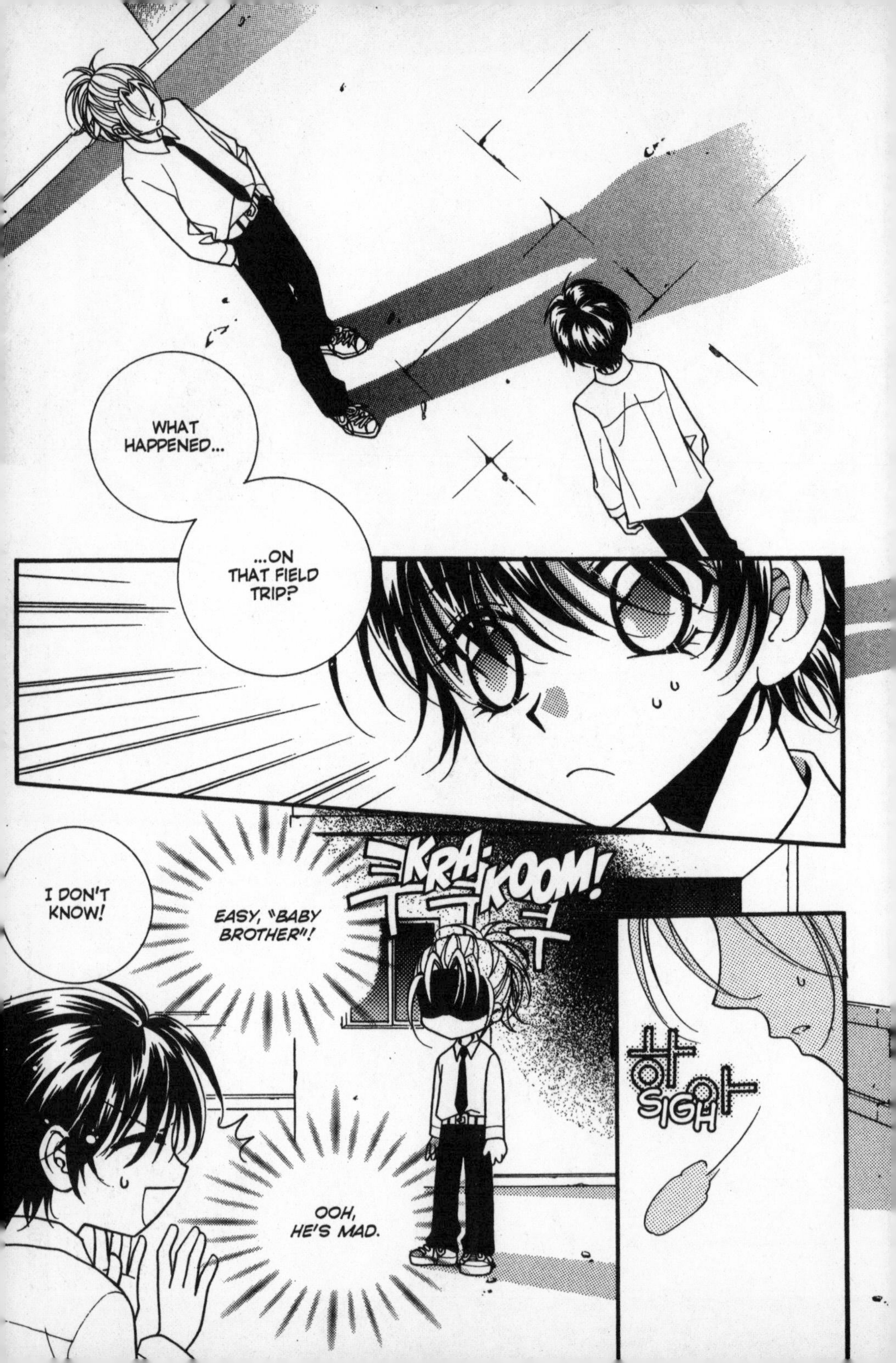
WHAT HAPPENED...
...ON THAT FIELD TRIP?
I DON'T KNOW!
KRA-KOOM!
EASY, "BABY BROTHER"!
OOH, HE'S MAD.
하아
SIGH

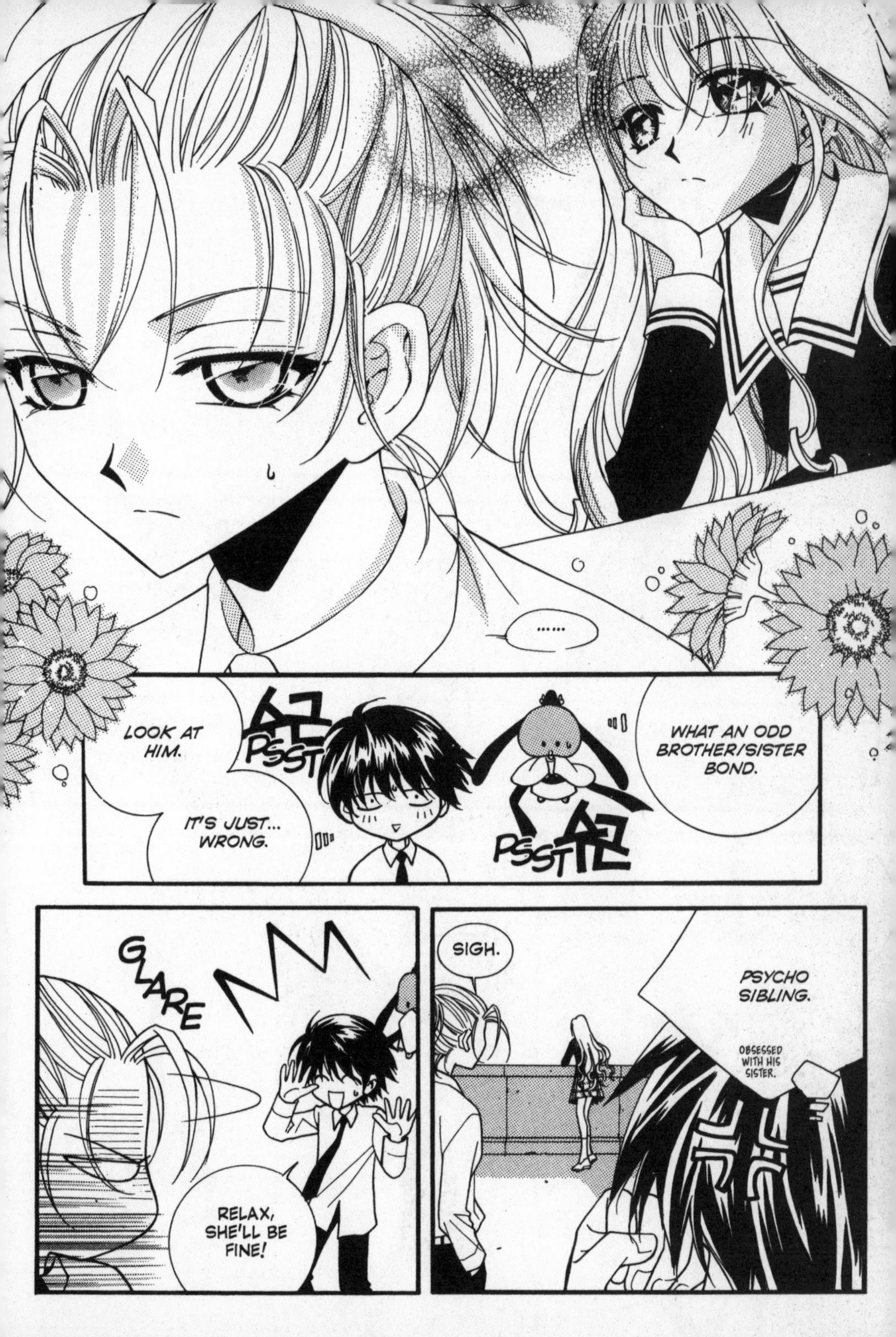
……
LOOK AT HIM.
PSSST
IT'S JUST... WRONG.
PSSST
WHAT AN ODD BROTHER/SISTER BOND.
GLARE
RELAX, SHE'LL BE FINE!
SIGH.
PSYCHO SIBLING.
OBSESSED WITH HIS SISTER.

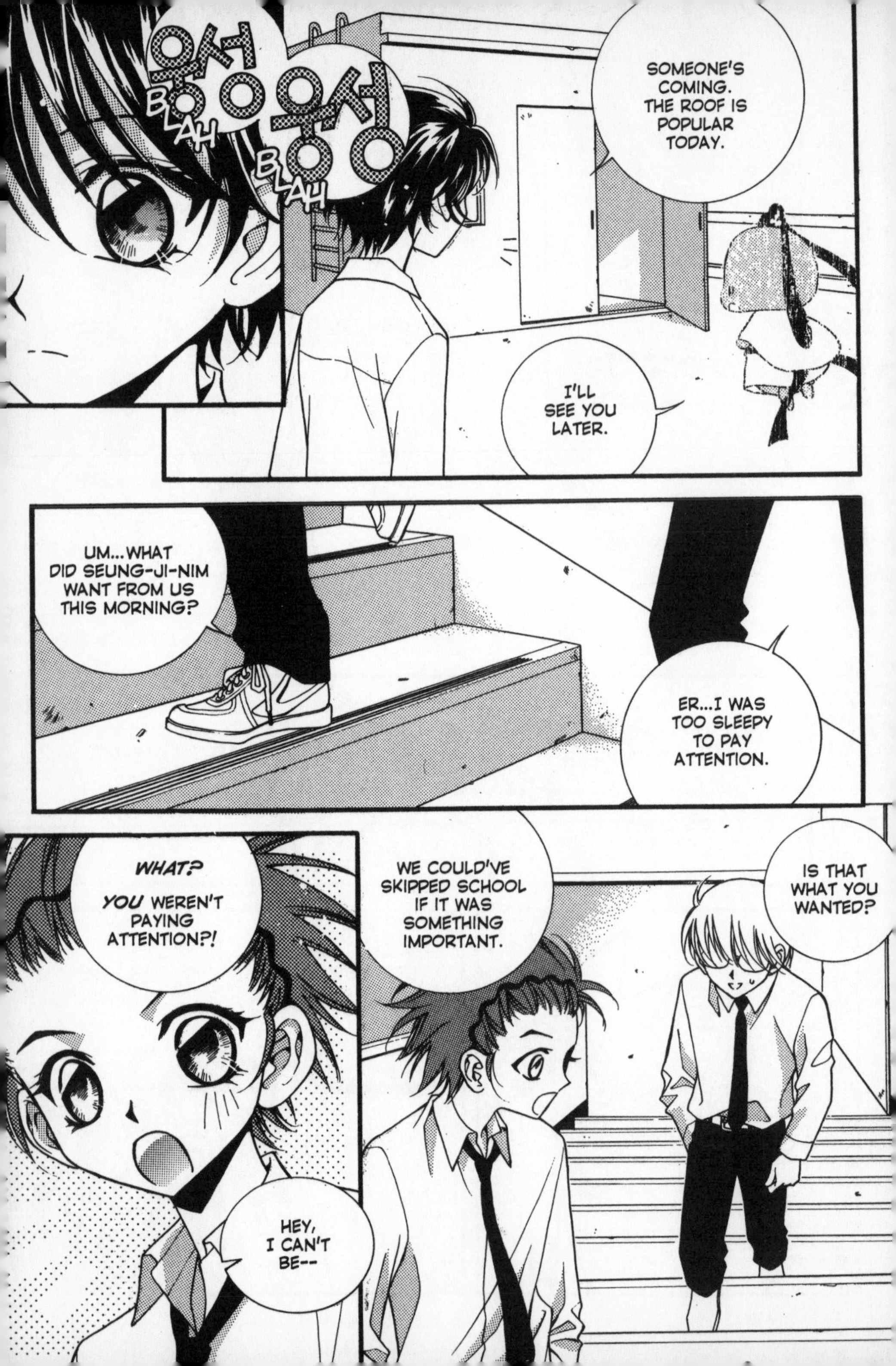
BLAH BLAH
BLAH BLAH
SOMEONE'S COMING. THE ROOF IS POPULAR TODAY.
I'LL SEE YOU LATER.
UM...WHAT DID SEUNG-JI-NIM WANT FROM US THIS MORNING?
ER...I WAS TOO SLEEPY TO PAY ATTENTION.
WHAT?
YOU WEREN'T PAYING ATTENTION?!
HEY, I CAN'T BE--
WE COULD'VE SKIPPED SCHOOL IF IT WAS SOMETHING IMPORTANT.
IS THAT WHAT YOU WANTED?

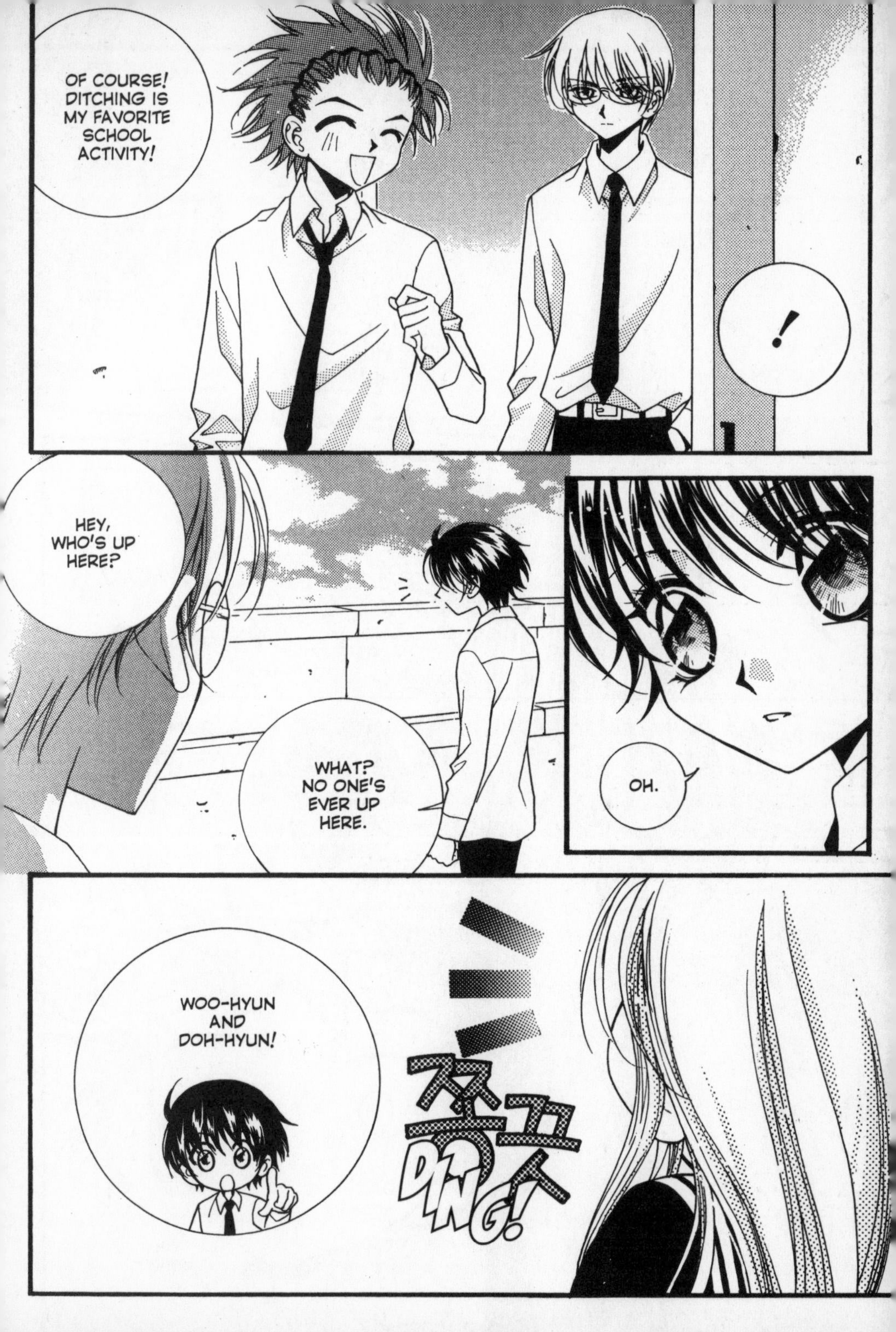
OF COURSE! DITCHING IS MY FAVORITE SCHOOL ACTIVITY!
!
HEY, WHO'S UP HERE?
WHAT? NO ONE'S EVER UP HERE.
OH.
WOO-HYUN AND DOH-HYUN!
DING!

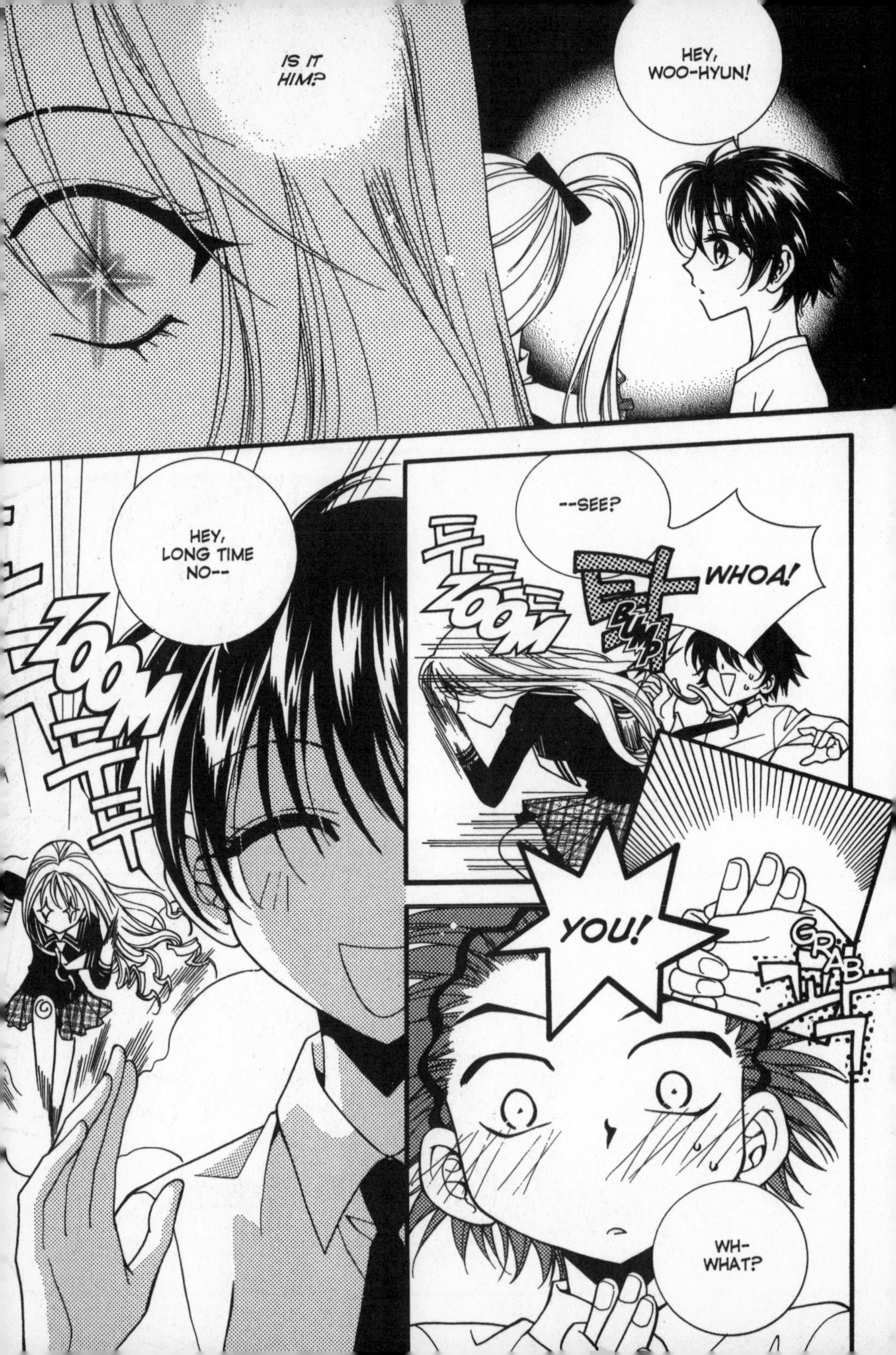
IS IT HIM?
HEY, WOO-HYUN!
HEY, LONG TIME NO--
ZOOM
--SEE?
ZOOM
BUMP
WHOA!
YOU!
GRAB
WH- WHAT?

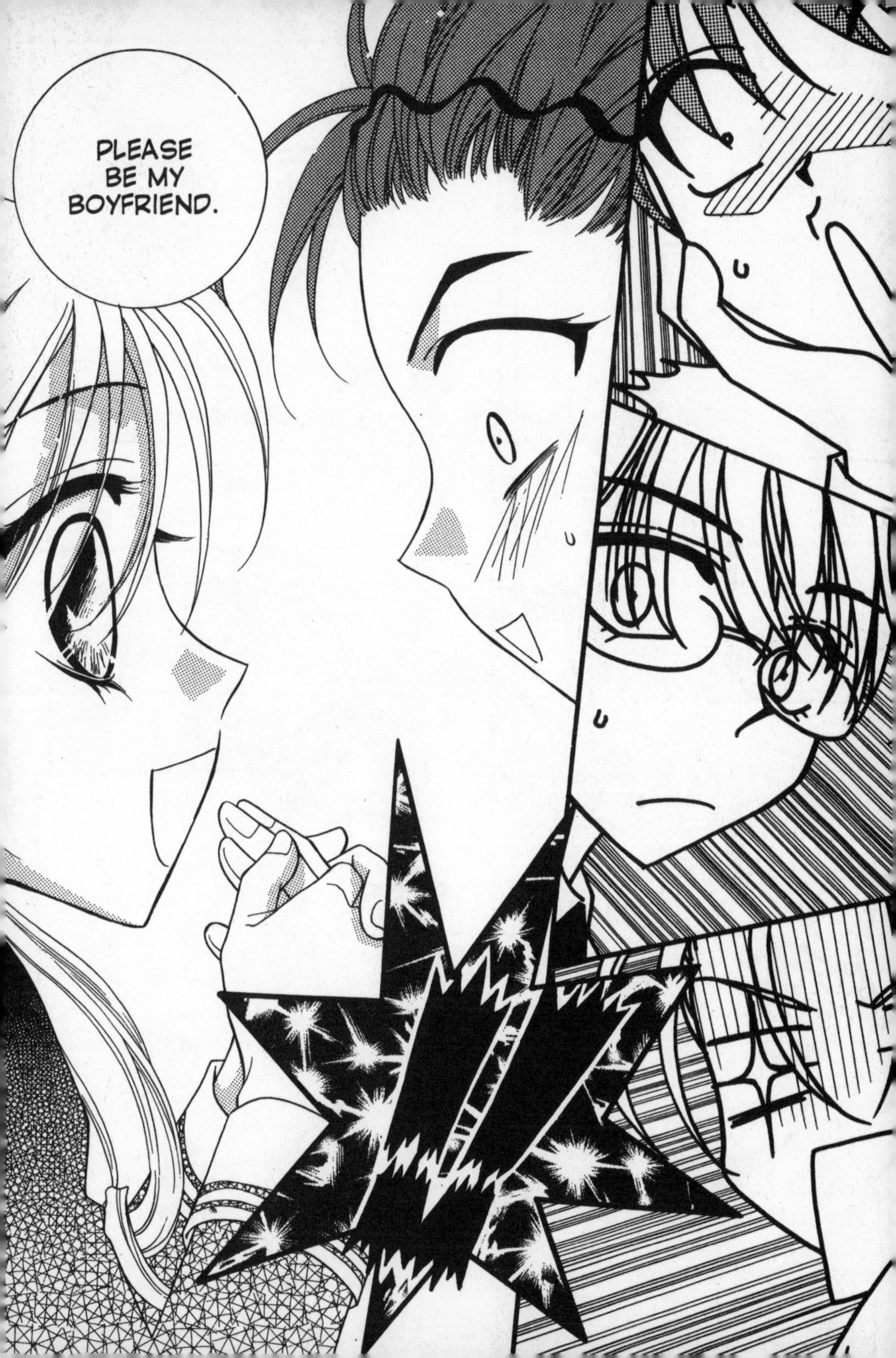
PLEASE BE MY BOYFRIEND.

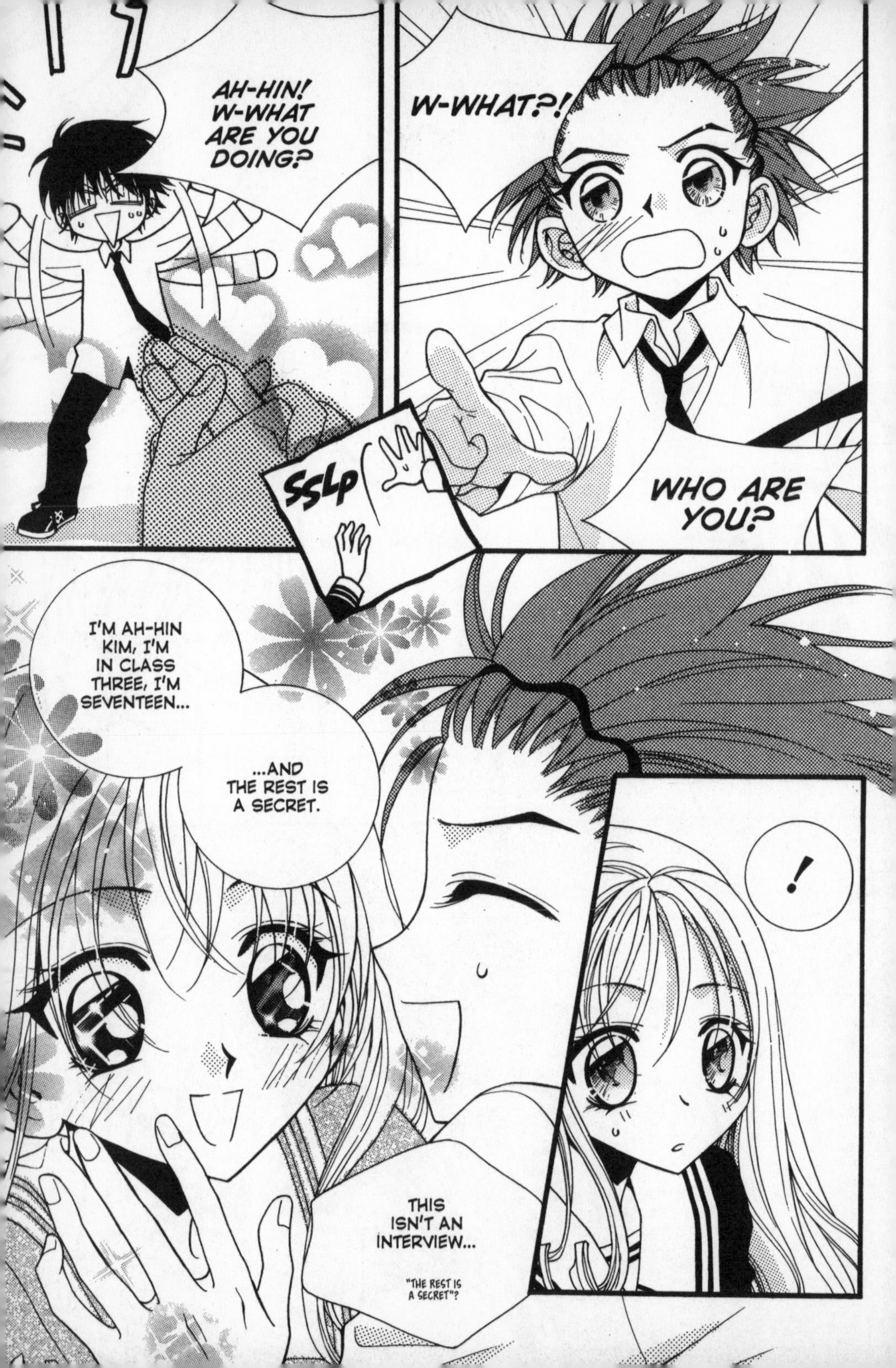
AH-HIN! W-WHAT ARE YOU DOING?
W-WHAT?!
SSLp
WHO ARE YOU?
I'M AH-HIN KIM, I'M IN CLASS THREE, I'M SEVENTEEN...
...AND THE REST IS A SECRET.
!
THIS ISN'T AN INTERVIEW...
"THE REST IS A SECRET"?

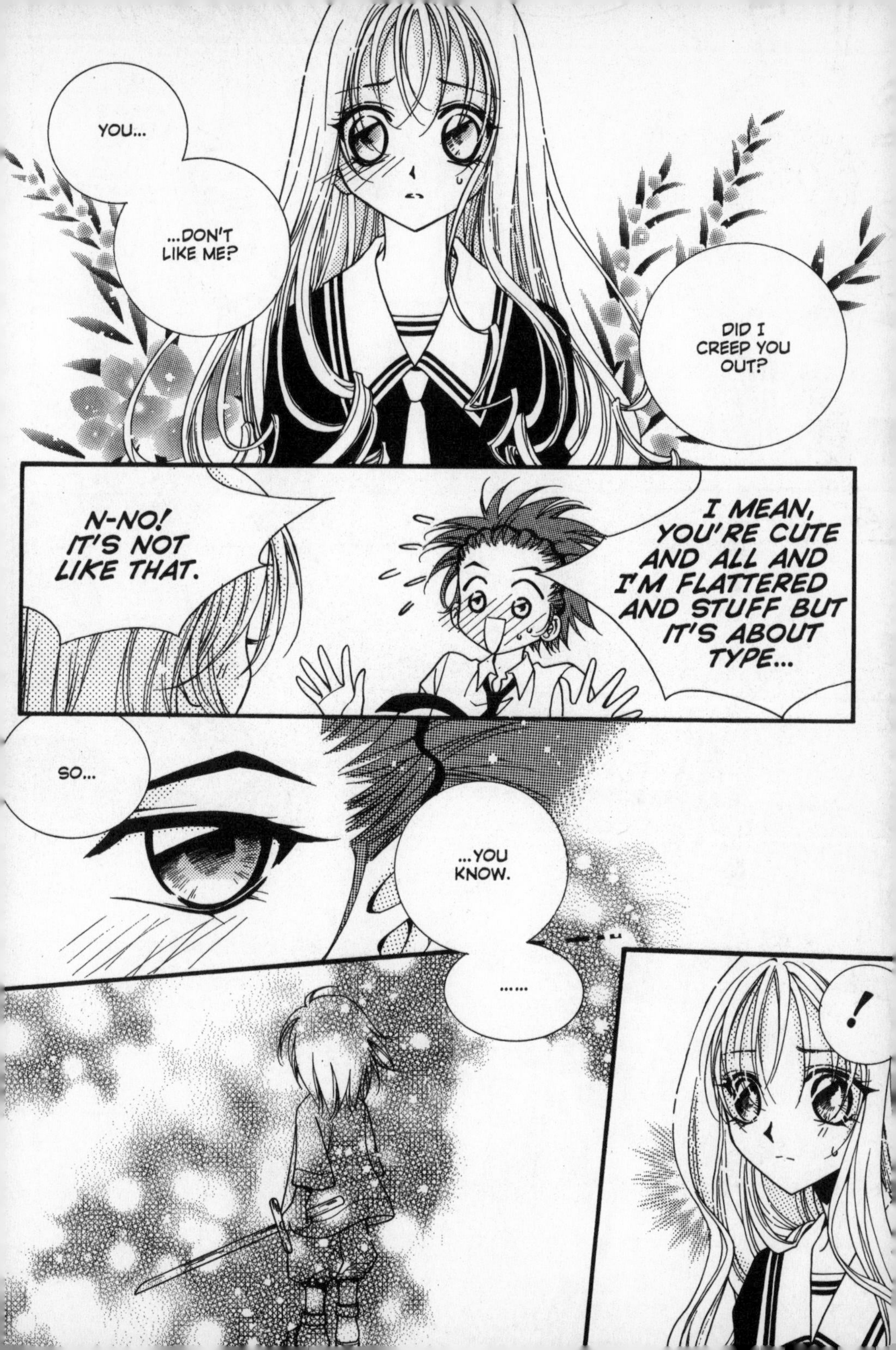
YOU...
...DON'T LIKE ME?
DID I CREEP YOU OUT?
N-NO! IT'S NOT LIKE THAT.
I MEAN, YOU'RE CUTE AND ALL AND I'M FLATTERED AND STUFF BUT IT'S ABOUT TYPE...
SO...
...YOU KNOW.
......
!

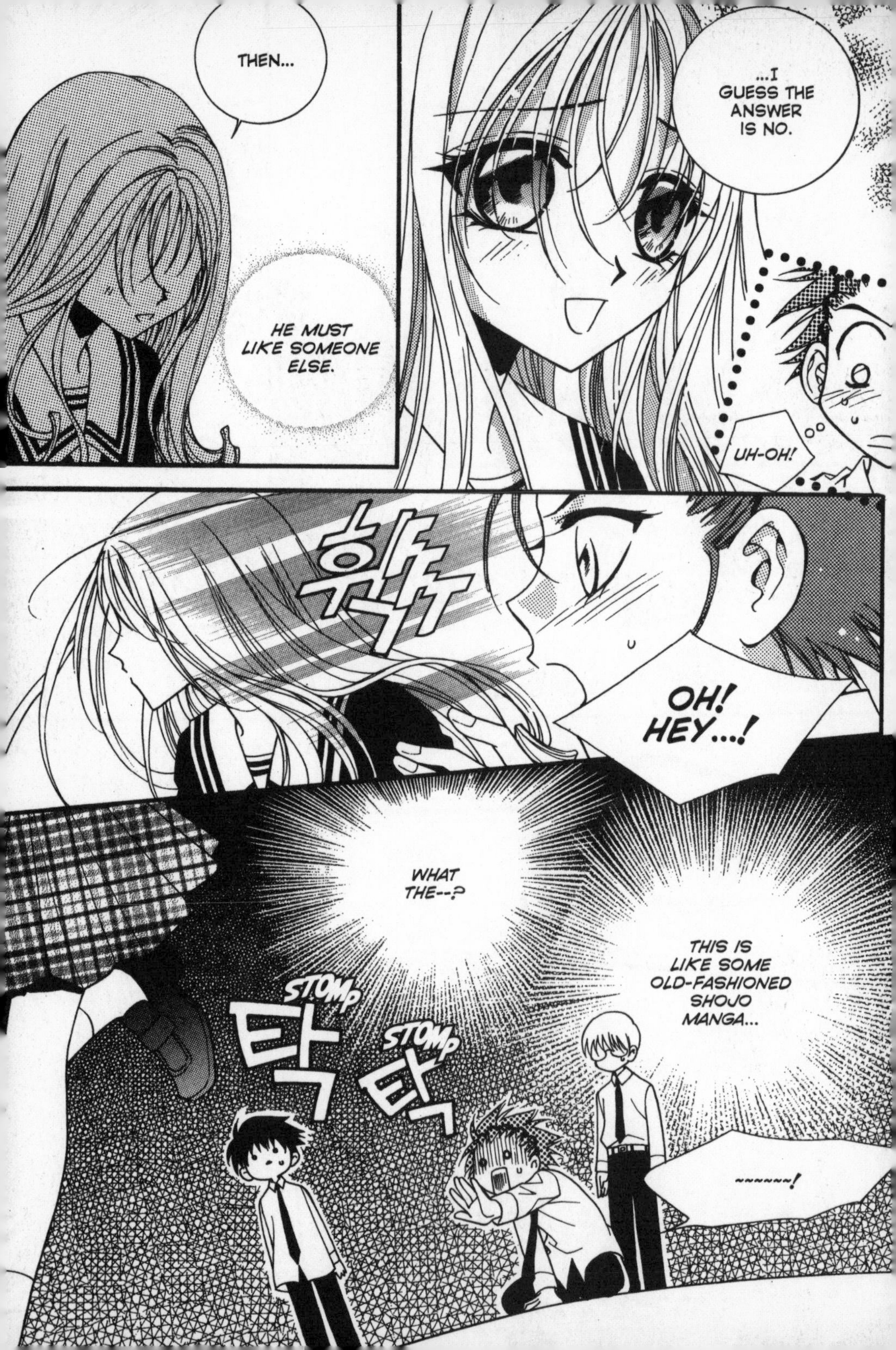
THEN...
HE MUST LIKE SOMEONE ELSE.
...I GUESS THE ANSWER IS NO.
UH-OH!
훽
OH! HEY...!
WHAT THE--?
THIS IS LIKE SOME OLD-FASHIONED SHOJO MANGA...
STOMP
탁
STOMP
탁
~~~~~~!
~~~~~~

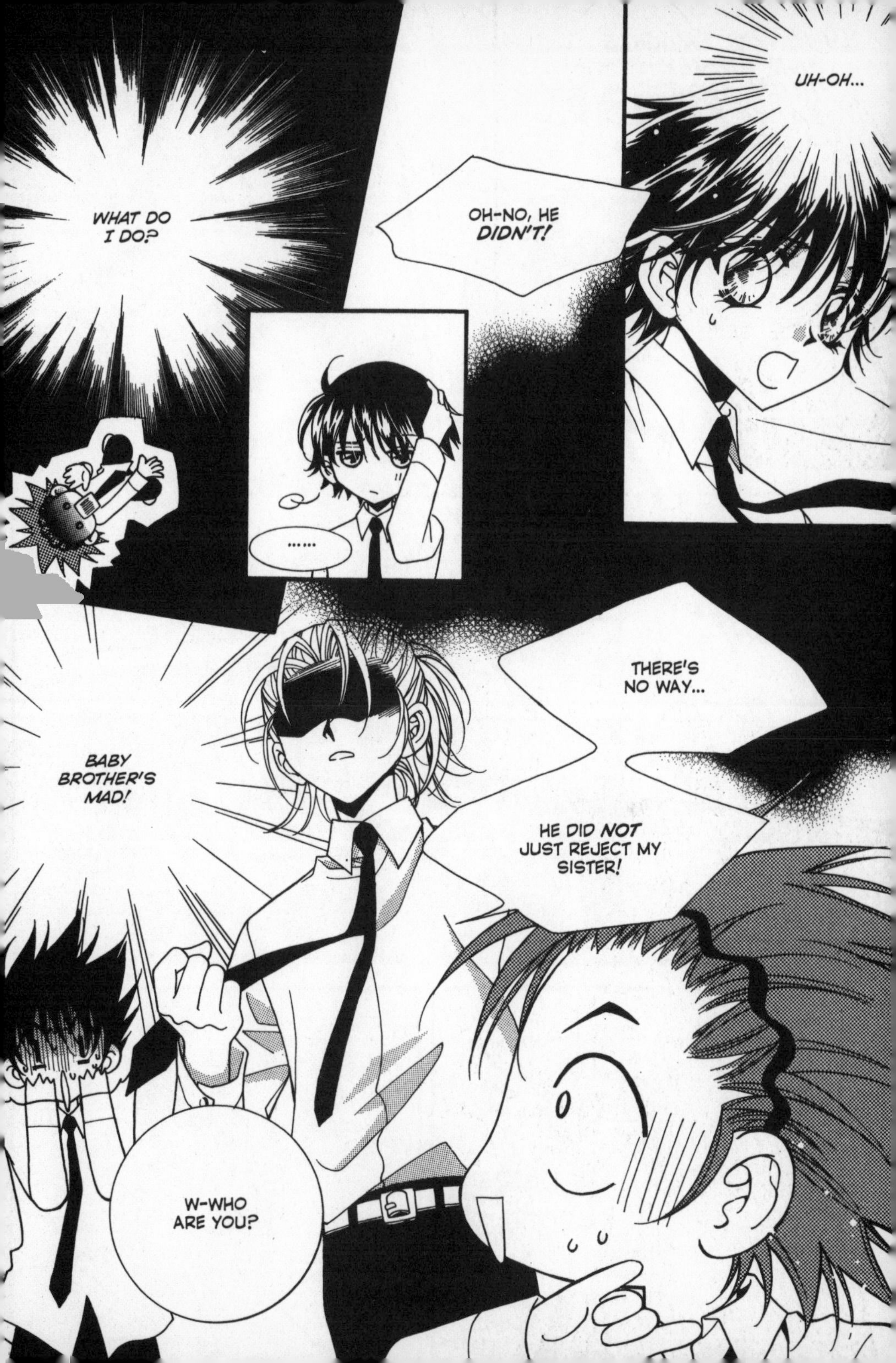
WHAT DO I DO?
......
UH-OH...
OH-NO, HE *DIDN'T!*
BABY BROTHER'S MAD!
THERE'S NO WAY...
HE DID *NOT* JUST REJECT MY SISTER!
W-WHO ARE YOU?

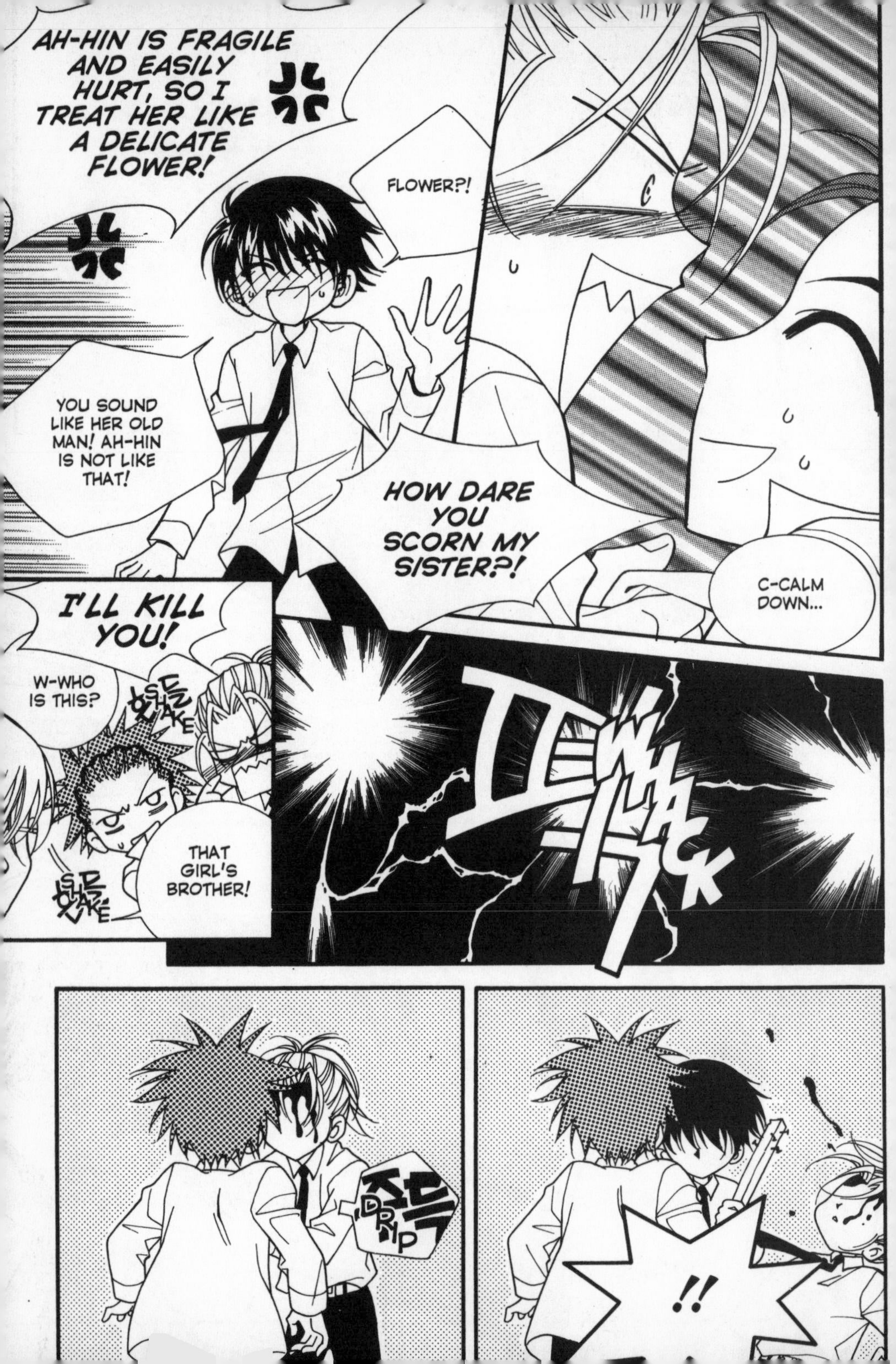
AH-HIN IS FRAGILE AND EASILY HURT, SO I TREAT HER LIKE A DELICATE FLOWER!
FLOWER?!
YOU SOUND LIKE HER OLD MAN! AH-HIN IS NOT LIKE THAT!
HOW DARE YOU SCORN MY SISTER?!
C-CALM DOWN...
I'LL KILL YOU!
W-WHO IS THIS?
SHAKE
THAT GIRL'S BROTHER!
SHAKE
WHACK
DRIP
!!

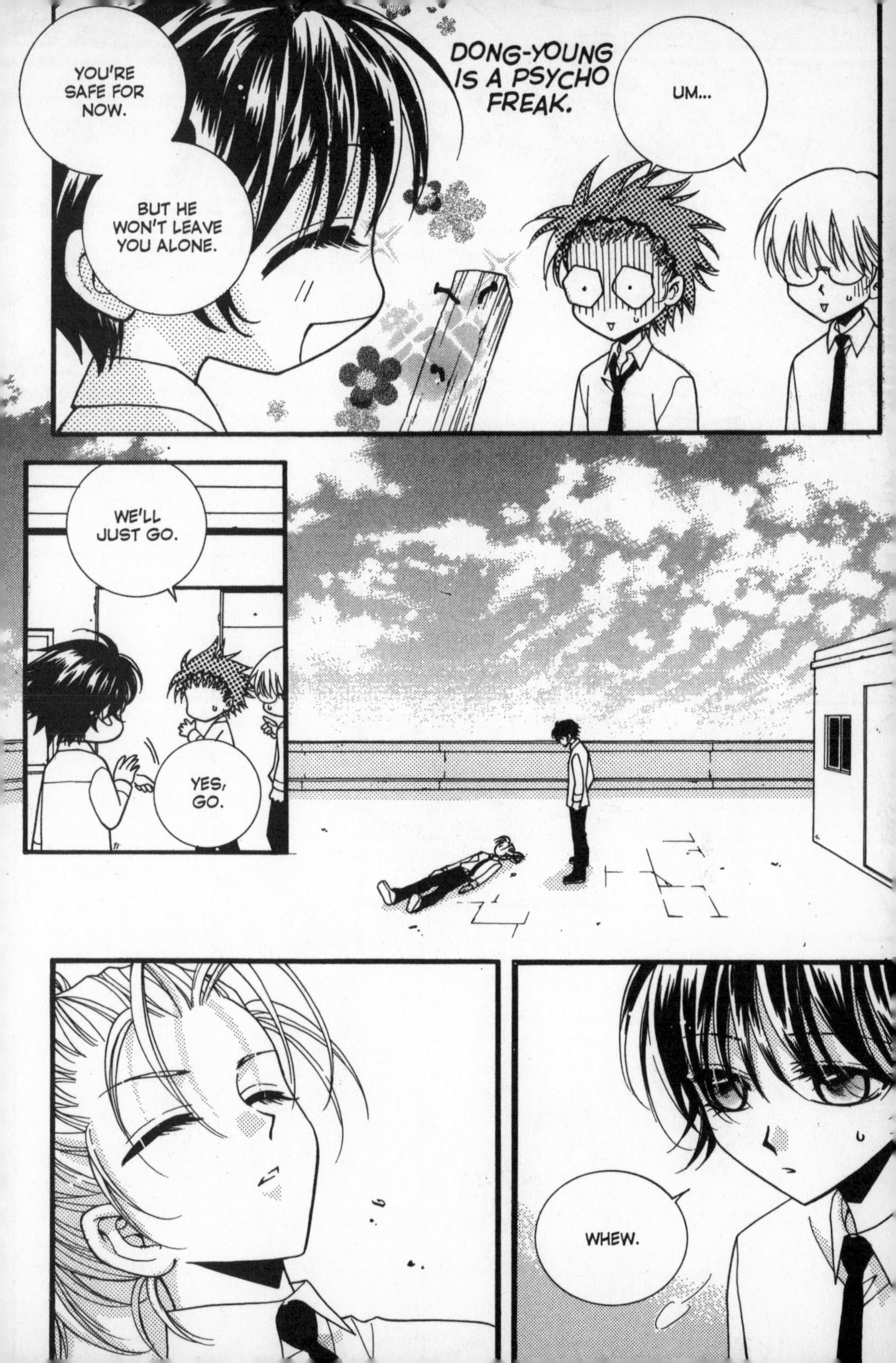
YOU'RE SAFE FOR NOW.
BUT HE WON'T LEAVE YOU ALONE.
DONG-YOUNG IS A PSYCHO FREAK.
UM...
WE'LL JUST GO.
YES, GO.
WHEW.

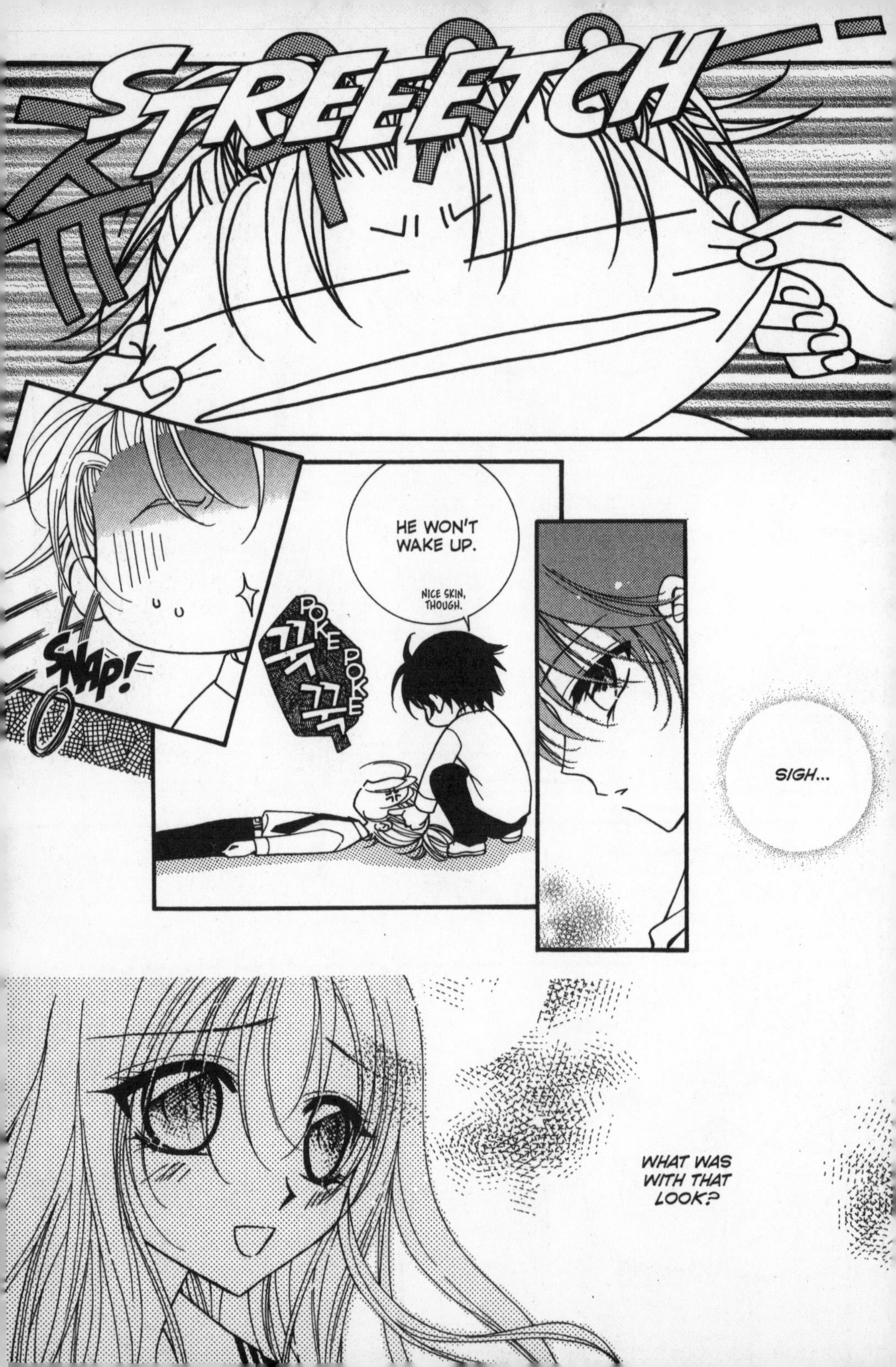
STREEETCH
SNAP!
POKE POKE
HE WON'T WAKE UP.
NICE SKIN, THOUGH.
SIGH...
WHAT WAS WITH THAT LOOK?

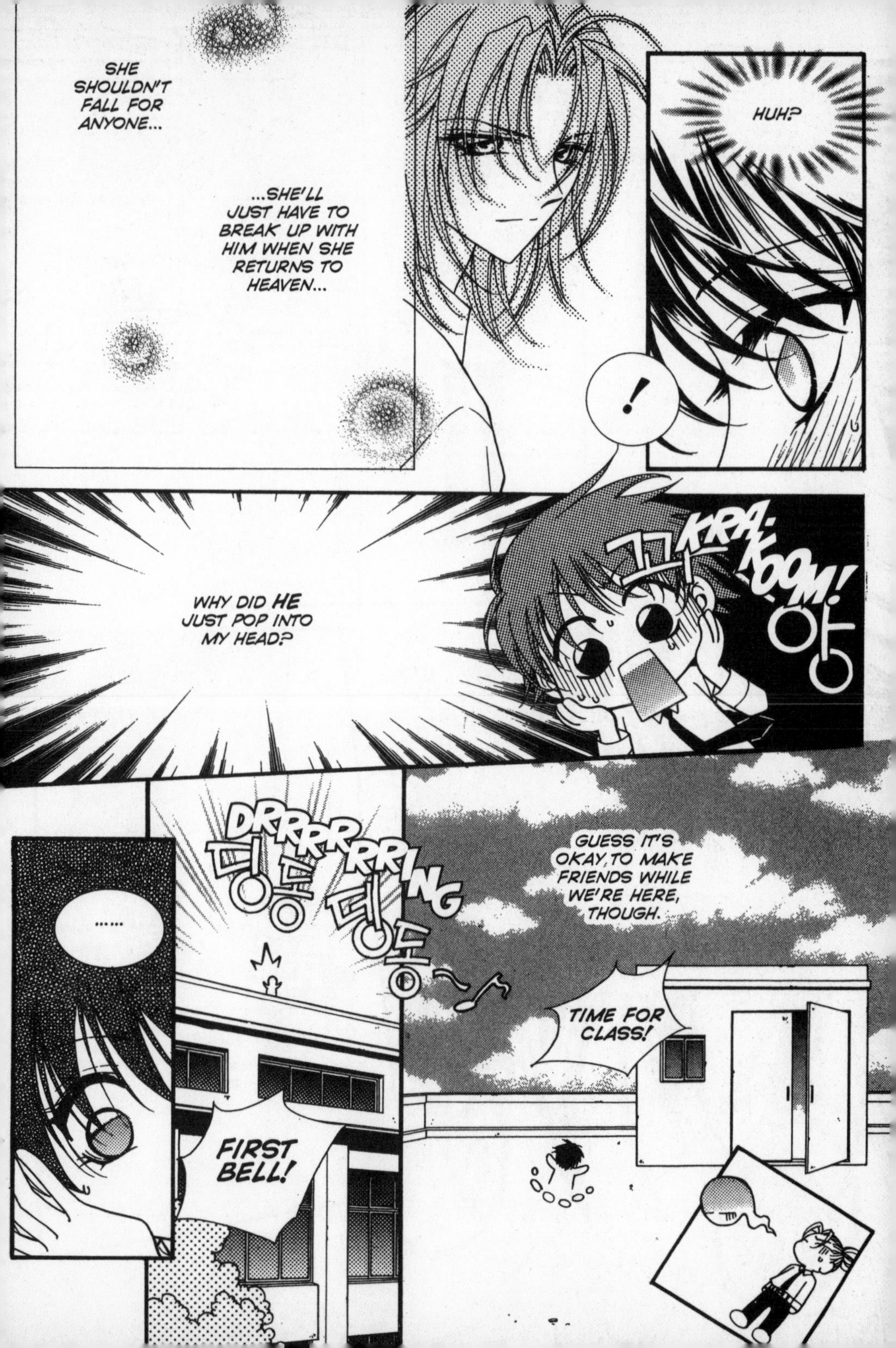

SHE SHOULDN'T FALL FOR ANYONE...
...SHE'LL JUST HAVE TO BREAK UP WITH HIM WHEN SHE RETURNS TO HEAVEN...
HUH?
!
WHY DID HE JUST POP INTO MY HEAD?
KRA-KOOM!
......
DRRRRRRRRING
FIRST BELL!
GUESS IT'S OKAY TO MAKE FRIENDS WHILE WE'RE HERE, THOUGH.
TIME FOR CLASS!

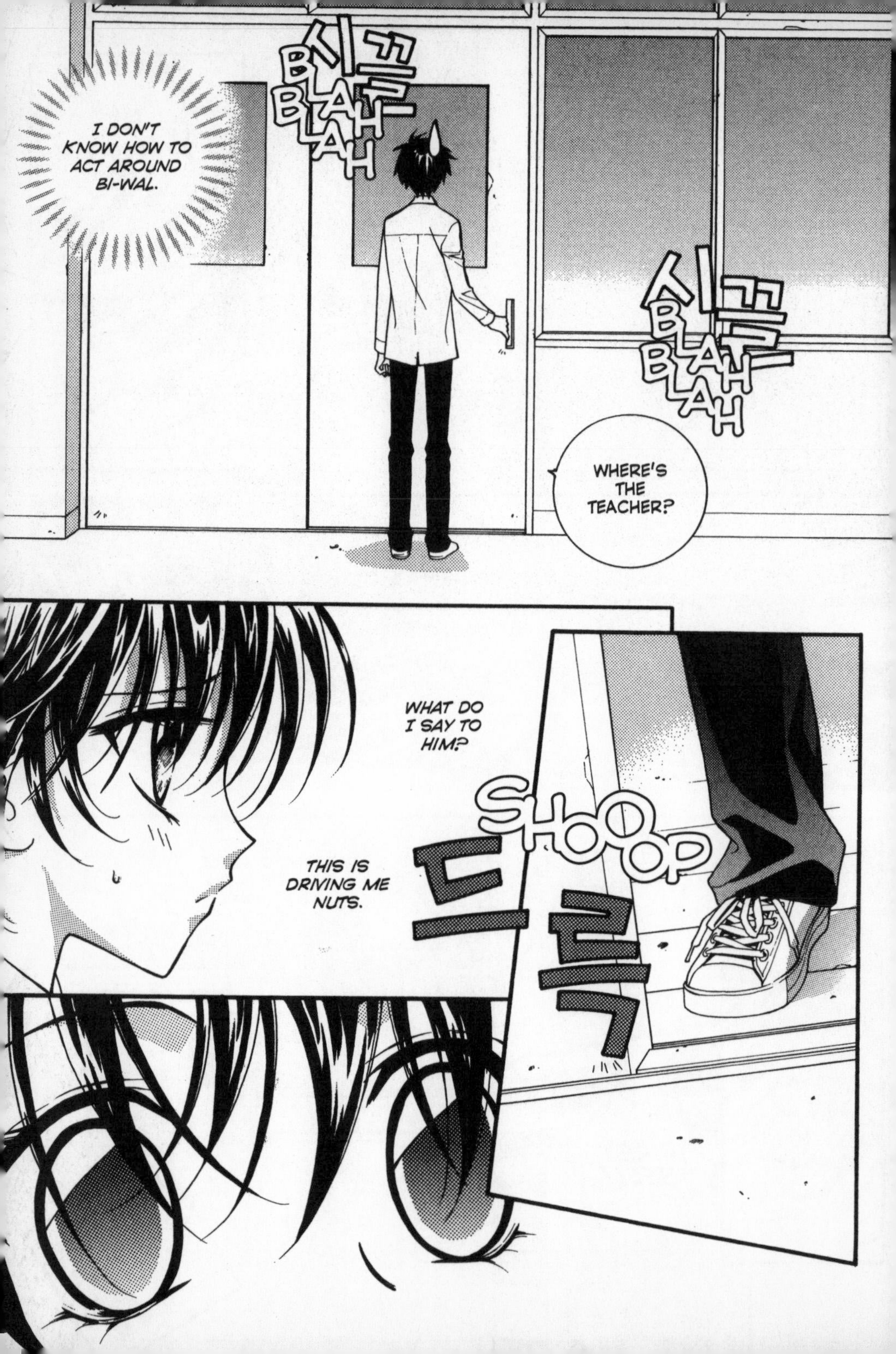
I DON'T KNOW HOW TO ACT AROUND BI-WAL.
BLAH BLAH
BLAH BLAH
WHERE'S THE TEACHER?
WHAT DO I SAY TO HIM?
THIS IS DRIVING ME NUTS.
SHOOOP

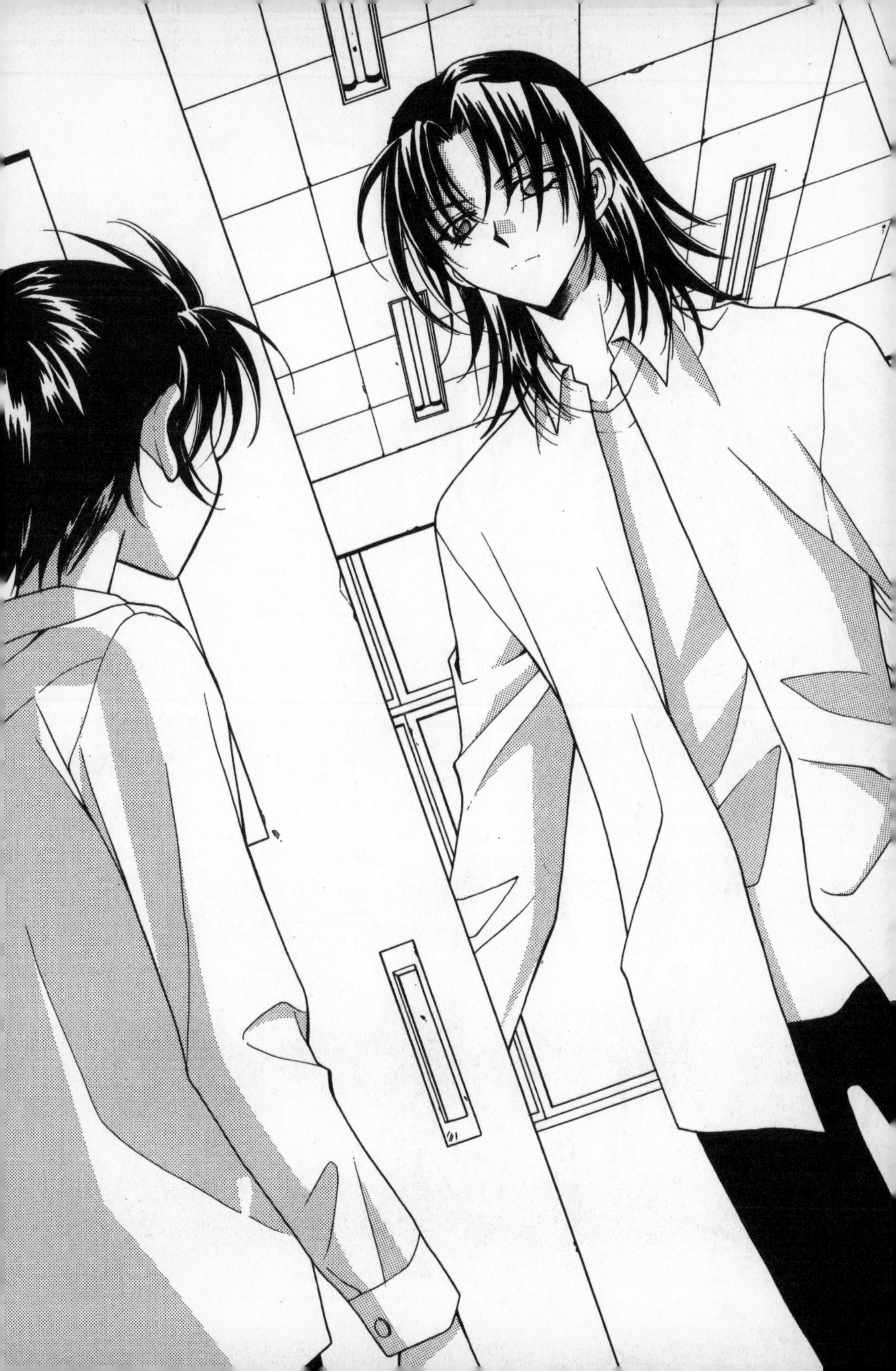

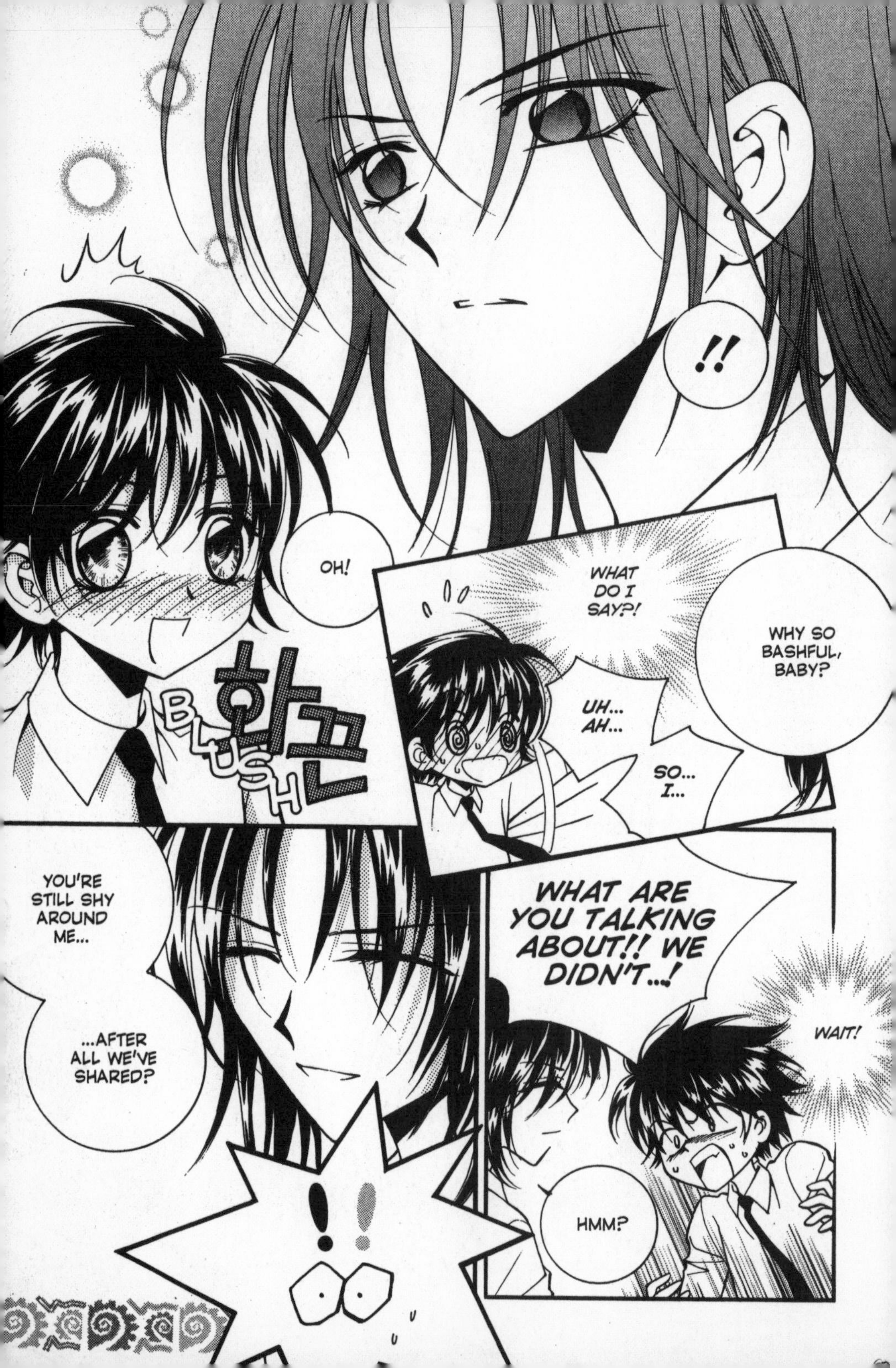

!!
OH!
BLUSH
화끈
WHAT DO I SAY?!
UH... AH...
SO... I...
WHY SO BASHFUL, BABY?
YOU'RE STILL SHY AROUND ME...
...AFTER ALL WE'VE SHARED?
!!
WHAT ARE YOU TALKING ABOUT!! WE DIDN'T...!
WAIT!
HMM?

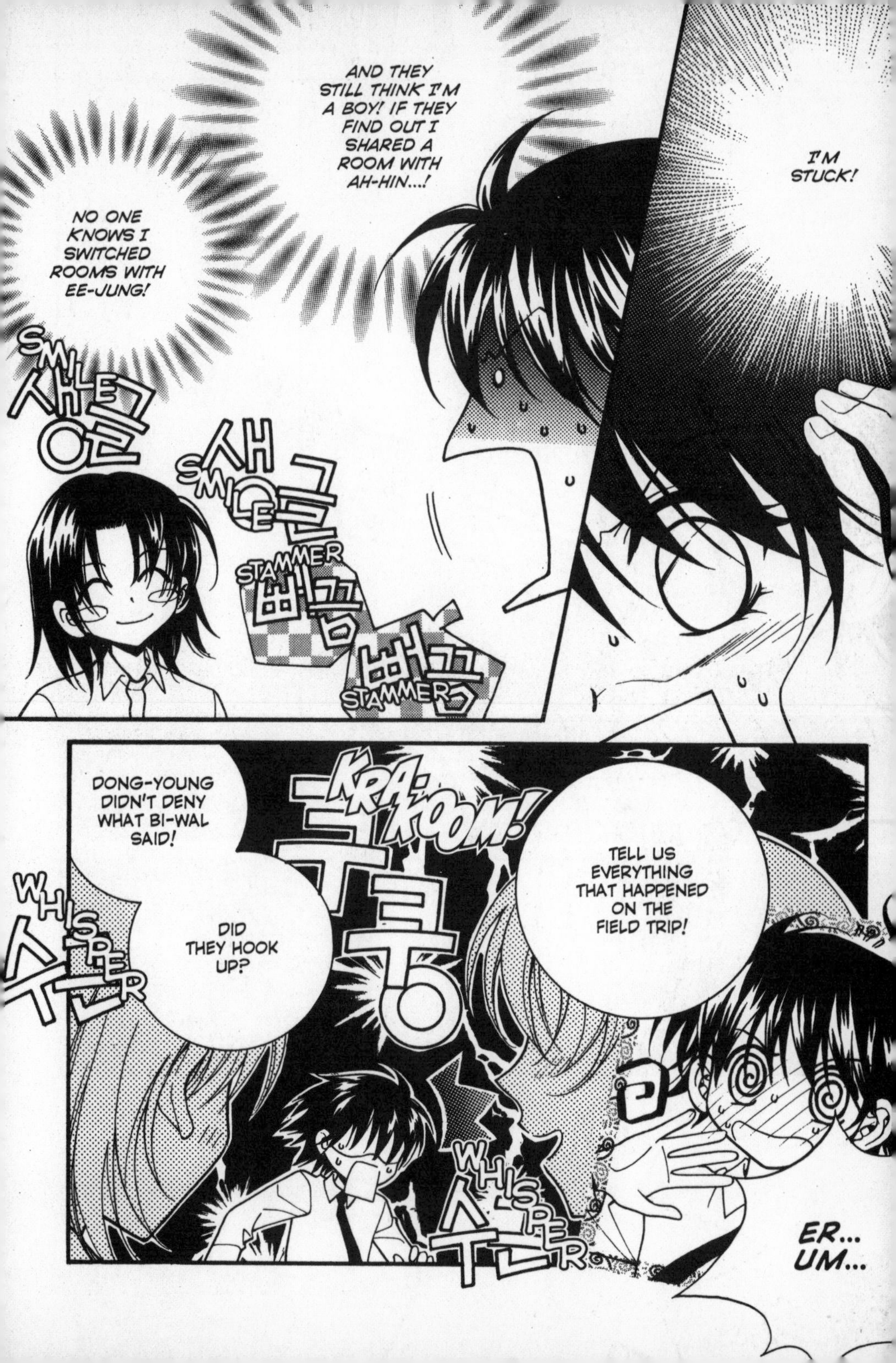
NO ONE KNOWS I SWITCHED ROOMS WITH EE-JUNG!
AND THEY STILL THINK I'M A BOY! IF THEY FIND OUT I SHARED A ROOM WITH AH-HIN...!
I'M STUCK!
생글 SMILE
생글 SMILE
STAMMER
STAMMER
DONG-YOUNG DIDN'T DENY WHAT BI-WAL SAID!
WHISPER
DID THEY HOOK UP?
KRA-KOOM!
TELL US EVERYTHING THAT HAPPENED ON THE FIELD TRIP!
WHISPER
ER... UM...

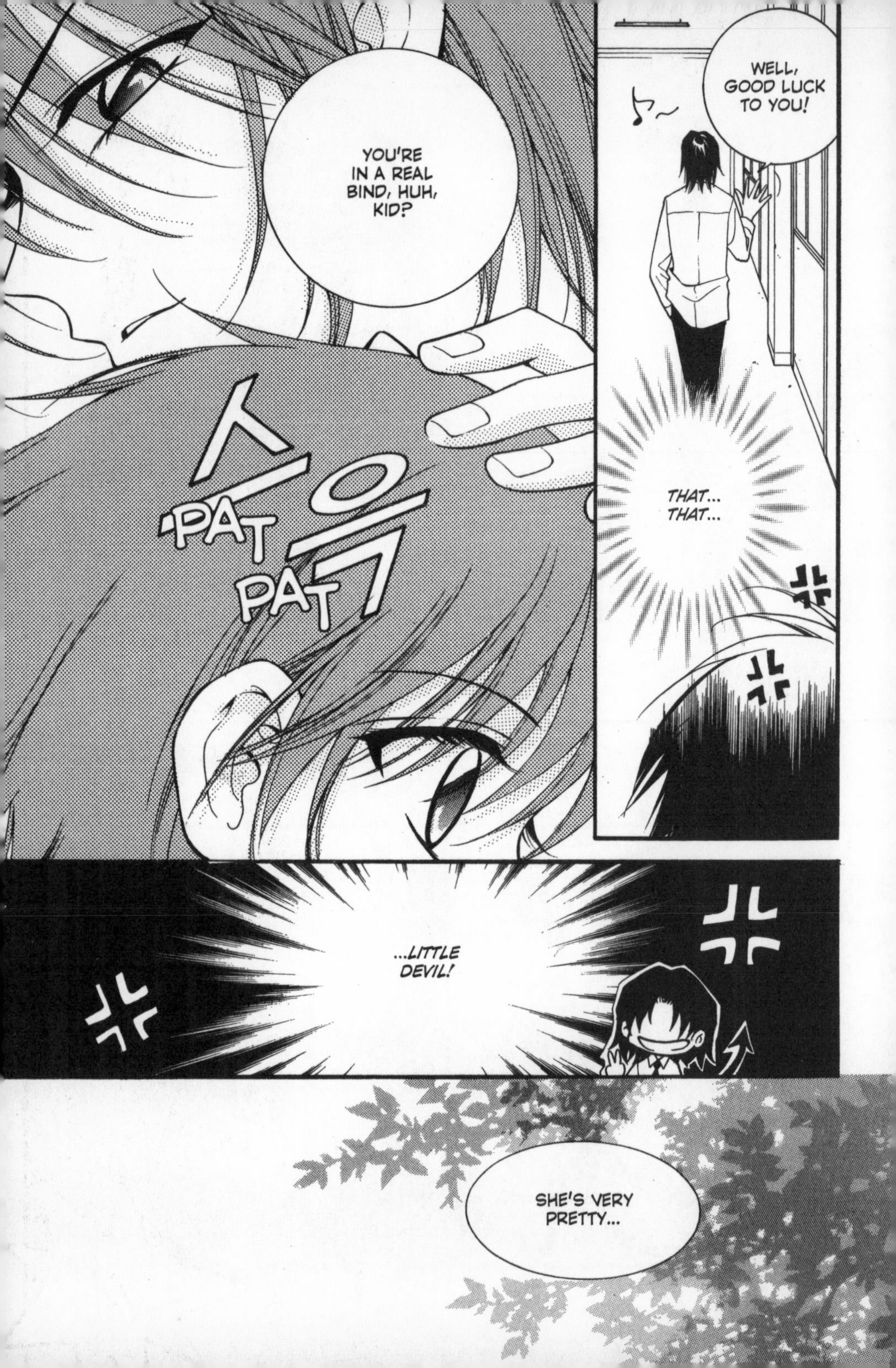
YOU'RE IN A REAL BIND, HUH, KID?
PAT PAT
WELL, GOOD LUCK TO YOU!
THAT... THAT...
...LITTLE DEVIL!
SHE'S VERY PRETTY...

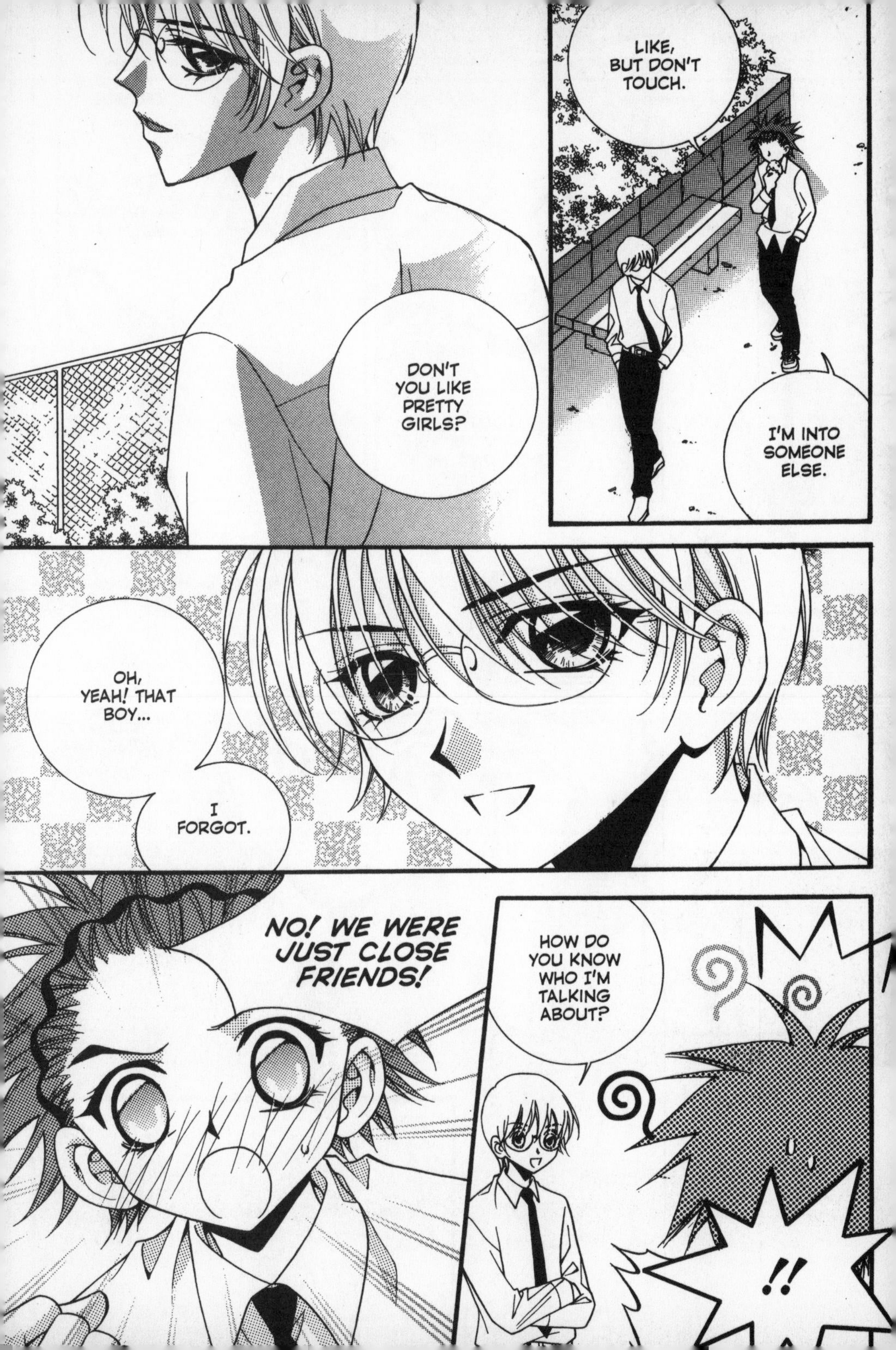
DON'T YOU LIKE PRETTY GIRLS?
LIKE, BUT DON'T TOUCH.
I'M INTO SOMEONE ELSE.
OH, YEAH! THAT BOY...
I FORGOT.
NO! WE WERE JUST CLOSE FRIENDS!
HOW DO YOU KNOW WHO I'M TALKING ABOUT?
!!

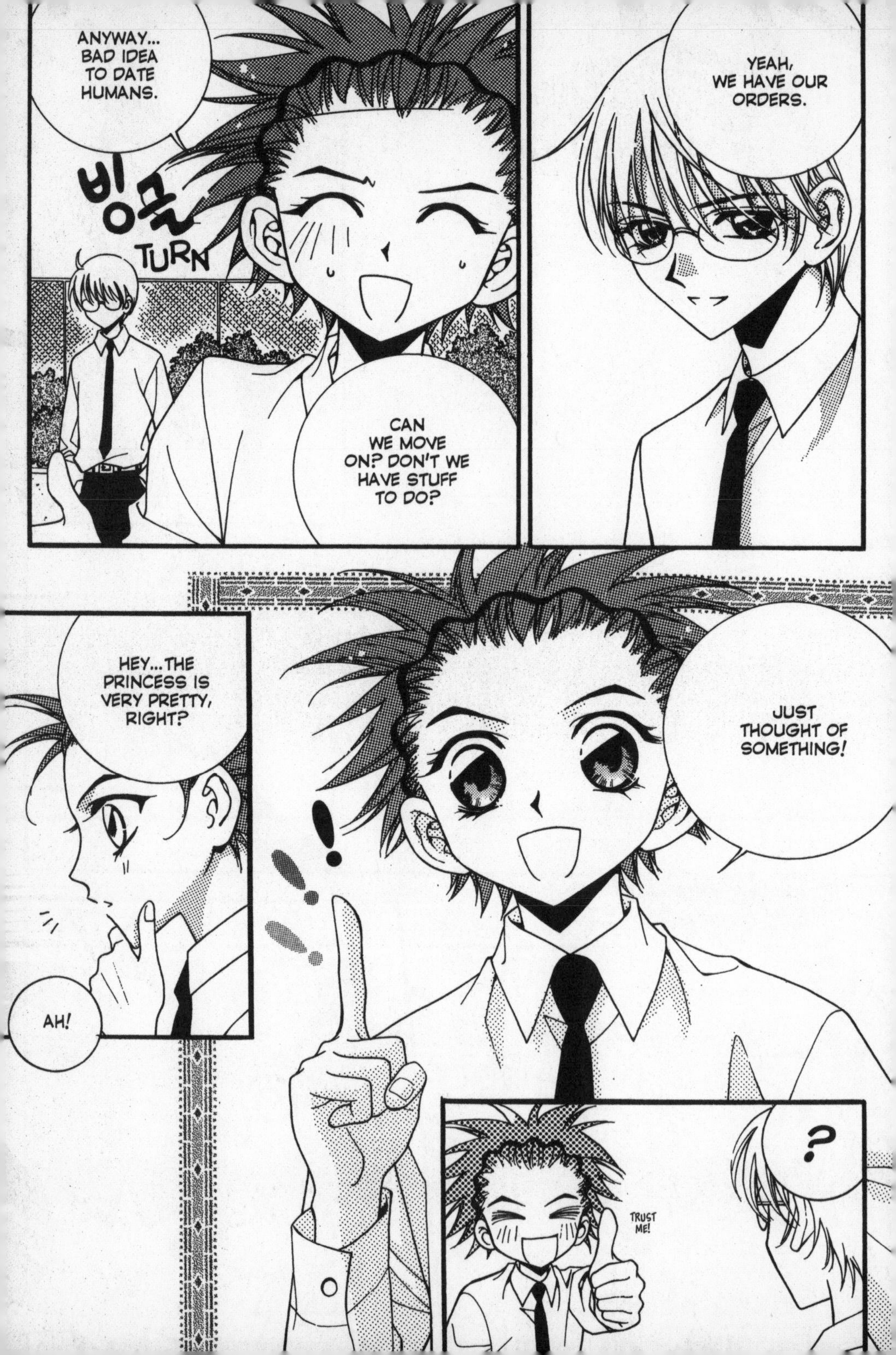
ANYWAY... BAD IDEA TO DATE HUMANS.
빙글
TURN
CAN WE MOVE ON? DON'T WE HAVE STUFF TO DO?
YEAH, WE HAVE OUR ORDERS.
HEY...THE PRINCESS IS VERY PRETTY, RIGHT?
AH!
JUST THOUGHT OF SOMETHING!
TRUST ME!
?

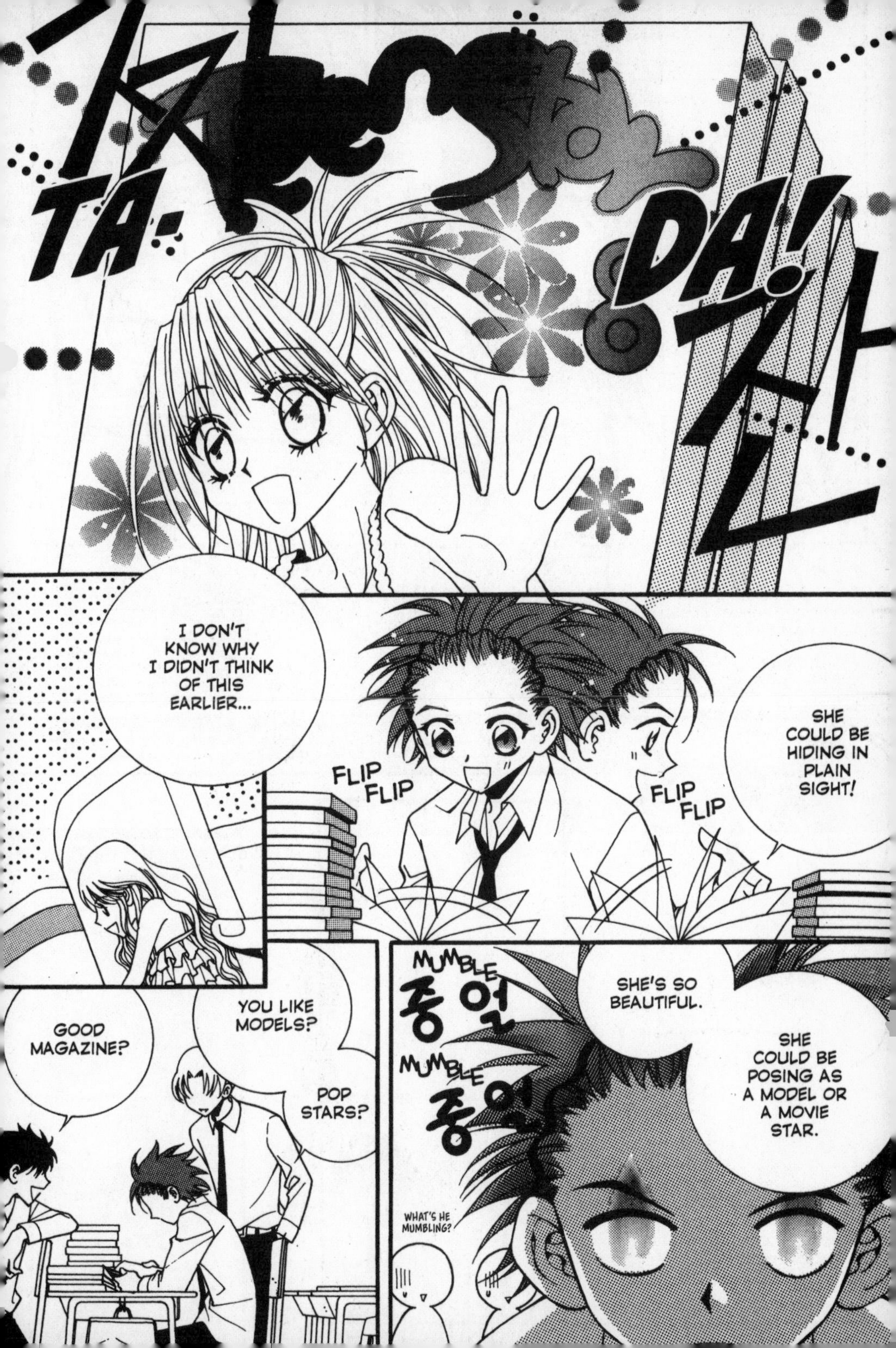
TA-
DA!
I DON'T KNOW WHY I DIDN'T THINK OF THIS EARLIER...
FLIP FLIP
FLIP FLIP
SHE COULD BE HIDING IN PLAIN SIGHT!
GOOD MAGAZINE?
YOU LIKE MODELS?
POP STARS?
MUMBLE
중얼
MUMBLE
중얼
SHE'S SO BEAUTIFUL.
SHE COULD BE POSING AS A MODEL OR A MOVIE STAR.
WHAT'S HE MUMBLING?

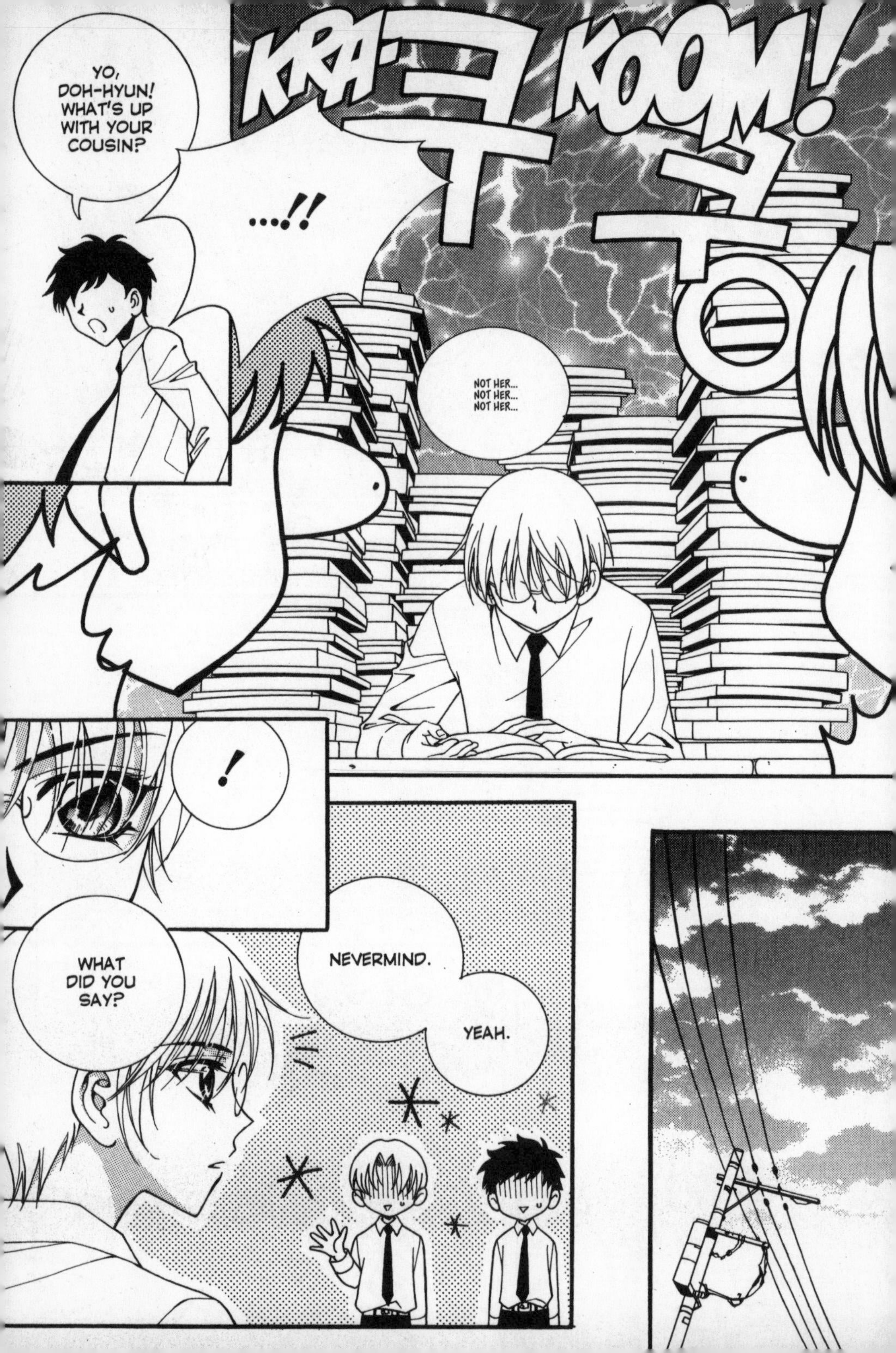
YO, DOH-HYUN! WHAT'S UP WITH YOUR COUSIN?
...!!
KRA- KOOM!
NOT HER... NOT HER... NOT HER...
!
WHAT DID YOU SAY?
NEVERMIND.
YEAH.

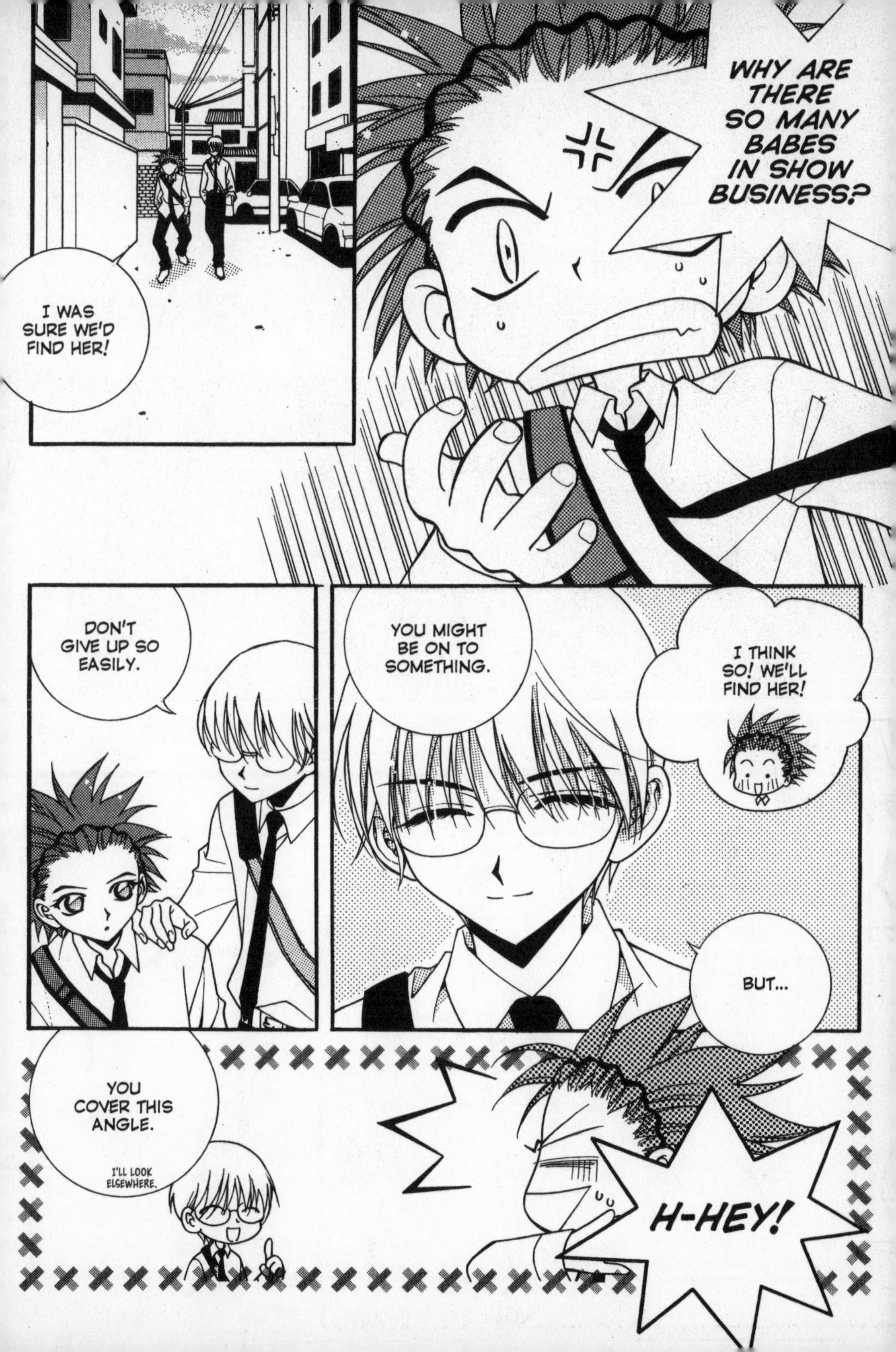
I WAS SURE WE'D FIND HER!
WHY ARE THERE SO MANY BABES IN SHOW BUSINESS?
DON'T GIVE UP SO EASILY.
YOU MIGHT BE ON TO SOMETHING.
I THINK SO! WE'LL FIND HER!
BUT...
YOU COVER THIS ANGLE.
I'LL LOOK ELSEWHERE.
H-HEY!

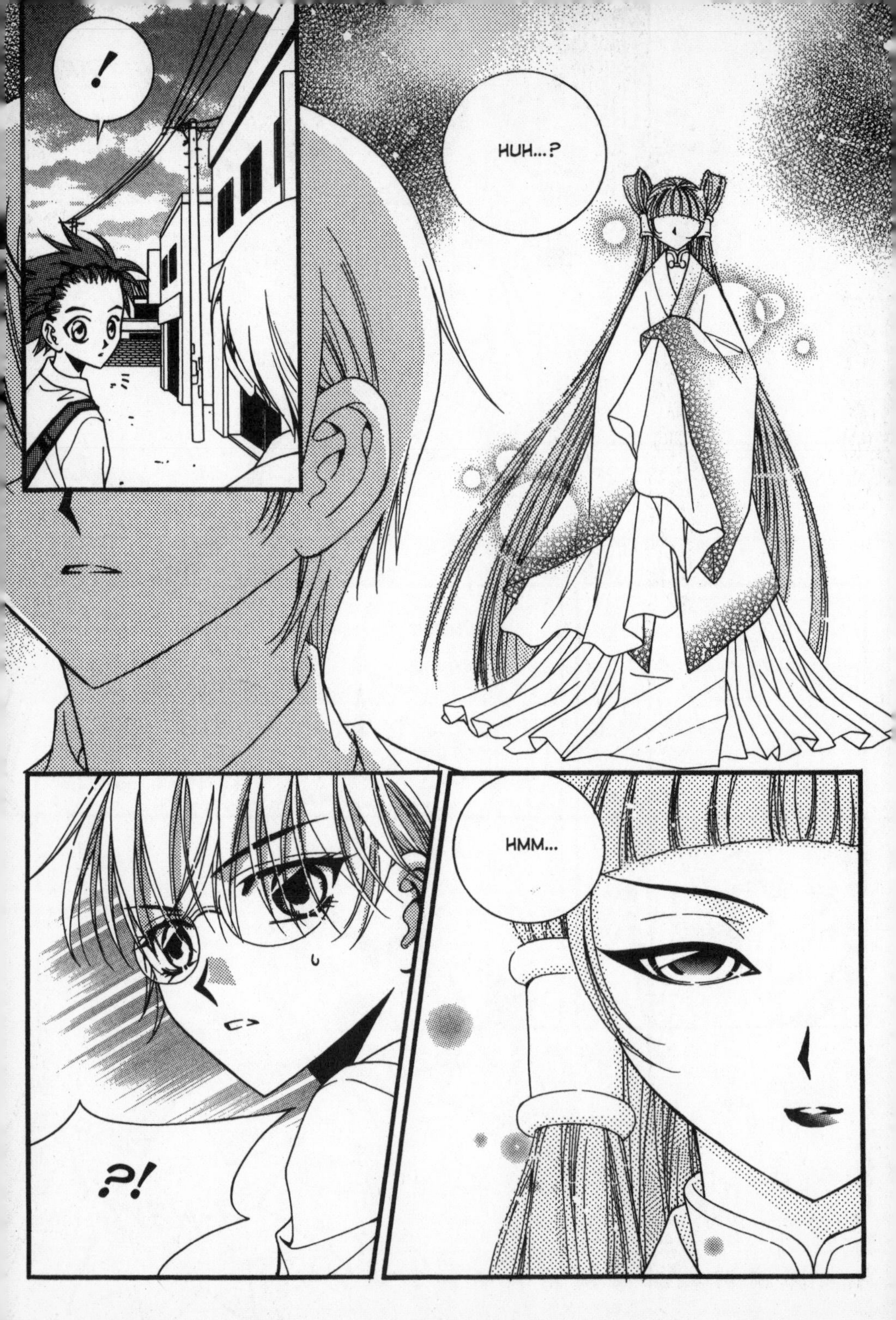
!
HUH...?
?!
HMM...

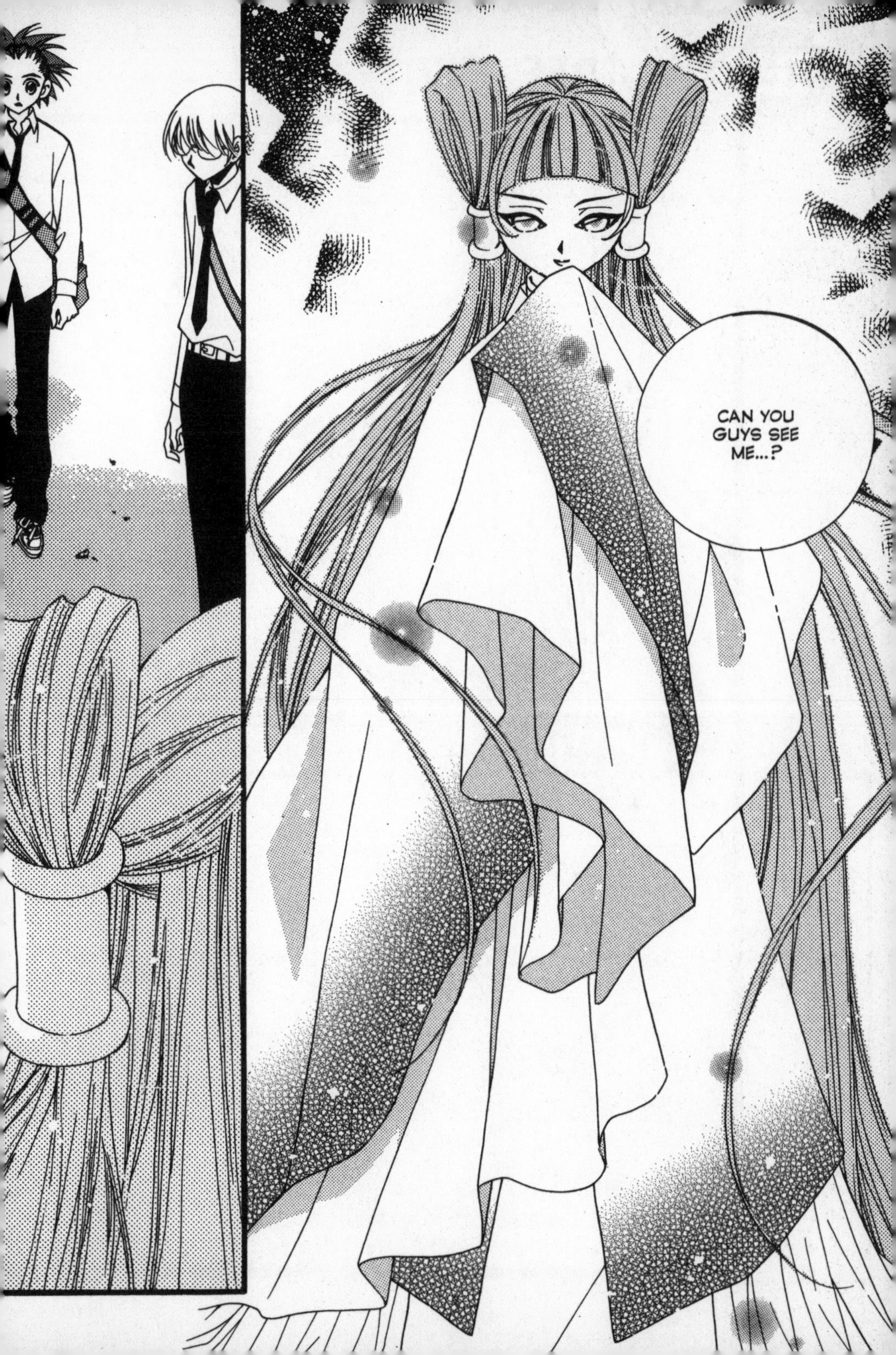
CAN YOU GUYS SEE ME...?

III THE TREE SPIRIT

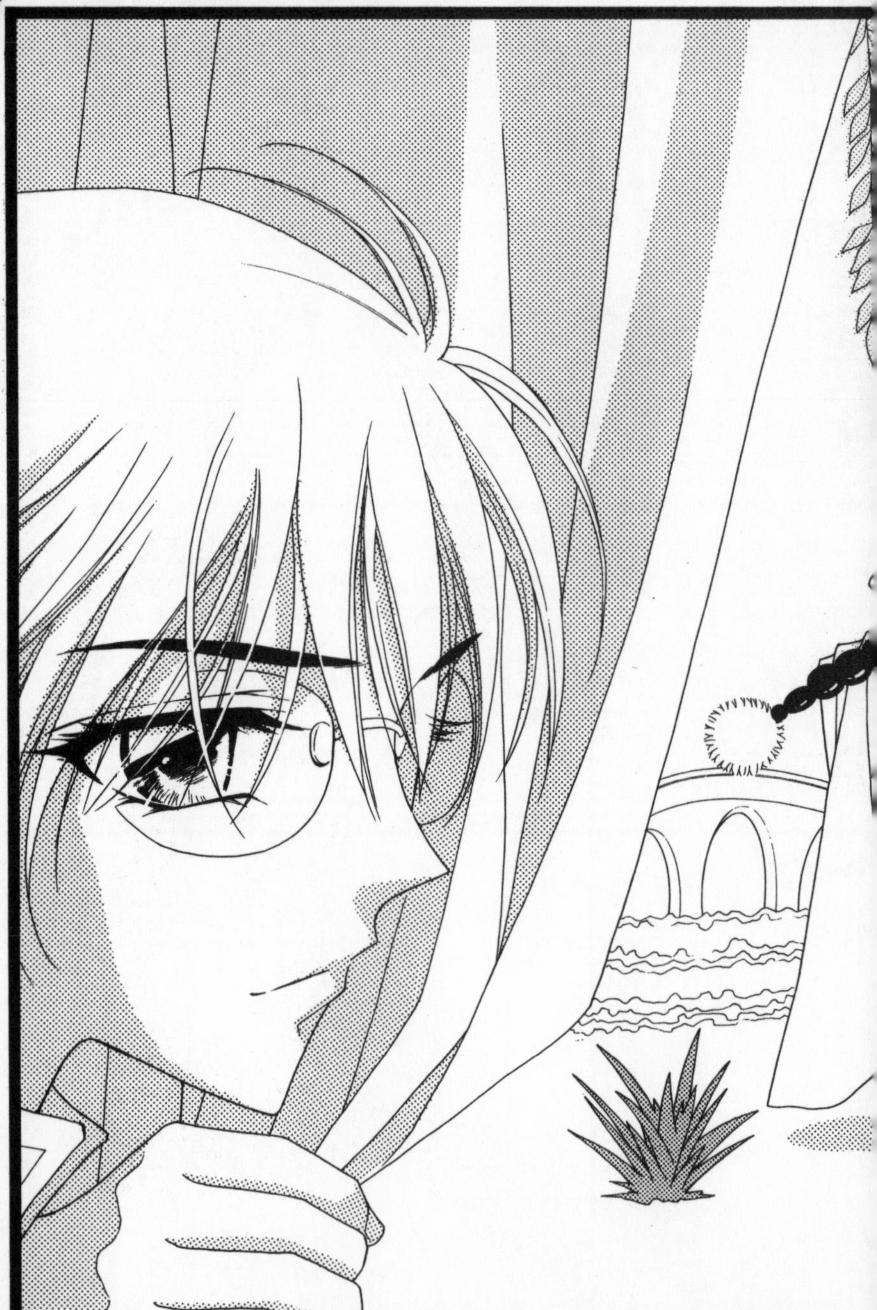

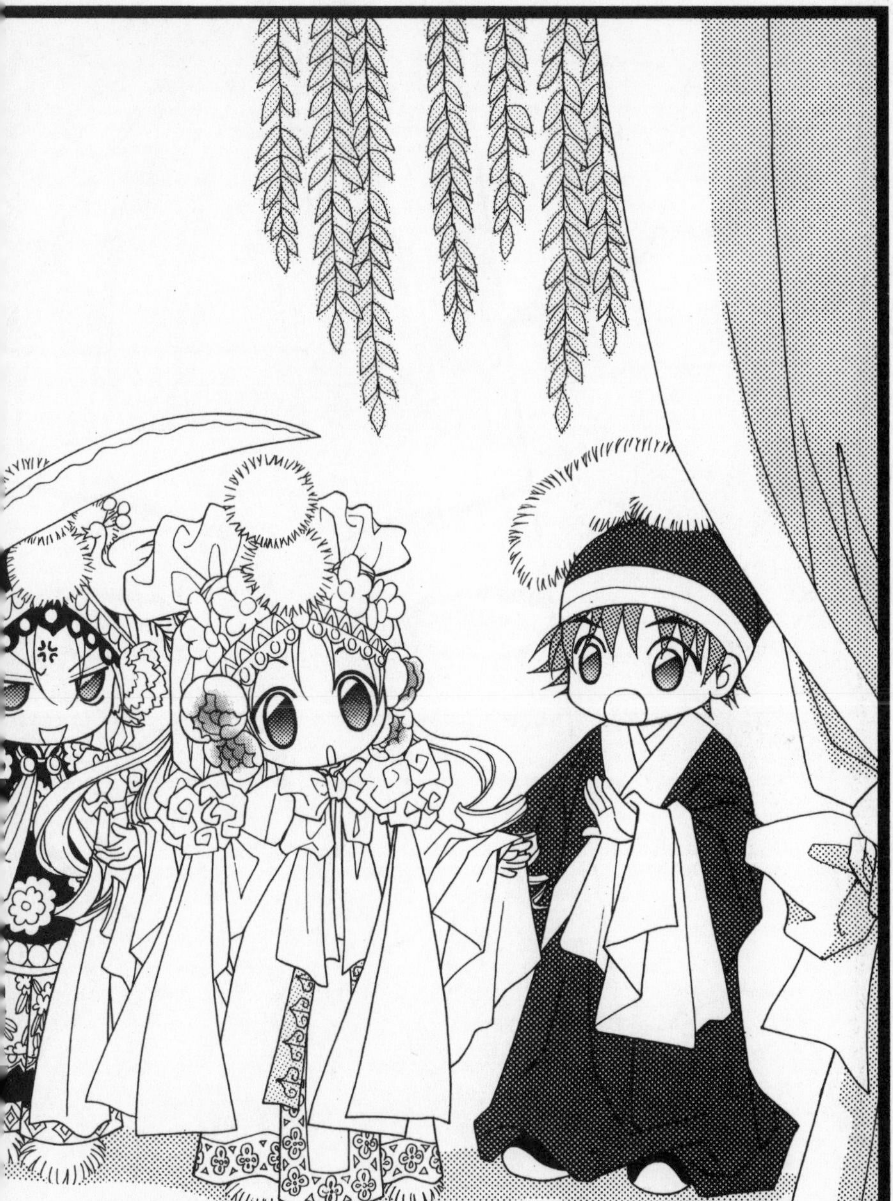

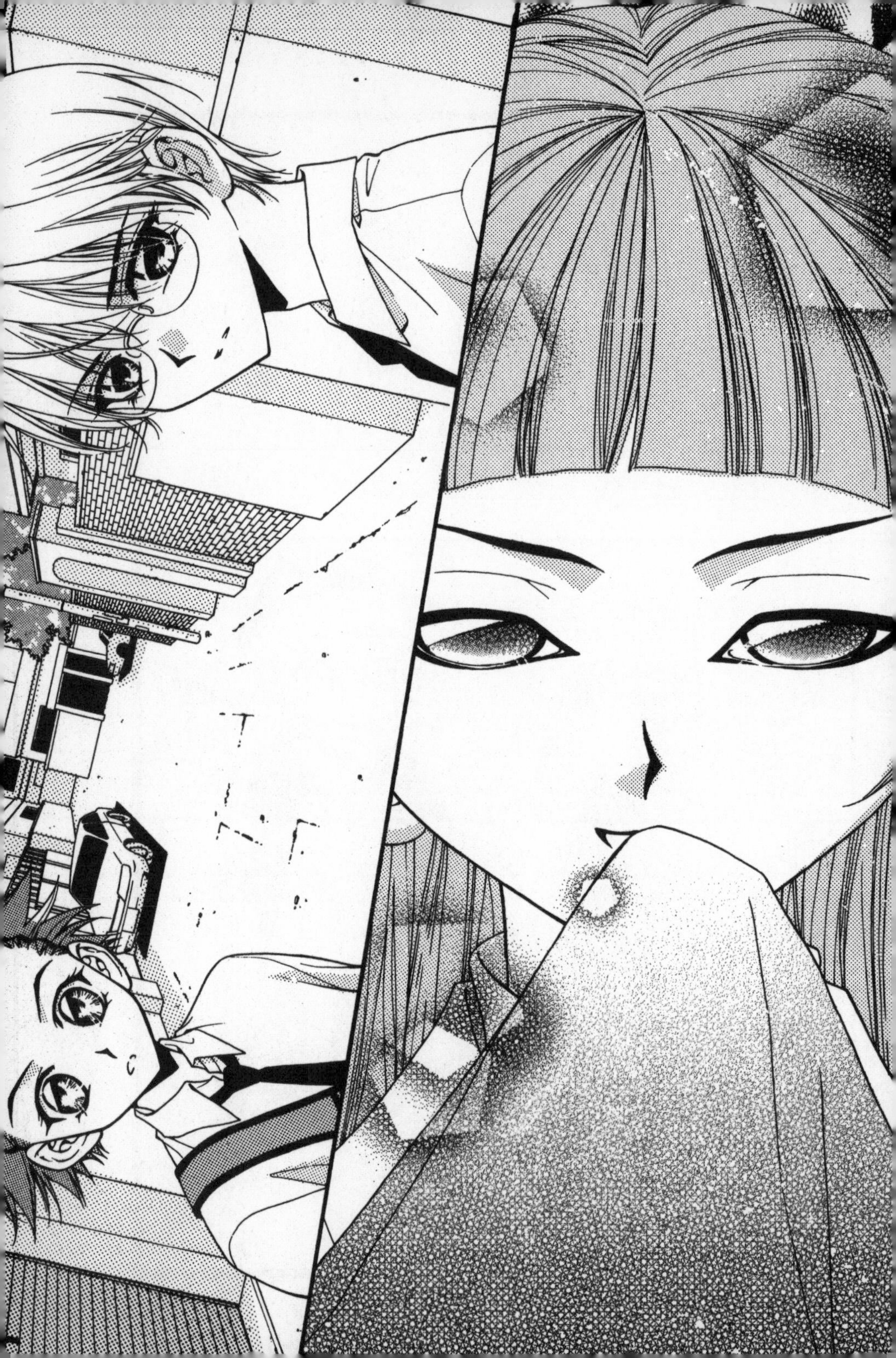

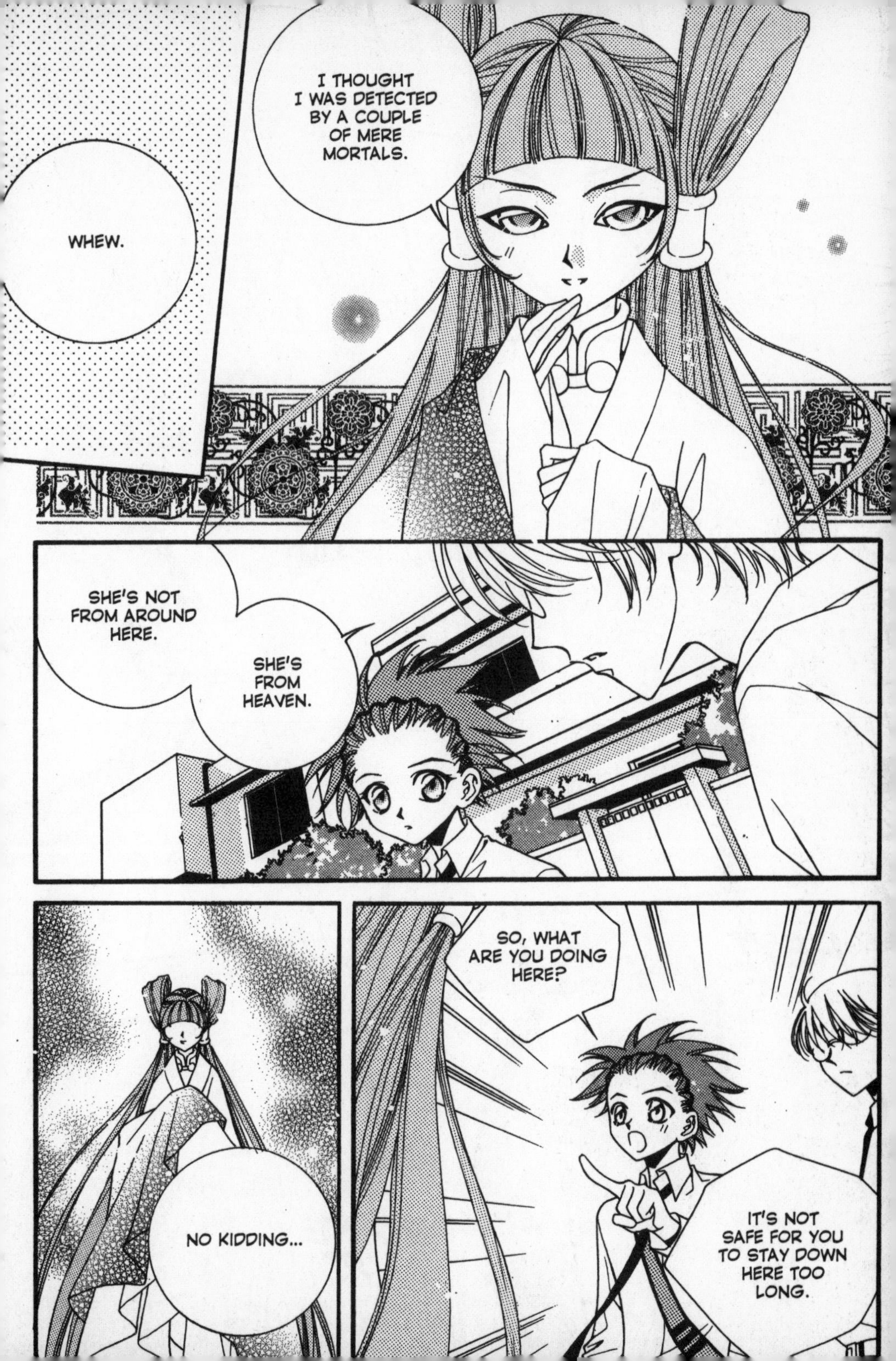
WHEW.
I THOUGHT I WAS DETECTED BY A COUPLE OF MERE MORTALS.
SHE'S NOT FROM AROUND HERE.
SHE'S FROM HEAVEN.
NO KIDDING...
SO, WHAT ARE YOU DOING HERE?
IT'S NOT SAFE FOR YOU TO STAY DOWN HERE TOO LONG.

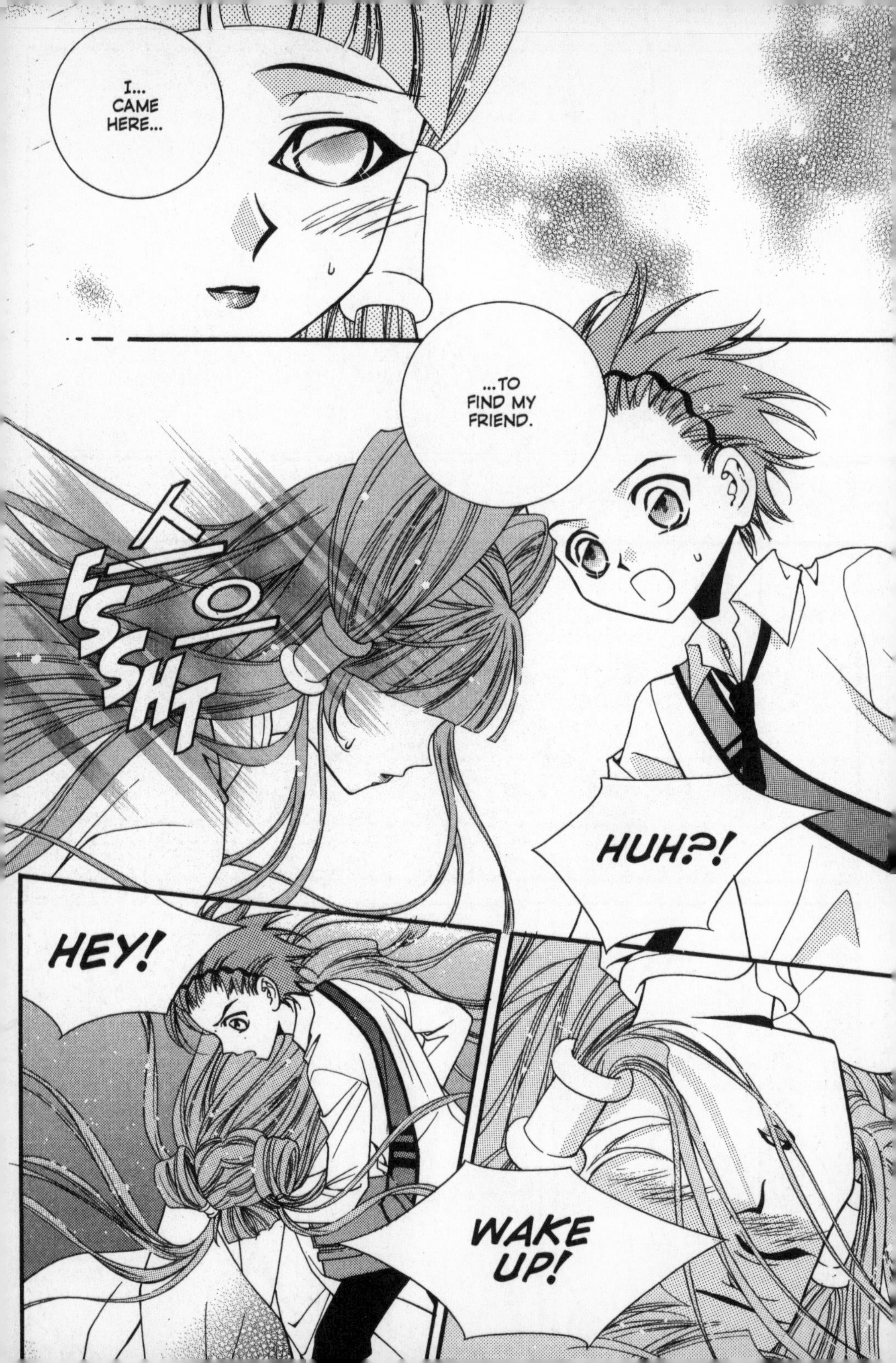
I... CAME HERE...
...TO FIND MY FRIEND.
FSSHT
HUH?!
HEY!
WAKE UP!

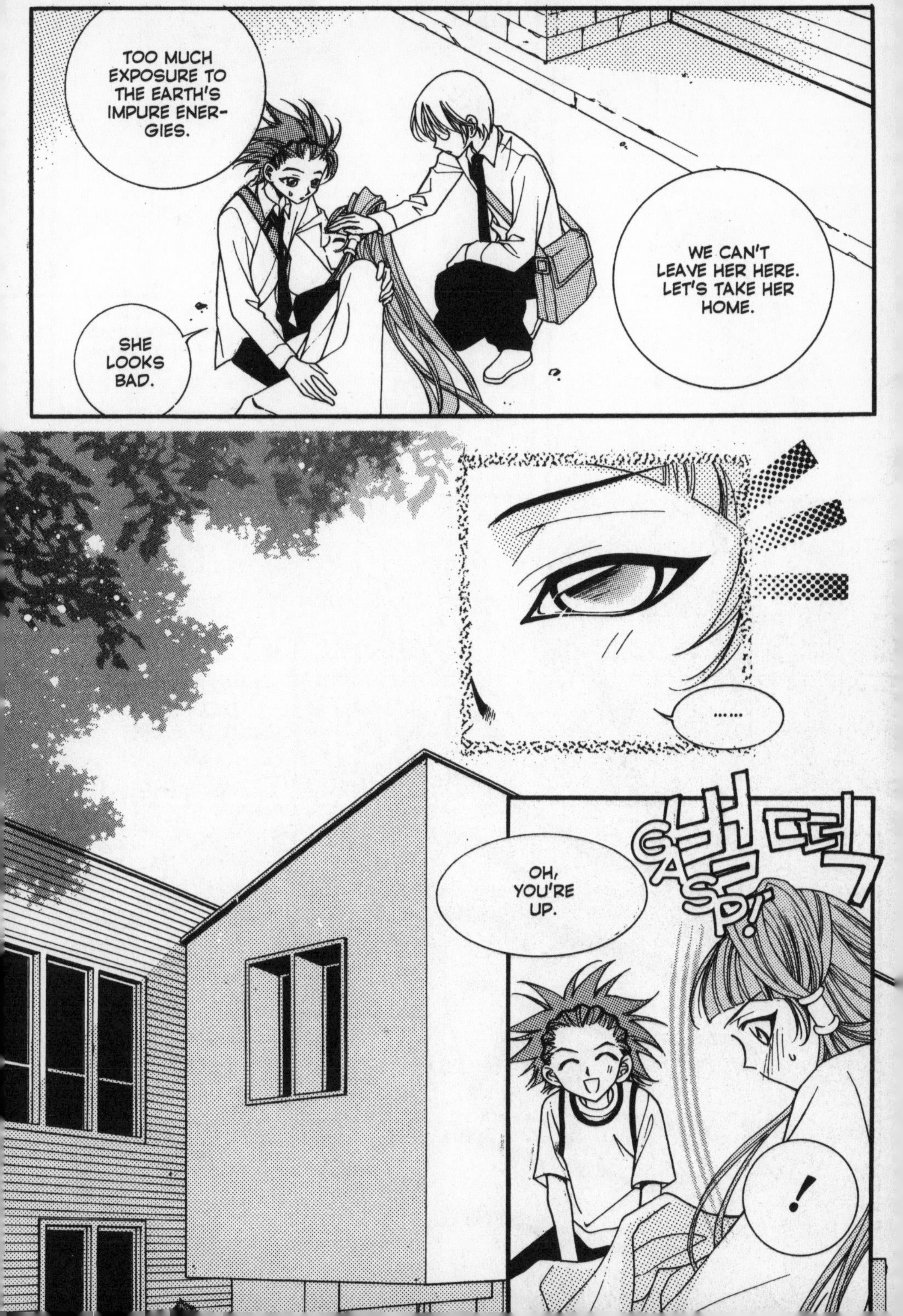
TOO MUCH EXPOSURE TO THE EARTH'S IMPURE ENER-GIES.
SHE LOOKS BAD.
WE CAN'T LEAVE HER HERE. LET'S TAKE HER HOME.
......
OH, YOU'RE UP.
GASP!
!

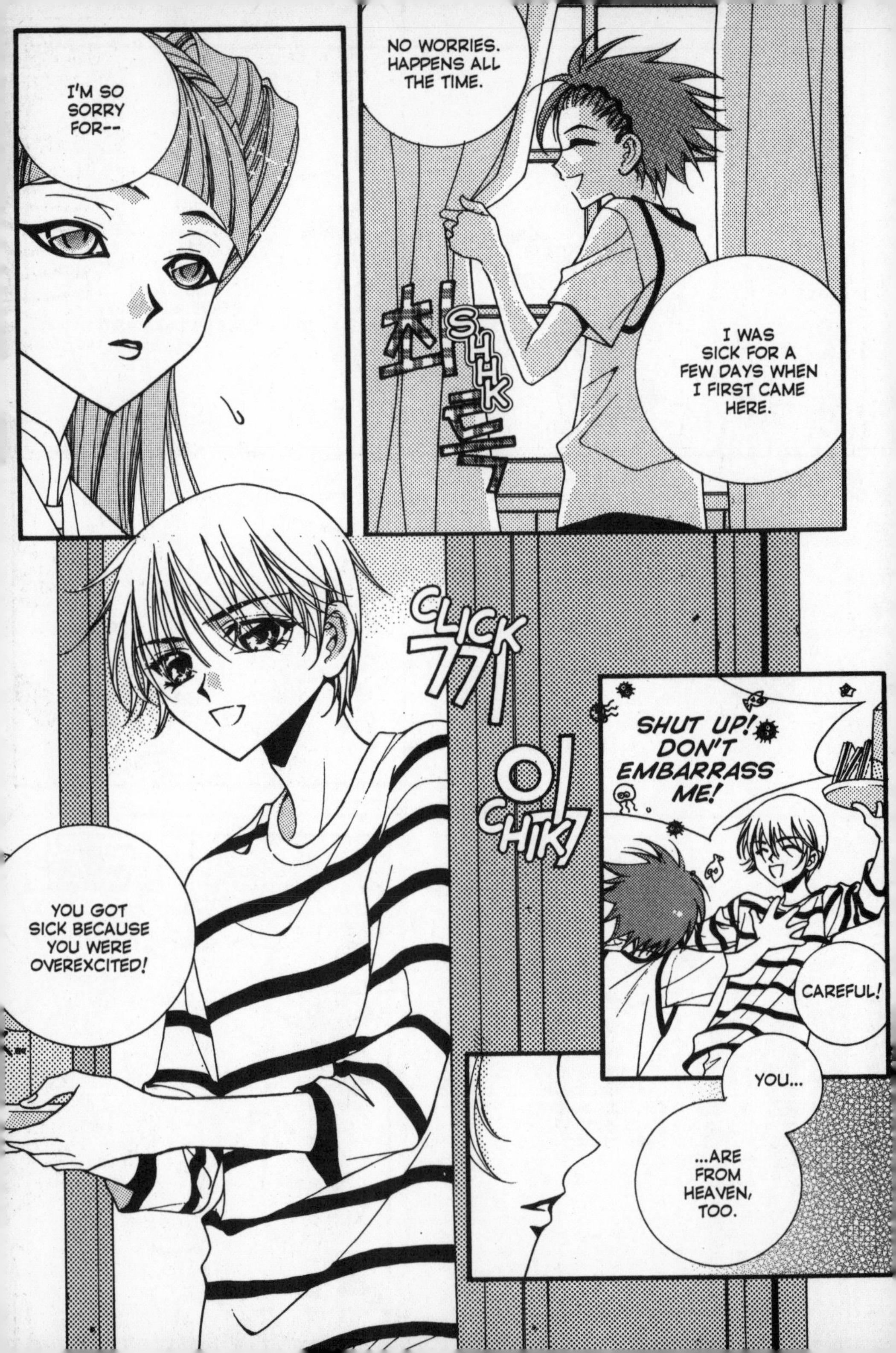
I'M SO SORRY FOR--
NO WORRIES. HAPPENS ALL THE TIME.
SHHK
I WAS SICK FOR A FEW DAYS WHEN I FIRST CAME HERE.
CLICK
CHIK
YOU GOT SICK BECAUSE YOU WERE OVEREXCITED!
SHUT UP! DON'T EMBARRASS ME!
CAREFUL!
YOU...
...ARE FROM HEAVEN, TOO.

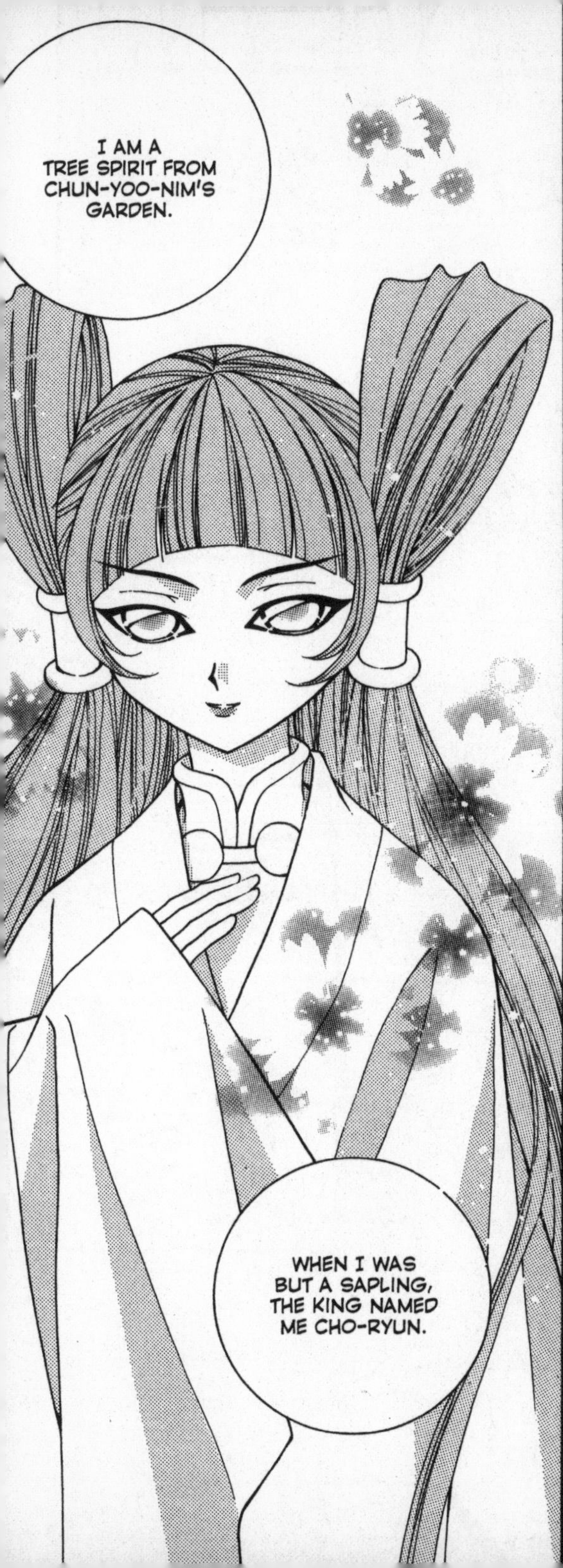
I AM A TREE SPIRIT FROM CHUN-YOO-NIM'S GARDEN.
WHEN I WAS BUT A SAPLING, THE KING NAMED ME CHO-RYUN.
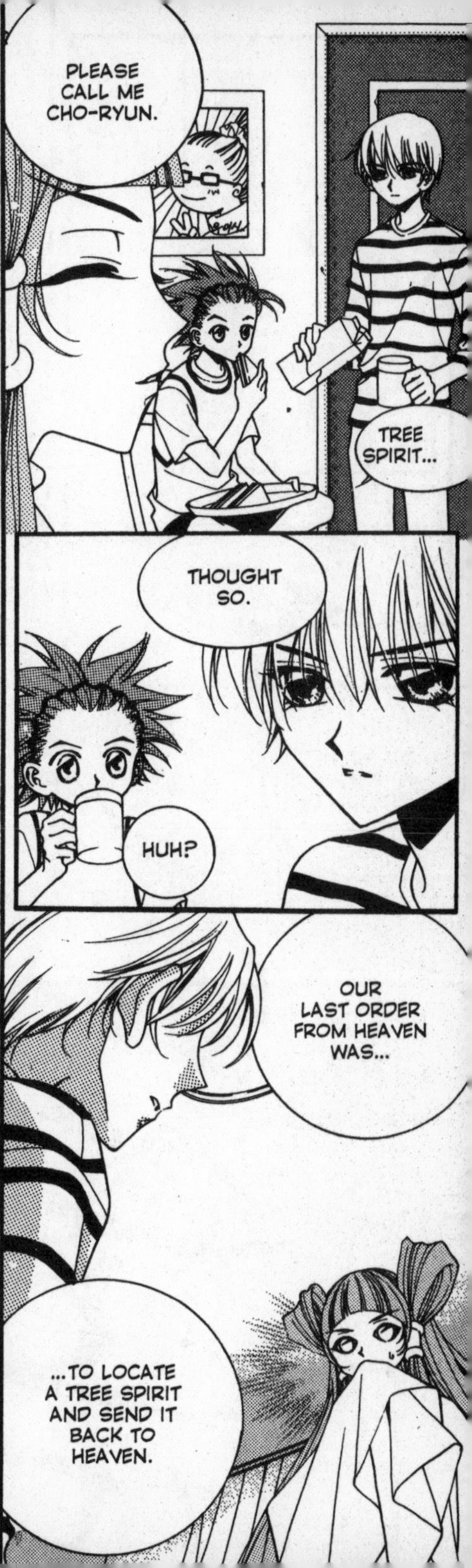
PLEASE CALL ME CHO-RYUN.
TREE SPIRIT...
THOUGHT SO.
HUH?
OUR LAST ORDER FROM HEAVEN WAS...
...TO LOCATE A TREE SPIRIT AND SEND IT BACK TO HEAVEN.

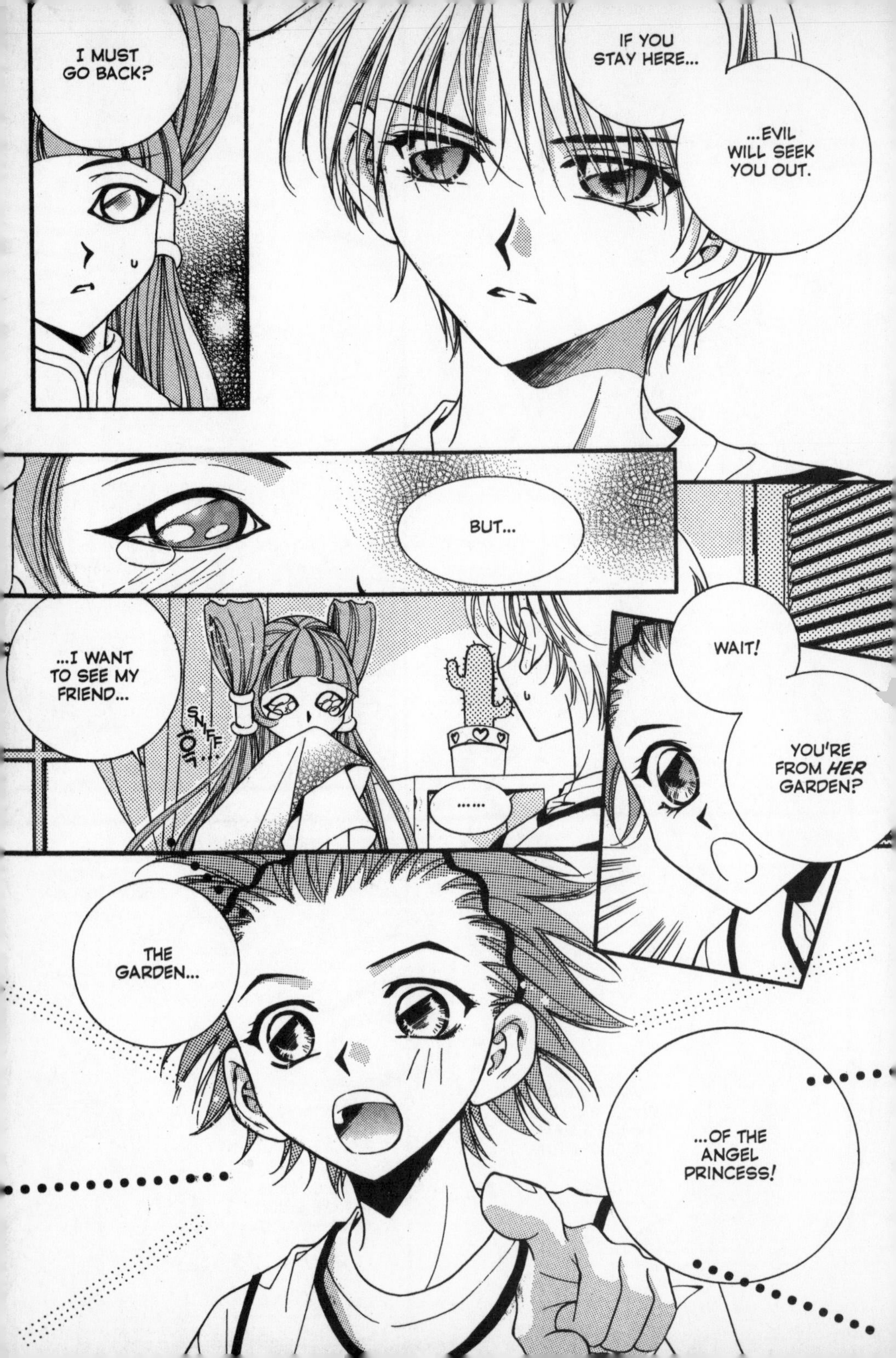
I MUST GO BACK?
IF YOU STAY HERE...
...EVIL WILL SEEK YOU OUT.
BUT...
...I WANT TO SEE MY FRIEND...
SNIFF
......
WAIT!
YOU'RE FROM *HER* GARDEN?
THE GARDEN...
...OF THE ANGEL PRINCESS!

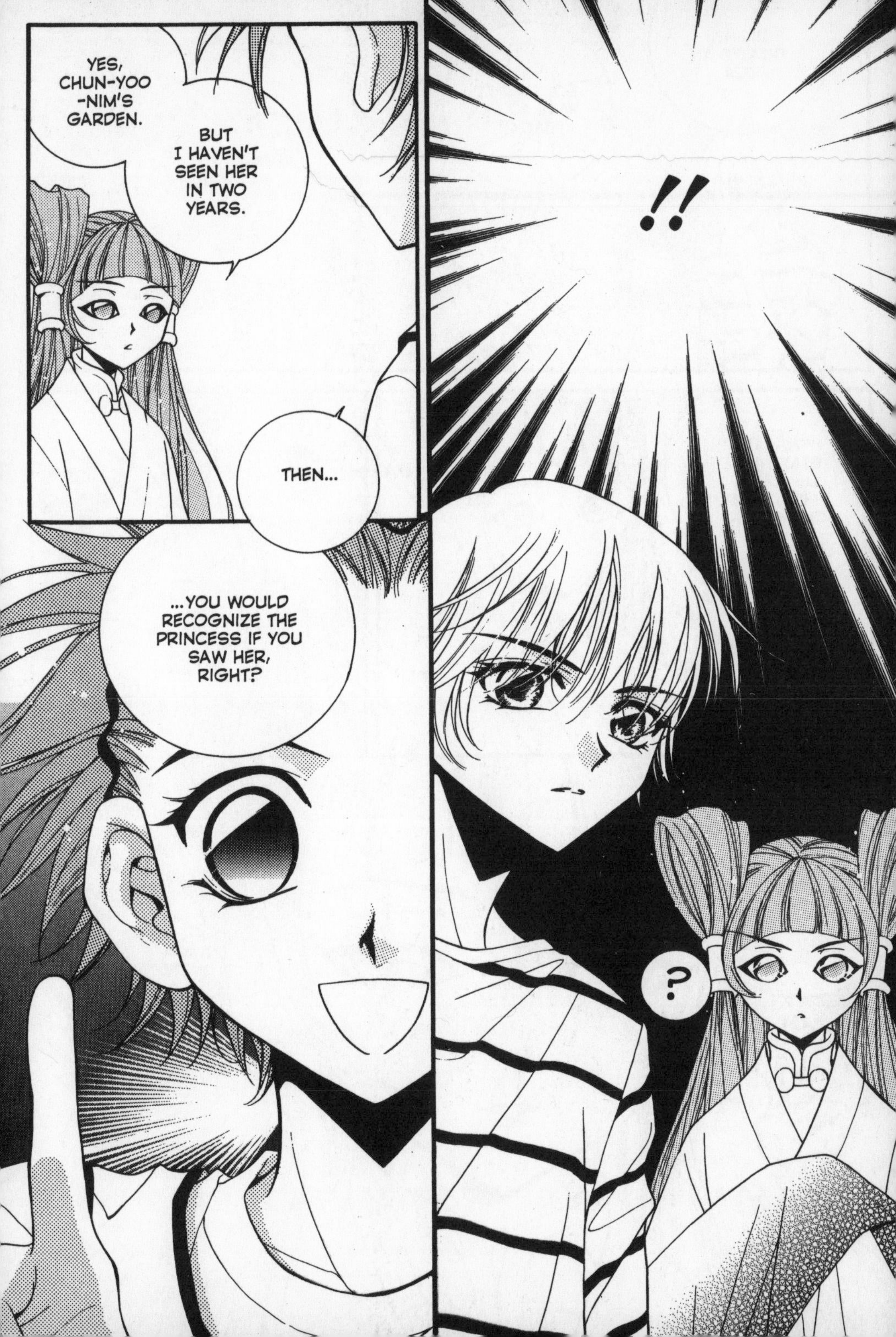
YES, CHUN-YOO -NIM'S GARDEN.
BUT I HAVEN'T SEEN HER IN TWO YEARS.
THEN...
...YOU WOULD RECOGNIZE THE PRINCESS IF YOU SAW HER, RIGHT?
!!
?

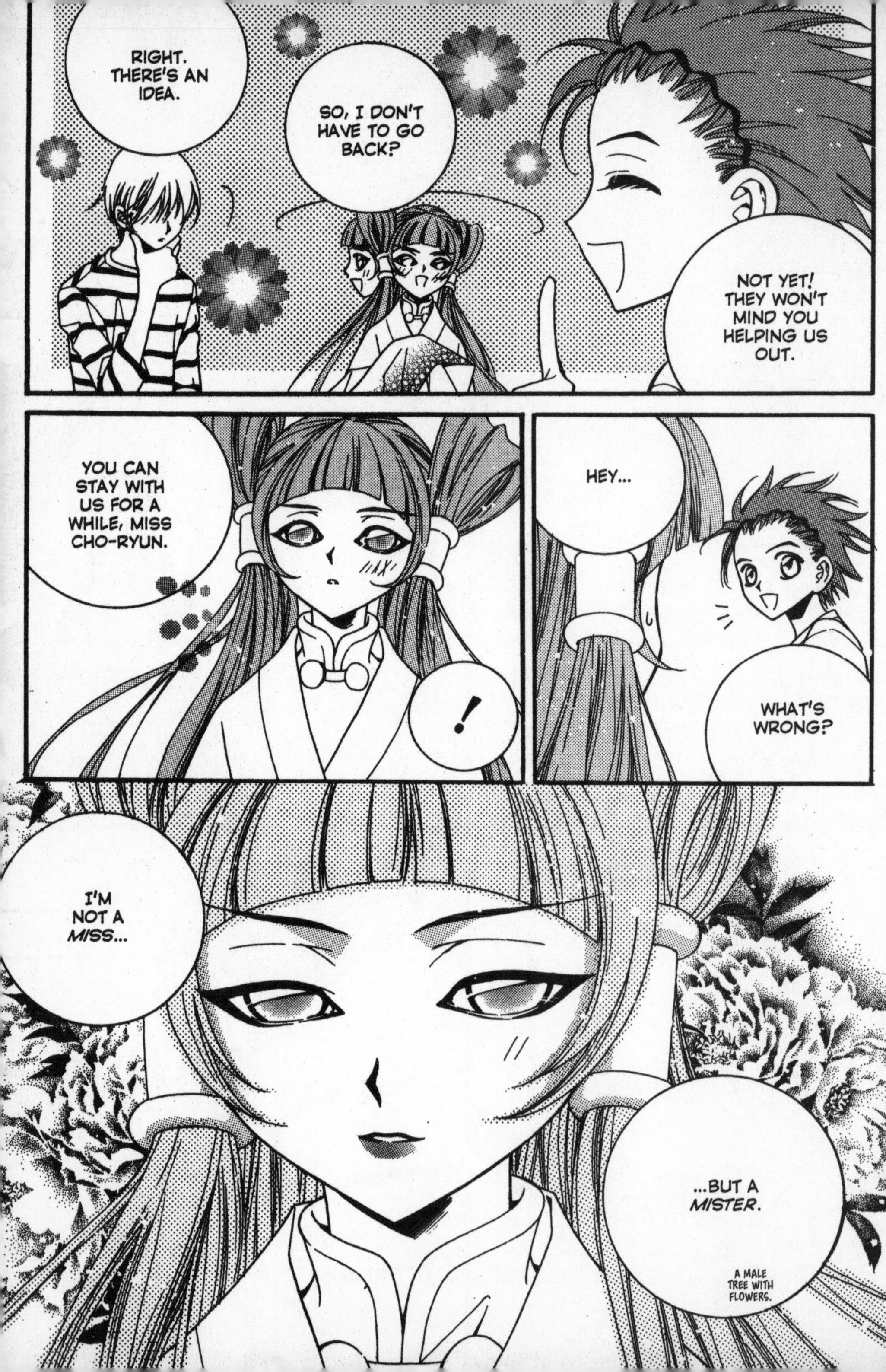
RIGHT. THERE'S AN IDEA.
SO, I DON'T HAVE TO GO BACK?
NOT YET! THEY WON'T MIND YOU HELPING US OUT.
YOU CAN STAY WITH US FOR A WHILE, MISS CHO-RYUN.
!
HEY...
WHAT'S WRONG?
I'M NOT A *MISS*...
...BUT A *MISTER*.
A MALE TREE WITH FLOWERS.

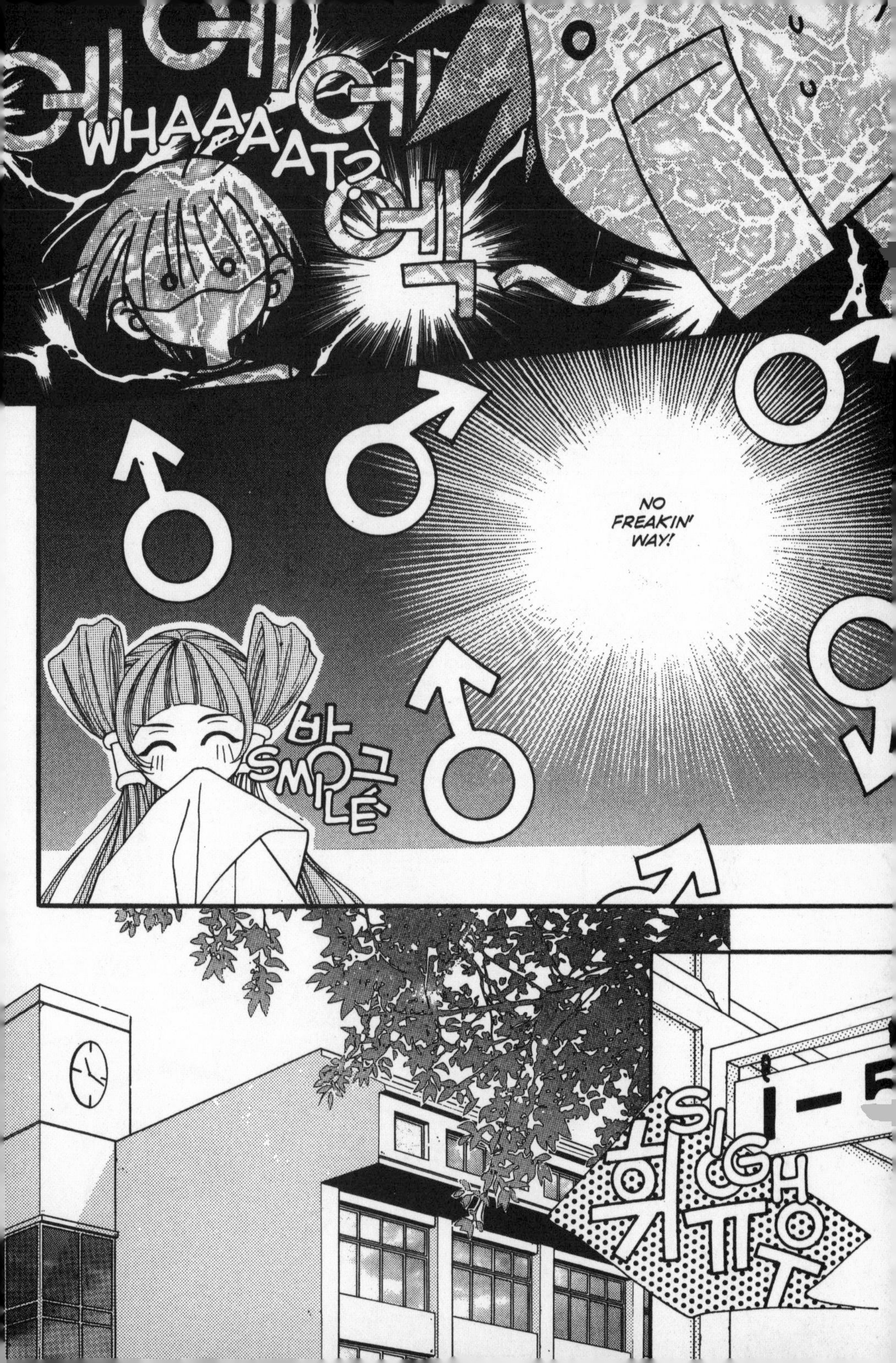

WHAAAAT?
NO FREAKIN' WAY!
SMILE
1-5
SIGH

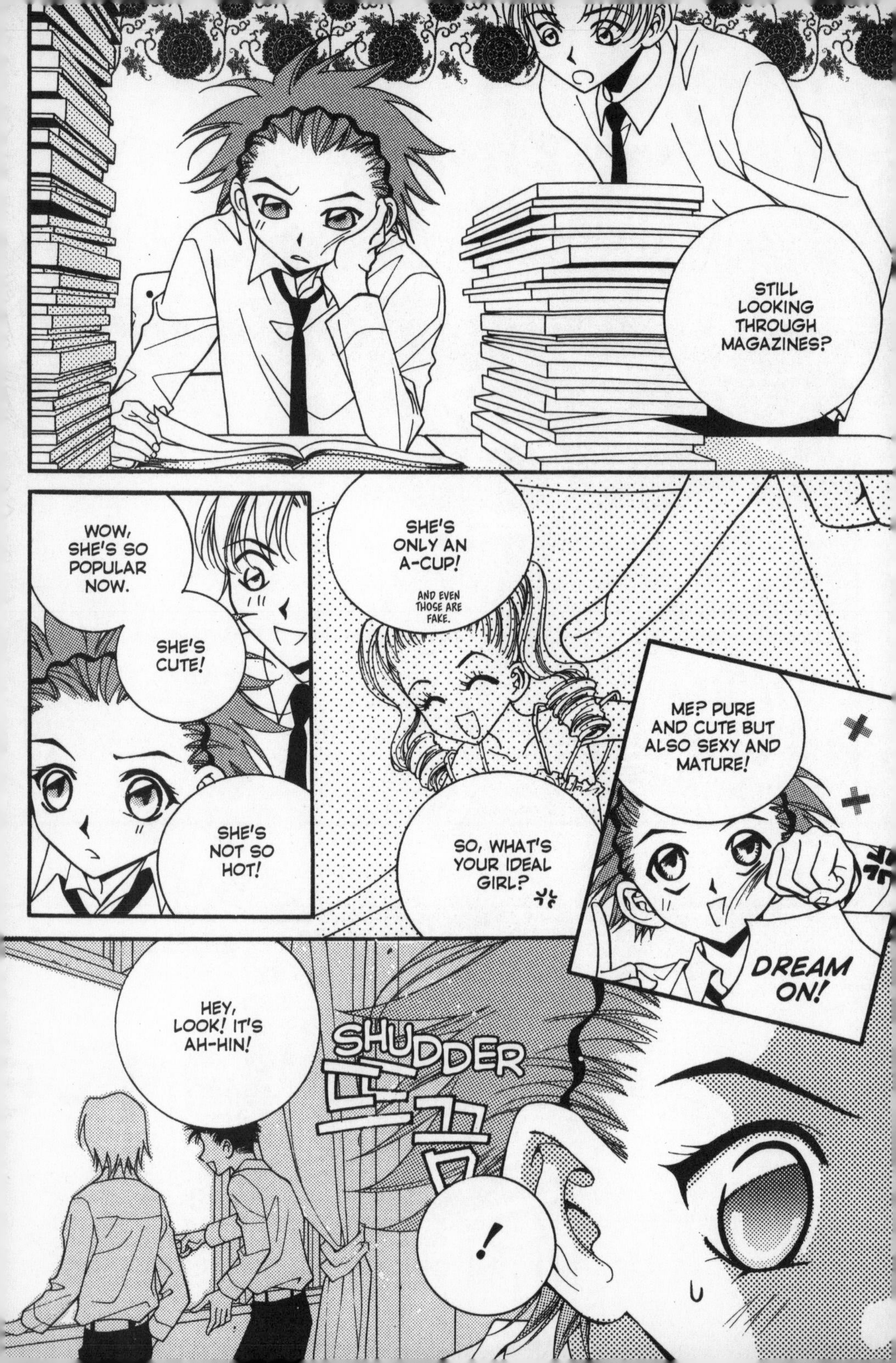
STILL LOOKING THROUGH MAGAZINES?
WOW, SHE'S SO POPULAR NOW.
SHE'S CUTE!
SHE'S NOT SO HOT!
SHE'S ONLY AN A-CUP!
AND EVEN THOSE ARE FAKE.
SO, WHAT'S YOUR IDEAL GIRL?
ME? PURE AND CUTE BUT ALSO SEXY AND MATURE!
DREAM ON!
HEY, LOOK! IT'S AH-HIN!
SHUDDER
!

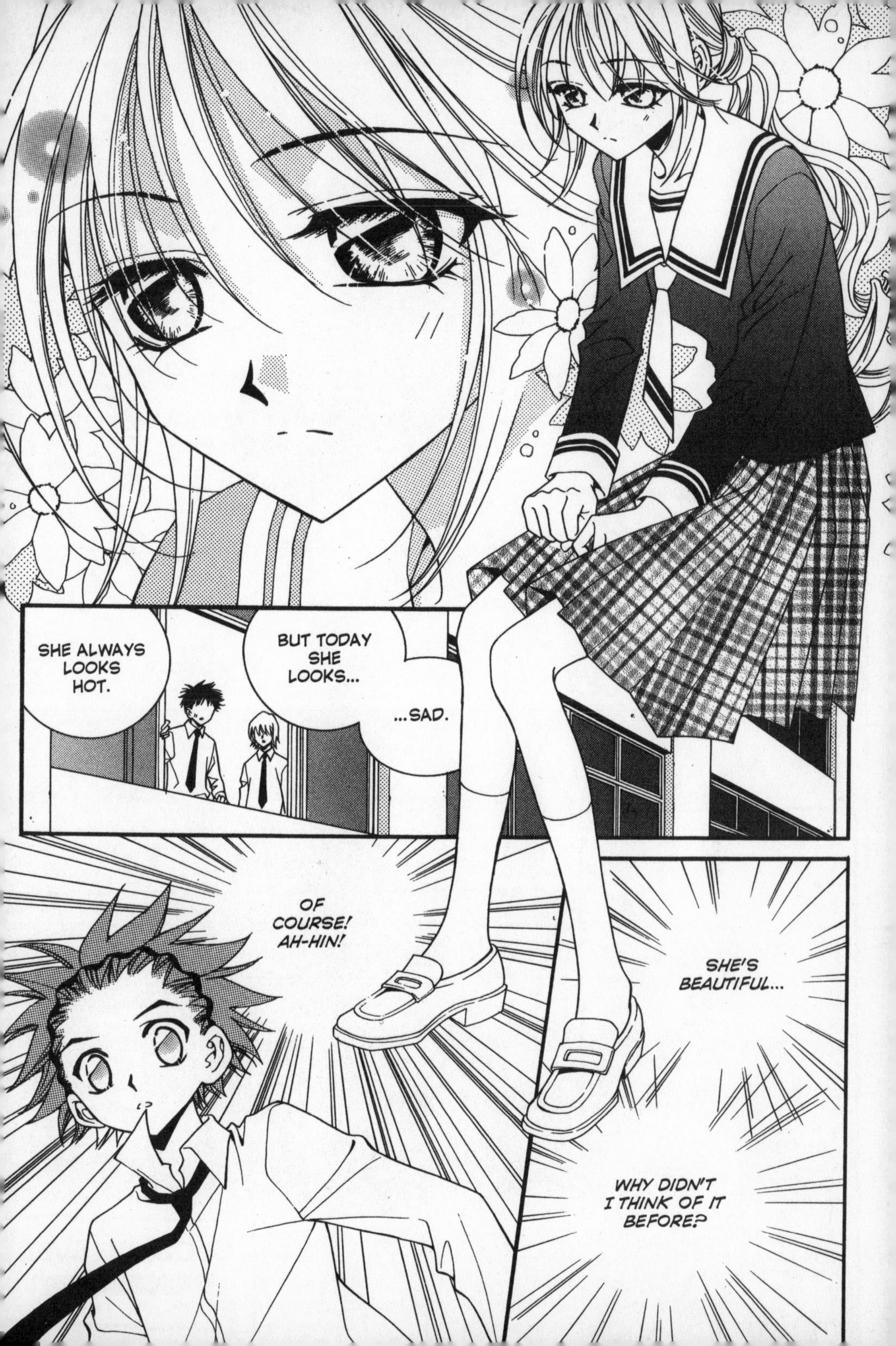
SHE ALWAYS LOOKS HOT.
BUT TODAY SHE LOOKS...
...SAD.
OF COURSE! AH-HIN!
SHE'S BEAUTIFUL...
WHY DIDN'T I THINK OF IT BEFORE?

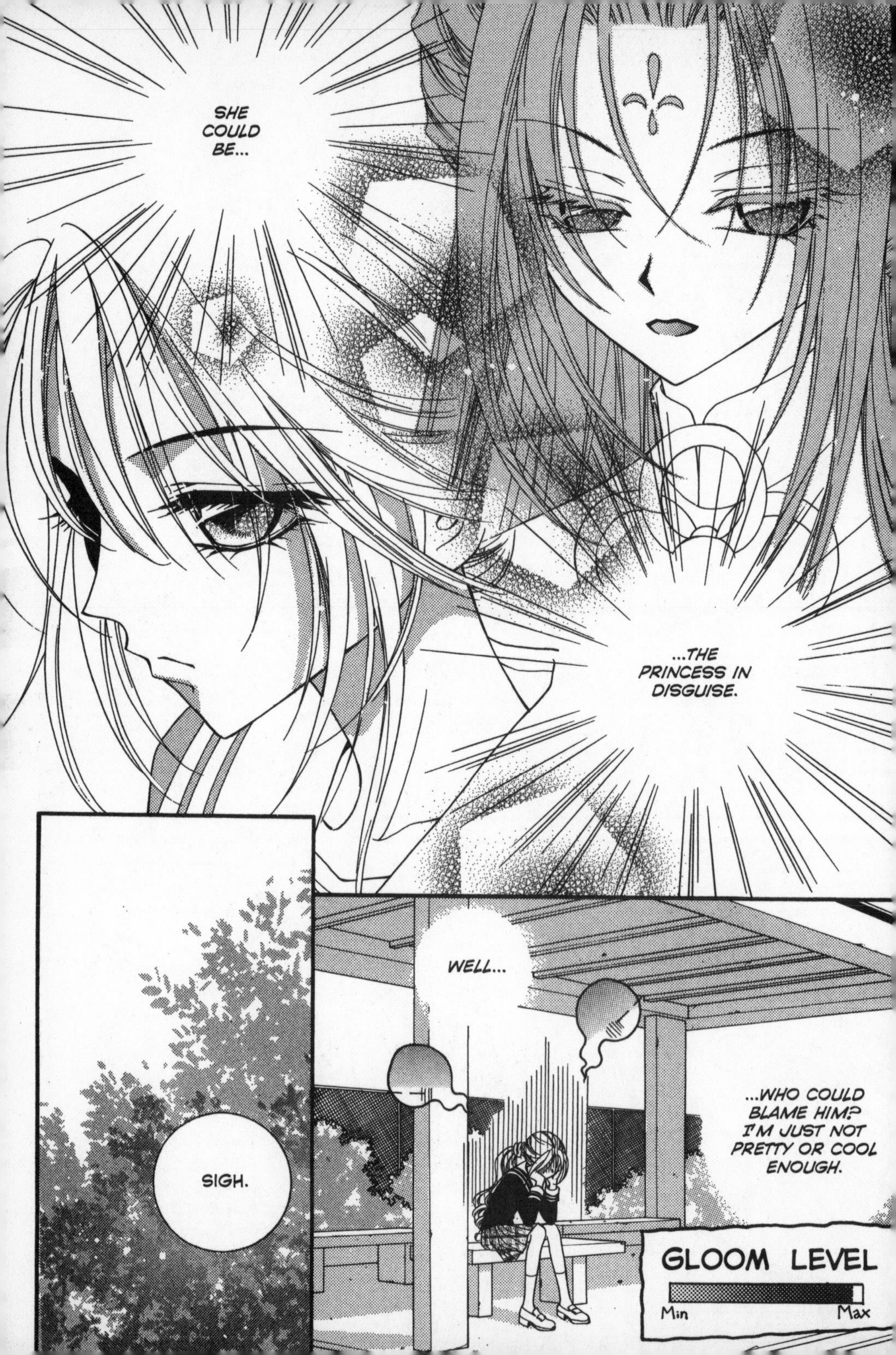
SHE COULD BE...
...THE PRINCESS IN DISGUISE.
SIGH.
WELL...
...WHO COULD BLAME HIM? I'M JUST NOT PRETTY OR COOL ENOUGH.
GLOOM LEVEL
Min
Max

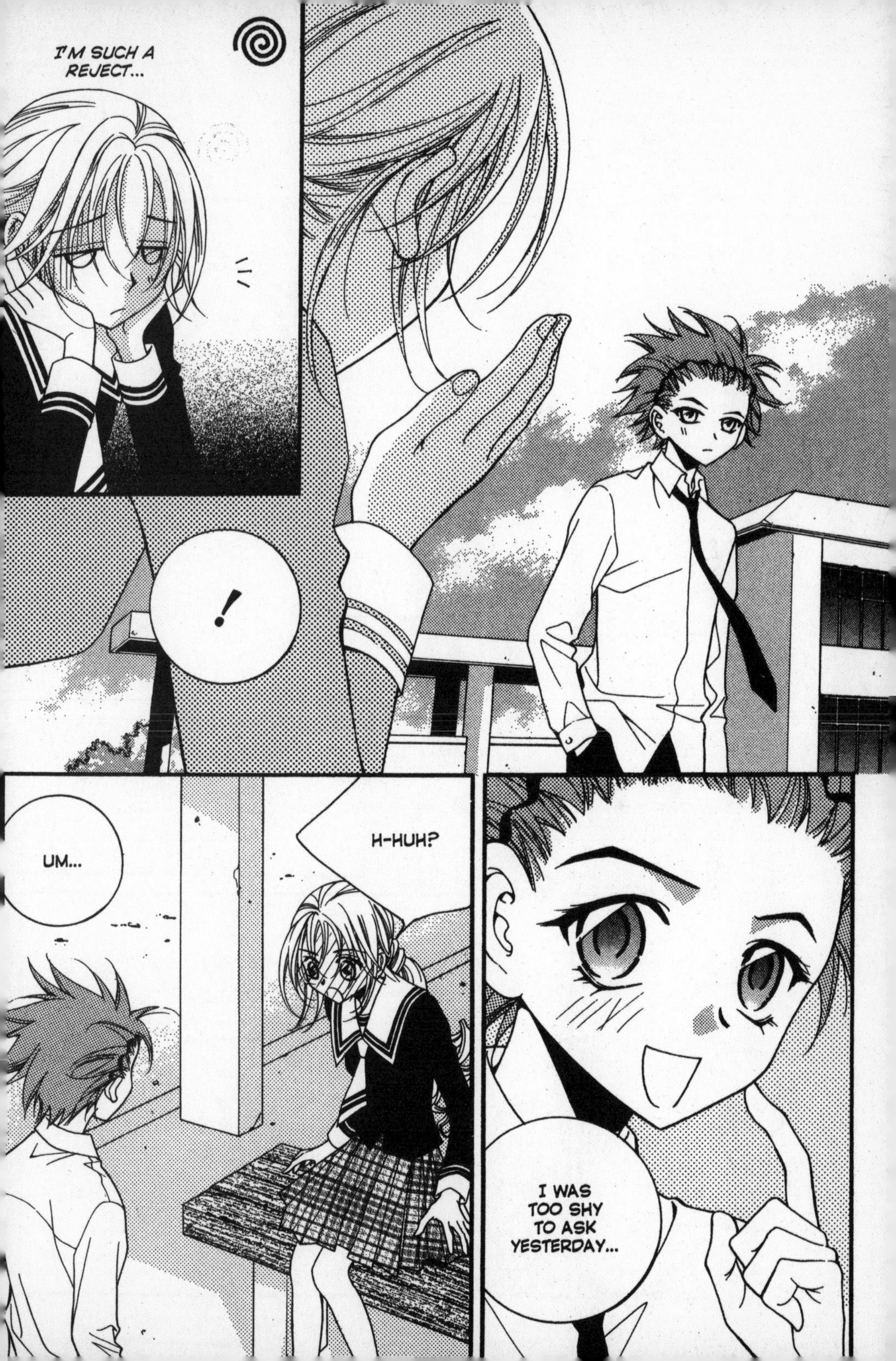
I'M SUCH A REJECT...
!
UM...
H-HUH?
I WAS TOO SHY TO ASK YESTERDAY...

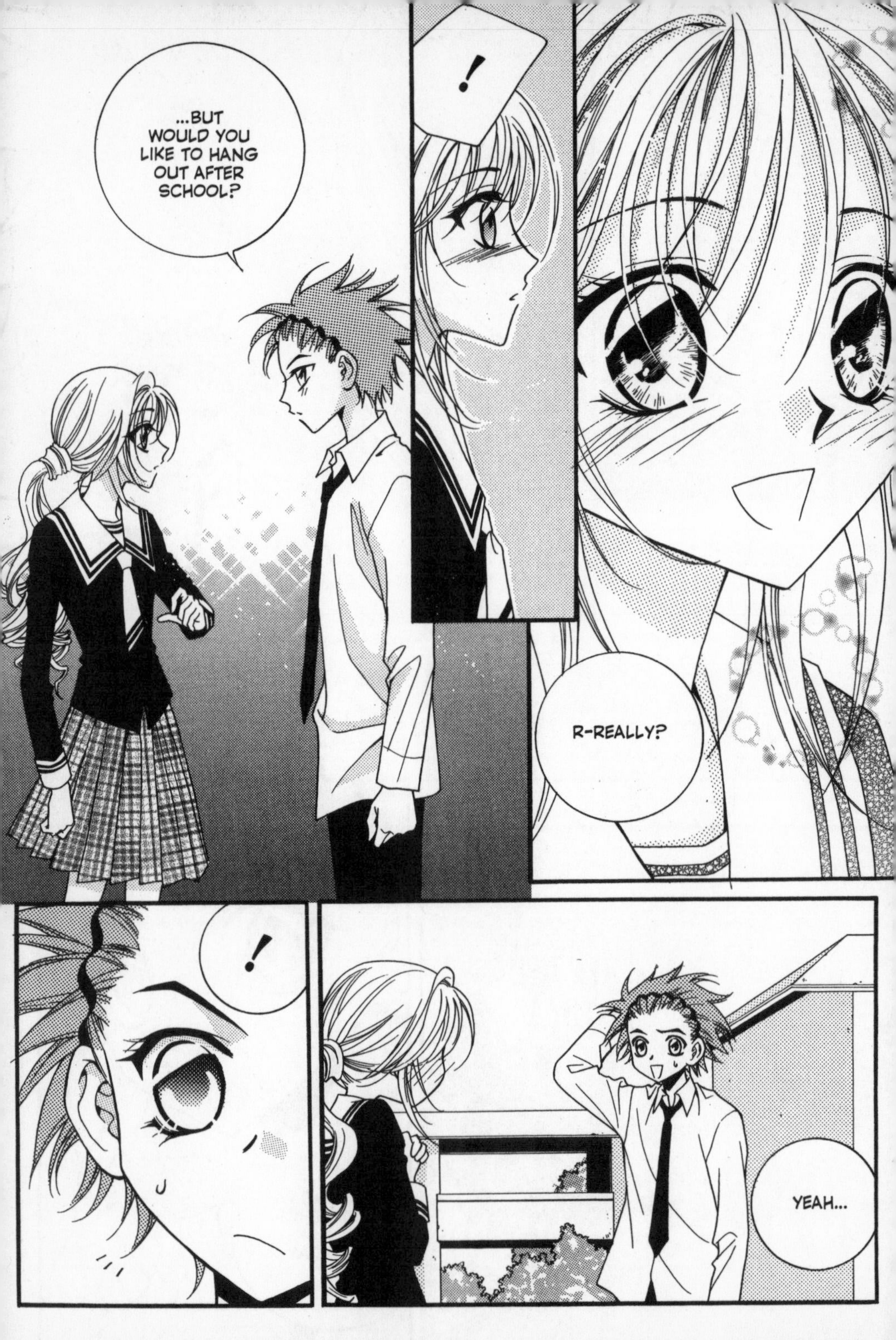
...BUT WOULD YOU LIKE TO HANG OUT AFTER SCHOOL?
!
R-REALLY?
!
YEAH...

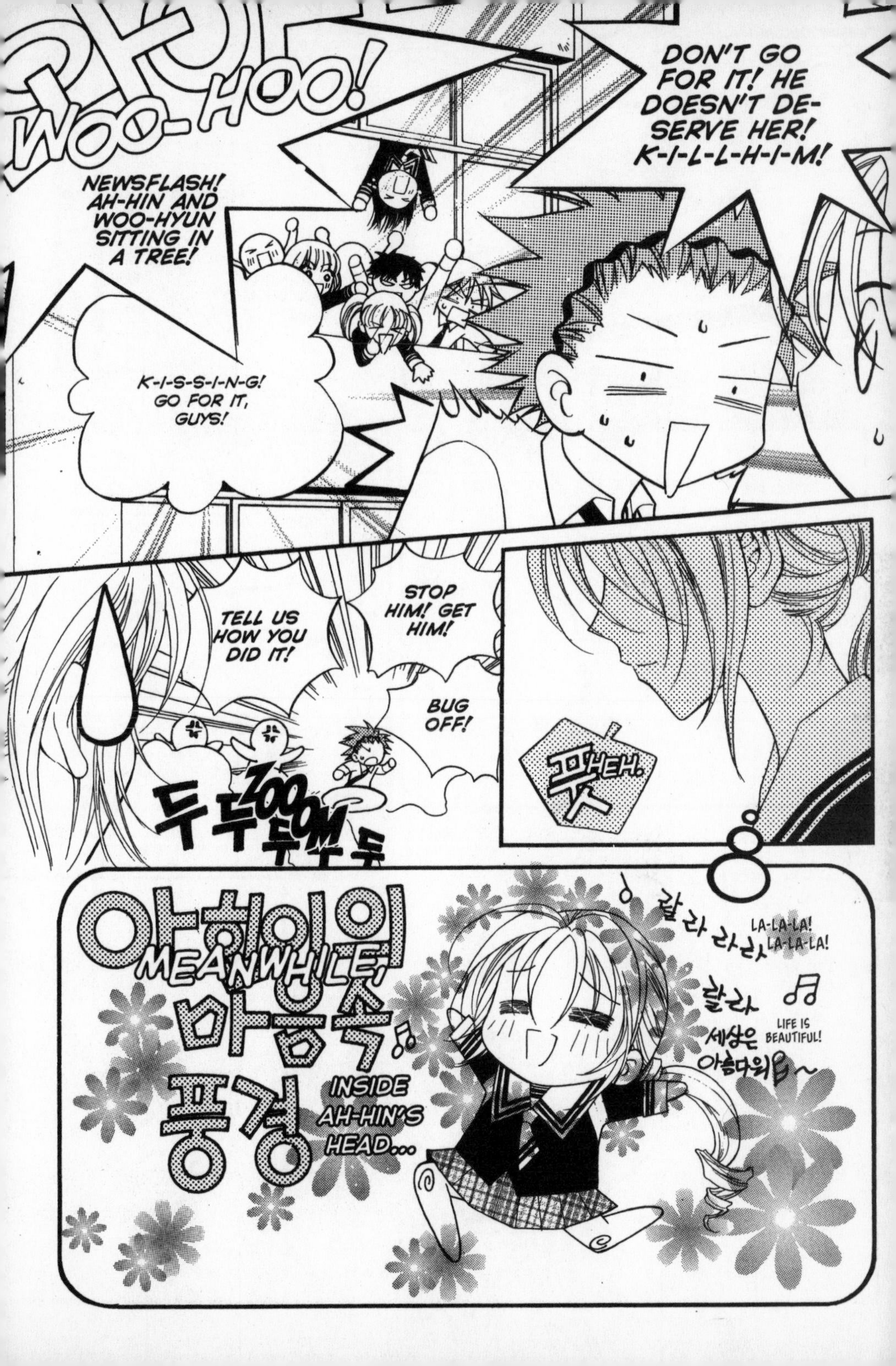

WOO-HOO!
NEWSFLASH! AH-HIN AND WOO-HYUN SITTING IN A TREE!
K-I-S-S-I-N-G! GO FOR IT, GUYS!
DON'T GO FOR IT! HE DOESN'T DE-SERVE HER! K-I-L-L-H-I-M!
TELL US HOW YOU DID IT!
STOP HIM! GET HIM!
BUG OFF!
ZOOOM
HEH.
MEANWHILE, INSIDE AH-HIN'S HEAD...
LA-LA-LA! LA-LA-LA!
LIFE IS BEAUTIFUL!

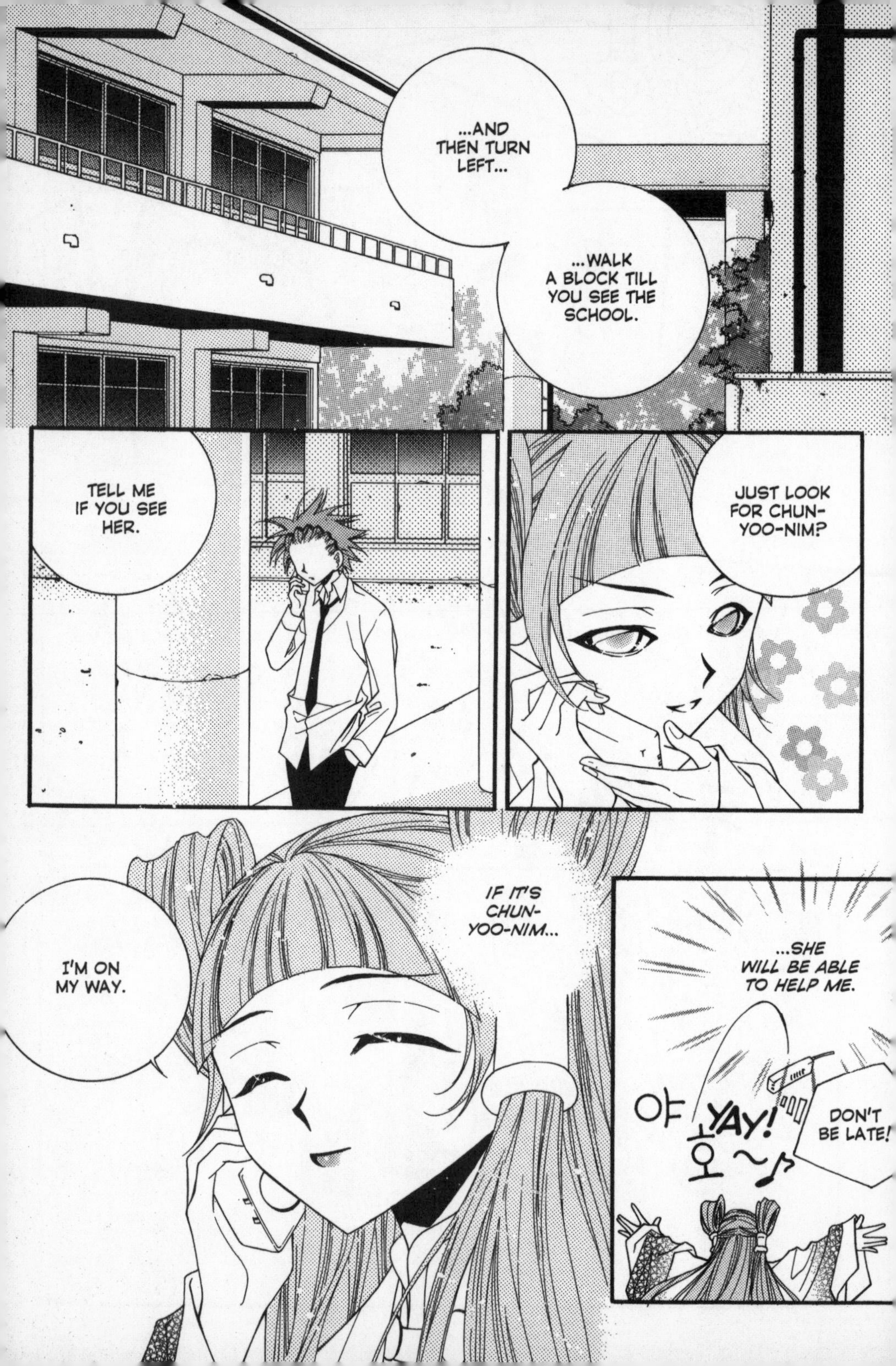

...AND THEN TURN LEFT...
...WALK A BLOCK TILL YOU SEE THE SCHOOL.
TELL ME IF YOU SEE HER.
JUST LOOK FOR CHUN-YOO-NIM?
I'M ON MY WAY.
IF IT'S CHUN-YOO-NIM...
...SHE WILL BE ABLE TO HELP ME.
야호~
YAY!
DON'T BE LATE!

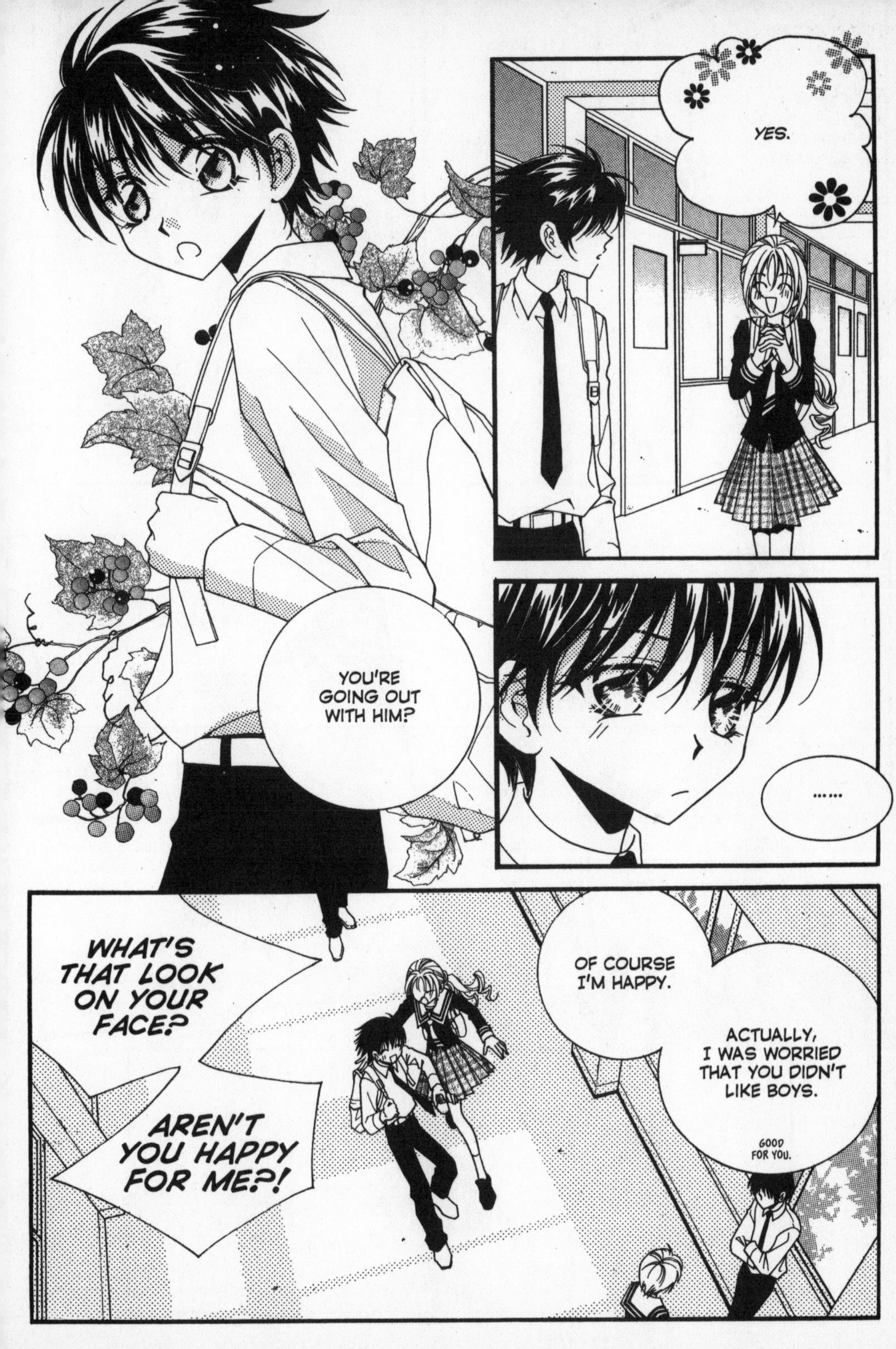
YOU'RE GOING OUT WITH HIM?
YES.
......
WHAT'S THAT LOOK ON YOUR FACE?
AREN'T YOU HAPPY FOR ME?!
OF COURSE I'M HAPPY.
ACTUALLY, I WAS WORRIED THAT YOU DIDN'T LIKE BOYS.
GOOD FOR YOU.

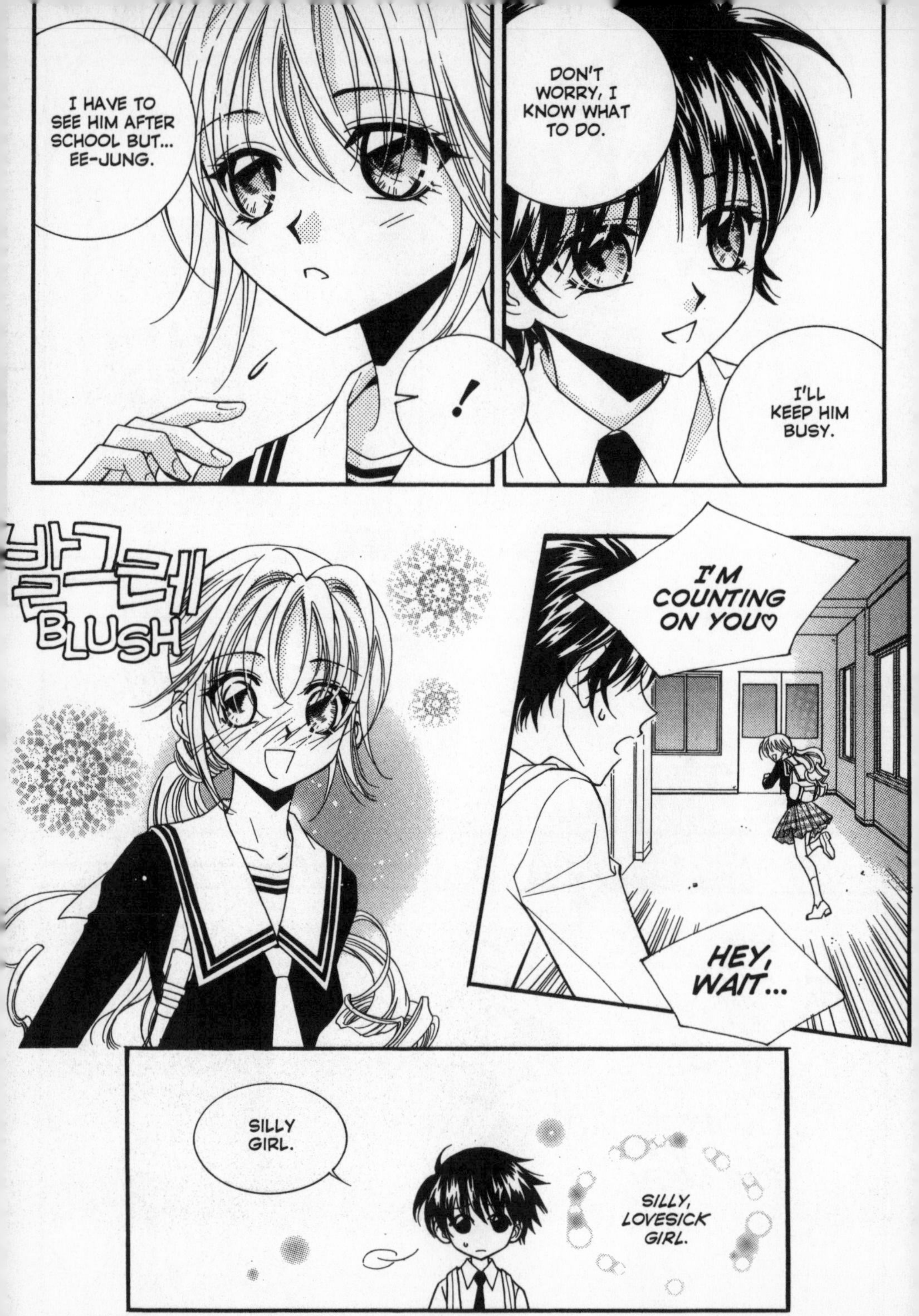
I HAVE TO SEE HIM AFTER SCHOOL BUT... EE-JUNG.
!
DON'T WORRY, I KNOW WHAT TO DO.
I'LL KEEP HIM BUSY.
발그레
BLUSH
I'M COUNTING ON YOU♡
HEY, WAIT...
SILLY GIRL.
SILLY, LOVESICK GIRL.

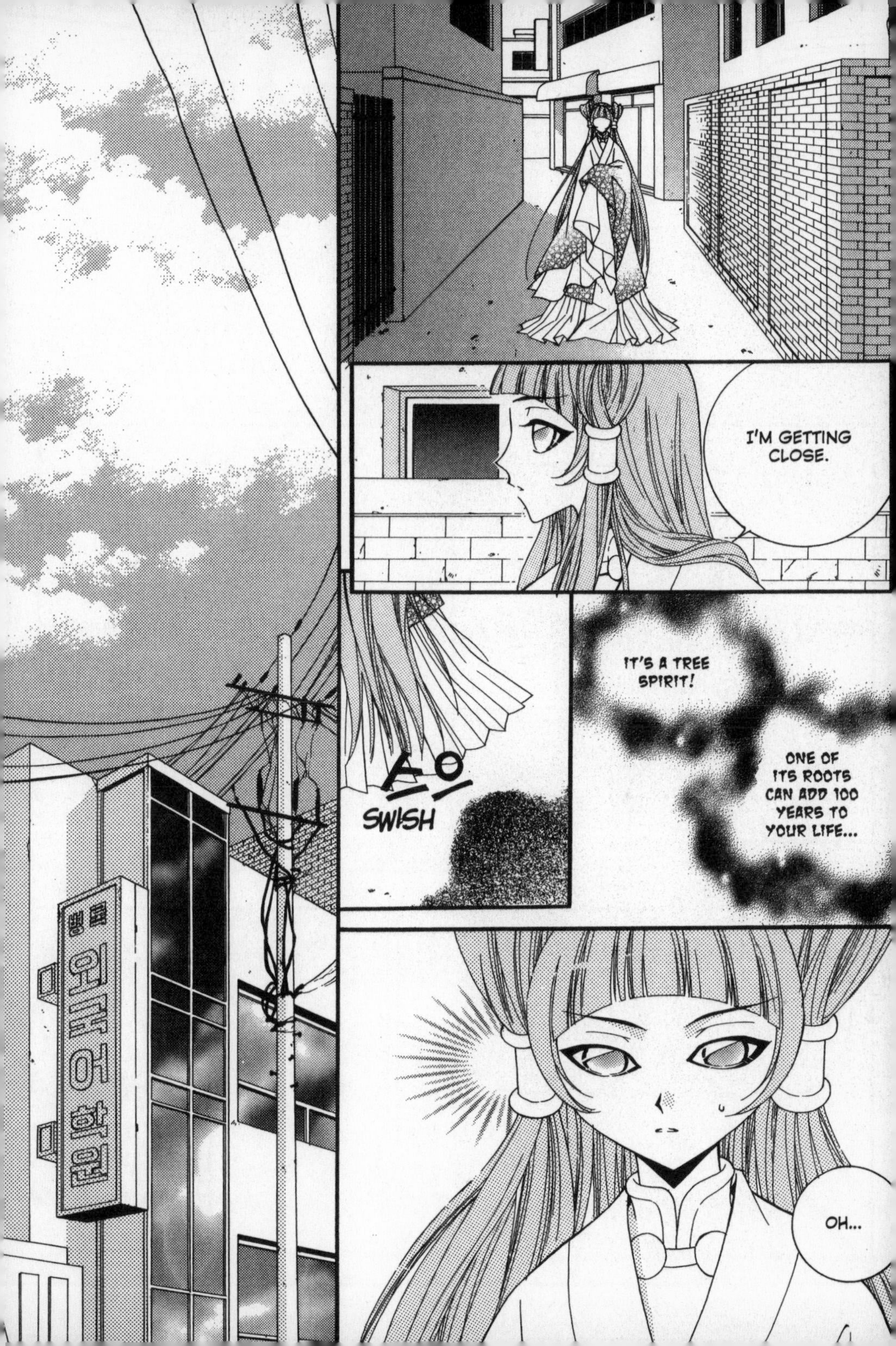

외국어학원
I'M GETTING CLOSE.
SWISH
IT'S A TREE SPIRIT!
ONE OF ITS ROOTS CAN ADD 100 YEARS TO YOUR LIFE...
OH...

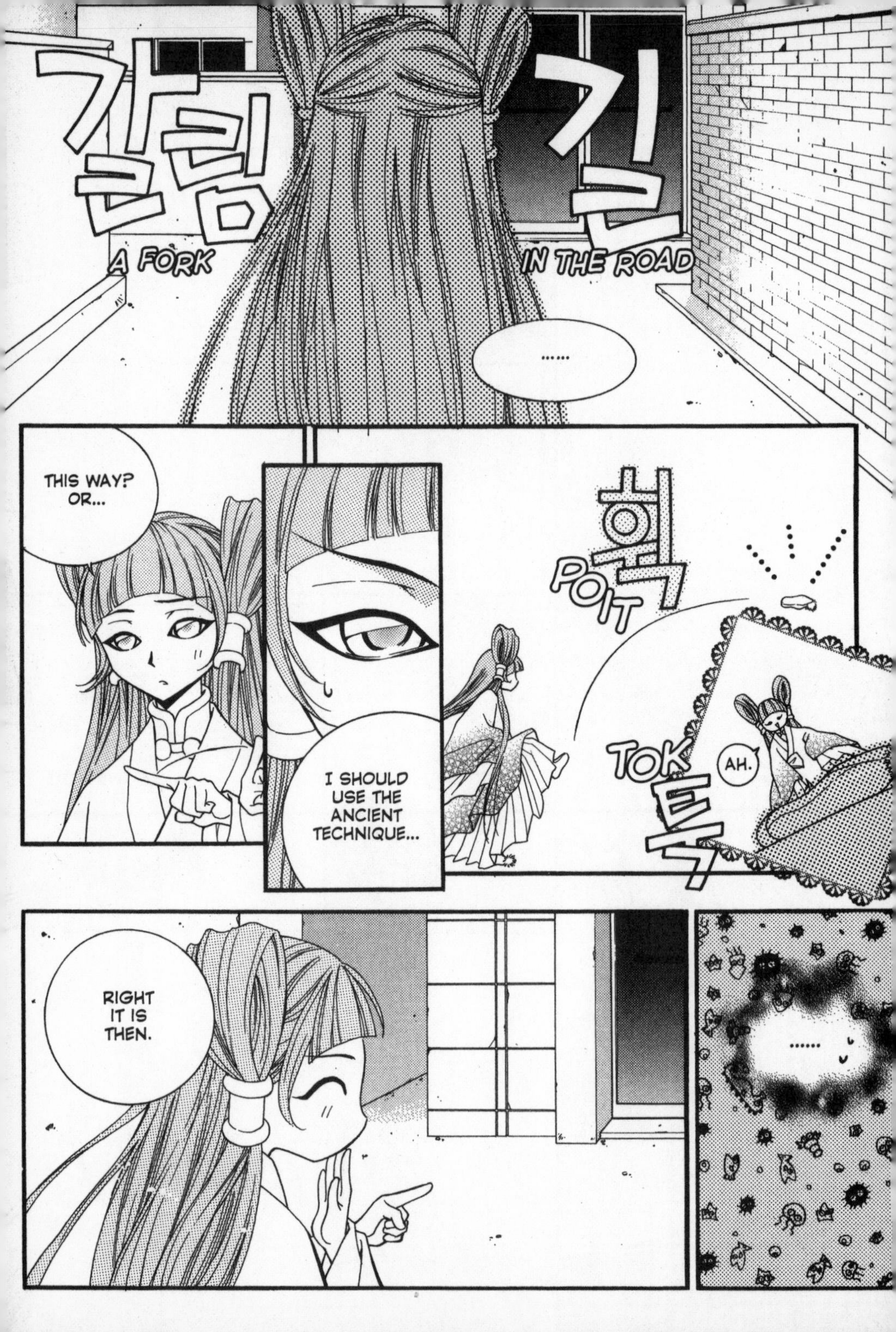
갈림
A FORK
길
IN THE ROAD
......
THIS WAY? OR...
I SHOULD USE THE ANCIENT TECHNIQUE...
휙
POIT
TOK
툭
AH.
RIGHT IT IS THEN.
......

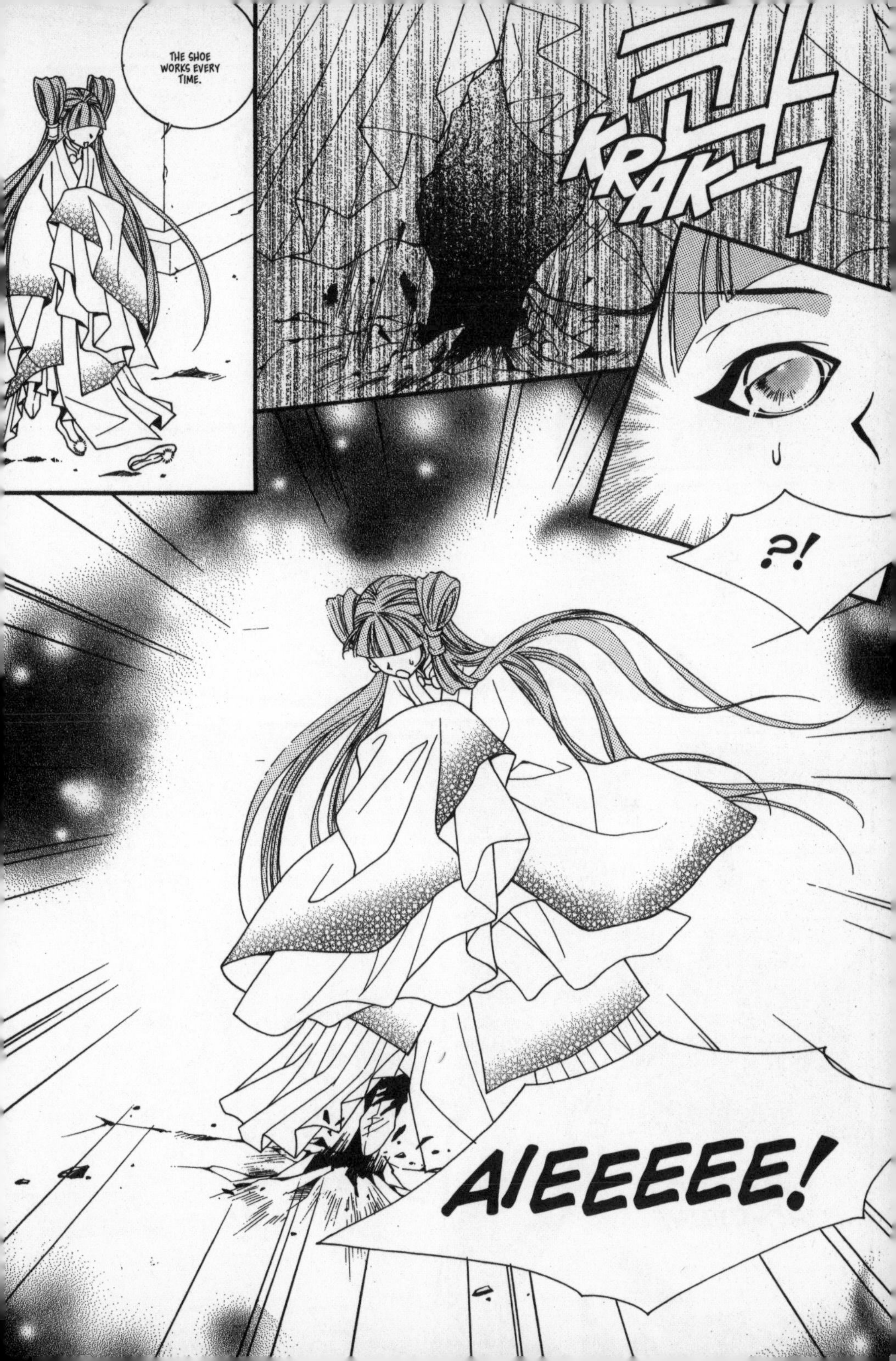
THE SHOE WORKS EVERY TIME.
KRAK
?!
AIEEEEEE!

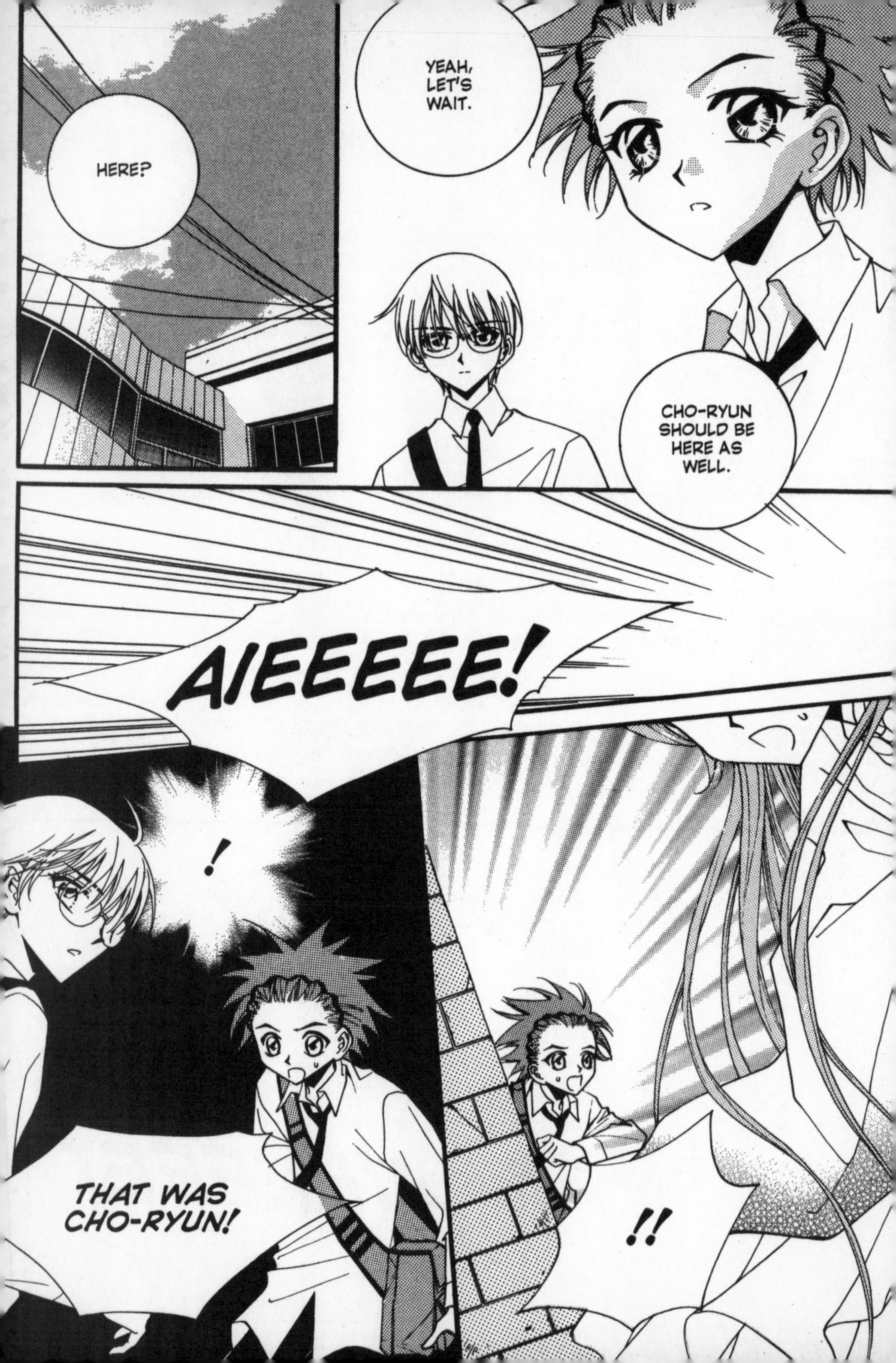
HERE?
YEAH, LET'S WAIT.
CHO-RYUN SHOULD BE HERE AS WELL.
AIEEEEEE!
!
THAT WAS CHO-RYUN!
!!

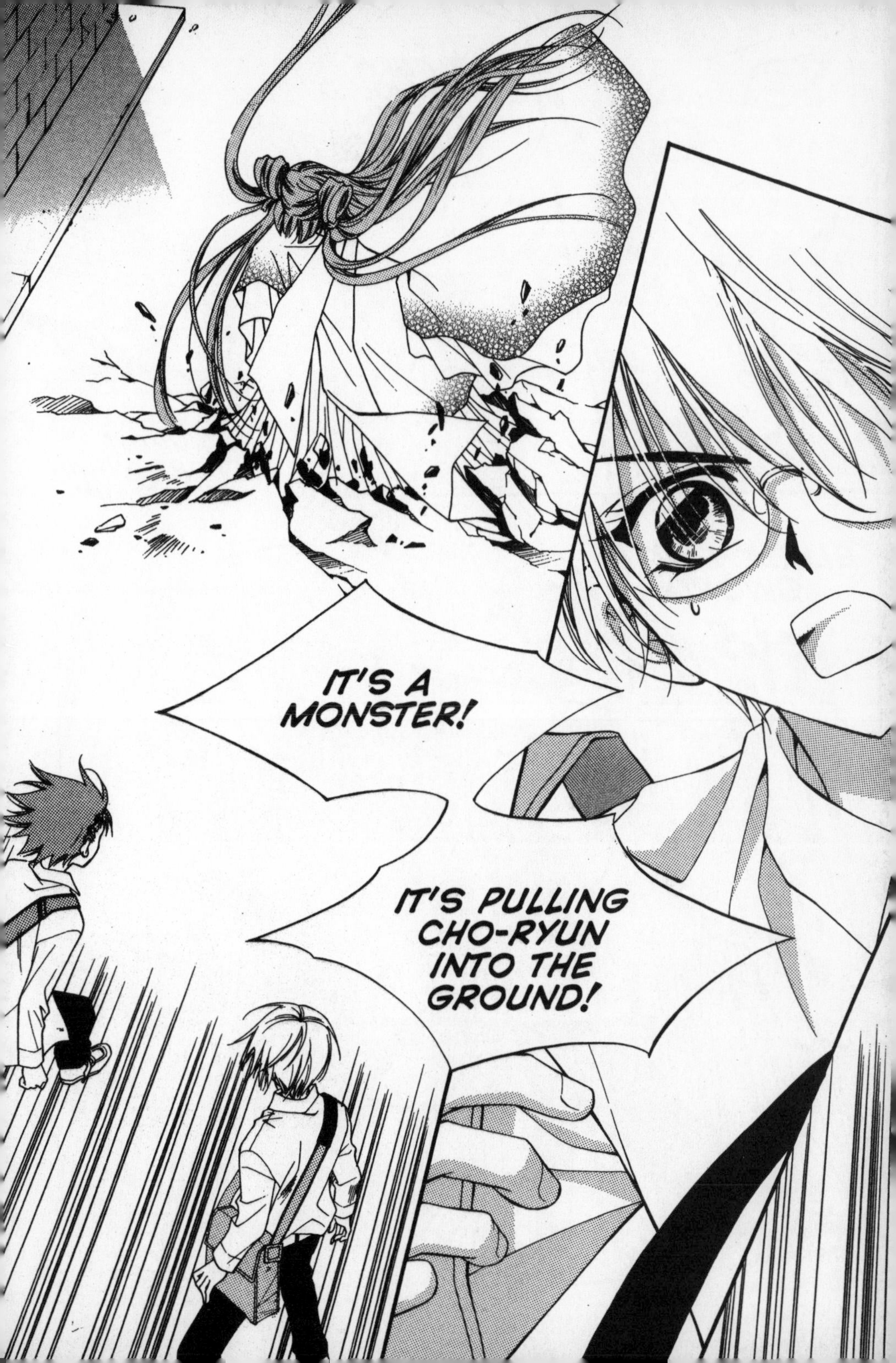
IT'S A MONSTER!
IT'S PULLING CHO-RYUN INTO THE GROUND!

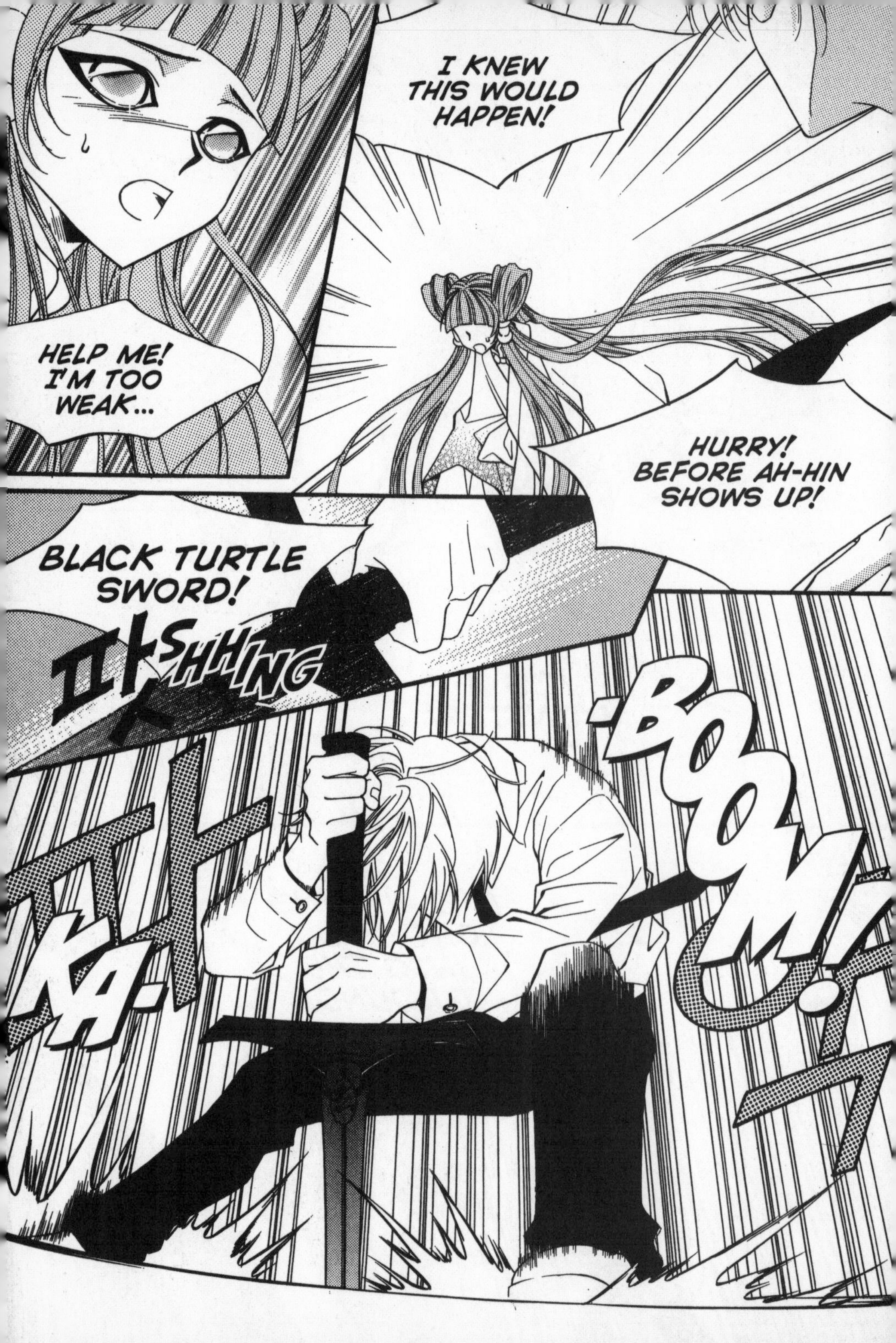
HELP ME! I'M TOO WEAK...
I KNEW THIS WOULD HAPPEN!
HURRY! BEFORE AH-HIN SHOWS UP!
BLACK TURTLE SWORD!
SHHING
KA-BOOM!

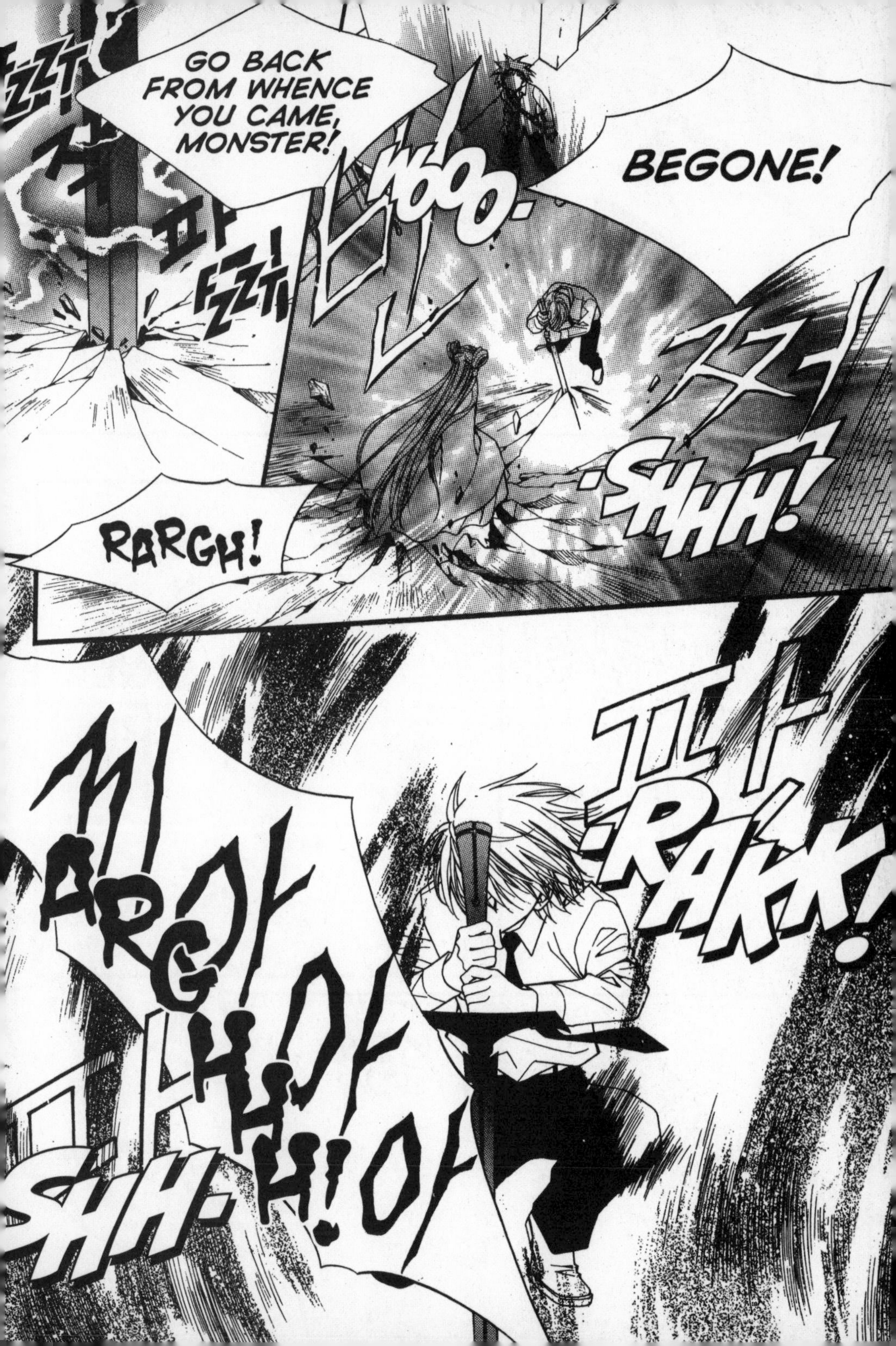
FZZT!
GO BACK FROM WHENCE YOU CAME, MONSTER!
FZZT!
WOOO-
BEGONE!
RARGH!
-SHHH!
ARGH!
SHH-H!
-RAKK!

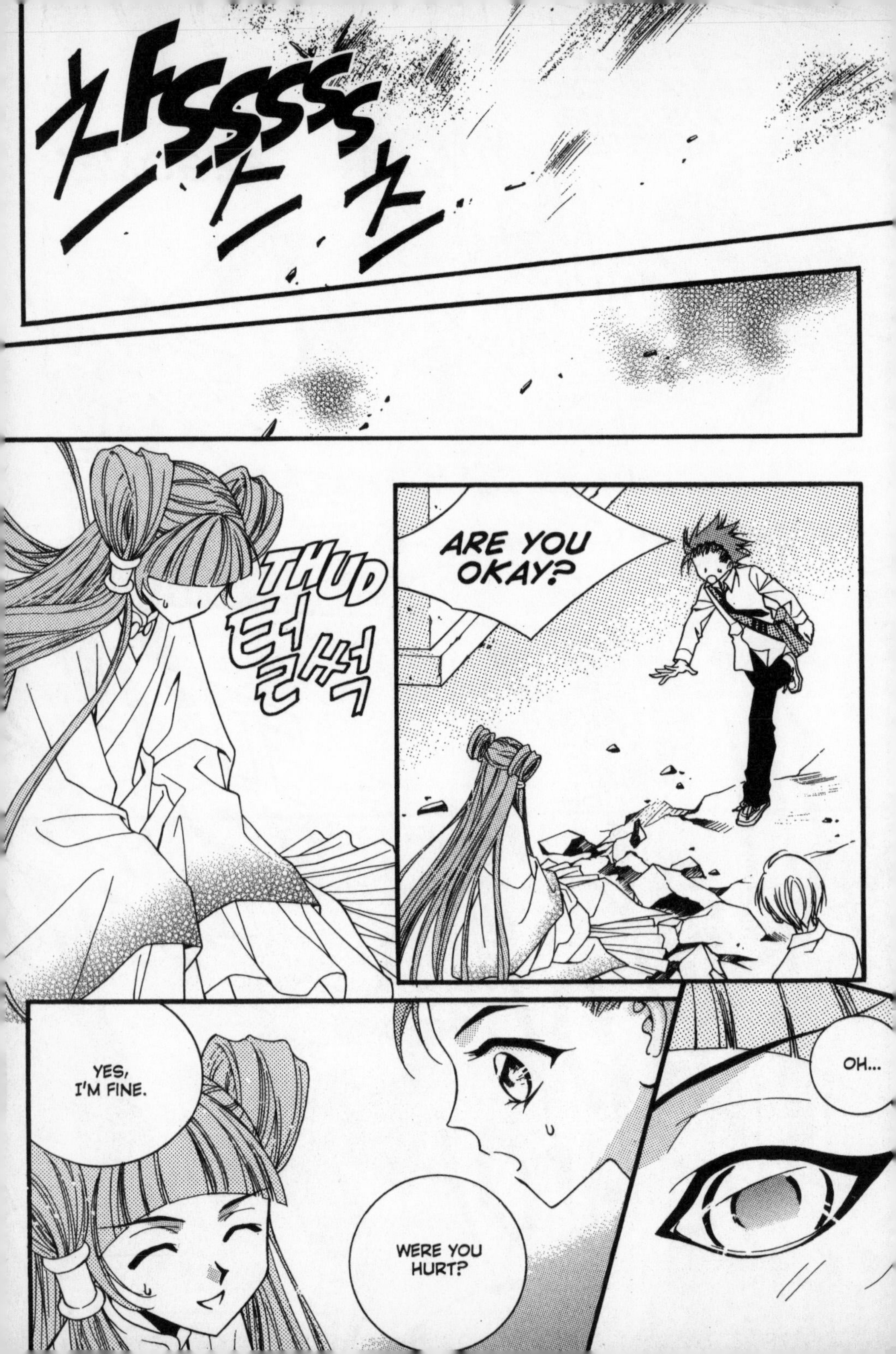
FSSSSS
THUD
털썩
ARE YOU OKAY?
YES, I'M FINE.
WERE YOU HURT?
OH...

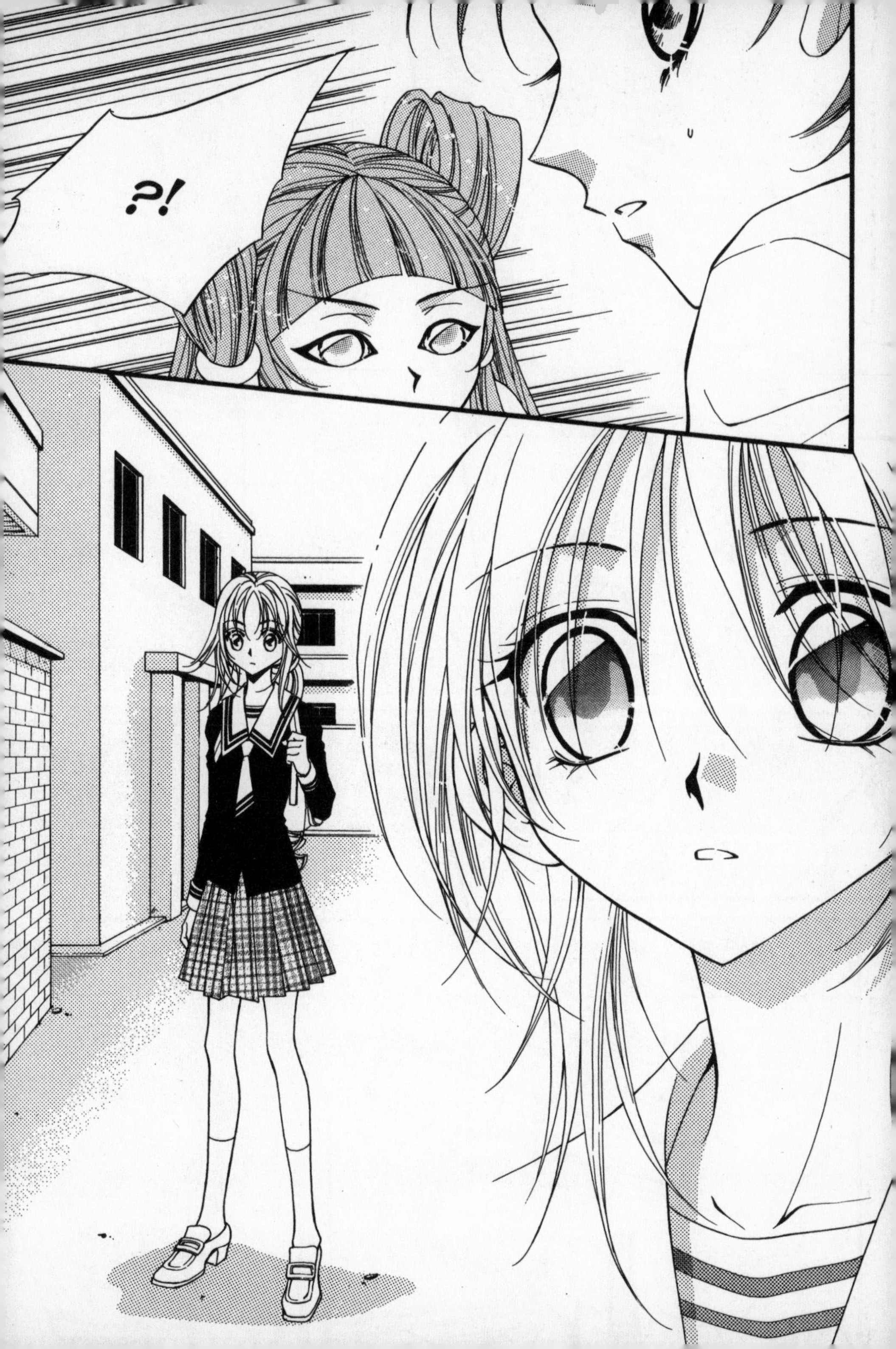
?!

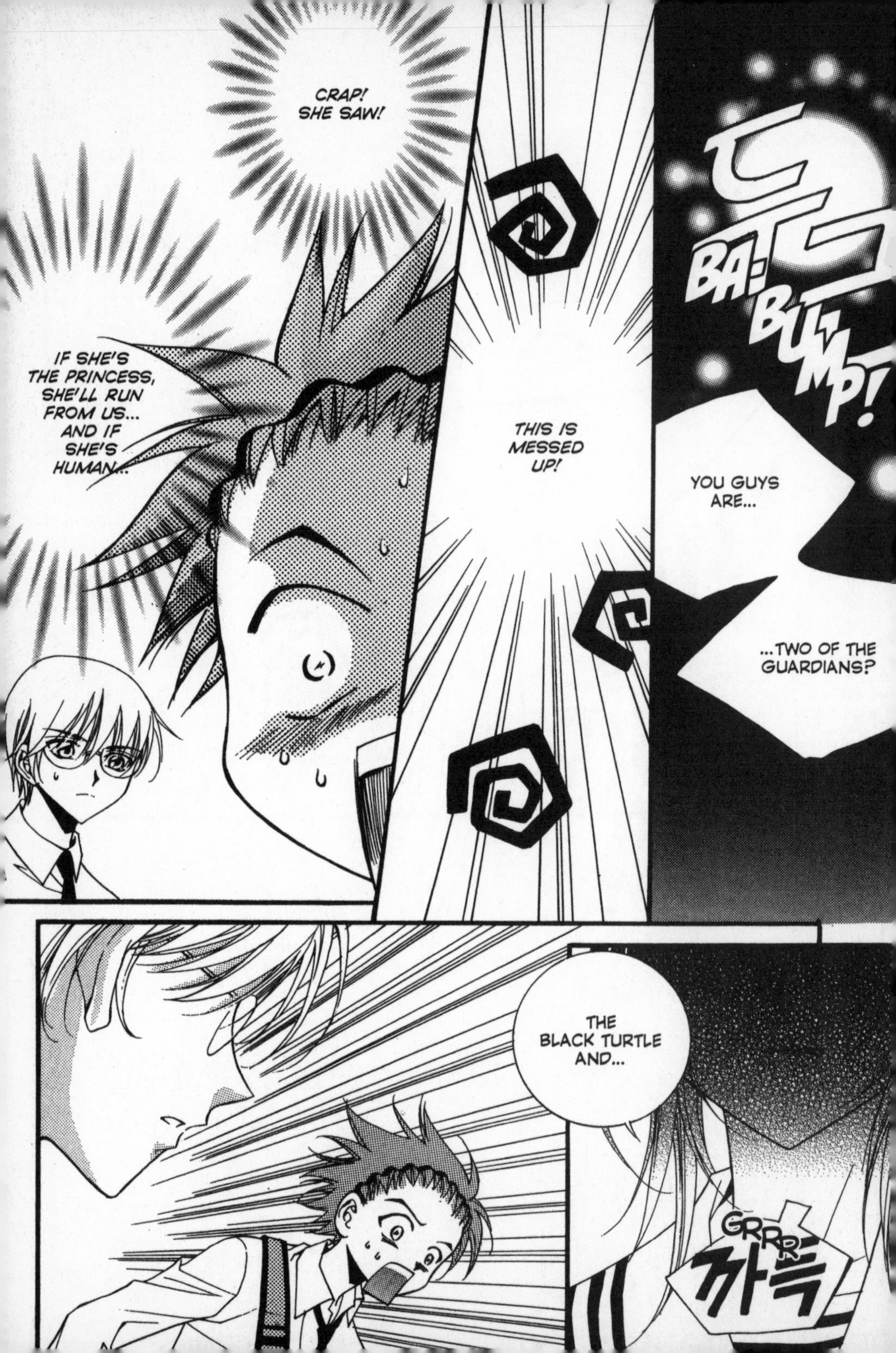

CRAP! SHE SAW!
IF SHE'S THE PRINCESS, SHE'LL RUN FROM US... AND IF SHE'S HUMAN...
THIS IS MESSED UP!
BA-BUMP!
YOU GUYS ARE...
...TWO OF THE GUARDIANS?
THE BLACK TURTLE AND...
GRRR

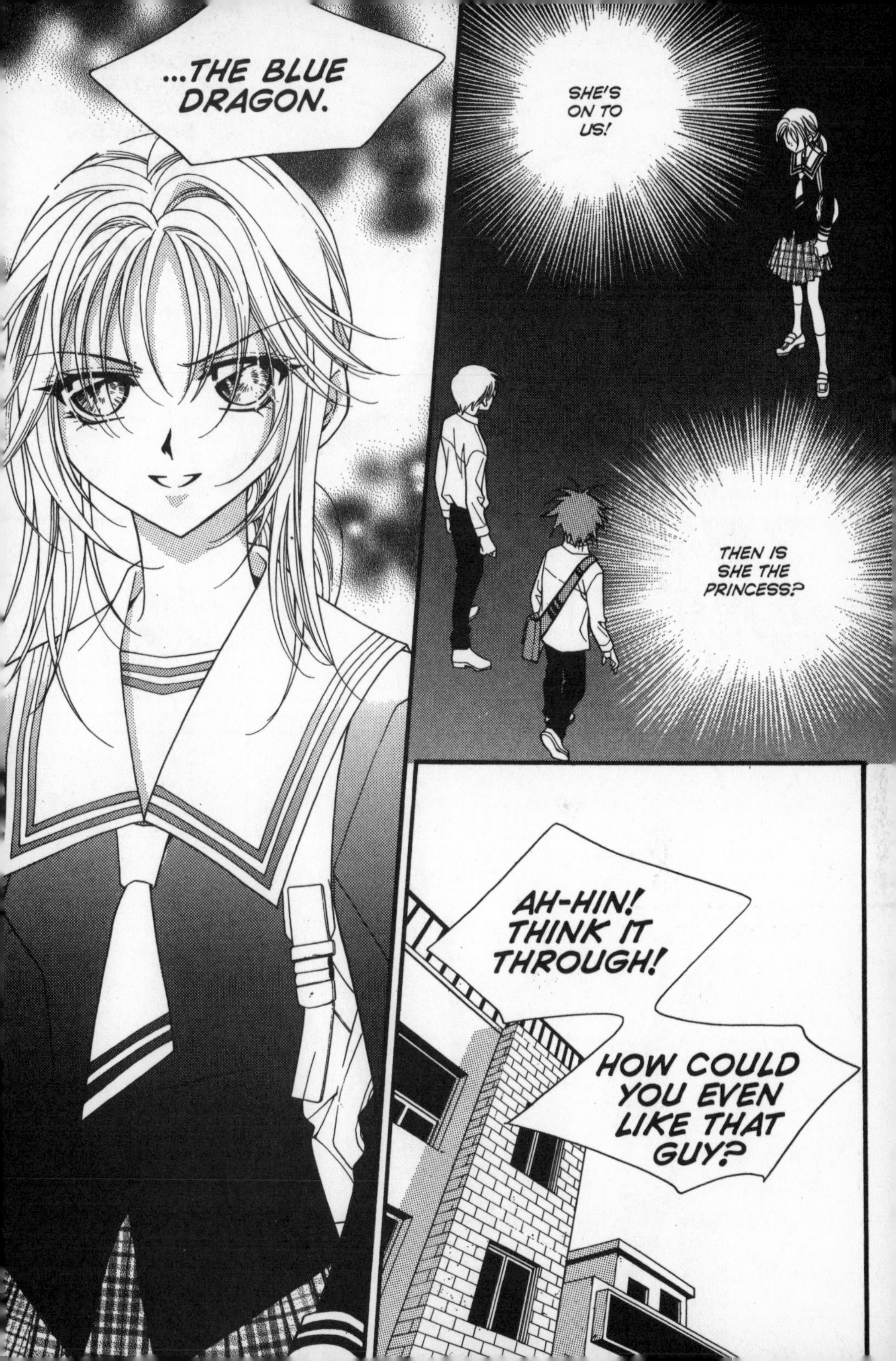
...THE BLUE DRAGON.
SHE'S ON TO US!
THEN IS SHE THE PRINCESS?
AH-HIN! THINK IT THROUGH!
HOW COULD YOU EVEN LIKE THAT GUY?

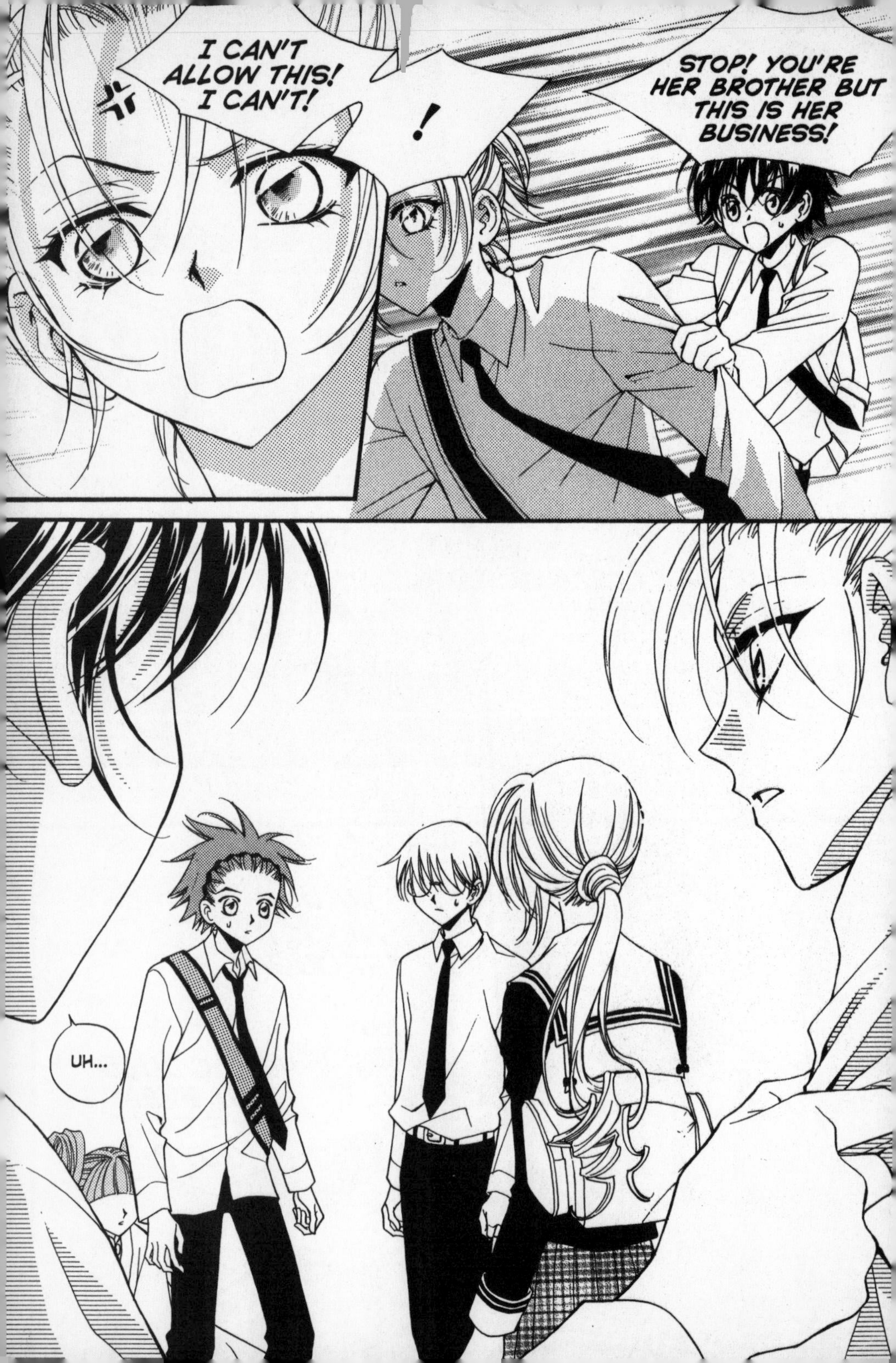
I CAN'T ALLOW THIS! I CAN'T!
!
STOP! YOU'RE HER BROTHER BUT THIS IS HER BUSINESS!
UH...

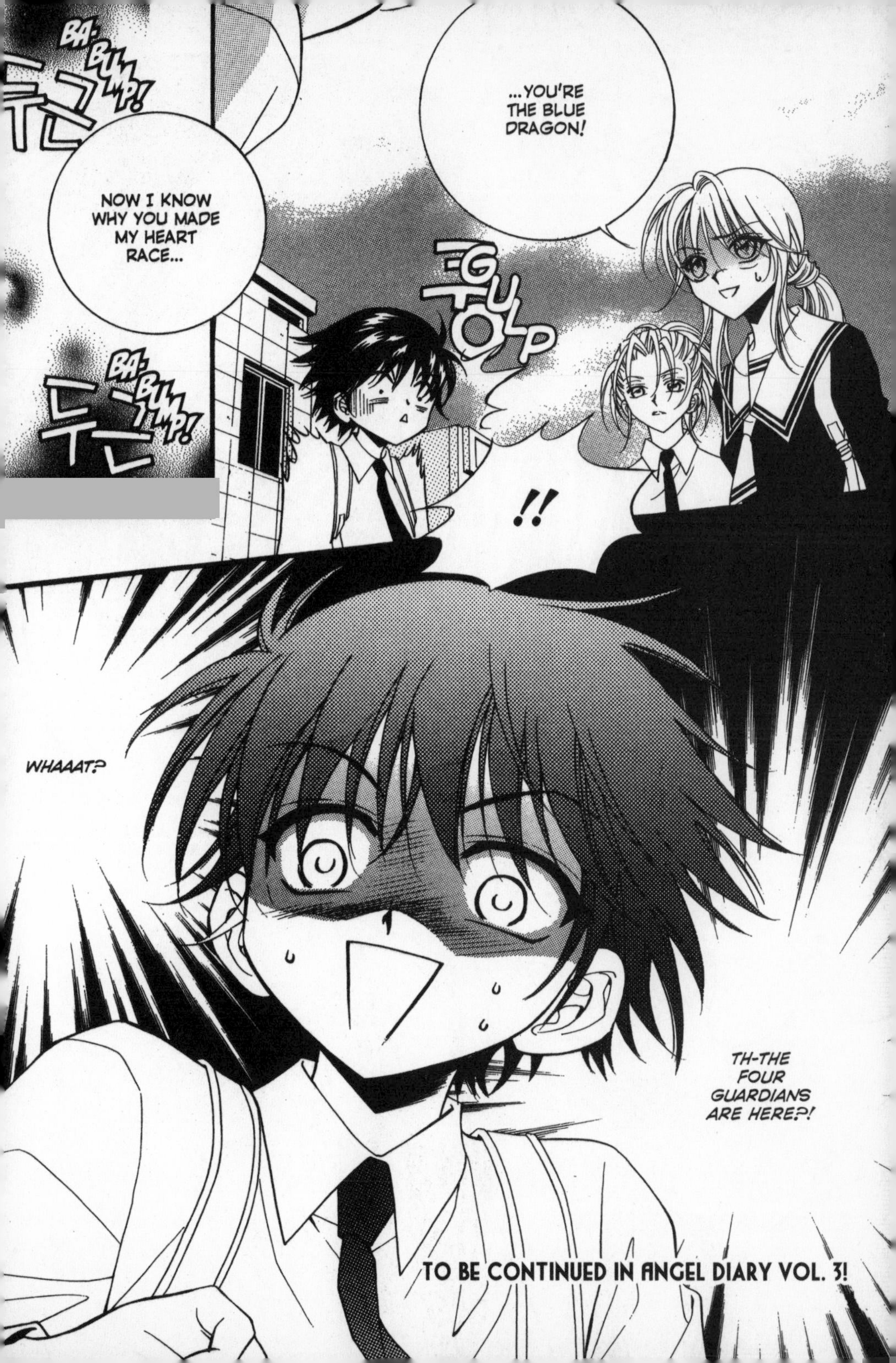
BA-BUMP!
NOW I KNOW WHY YOU MADE MY HEART RACE...
BA-BUMP!
...YOU'RE THE BLUE DRAGON!
GULP
!!
WHAAAT?
TH-THE FOUR GUARDIANS ARE HERE?!
TO BE CONTINUED IN ANGEL DIARY VOL. 3!

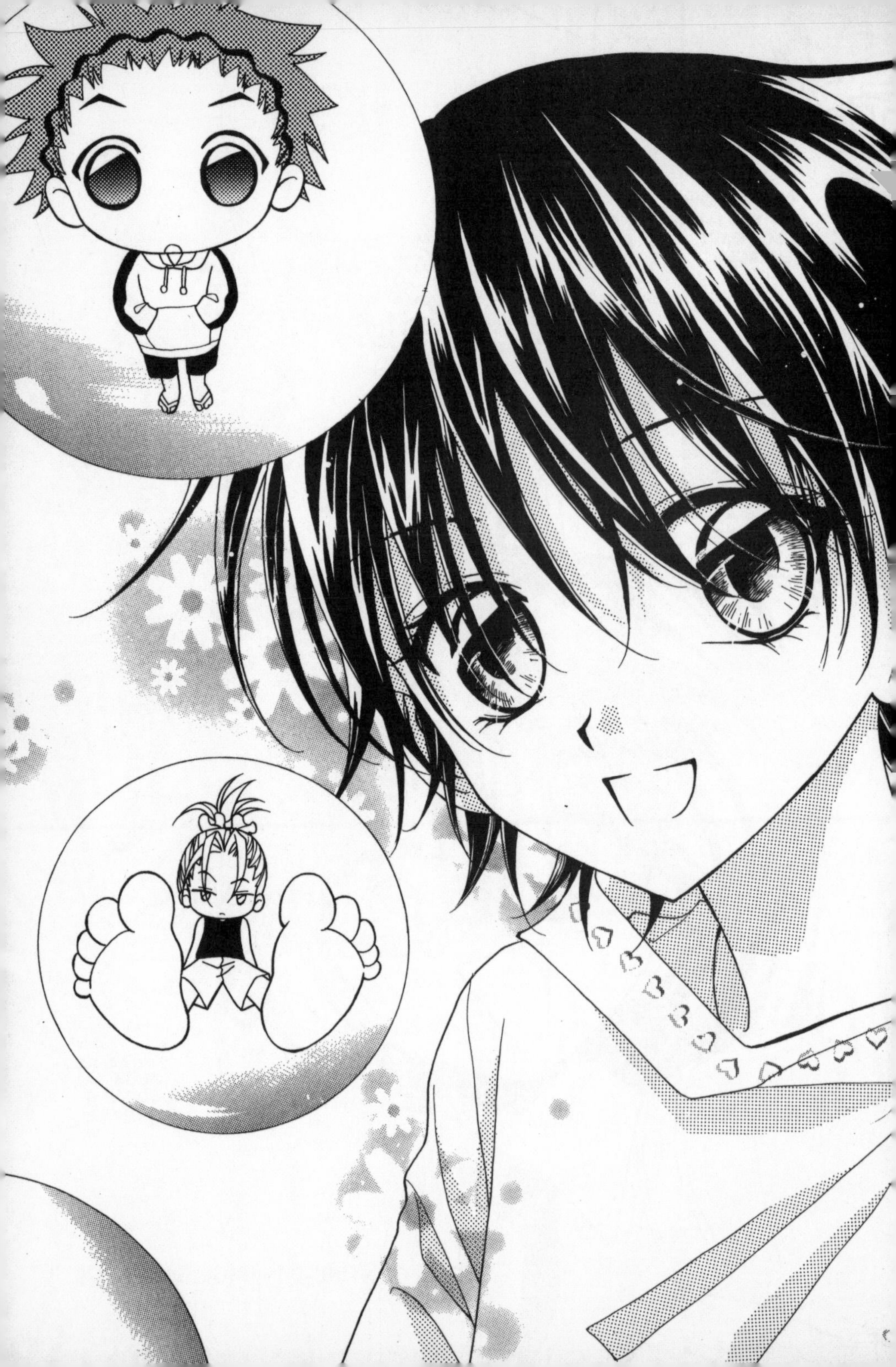

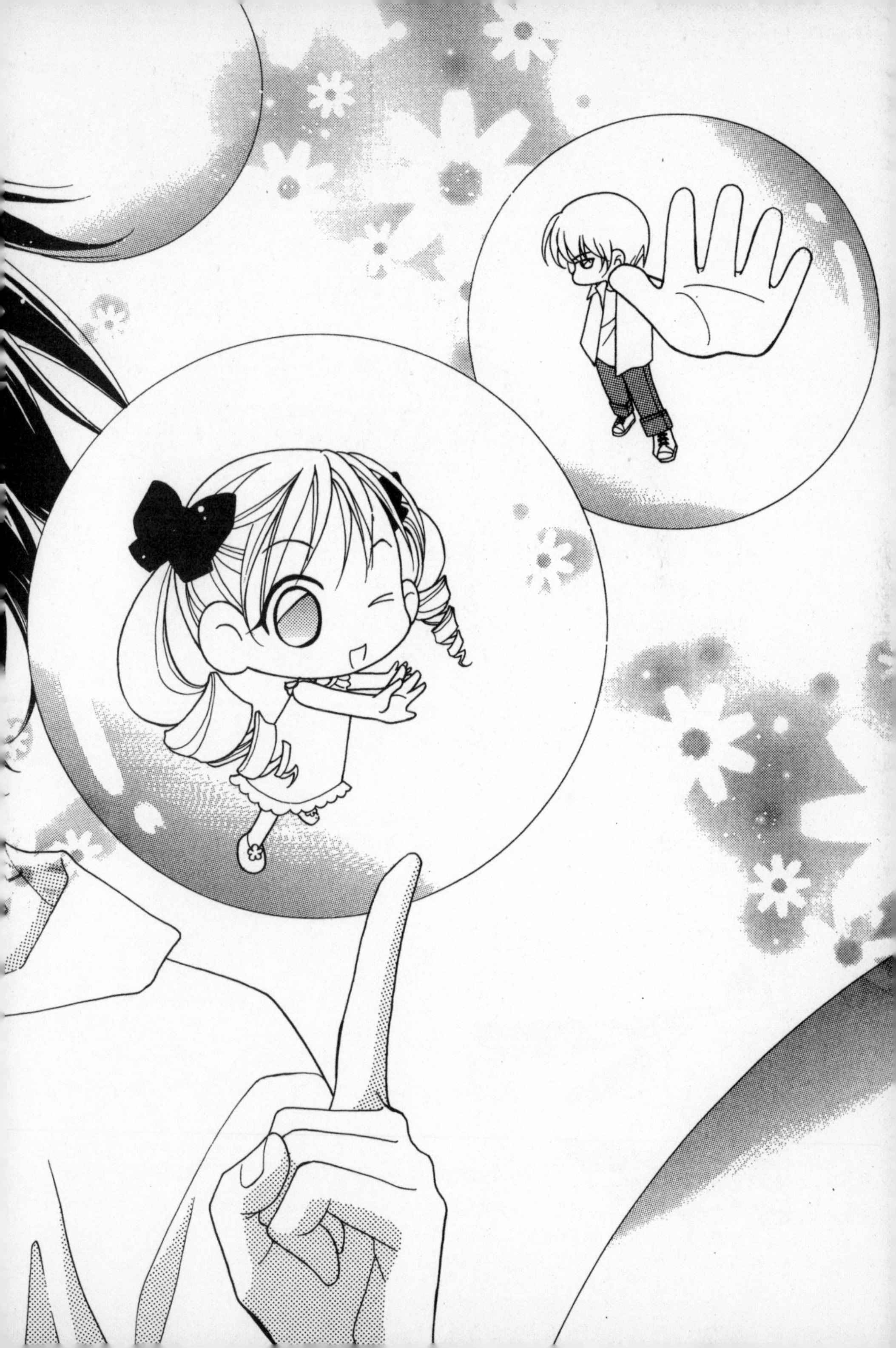

11th CAT

vol.2

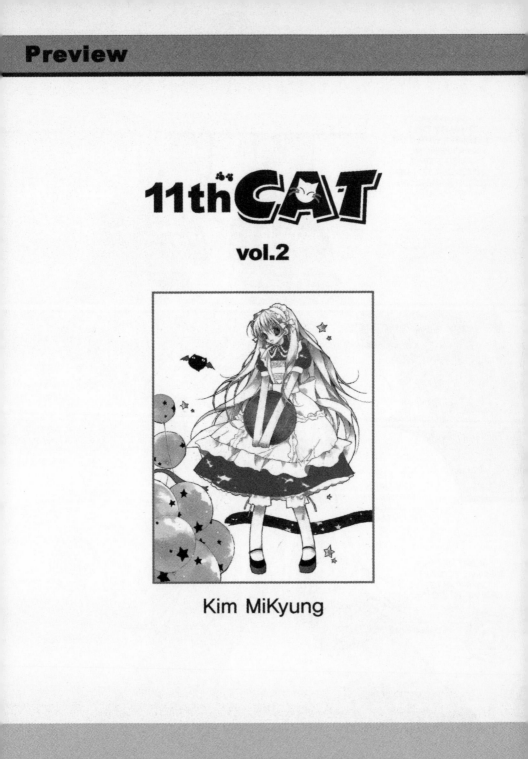

Kim MiKyung

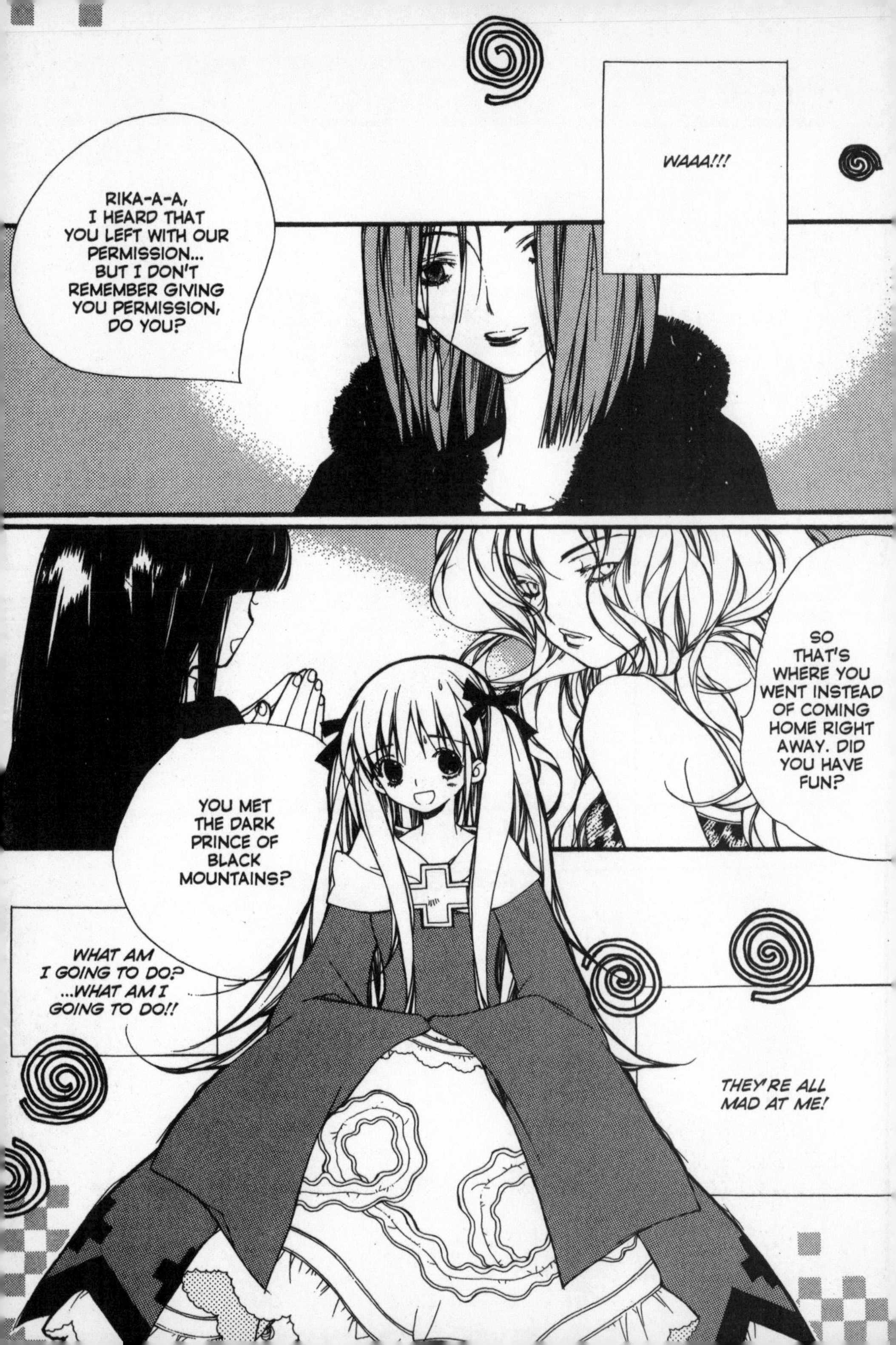
WAAA!!!
RIKA-A-A, I HEARD THAT YOU LEFT WITH OUR PERMISSION... BUT I DON'T REMEMBER GIVING YOU PERMISSION, DO YOU?
YOU MET THE DARK PRINCE OF BLACK MOUNTAINS?
SO THAT'S WHERE YOU WENT INSTEAD OF COMING HOME RIGHT AWAY. DID YOU HAVE FUN?
WHAT AM I GOING TO DO? ...WHAT AM I GOING TO DO!!
THEY'RE ALL MAD AT ME!

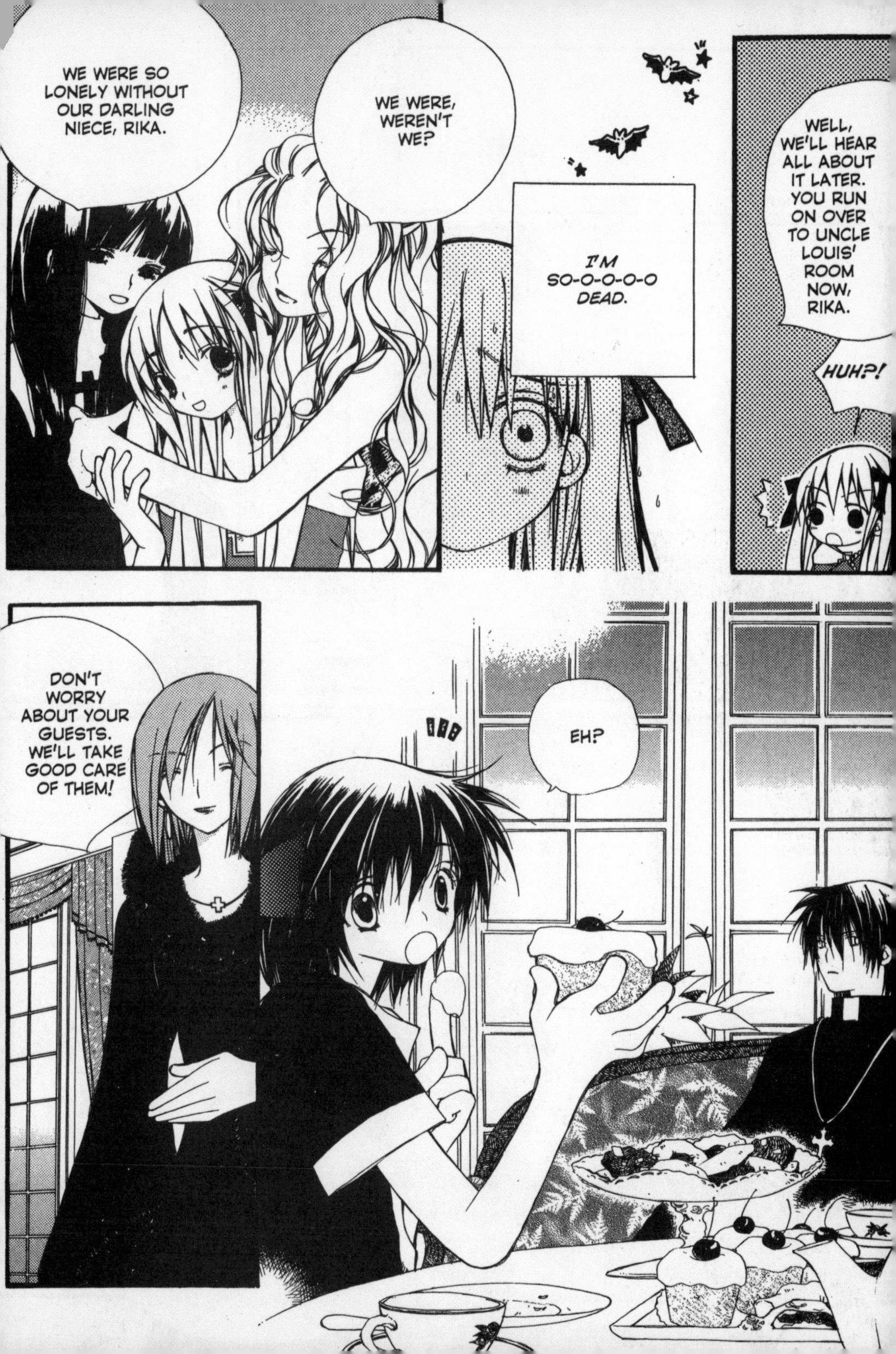
WE WERE SO LONELY WITHOUT OUR DARLING NIECE, RIKA.
WE WERE, WEREN'T WE?
I'M SO-O-O-O-O DEAD.
WELL, WE'LL HEAR ALL ABOUT IT LATER. YOU RUN ON OVER TO UNCLE LOUIS' ROOM NOW, RIKA.
HUH?!
DON'T WORRY ABOUT YOUR GUESTS. WE'LL TAKE GOOD CARE OF THEM!
EH?

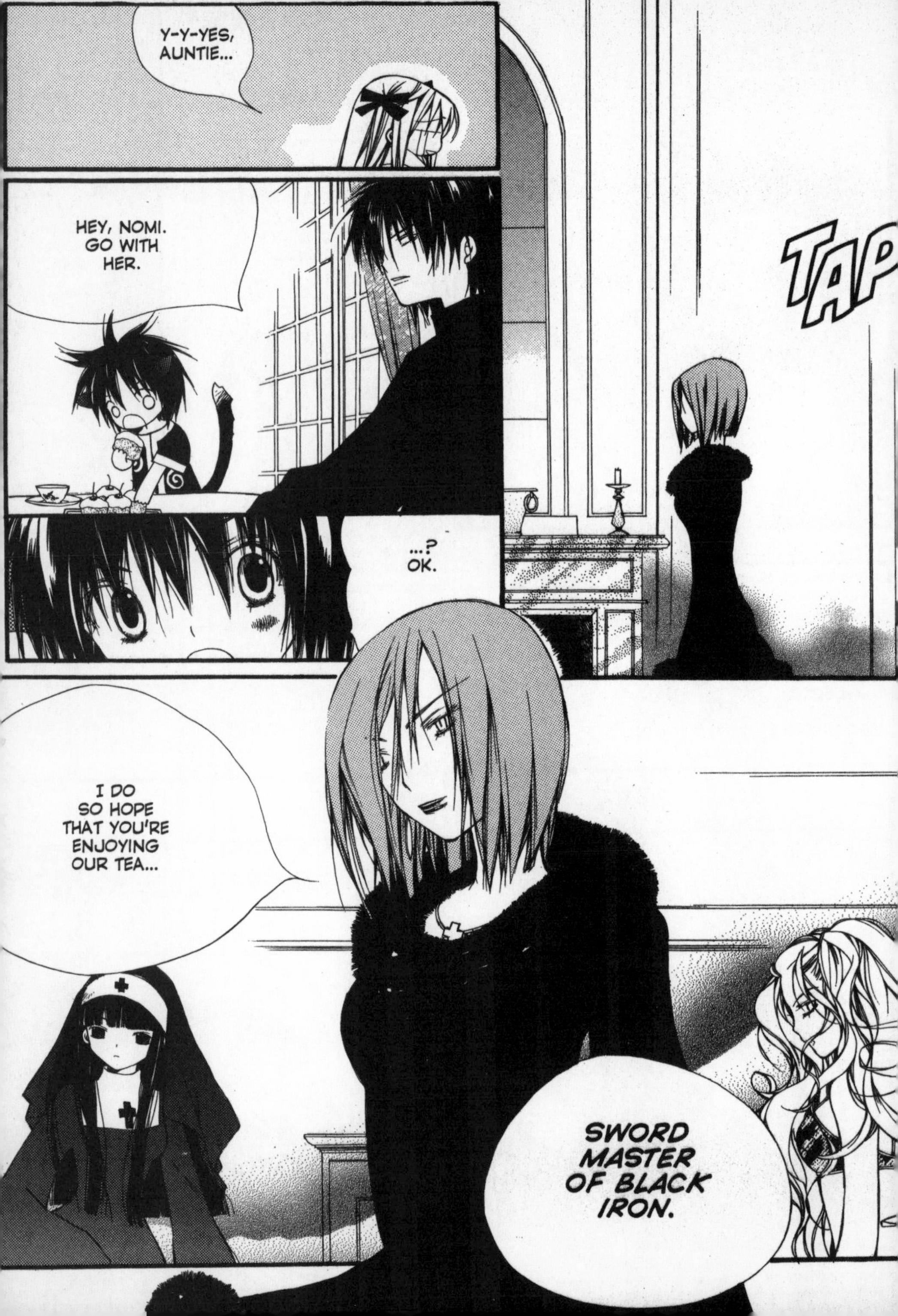
Y-Y-YES, AUNTIE...
HEY, NOMI. GO WITH HER.
...? OK.
TAP
I DO SO HOPE THAT YOU'RE ENJOYING OUR TEA...
SWORD MASTER OF BLACK IRON.

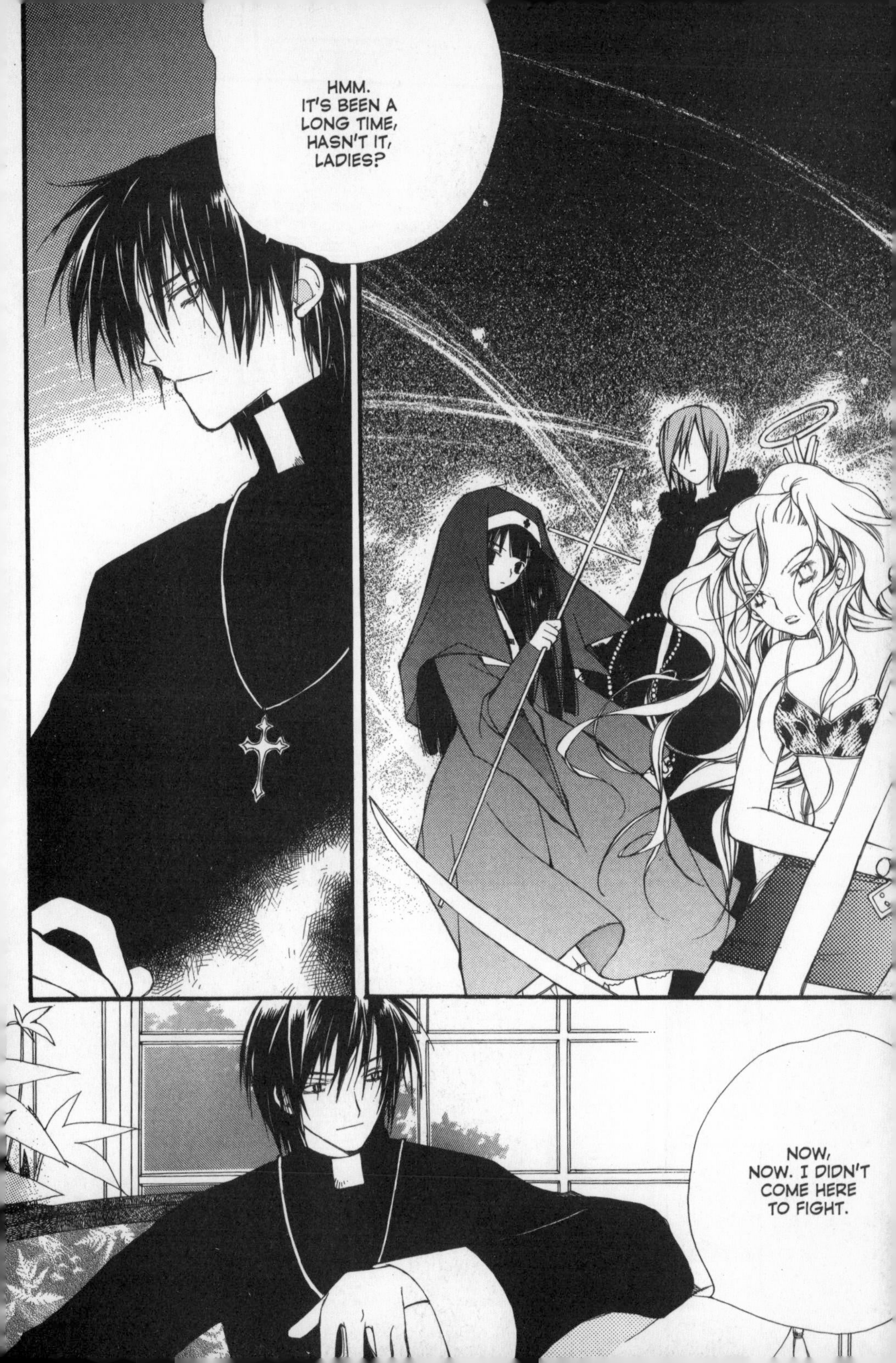
HMM. IT'S BEEN A LONG TIME, HASN'T IT, LADIES?
NOW, NOW. I DIDN'T COME HERE TO FIGHT.

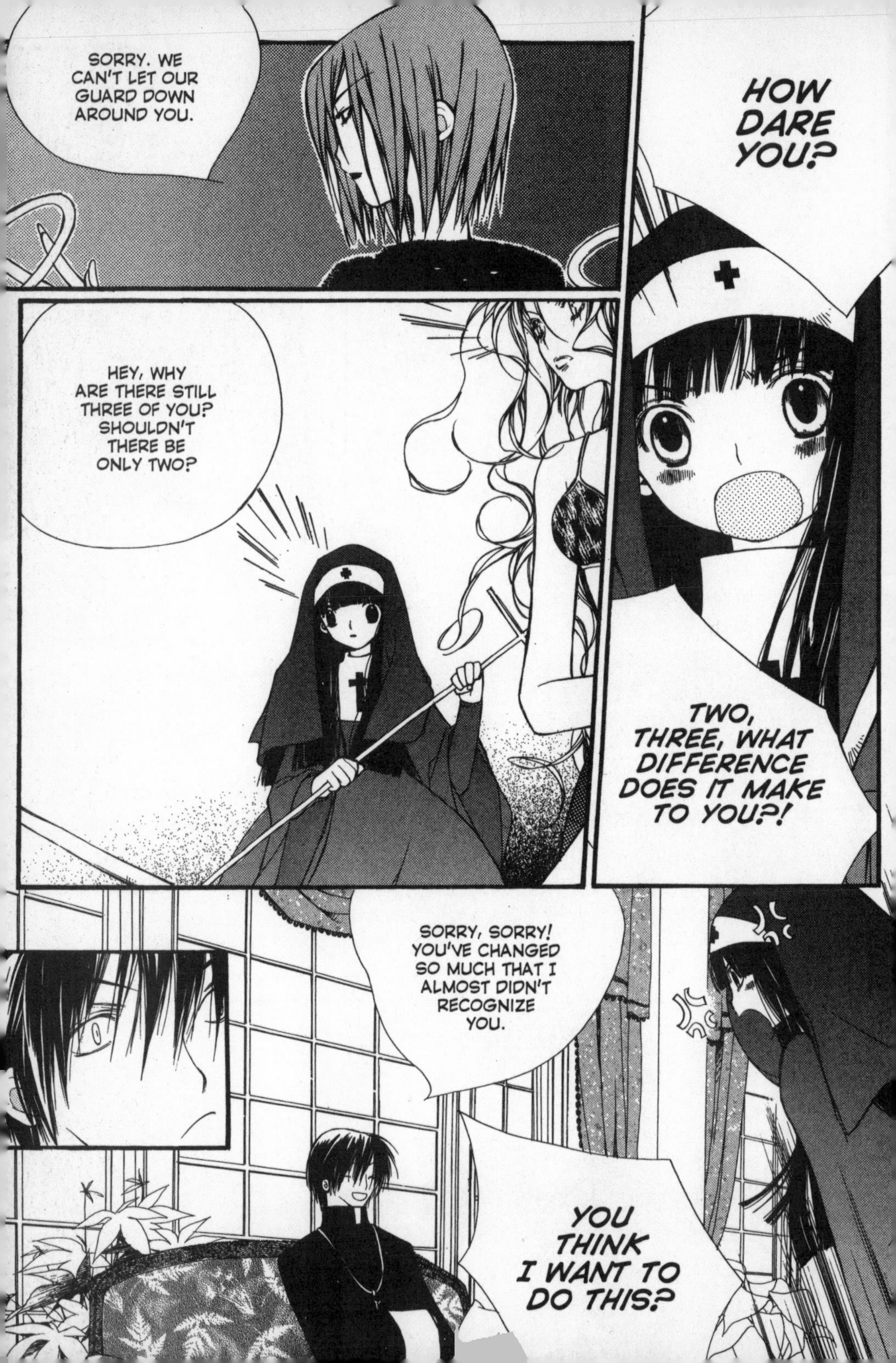
SORRY. WE CAN'T LET OUR GUARD DOWN AROUND YOU.
HEY, WHY ARE THERE STILL THREE OF YOU? SHOULDN'T THERE BE ONLY TWO?
HOW DARE YOU?
TWO, THREE, WHAT DIFFERENCE DOES IT MAKE TO YOU?!
SORRY, SORRY! YOU'VE CHANGED SO MUCH THAT I ALMOST DIDN'T RECOGNIZE YOU.
YOU THINK I WANT TO DO THIS?

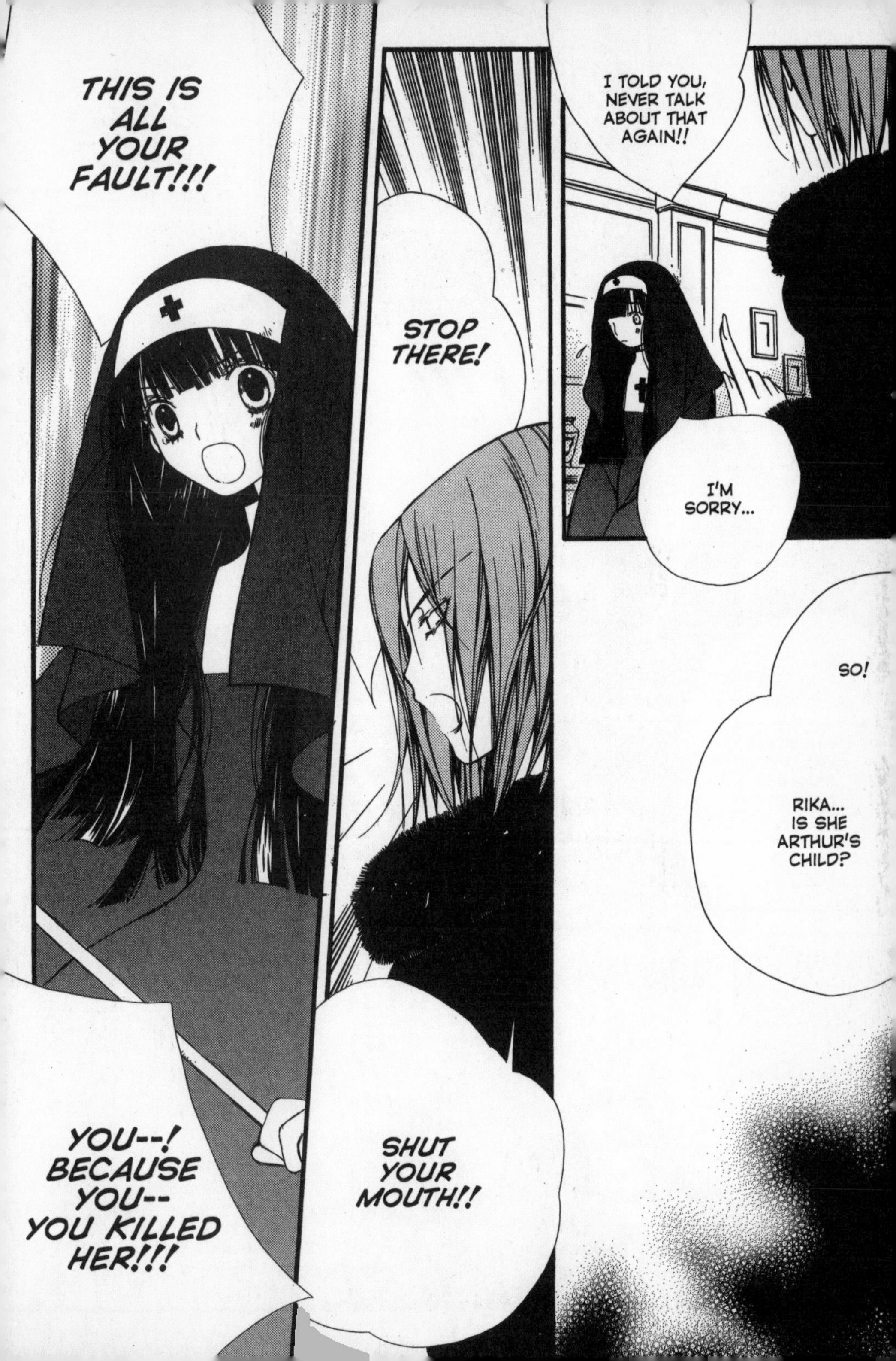
THIS IS ALL YOUR FAULT!!!
YOU--! BECAUSE YOU-- YOU KILLED HER!!!
STOP THERE!
SHUT YOUR MOUTH!!
I TOLD YOU, NEVER TALK ABOUT THAT AGAIN!!
I'M SORRY...
SO!
RIKA... IS SHE ARTHUR'S CHILD?

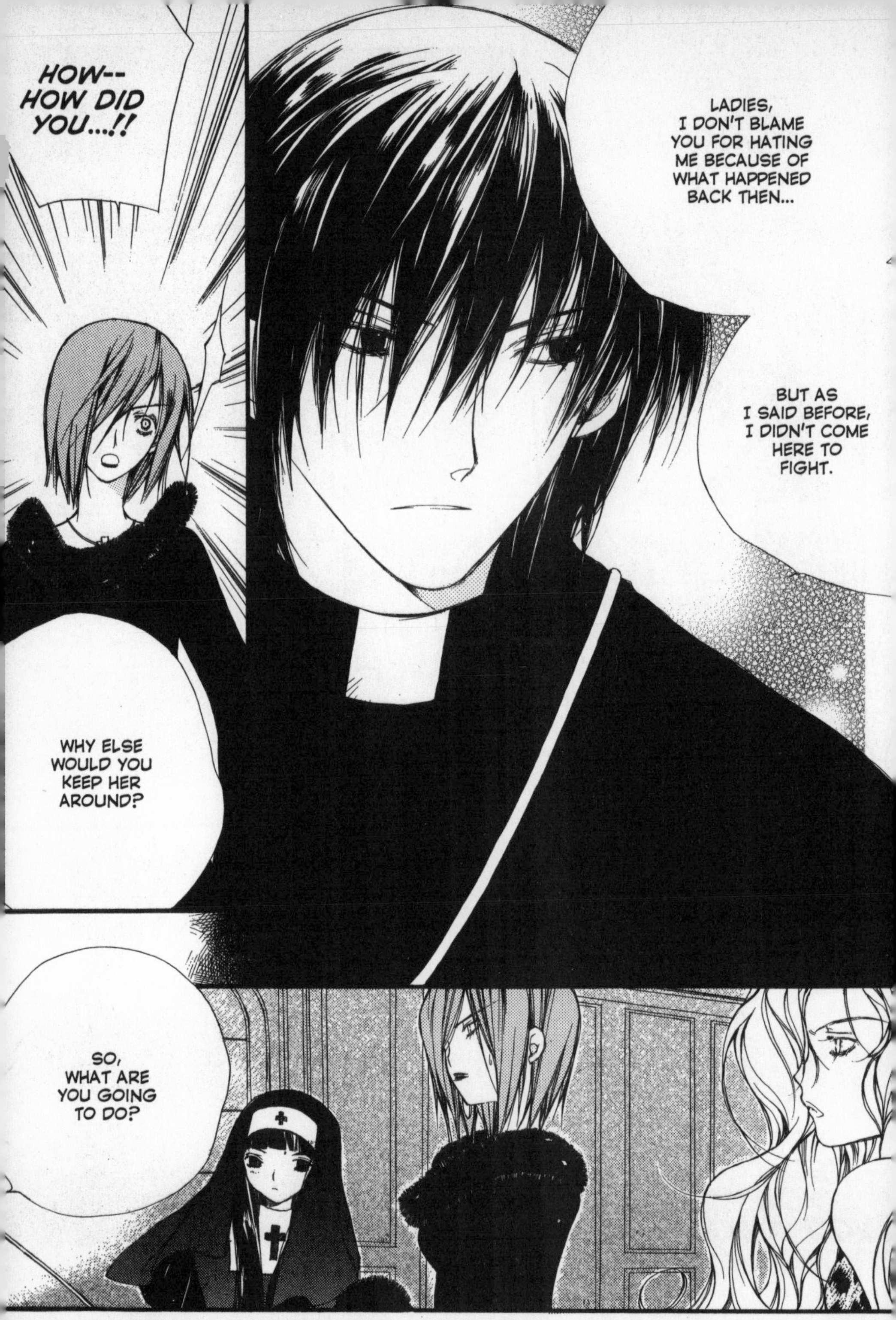
HOW--
HOW DID YOU...!!
WHY ELSE WOULD YOU KEEP HER AROUND?
LADIES, I DON'T BLAME YOU FOR HATING ME BECAUSE OF WHAT HAPPENED BACK THEN...
BUT AS I SAID BEFORE, I DIDN'T COME HERE TO FIGHT.
SO, WHAT ARE YOU GOING TO DO?

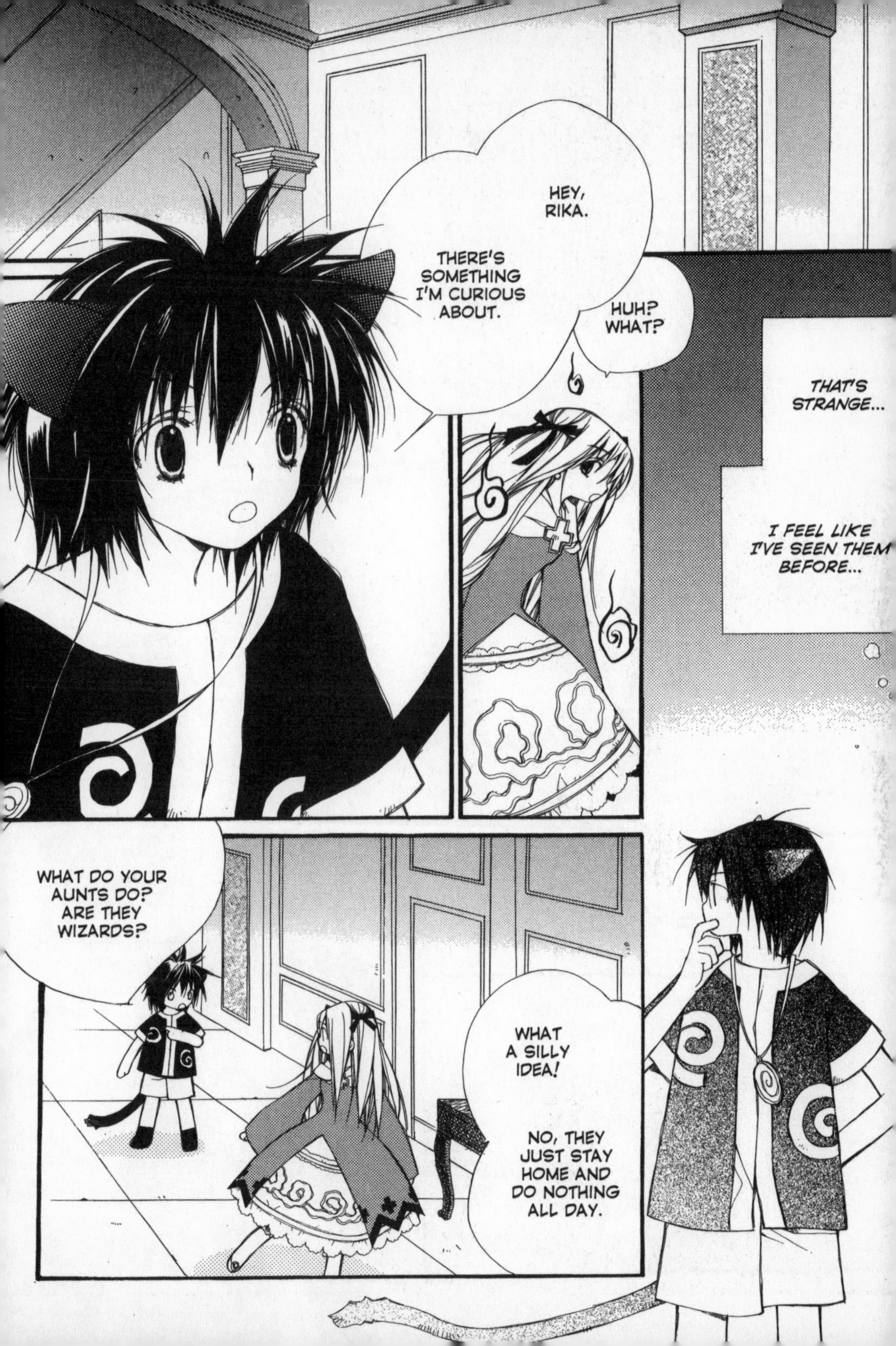
HEY, RIKA.
THERE'S SOMETHING I'M CURIOUS ABOUT.
HUH? WHAT?
THAT'S STRANGE...
I FEEL LIKE I'VE SEEN THEM BEFORE...
WHAT DO YOUR AUNTS DO? ARE THEY WIZARDS?
WHAT A SILLY IDEA!
NO, THEY JUST STAY HOME AND DO NOTHING ALL DAY.

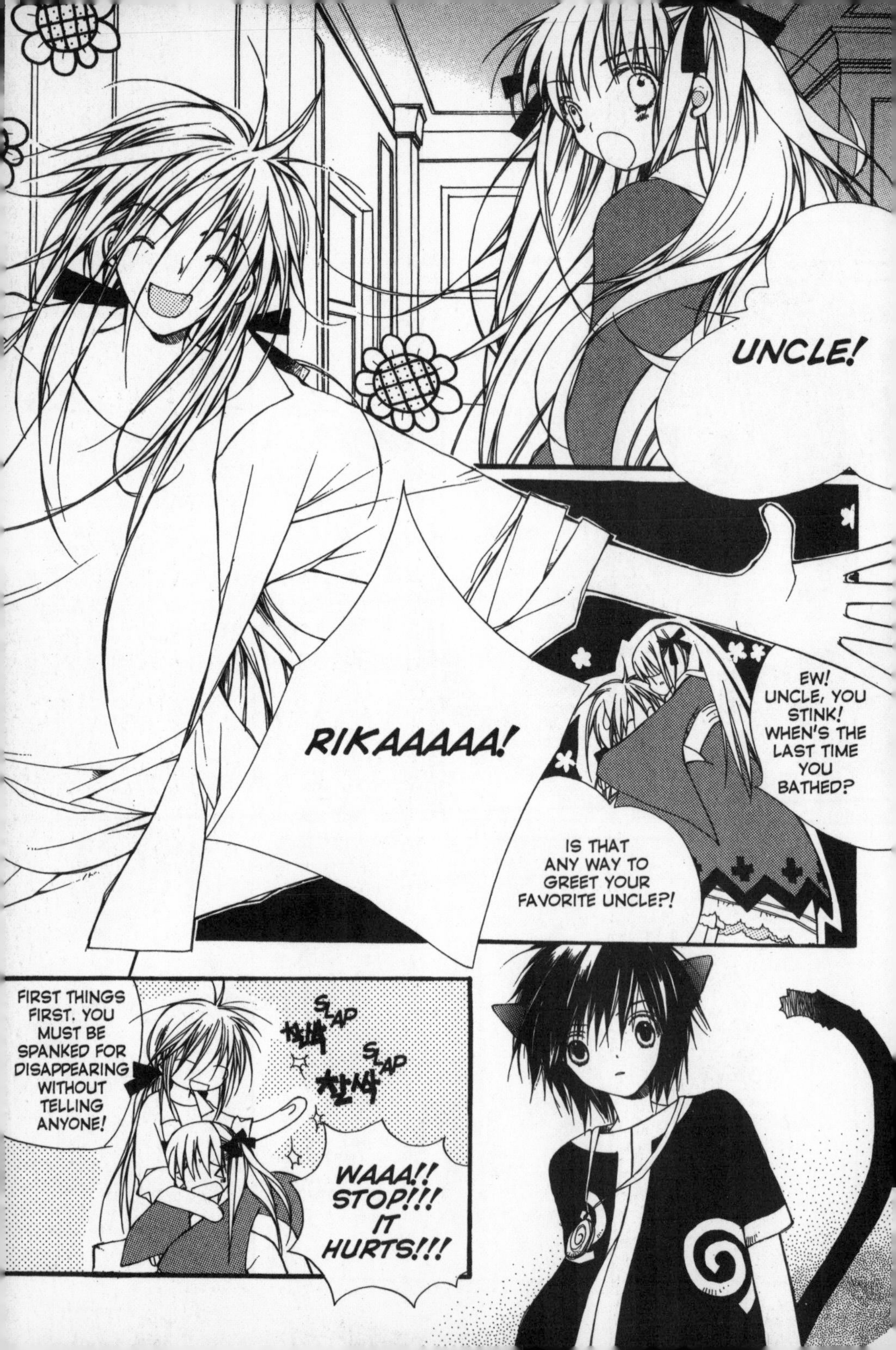
UNCLE!
RIKAAAAA!
EW! UNCLE, YOU STINK! WHEN'S THE LAST TIME YOU BATHED?
IS THAT ANY WAY TO GREET YOUR FAVORITE UNCLE?!
FIRST THINGS FIRST. YOU MUST BE SPANKED FOR DISAPPEARING WITHOUT TELLING ANYONE!
SLAP
SLAP
WAAA!! STOP!!! IT HURTS!!!

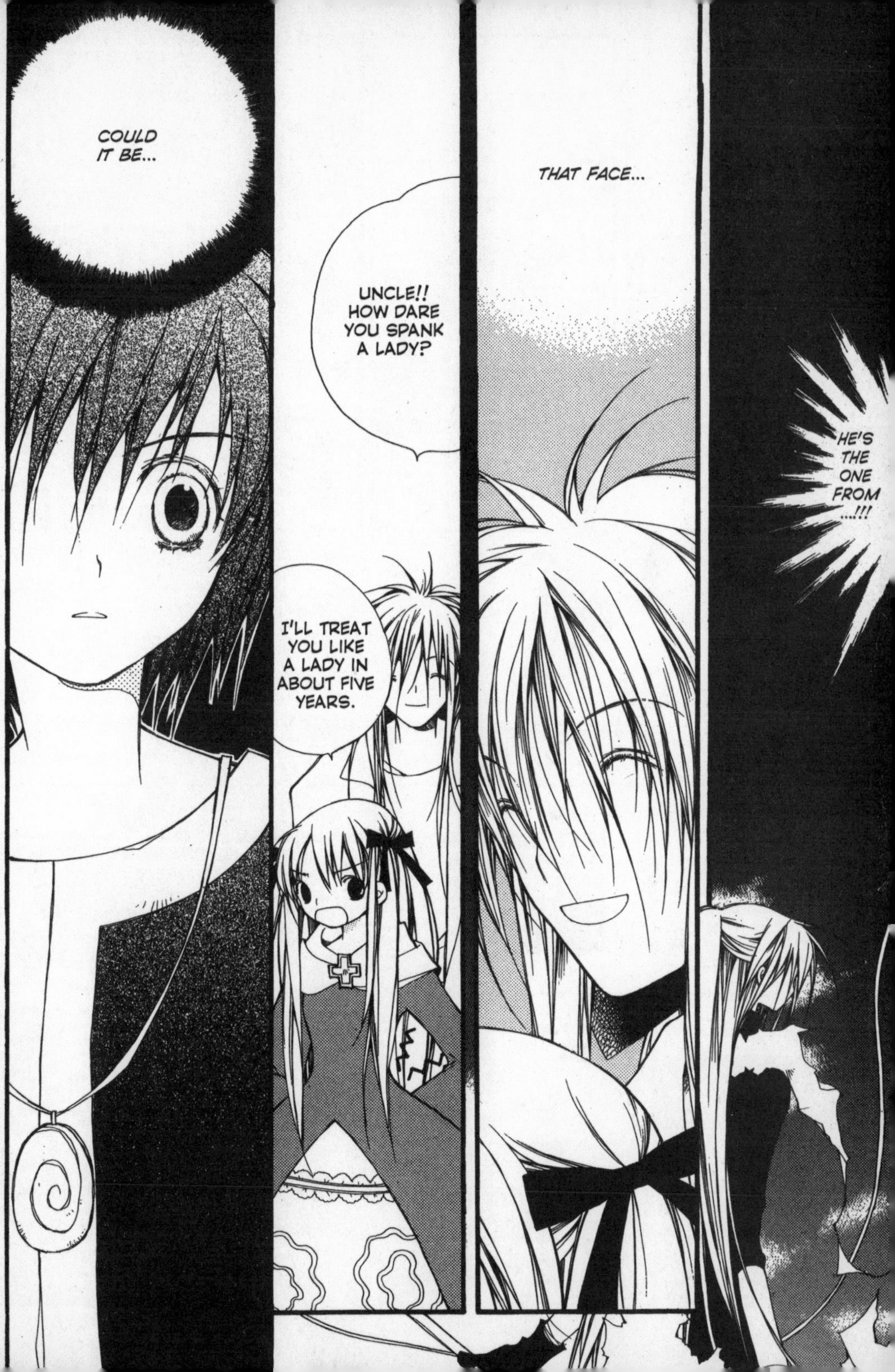
COULD IT BE...
UNCLE!! HOW DARE YOU SPANK A LADY?
I'LL TREAT YOU LIKE A LADY IN ABOUT FIVE YEARS.
THAT FACE...
HE'S THE ONE FROM ...!!!

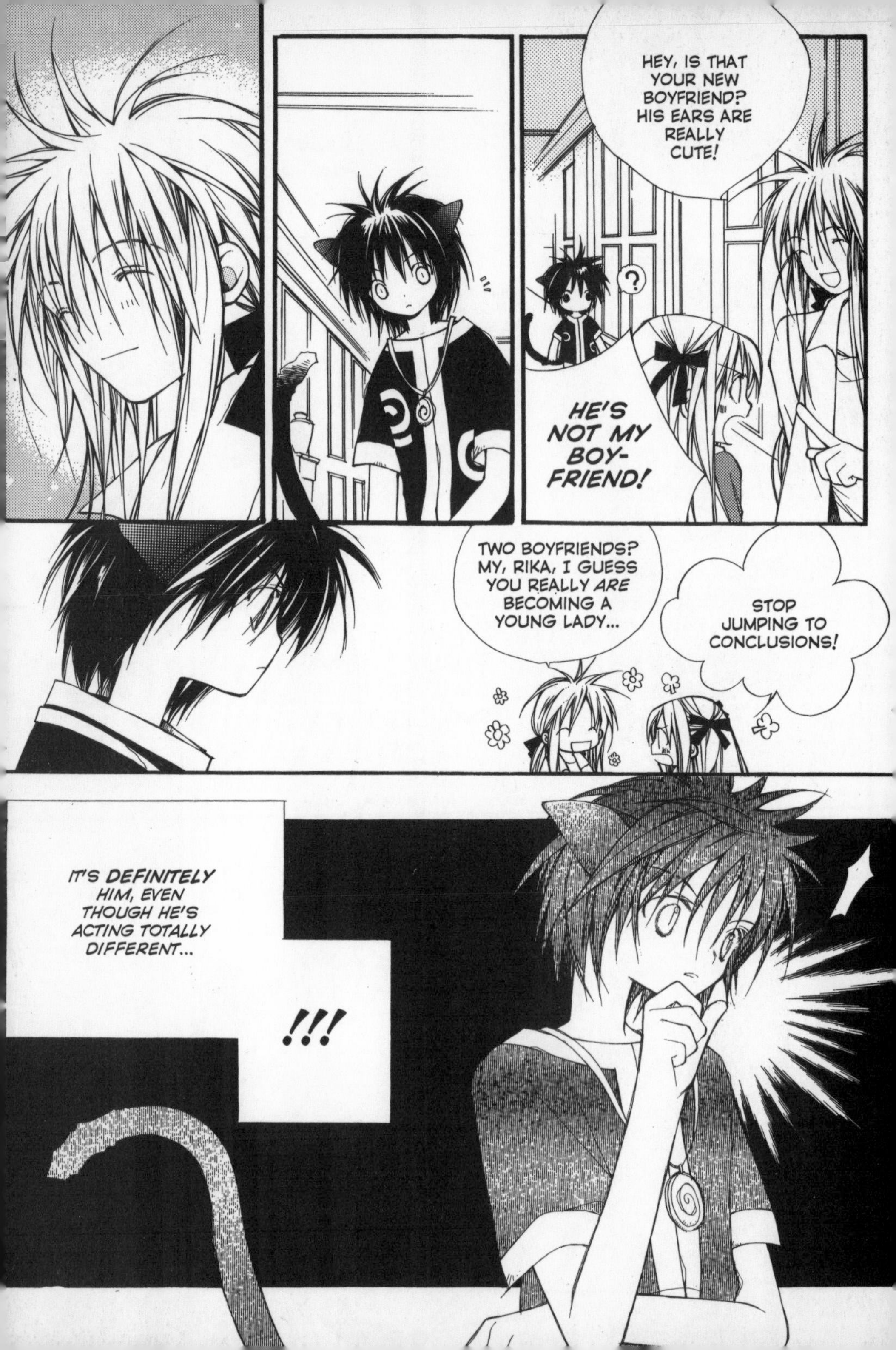
HEY, IS THAT YOUR NEW BOYFRIEND? HIS EARS ARE REALLY CUTE!
?
HE'S NOT MY BOY-FRIEND!
TWO BOYFRIENDS? MY, RIKA, I GUESS YOU REALLY ARE BECOMING A YOUNG LADY...
STOP JUMPING TO CONCLUSIONS!
IT'S DEFINITELY HIM, EVEN THOUGH HE'S ACTING TOTALLY DIFFERENT...
!!!

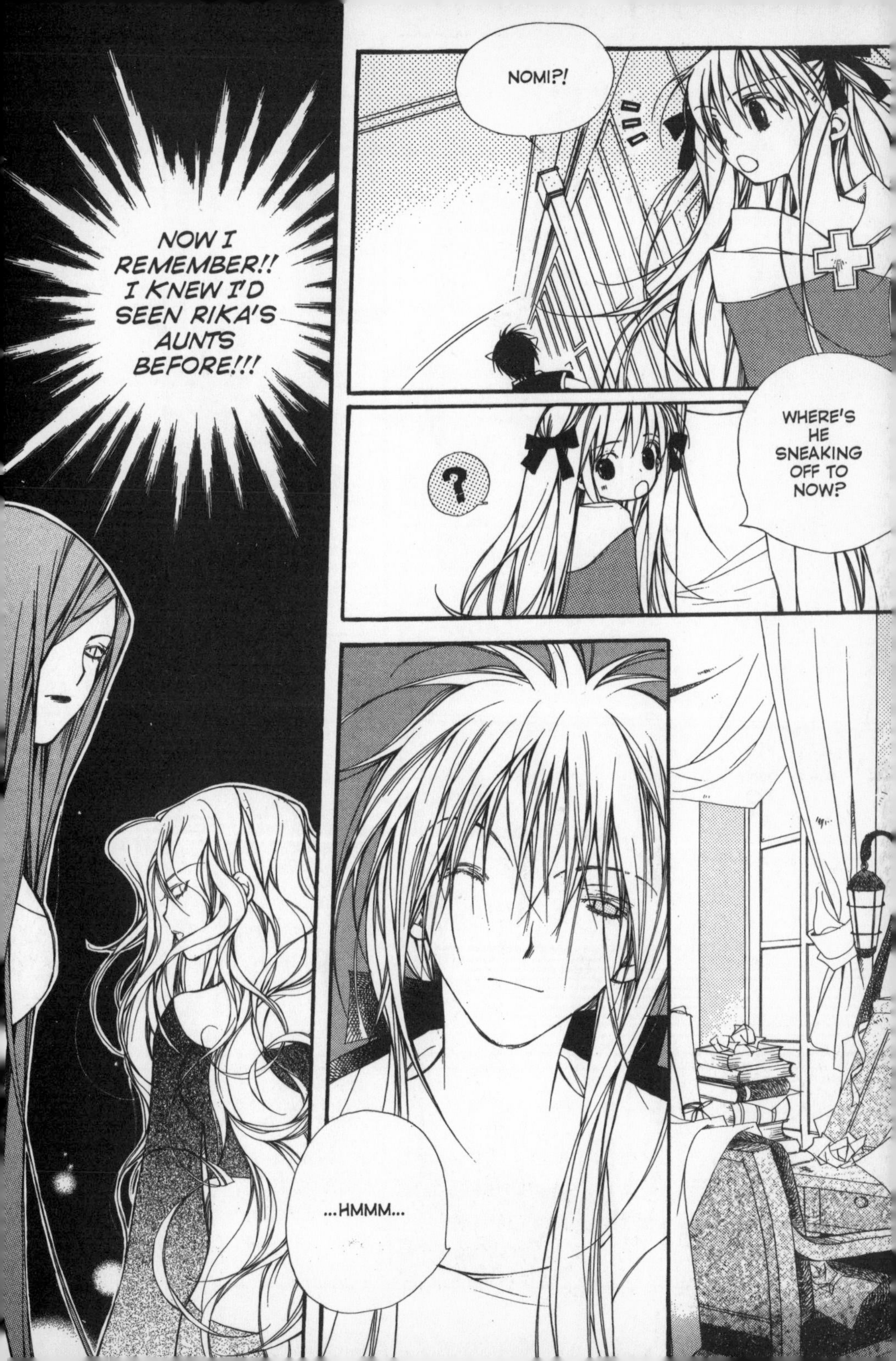
NOW I REMEMBER!! I KNEW I'D SEEN RIKA'S AUNTS BEFORE!!!
NOMI?!
?
WHERE'S HE SNEAKING OFF TO NOW?
...HMMM...

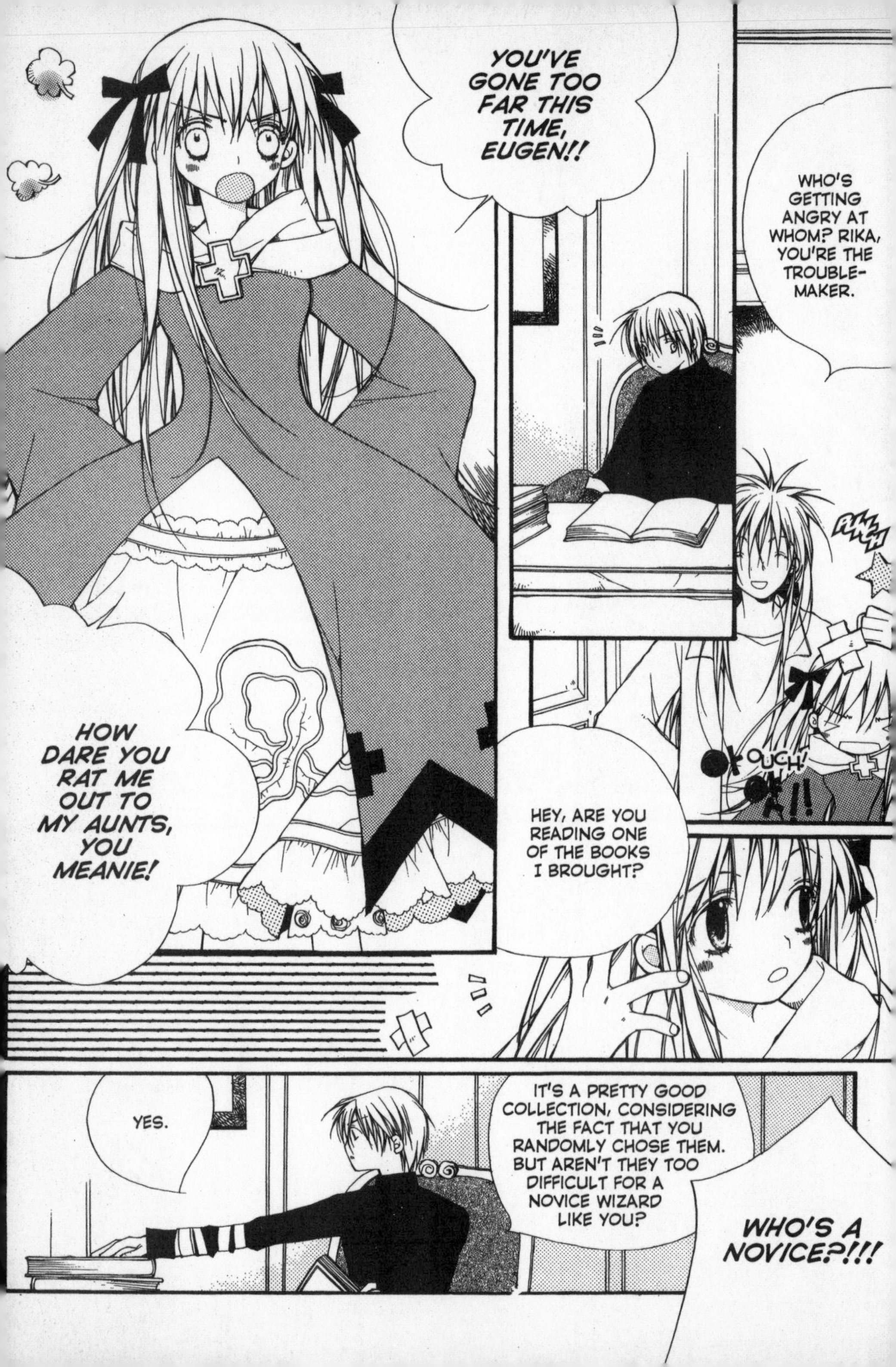

YOU'VE GONE TOO FAR THIS TIME, EUGEN!!
HOW DARE YOU RAT ME OUT TO MY AUNTS, YOU MEANIE!
WHO'S GETTING ANGRY AT WHOM? RIKA, YOU'RE THE TROUBLE-MAKER.
OUCH!
HEY, ARE YOU READING ONE OF THE BOOKS I BROUGHT?
YES.
IT'S A PRETTY GOOD COLLECTION, CONSIDERING THE FACT THAT YOU RANDOMLY CHOSE THEM. BUT AREN'T THEY TOO DIFFICULT FOR A NOVICE WIZARD LIKE YOU?
WHO'S A NOVICE?!!!

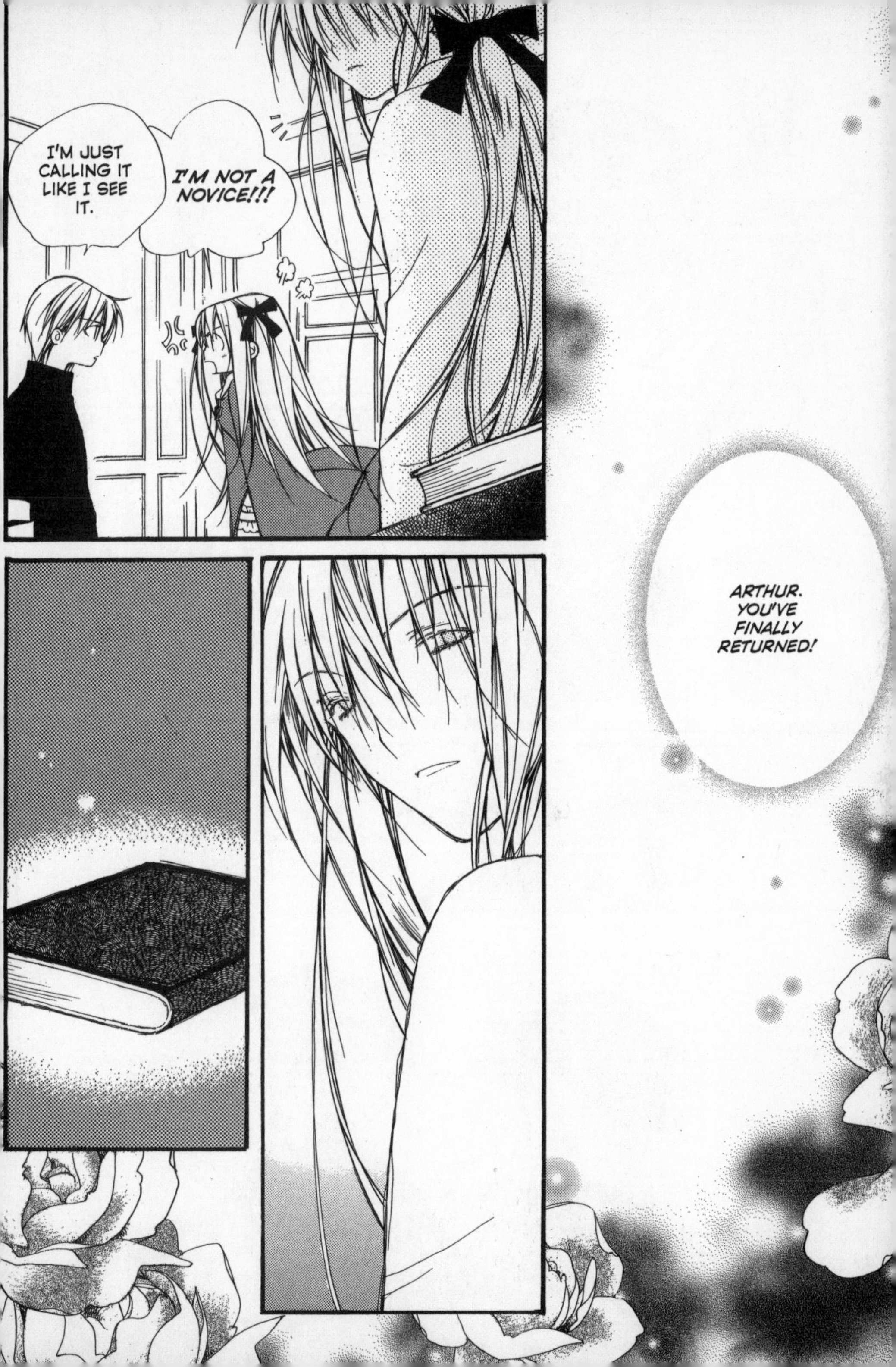
I'M JUST CALLING IT LIKE I SEE IT.
I'M NOT A NOVICE!!!
ARTHUR. YOU'VE FINALLY RETURNED!

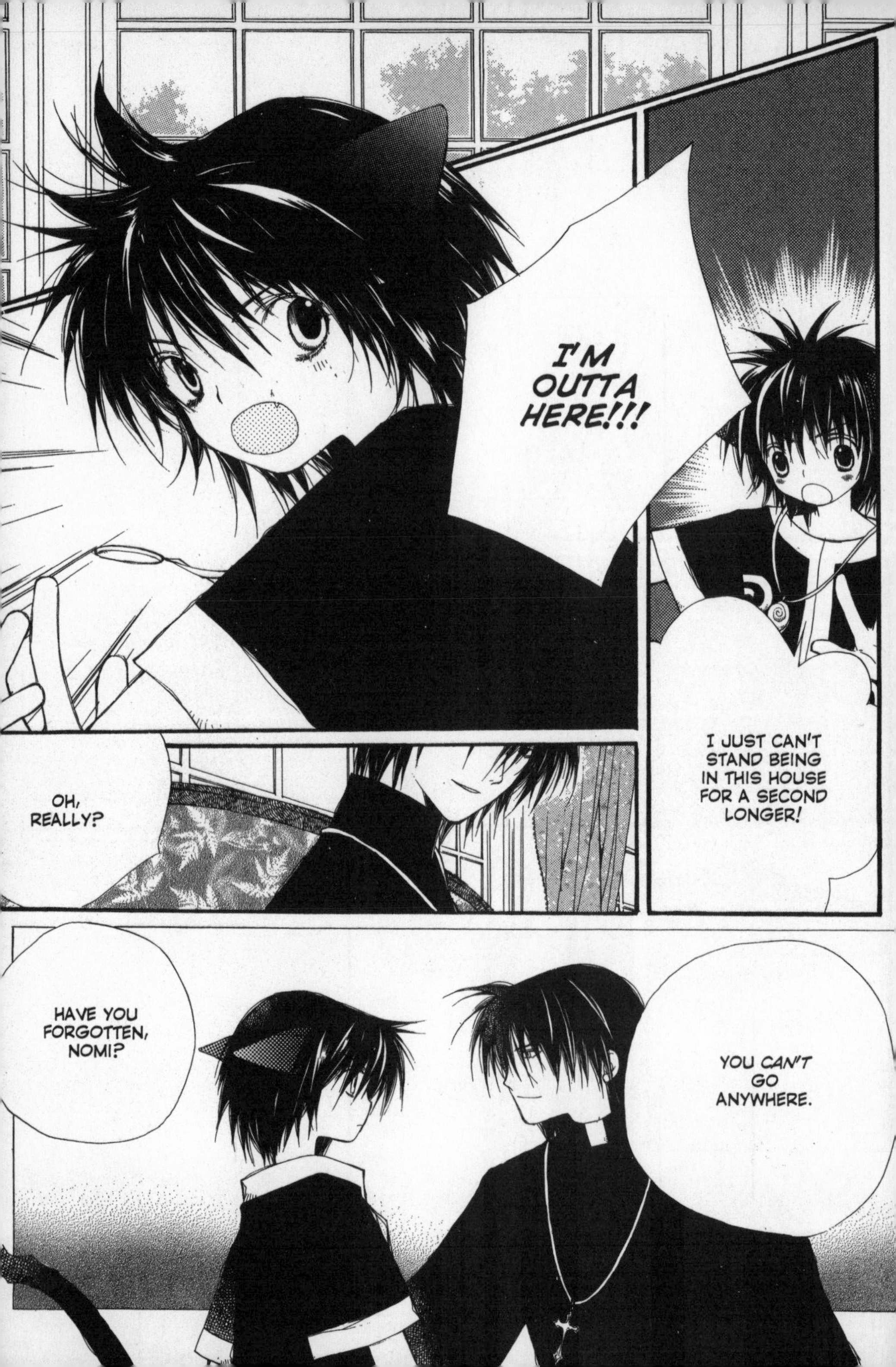
I'M OUTTA HERE!!!
OH, REALLY?
I JUST CAN'T STAND BEING IN THIS HOUSE FOR A SECOND LONGER!
HAVE YOU FORGOTTEN, NOMI?
YOU CAN'T GO ANYWHERE.

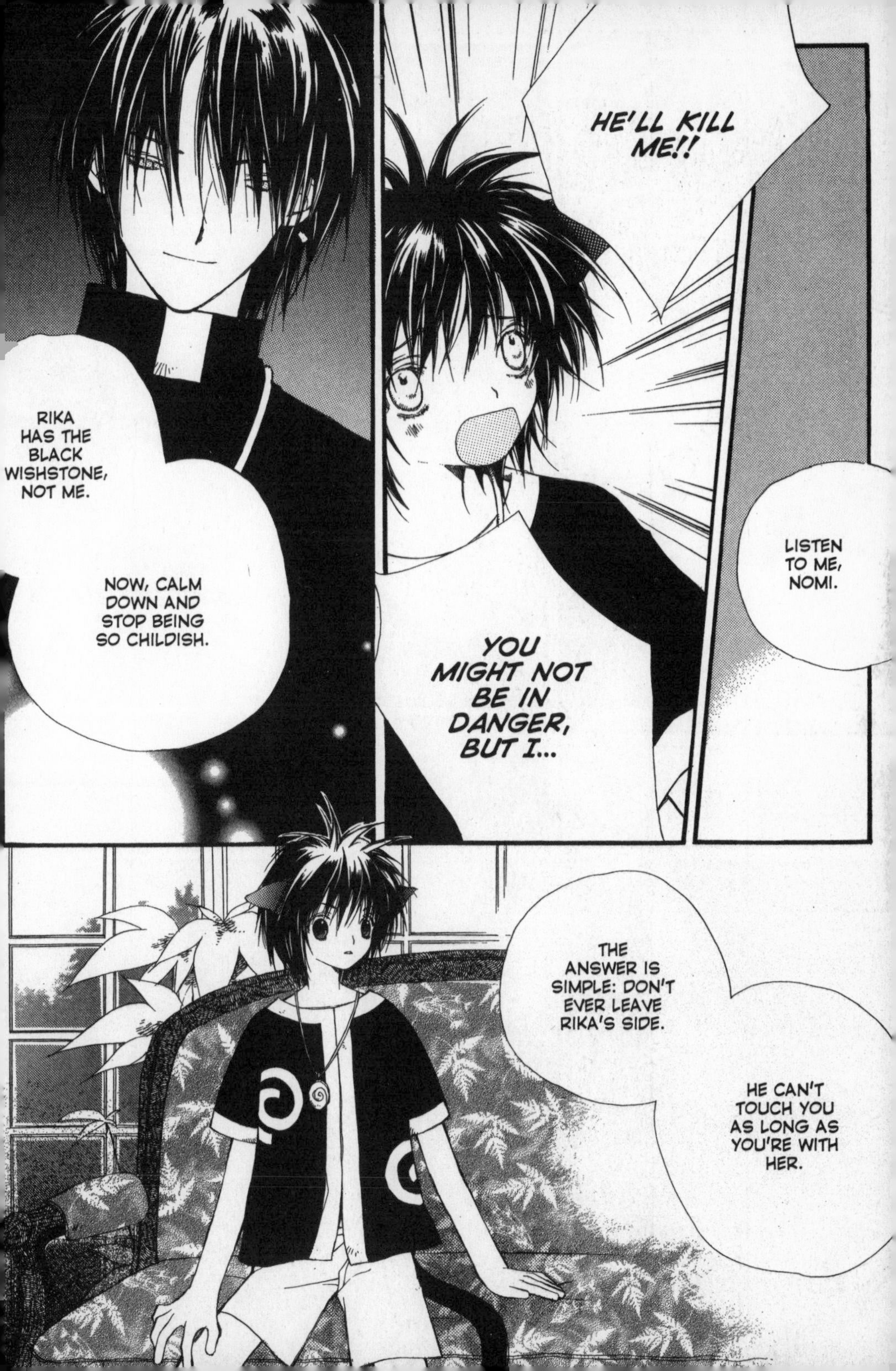
RIKA HAS THE BLACK WISHSTONE, NOT ME.
NOW, CALM DOWN AND STOP BEING SO CHILDISH.
HE'LL KILL ME!!
YOU MIGHT NOT BE IN DANGER, BUT I...
LISTEN TO ME, NOMI.
THE ANSWER IS SIMPLE: DON'T EVER LEAVE RIKA'S SIDE.
HE CAN'T TOUCH YOU AS LONG AS YOU'RE WITH HER.

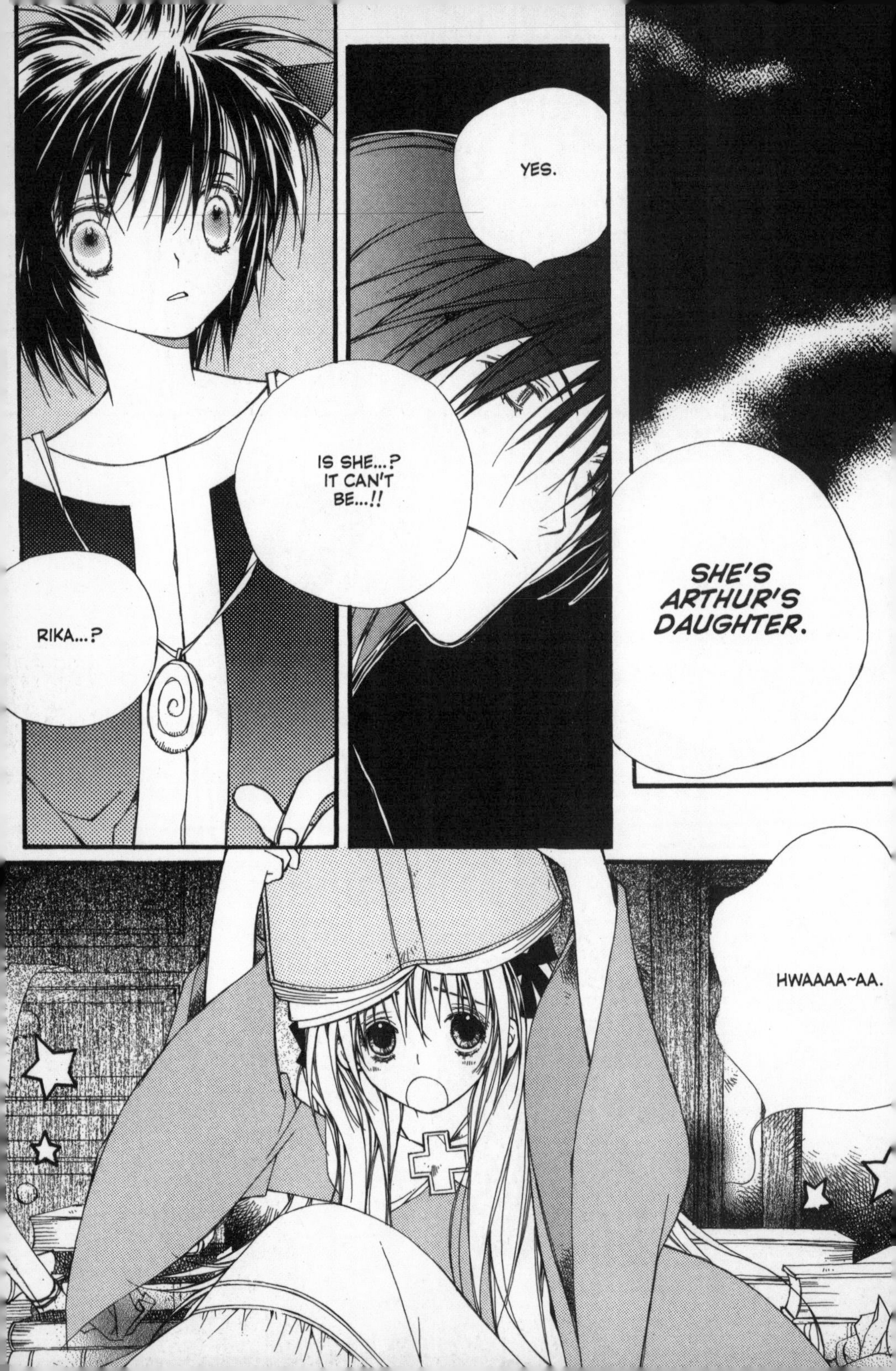
RIKA...?
IS SHE...? IT CAN'T BE...!!
YES.
SHE'S ARTHUR'S DAUGHTER.
HWAAAA~AA.

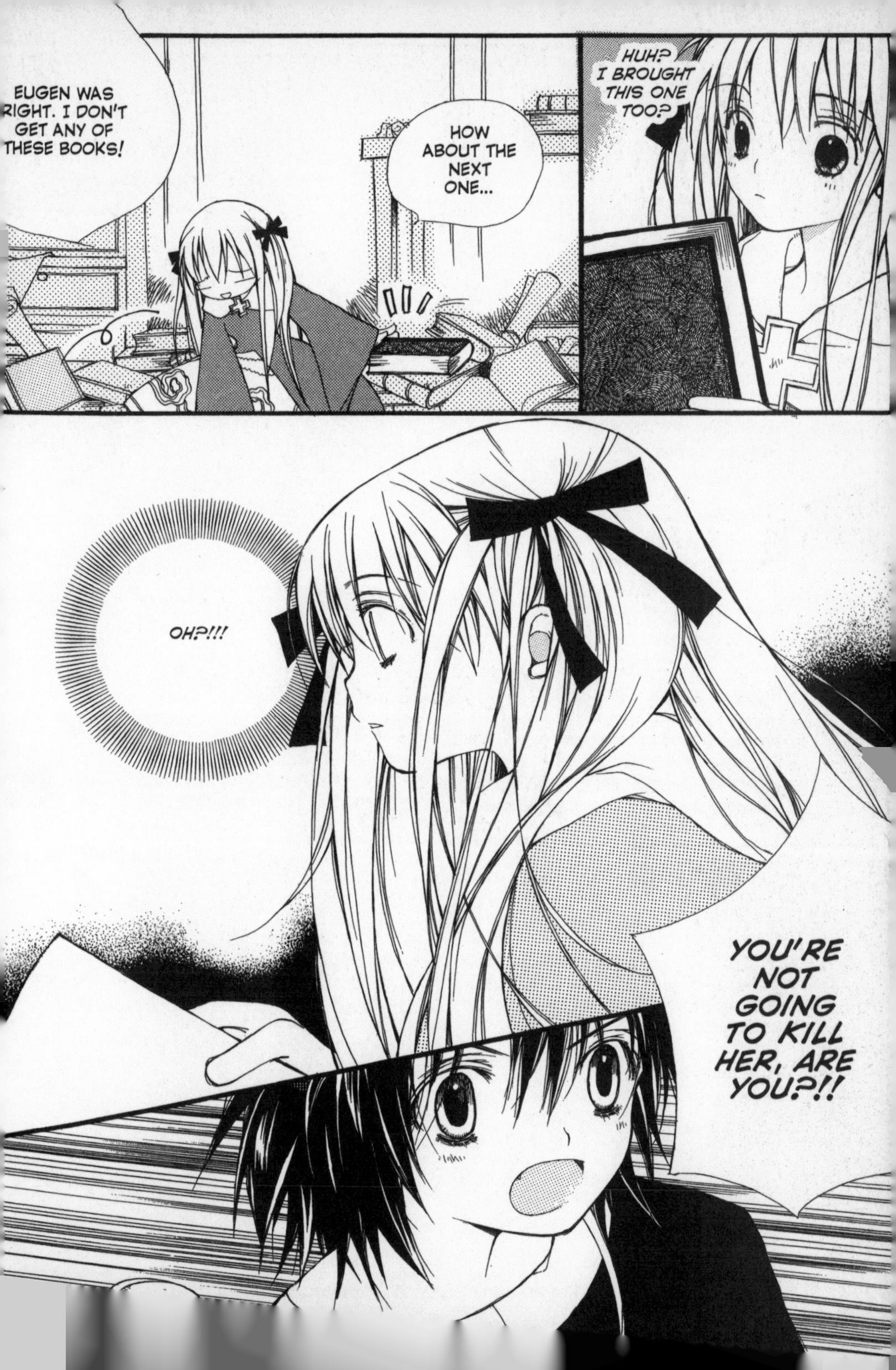
EUGEN WAS RIGHT. I DON'T GET ANY OF THESE BOOKS!
HOW ABOUT THE NEXT ONE...
HUH? I BROUGHT THIS ONE TOO?
OH?!!!
YOU'RE NOT GOING TO KILL HER, ARE YOU?!!

Danbi Original

Angel Diary vol.2

Story by YunHee Lee
Art by KARA

Translation HyeYoung Im · J. Torres
English Adaptation J. Torres
Touch-up and Lettering Marshall Dillon
Graphic Design EunKyung Kim
Editor JuYoun Lee

ICE Kunion

Project Manager Chan Park
Managing Editor Marshall Dillon
Marketing Manager Erik Ko
Editor in Chief Eddie Yu
Publishing Director JeongHyun Chin
Publisher and C.E.O. JaeKook Chun

Angel Diary © 2005 Kara · YunHee Lee
First published in Korea in 2003 by SIGONGSA Co., Ltd.
English text translation rights arranged by SIGONGSA Co., Ltd.
English text © 2005 ICE KUNION

Published by ICE Kunion.
SIGONGSA 2F Yeil Bldg. 1619-4, Seocho-dong, Seocho-gu, Seoul, 137-878, Korea

ISBN : 89-527-4474-8

First printing, January 2006
10 9 8 7 6 5 4 3 2 1
Printed in Canada

www.ICEkunion.com/www.koreanmanhwa.com